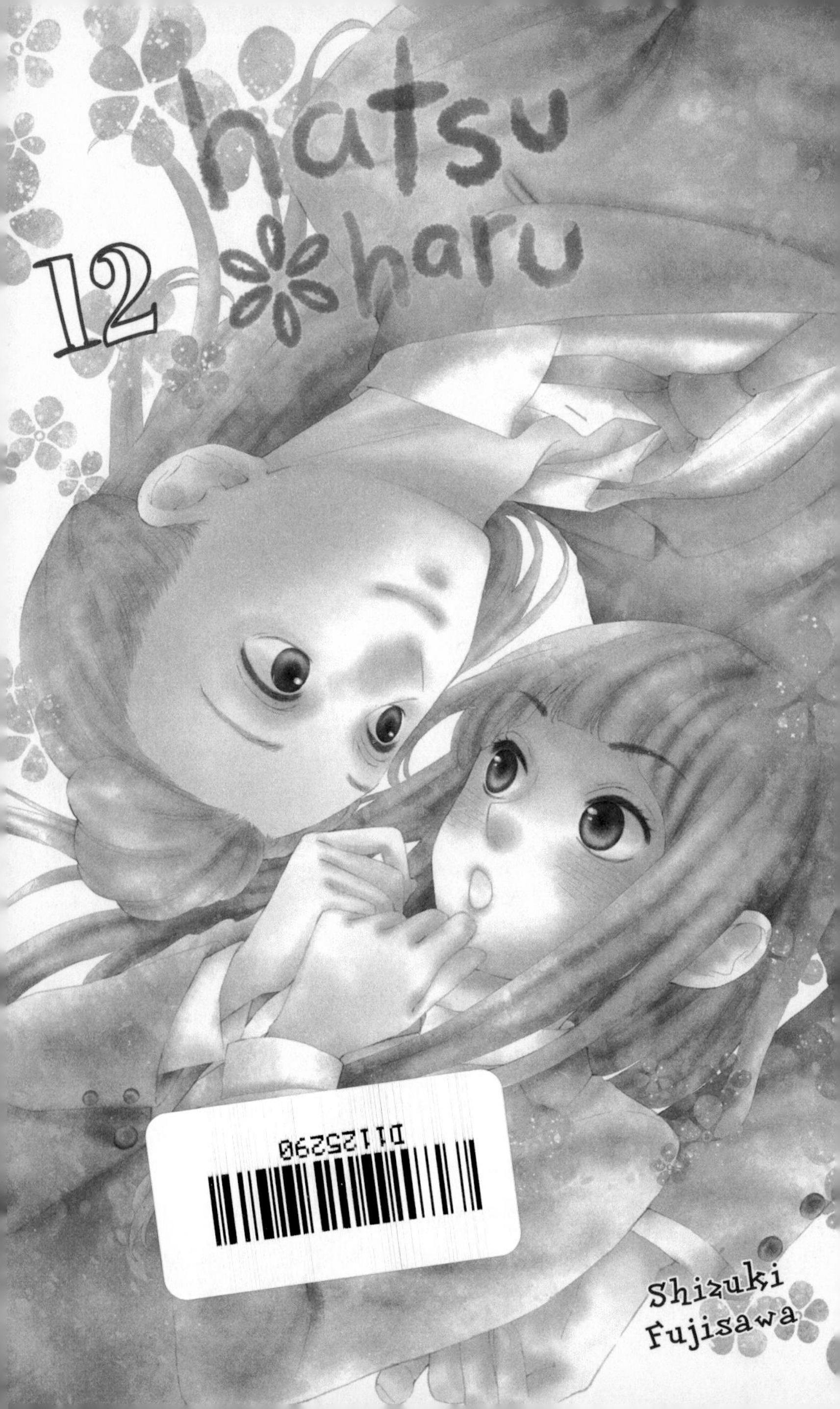
hatsu
haru
12
Shizuki
Fujisawa

CONTENTS

hatsu  haru

12

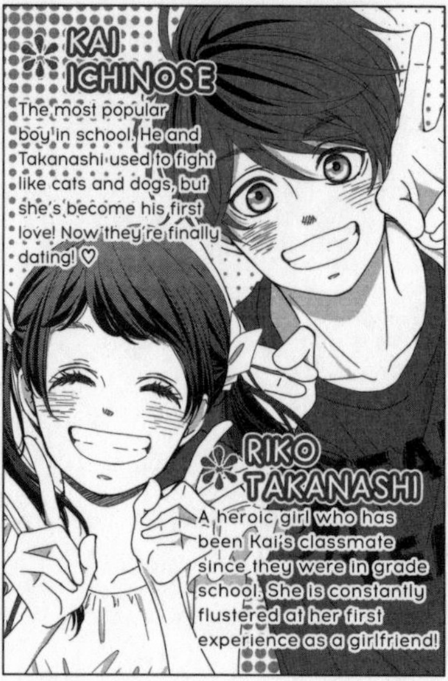
KAI ICHINOSE
The most popular boy in school. He and Takanashi used to fight like cats and dogs, but she's become his first love! Now they're finally dating! ♡
RIKO TAKANASHI
A heroic girl who has been Kai's classmate since they were in grade school. She is constantly flustered at her first experience as a girlfriend!

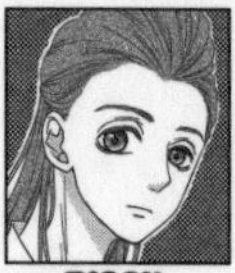
TAROU TORAMARU

The heir to a Buddhist temple and the heiress to a Shinto shrine. Childhood friends. Kagura has an instinctual disdain for playboy Tora, but...!?

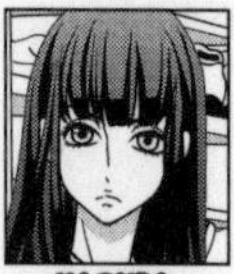
KAGURA TATSUNAMI

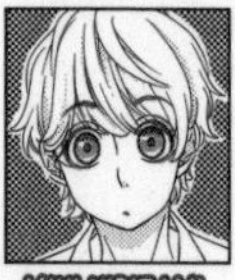
MIKI KIRITANI

A pure and innocent couple whose love level is always rising. ♡ Their height difference doesn't bother them one bit. ♡

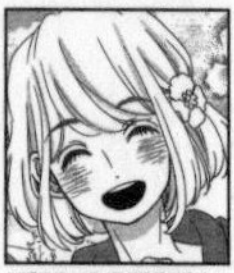
KIYO OOSHIMA

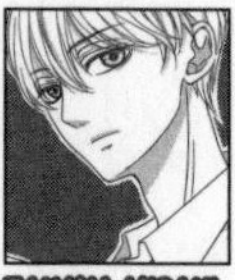
TAKAYA MISAKI

They became a fake couple to help Kai and Riko get together, but...?

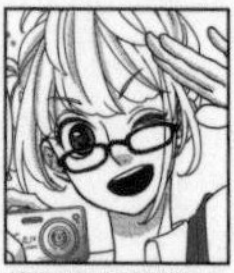
AYUMI SHIMURA

STORY

● Kai, the school's most popular playboy, falls in love for the first time with his combative and short-tempered childhood friend, Riko Takanashi! After some time struggling with their feelings for each other, they have finally started dating! ♡ Despite an awkward start, they gradually grow closer. However, with spring's arrival, Kai and Riko become second-years and are assigned to different classes!

● Ayumi, meanwhile, is distressed over her inability to put Taka out of her mind. She has no idea what is causing it, but after Taka's persistent advances, she realizes she is in love, and the two become a couple.

● Then, with the school trip on the horizon, Kai encourages Kagura to act on her feelings for Tora. She asks him out on a date, but her attempt is an abysmal failure. She tries to get over him and move on, but ultimately takes the advice of Father John and confesses her love to him on the school trip...!

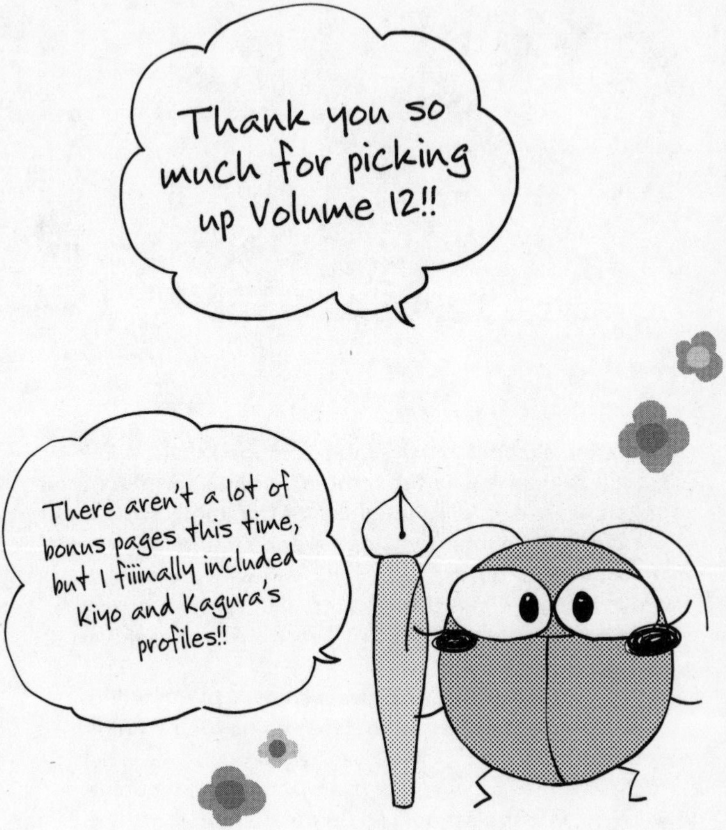
Thank you so much for picking up Volume 12!!
There aren't a lot of bonus pages this time, but I fiiinally included Kiyo and Kagura's profiles!!

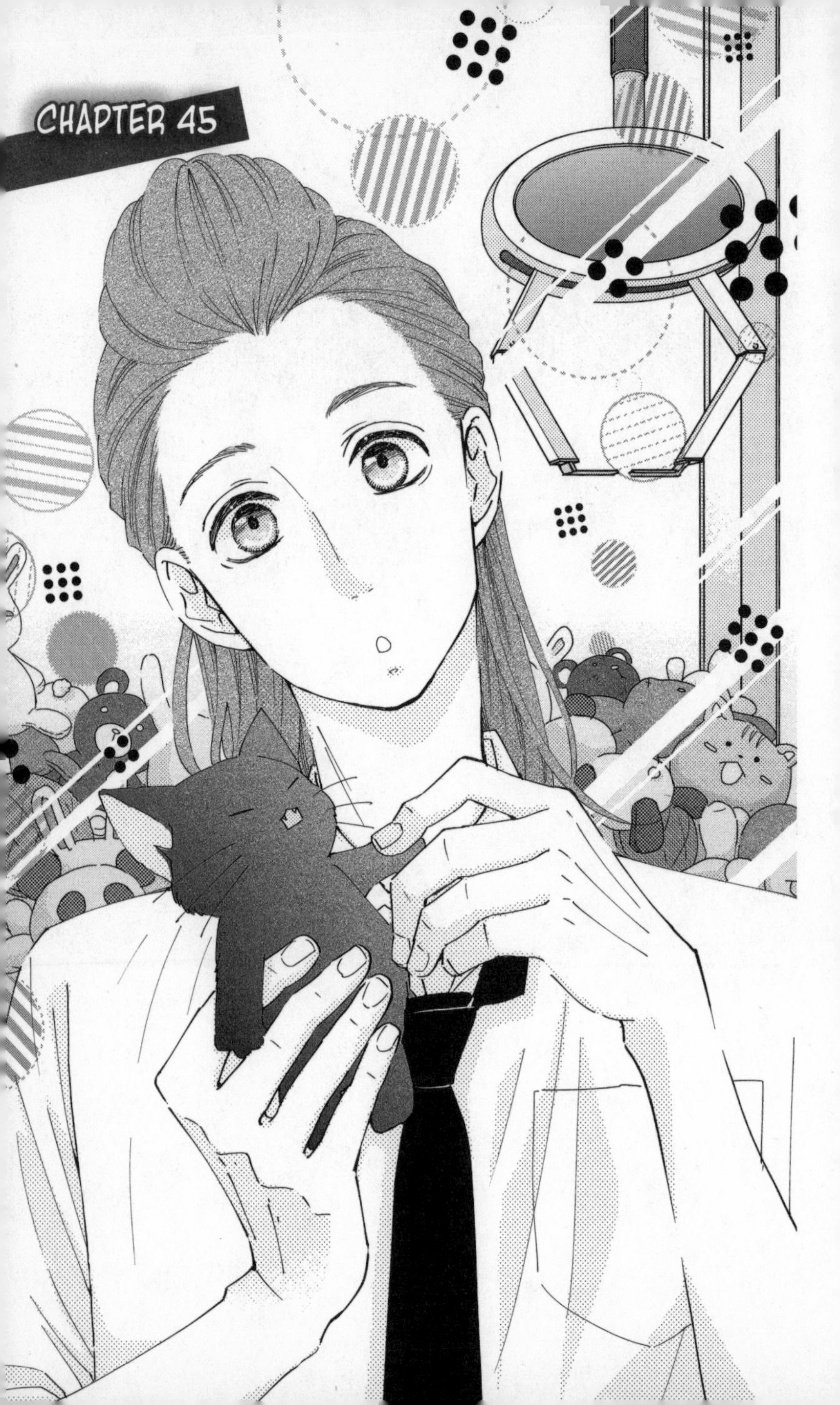
CHAPTER 45

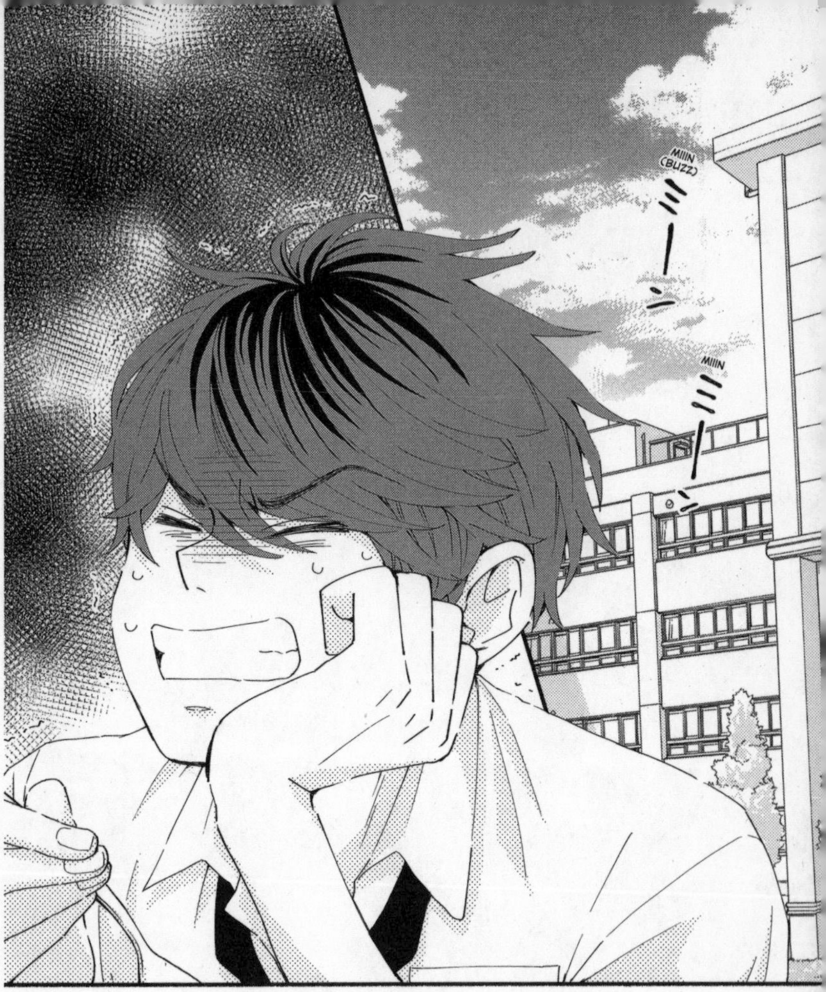
MIIN (BUZZ)
MIIN

hatsu haru

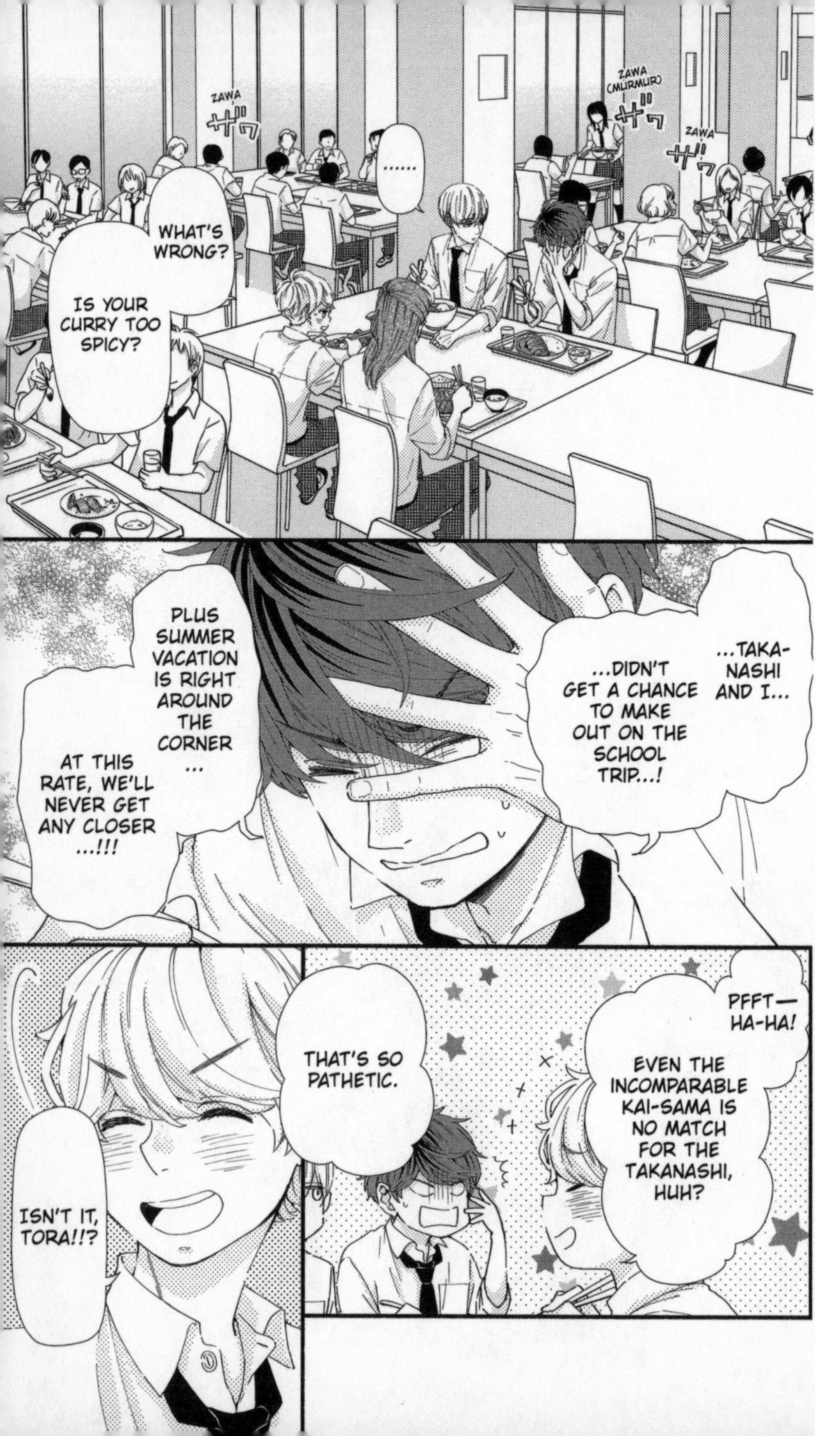
ZAWA (MURMUR)
ザワ
ZAWA
ザワ
......
ZAWA
ザワ
WHAT'S WRONG?
IS YOUR CURRY TOO SPICY?
...TAKA-NASHI AND I...
...DIDN'T GET A CHANCE TO MAKE OUT ON THE SCHOOL TRIP...!
PLUS SUMMER VACATION IS RIGHT AROUND THE CORNER...
AT THIS RATE, WE'LL NEVER GET ANY CLOSER...!!!
PFFT—HA-HA!
EVEN THE INCOMPARABLE KAI-SAMA IS NO MATCH FOR THE TAKANASHI, HUH?
THAT'S SO PATHETIC.
ISN'T IT, TORA!!?

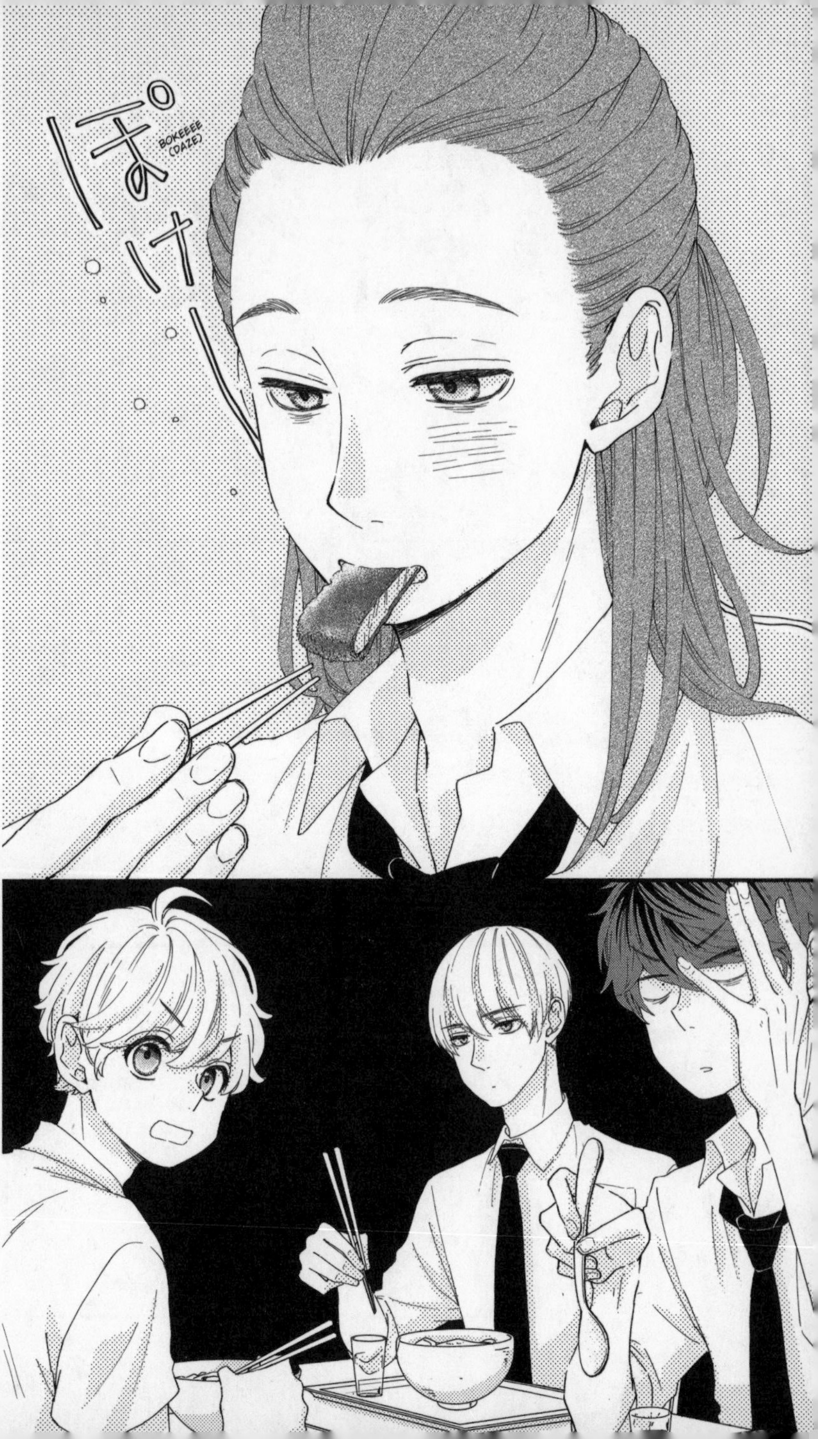
ぽけーー
BOKEEEE
(DAZE)

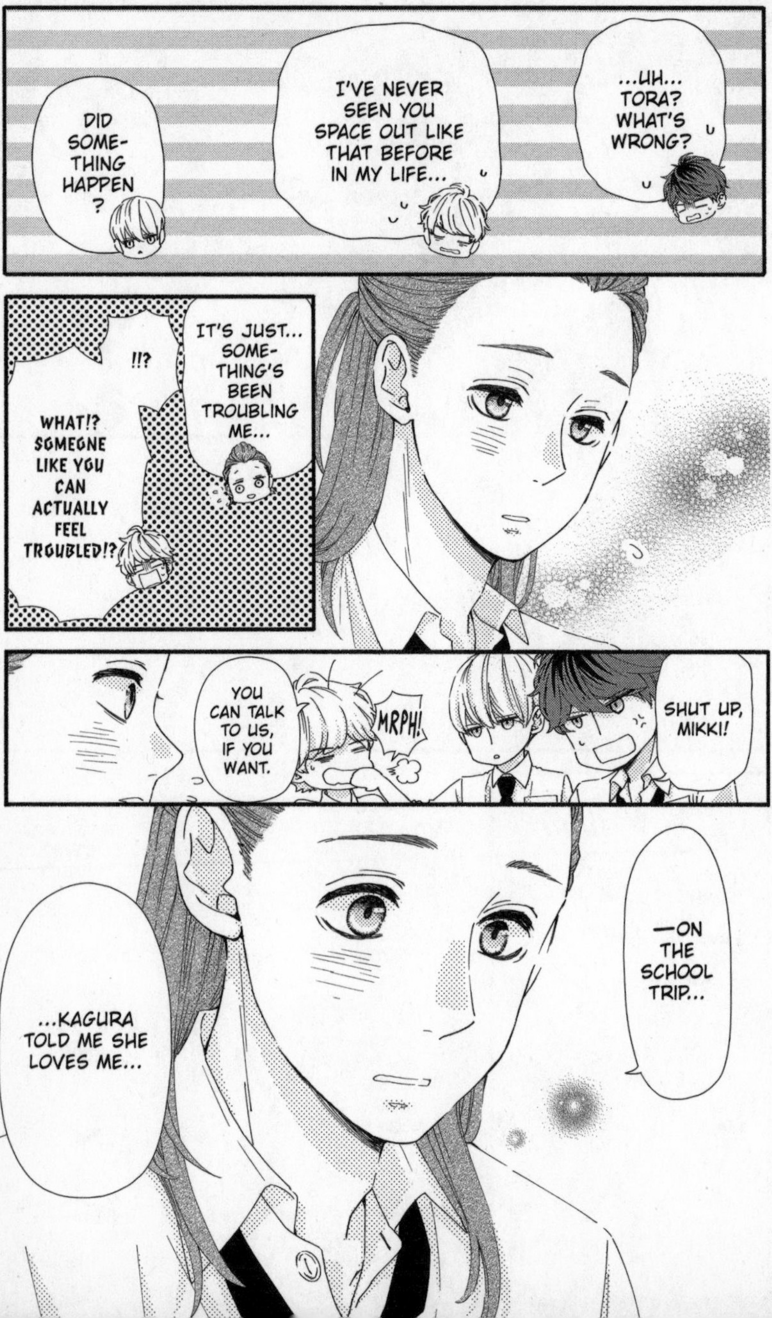
...UH... TORA? WHAT'S WRONG?
I'VE NEVER SEEN YOU SPACE OUT LIKE THAT BEFORE IN MY LIFE...
DID SOME-THING HAPPEN?
IT'S JUST... SOME-THING'S BEEN TROUBLING ME...
!!?
WHAT!? SOMEONE LIKE YOU CAN ACTUALLY FEEL TROUBLED!?
SHUT UP, MIKKI!
MRPH!
YOU CAN TALK TO US, IF YOU WANT.
—ON THE SCHOOL TRIP...
...KAGURA TOLD ME SHE LOVES ME...

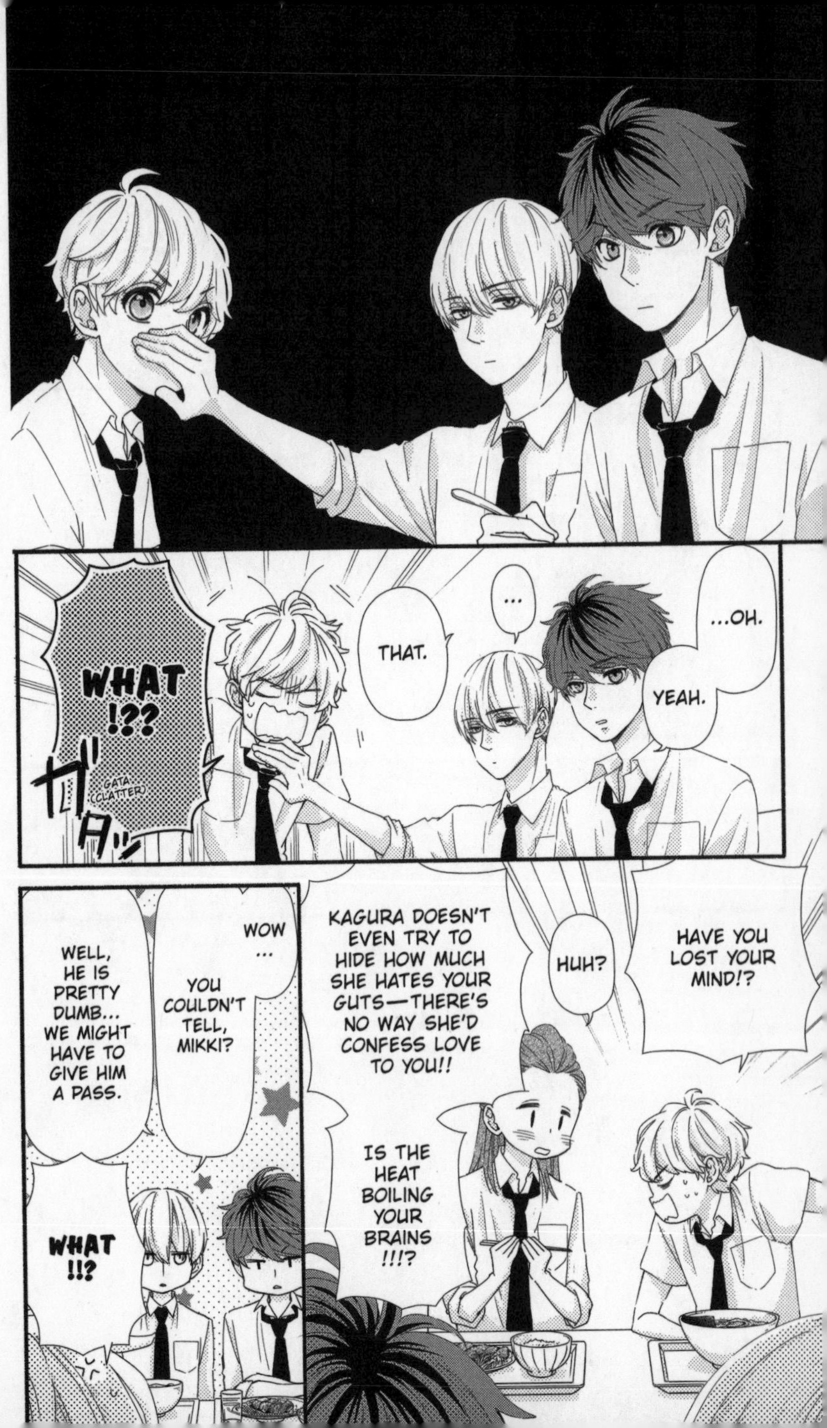
...OH.
YEAH.
...
THAT.
WHAT!??
GATA (CLATTER)
HAVE YOU LOST YOUR MIND!?
HUH?
KAGURA DOESN'T EVEN TRY TO HIDE HOW MUCH SHE HATES YOUR GUTS—THERE'S NO WAY SHE'D CONFESS LOVE TO YOU!!
IS THE HEAT BOILING YOUR BRAINS!!!?
WOW... YOU COULDN'T TELL, MIKKI?
WELL, HE IS PRETTY DUMB... WE MIGHT HAVE TO GIVE HIM A PASS.
WHAT!!?

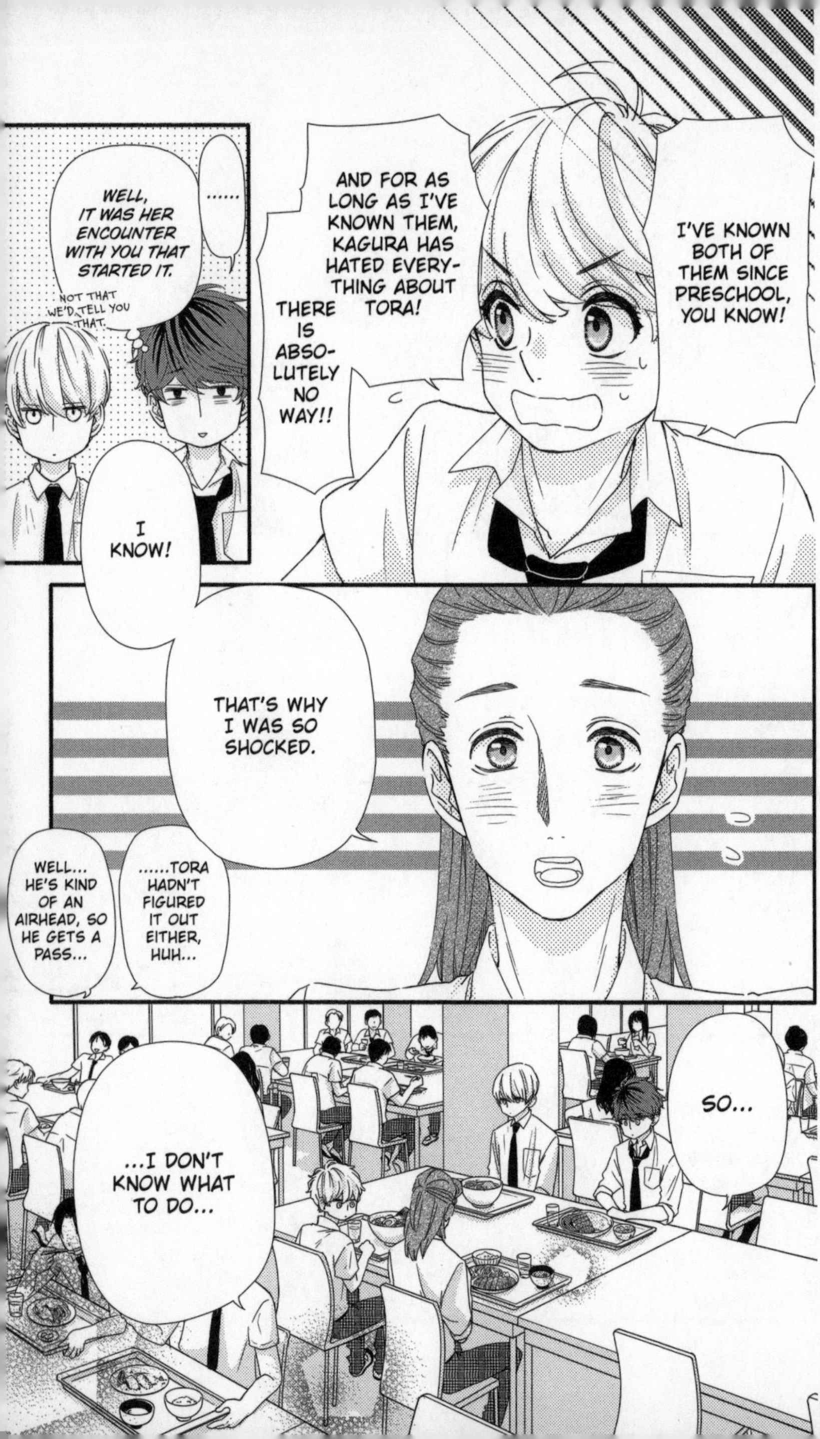
I'VE KNOWN BOTH OF THEM SINCE PRESCHOOL, YOU KNOW!
AND FOR AS LONG AS I'VE KNOWN THEM, KAGURA HAS HATED EVERYTHING ABOUT TORA!
THERE IS ABSOLUTELY NO WAY!!
......
WELL, IT WAS HER ENCOUNTER WITH YOU THAT STARTED IT.
NOT THAT WE'D TELL YOU THAT.
I KNOW!
THAT'S WHY I WAS SO SHOCKED.
......TORA HADN'T FIGURED IT OUT EITHER, HUH...
WELL... HE'S KIND OF AN AIRHEAD, SO HE GETS A PASS...
SO...
...I DON'T KNOW WHAT TO DO...

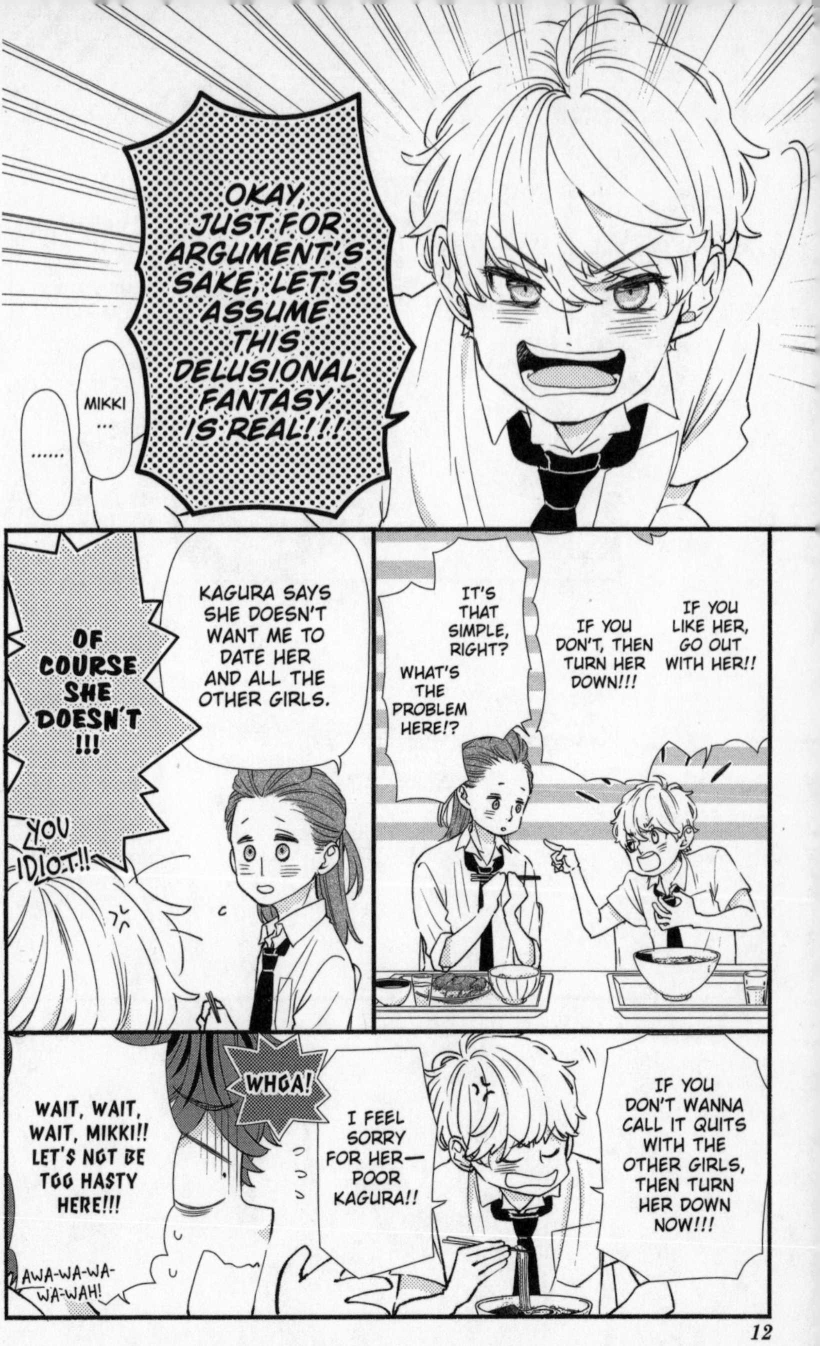

OKAY, JUST FOR ARGUMENT'S SAKE, LET'S ASSUME THIS DELUSIONAL FANTASY IS REAL!!!
MIKKI...
......
IF YOU LIKE HER, GO OUT WITH HER!!
IF YOU DON'T, THEN TURN HER DOWN!!!
IT'S THAT SIMPLE, RIGHT? WHAT'S THE PROBLEM HERE!?
KAGURA SAYS SHE DOESN'T WANT ME TO DATE HER AND ALL THE OTHER GIRLS.
OF COURSE SHE DOESN'T!!!
YOU IDIOT!!
IF YOU DON'T WANNA CALL IT QUITS WITH THE OTHER GIRLS, THEN TURN HER DOWN NOW!!!
I FEEL SORRY FOR HER— POOR KAGURA!!
WHOA!
WAIT, WAIT, WAIT, MIKKI!! LET'S NOT BE TOO HASTY HERE!!!
AWA-WA-WA-WA-WAH!

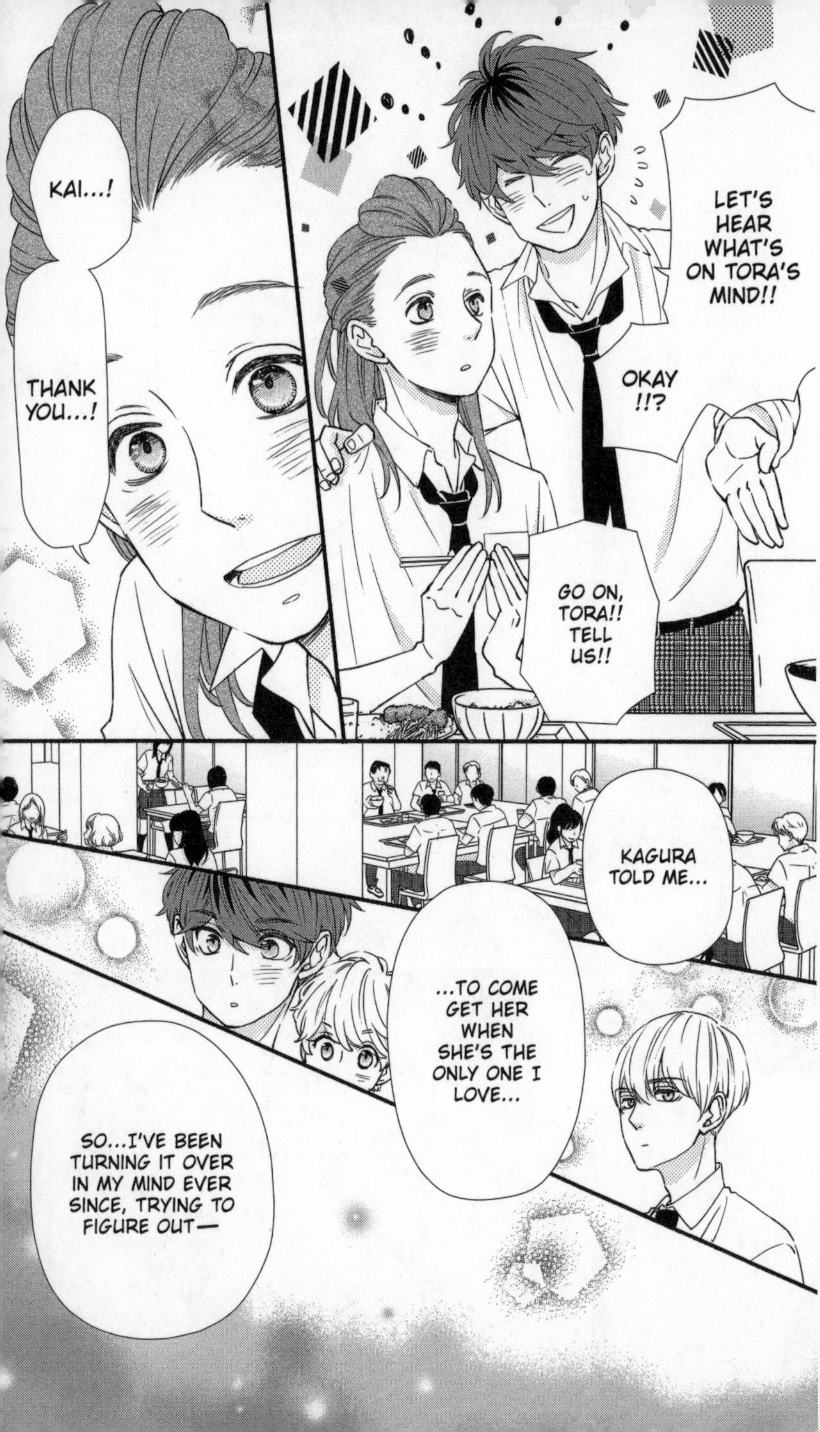
LET'S HEAR WHAT'S ON TORA'S MIND!!
OKAY!!?
GO ON, TORA!! TELL US!!
KAI...!
THANK YOU...!
KAGURA TOLD ME...
...TO COME GET HER WHEN SHE'S THE ONLY ONE I LOVE...
SO...I'VE BEEN TURNING IT OVER IN MY MIND EVER SINCE, TRYING TO FIGURE OUT—

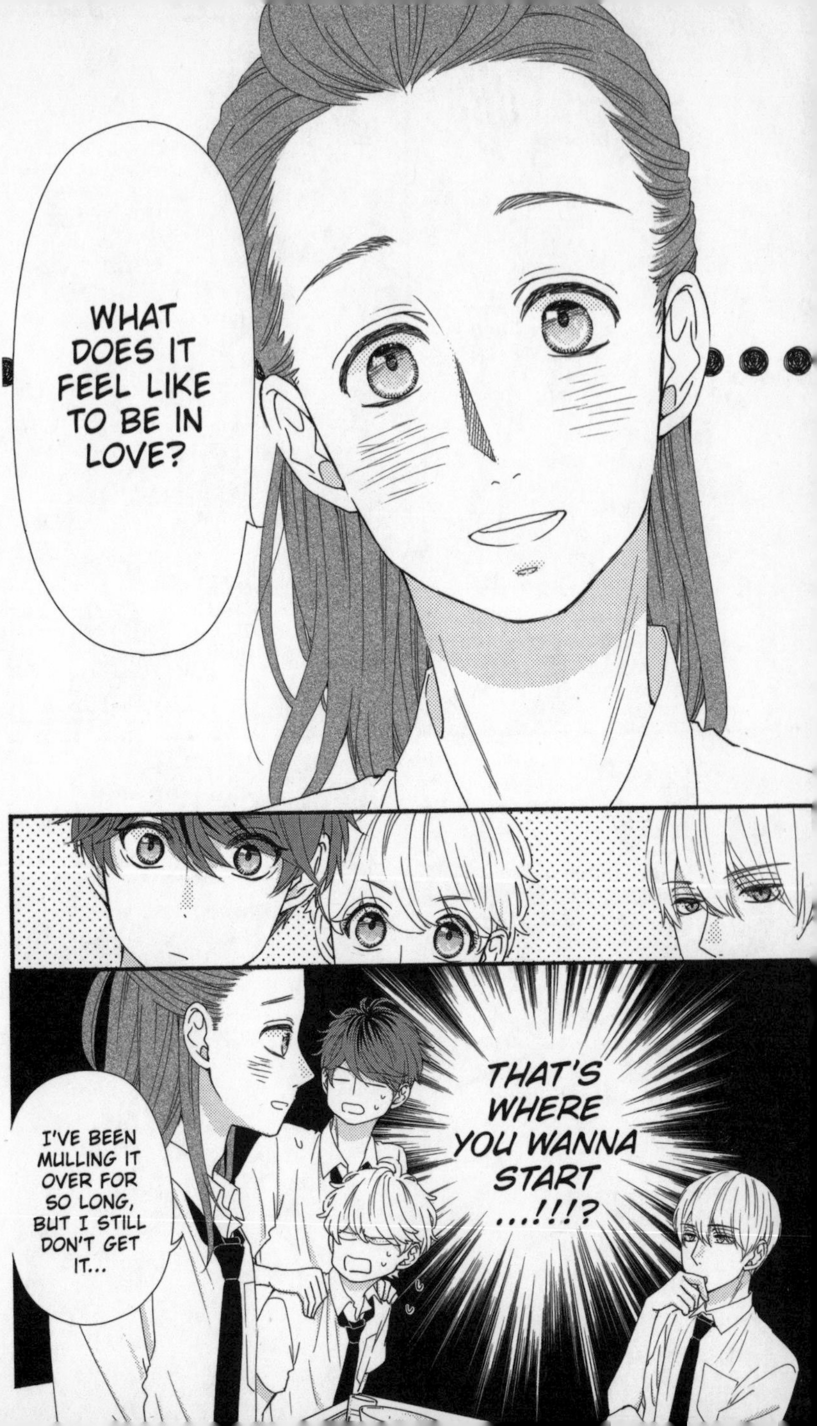
WHAT DOES IT FEEL LIKE TO BE IN LOVE?
THAT'S WHERE YOU WANNA START ...!!!?
I'VE BEEN MULLING IT OVER FOR SO LONG, BUT I STILL DON'T GET IT...

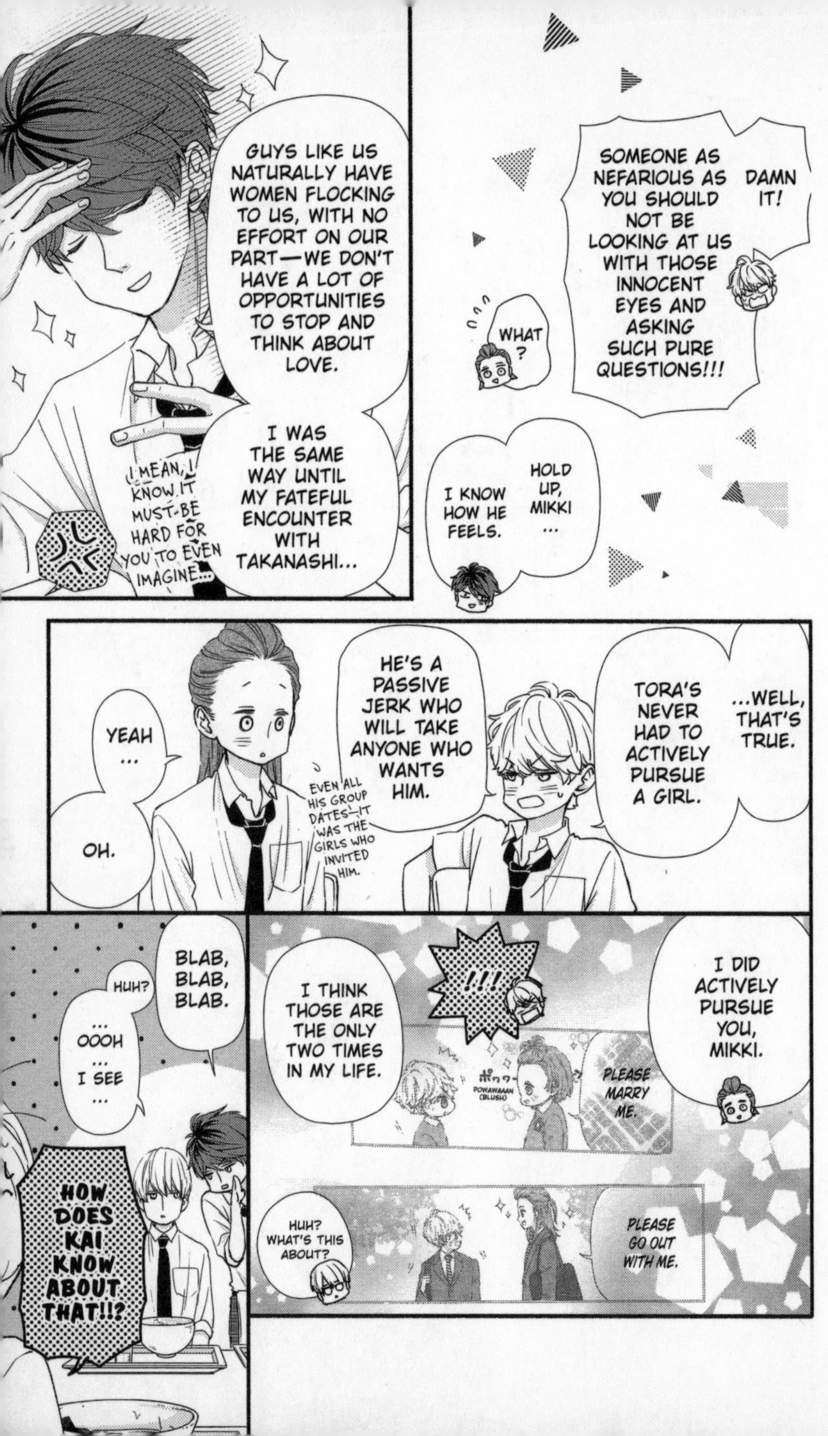
DAMN IT!
SOMEONE AS NEFARIOUS AS YOU SHOULD NOT BE LOOKING AT US WITH THOSE INNOCENT EYES AND ASKING SUCH PURE QUESTIONS!!!
WHAT?
HOLD UP, MIKKI...
I KNOW HOW HE FEELS.
GUYS LIKE US NATURALLY HAVE WOMEN FLOCKING TO US, WITH NO EFFORT ON OUR PART—WE DON'T HAVE A LOT OF OPPORTUNITIES TO STOP AND THINK ABOUT LOVE.
I WAS THE SAME WAY UNTIL MY FATEFUL ENCOUNTER WITH TAKANASHI...
I MEAN, I KNOW IT MUST BE HARD FOR YOU TO EVEN IMAGINE...
...WELL, THAT'S TRUE.
TORA'S NEVER HAD TO ACTIVELY PURSUE A GIRL.
HE'S A PASSIVE JERK WHO WILL TAKE ANYONE WHO WANTS HIM.
EVEN ALL HIS GROUP DATES—IT WAS THE GIRLS WHO INVITED HIM.
YEAH...
OH.
I DID ACTIVELY PURSUE YOU, MIKKI.
!!!
PLEASE MARRY ME.
POWAWAAAN (BLUSH)
I THINK THOSE ARE THE ONLY TWO TIMES IN MY LIFE.
PLEASE GO OUT WITH ME.
HUH? WHAT'S THIS ABOUT?
BLAB, BLAB, BLAB.
HUH?
...OOOH... I SEE...
HOW DOES KAI KNOW ABOUT THAT!!?

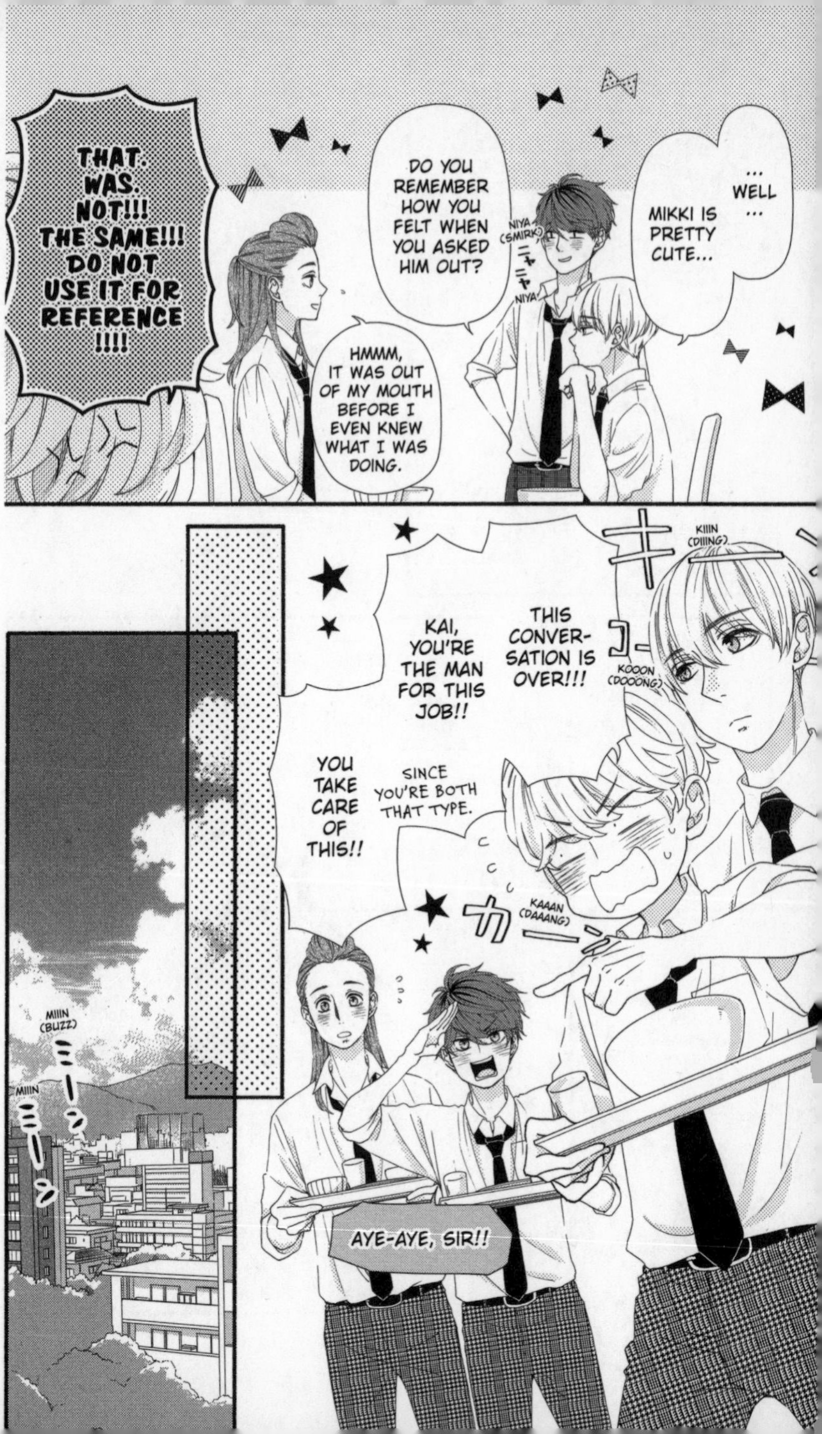
... WELL ... MIKKI IS PRETTY CUTE...
NIYA (SMIRK)
NIYA
DO YOU REMEMBER HOW YOU FELT WHEN YOU ASKED HIM OUT?
HMMM, IT WAS OUT OF MY MOUTH BEFORE I EVEN KNEW WHAT I WAS DOING.
THAT. WAS. NOT!!! THE SAME!!! DO NOT USE IT FOR REFERENCE !!!!
KIIN (DIIING)
KOOON (DOOONG)
THIS CONVER-SATION IS OVER!!!
KAI, YOU'RE THE MAN FOR THIS JOB!!
SINCE YOU'RE BOTH THAT TYPE.
YOU TAKE CARE OF THIS!!
KAAAN (DAAANG)
AYE-AYE, SIR!!
MIIN (BUZZ)
MIIN

MIIIN
ミーー♪

MIIN
ミーー♪

......

KASA
(RUSTLE)
カサ

上

CHARM: GOOD LUCK, ENVELOPE: FRONT

URO
(PACE)
ウロ

URO
(PACE)
ウロ

KAGURA-CHAN!

KARAN
(CLINK)
カラ…ン…

WEL-COME!

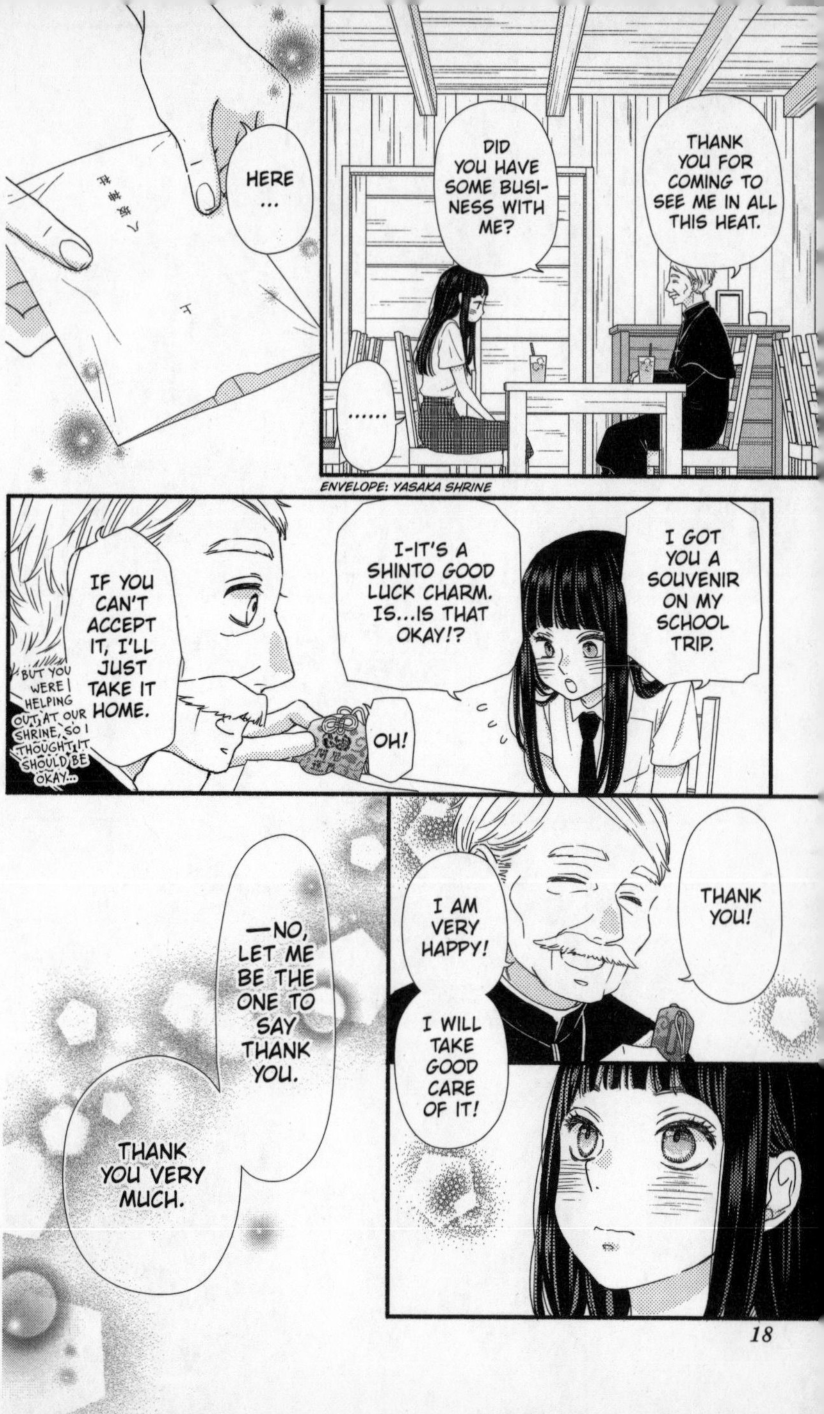
THANK YOU FOR COMING TO SEE ME IN ALL THIS HEAT.
DID YOU HAVE SOME BUSINESS WITH ME?
......
HERE ...
ENVELOPE: YASAKA SHRINE
I GOT YOU A SOUVENIR ON MY SCHOOL TRIP.
I-IT'S A SHINTO GOOD LUCK CHARM. IS...IS THAT OKAY!?
OH!
IF YOU CAN'T ACCEPT IT, I'LL JUST TAKE IT HOME.
BUT YOU WERE HELPING OUT AT OUR SHRINE, SO I THOUGHT IT SHOULD BE OKAY...
THANK YOU!
I AM VERY HAPPY!
I WILL TAKE GOOD CARE OF IT!
—NO, LET ME BE THE ONE TO SAY THANK YOU.
THANK YOU VERY MUCH.

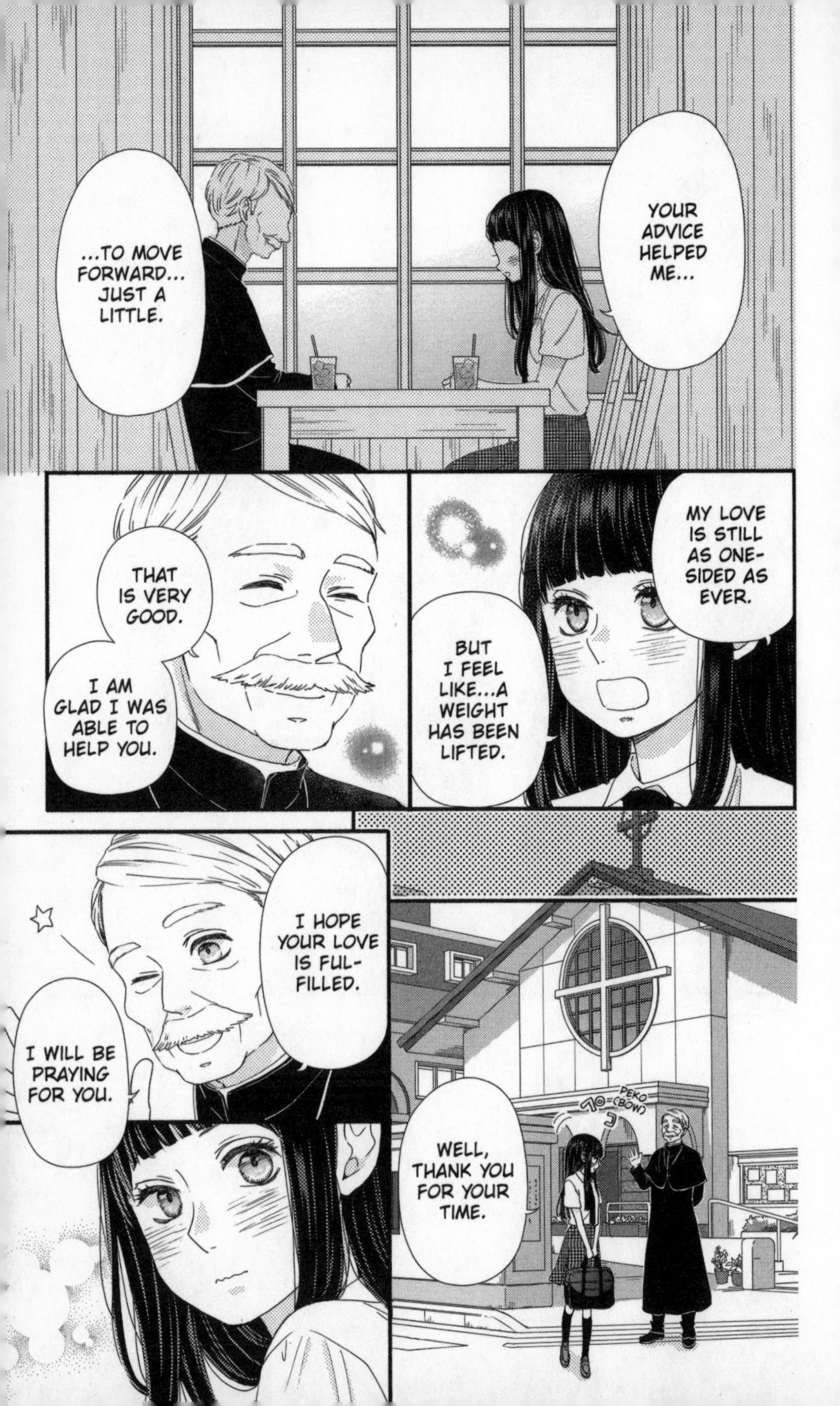
YOUR ADVICE HELPED ME...
...TO MOVE FORWARD... JUST A LITTLE.
MY LOVE IS STILL AS ONE-SIDED AS EVER.
BUT I FEEL LIKE...A WEIGHT HAS BEEN LIFTED.
THAT IS VERY GOOD.
I AM GLAD I WAS ABLE TO HELP YOU.
PEKO (BOW)
WELL, THANK YOU FOR YOUR TIME.
I HOPE YOUR LOVE IS FUL-FILLED.
I WILL BE PRAYING FOR YOU.

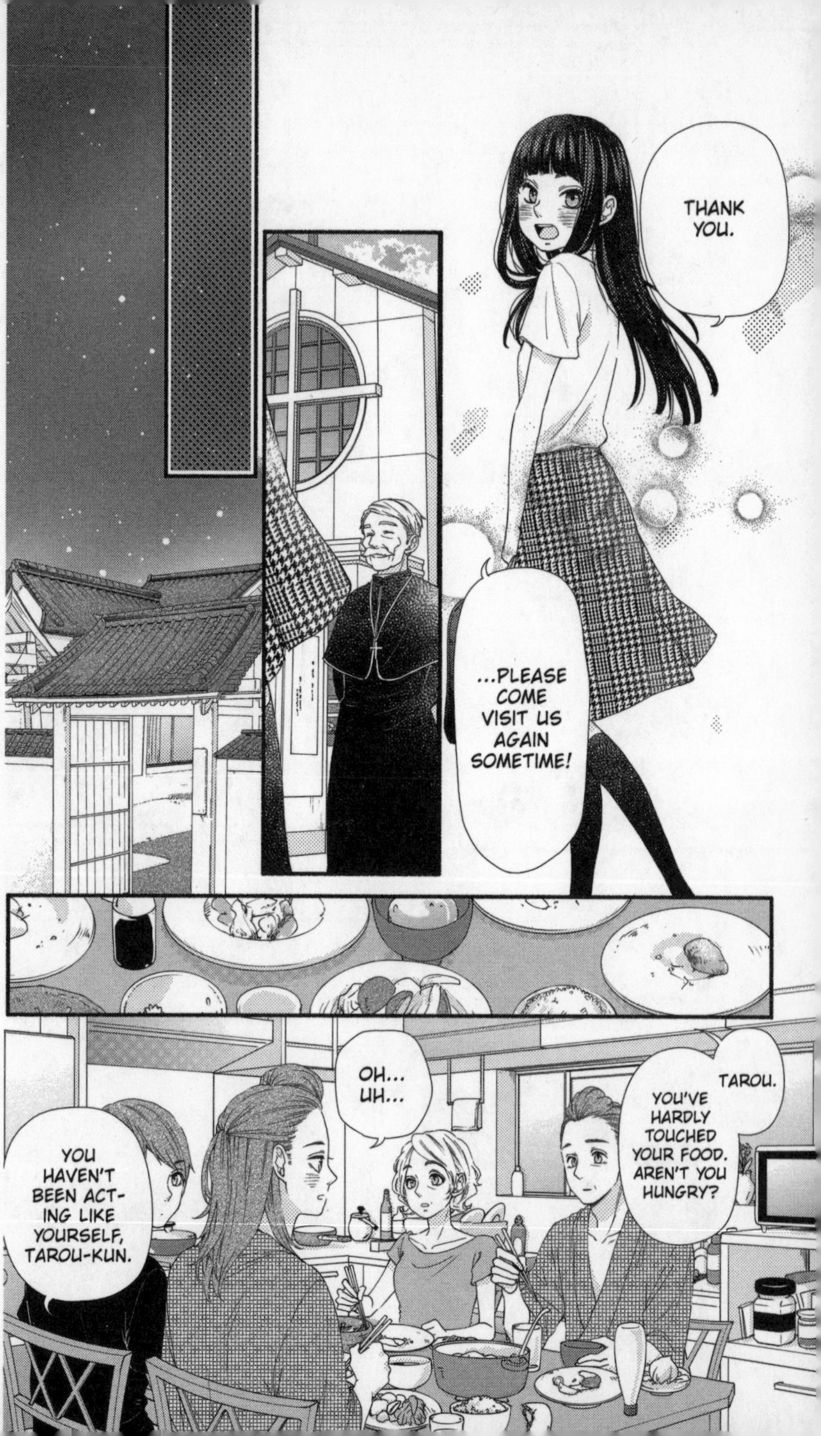
THANK YOU.
...PLEASE COME VISIT US AGAIN SOMETIME!
TAROU.
YOU'VE HARDLY TOUCHED YOUR FOOD. AREN'T YOU HUNGRY?
OH... UH...
YOU HAVEN'T BEEN ACT-ING LIKE YOURSELF, TAROU-KUN.

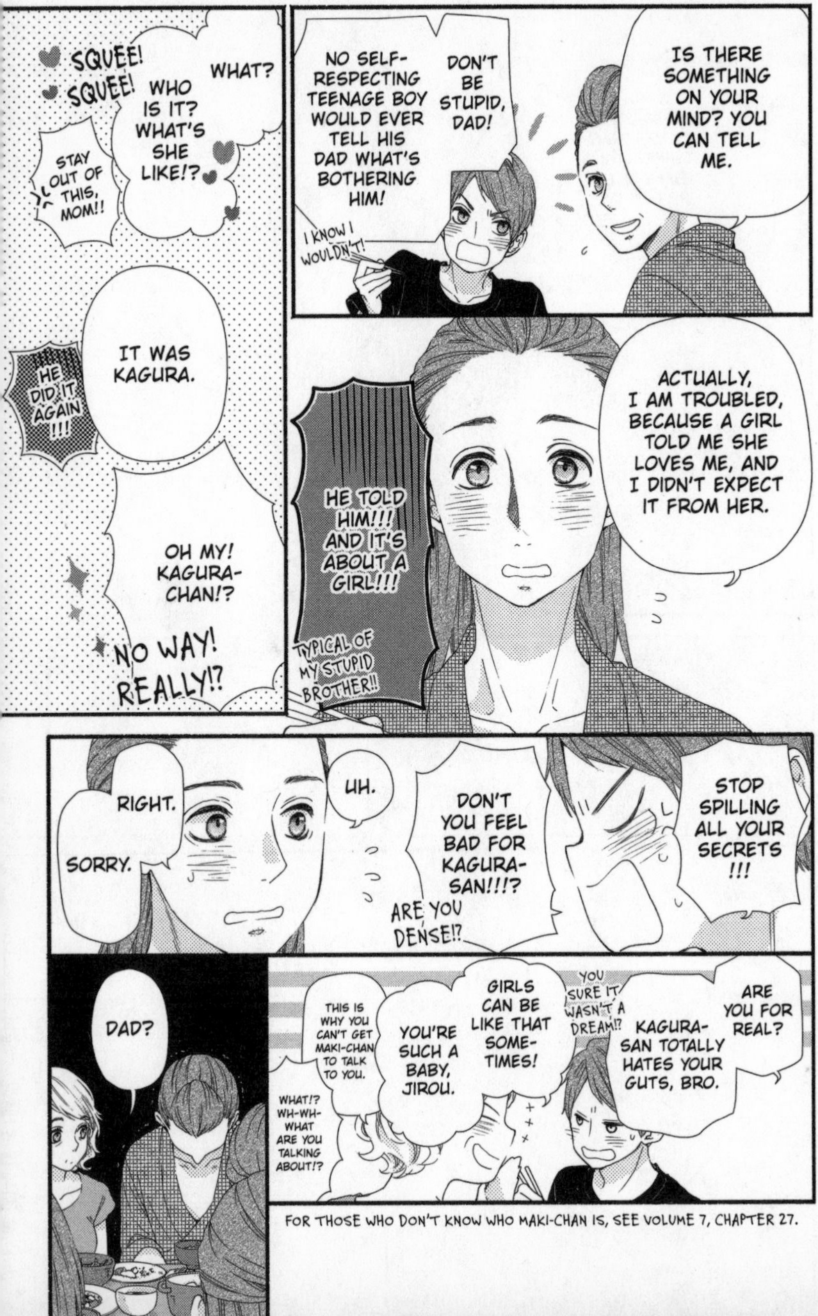
IS THERE SOMETHING ON YOUR MIND? YOU CAN TELL ME.
DON'T BE STUPID, DAD!
NO SELF-RESPECTING TEENAGE BOY WOULD EVER TELL HIS DAD WHAT'S BOTHERING HIM!
I KNOW I WOULDN'T!
ACTUALLY, I AM TROUBLED, BECAUSE A GIRL TOLD ME SHE LOVES ME, AND I DIDN'T EXPECT IT FROM HER.
HE TOLD HIM!!! AND IT'S ABOUT A GIRL!!!
TYPICAL OF MY STUPID BROTHER!!
WHAT?
WHO IS IT? WHAT'S SHE LIKE!?
SQUEE! SQUEE!
STAY OUT OF THIS, MOM!!
IT WAS KAGURA.
HE DID IT AGAIN!!!
OH MY! KAGURA-CHAN!?
NO WAY! REALLY!?
STOP SPILLING ALL YOUR SECRETS!!!
DON'T YOU FEEL BAD FOR KAGURA-SAN!!!?
ARE YOU DENSE!?
UH.
RIGHT.
SORRY.
ARE YOU FOR REAL?
KAGURA-SAN TOTALLY HATES YOUR GUTS, BRO.
YOU SURE IT WASN'T A DREAM!?
GIRLS CAN BE LIKE THAT SOMETIMES!
YOU'RE SUCH A BABY, JIROU.
THIS IS WHY YOU CAN'T GET MAKI-CHAN TO TALK TO YOU.
WHAT!? WH-WH-WHAT ARE YOU TALKING ABOUT!?
DAD?
FOR THOSE WHO DON'T KNOW WHO MAKI-CHAN IS, SEE VOLUME 7, CHAPTER 27.

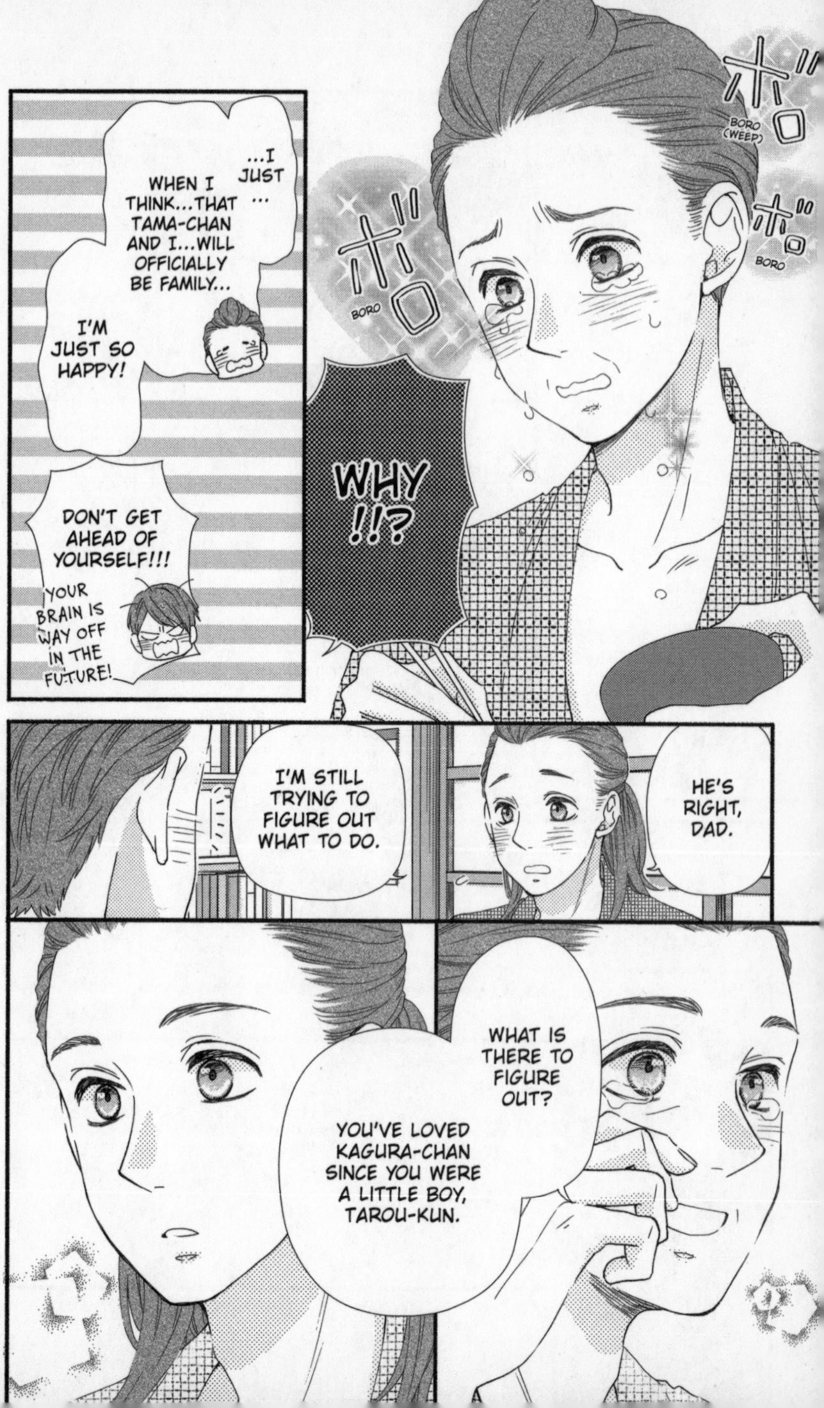

BORO (WEEP)
BORO
BORO
WHY!!?
...I JUST...
WHEN I THINK...THAT TAMA-CHAN AND I...WILL OFFICIALLY BE FAMILY...
I'M JUST SO HAPPY!
DON'T GET AHEAD OF YOURSELF!!!
YOUR BRAIN IS WAY OFF IN THE FUTURE!
HE'S RIGHT, DAD.
I'M STILL TRYING TO FIGURE OUT WHAT TO DO.
WHAT IS THERE TO FIGURE OUT?
YOU'VE LOVED KAGURA-CHAN SINCE YOU WERE A LITTLE BOY, TAROU-KUN.

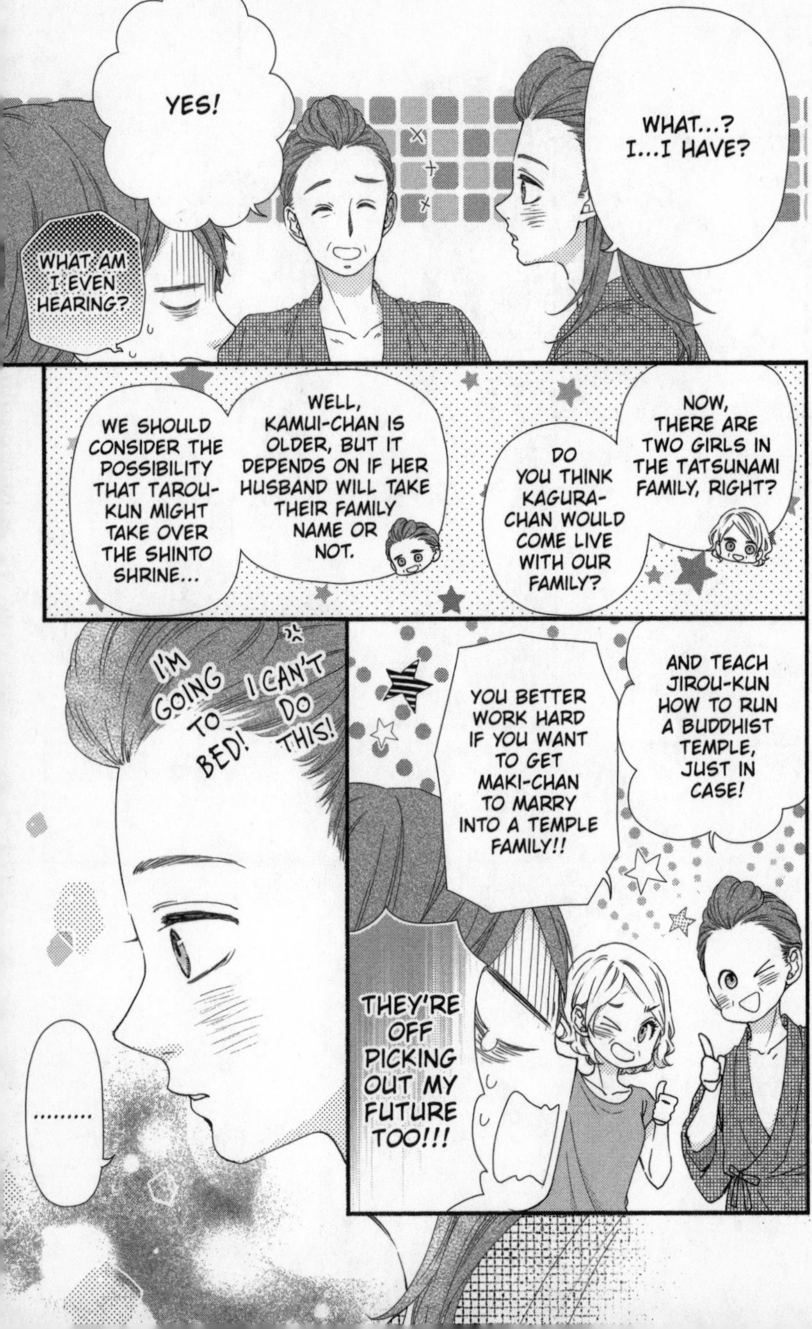
WHAT...? I...I HAVE?
YES!
WHAT AM I EVEN HEARING?
NOW, THERE ARE TWO GIRLS IN THE TATSUNAMI FAMILY, RIGHT?
DO YOU THINK KAGURA-CHAN WOULD COME LIVE WITH OUR FAMILY?
WELL, KAMUI-CHAN IS OLDER, BUT IT DEPENDS ON IF HER HUSBAND WILL TAKE THEIR FAMILY NAME OR NOT.
WE SHOULD CONSIDER THE POSSIBILITY THAT TAROU-KUN MIGHT TAKE OVER THE SHINTO SHRINE...
AND TEACH JIROU-KUN HOW TO RUN A BUDDHIST TEMPLE, JUST IN CASE!
YOU BETTER WORK HARD IF YOU WANT TO GET MAKI-CHAN TO MARRY INTO A TEMPLE FAMILY!!
THEY'RE OFF PICKING OUT MY FUTURE TOO!!!
I CAN'T DO THIS!
I'M GOING TO BED!
....

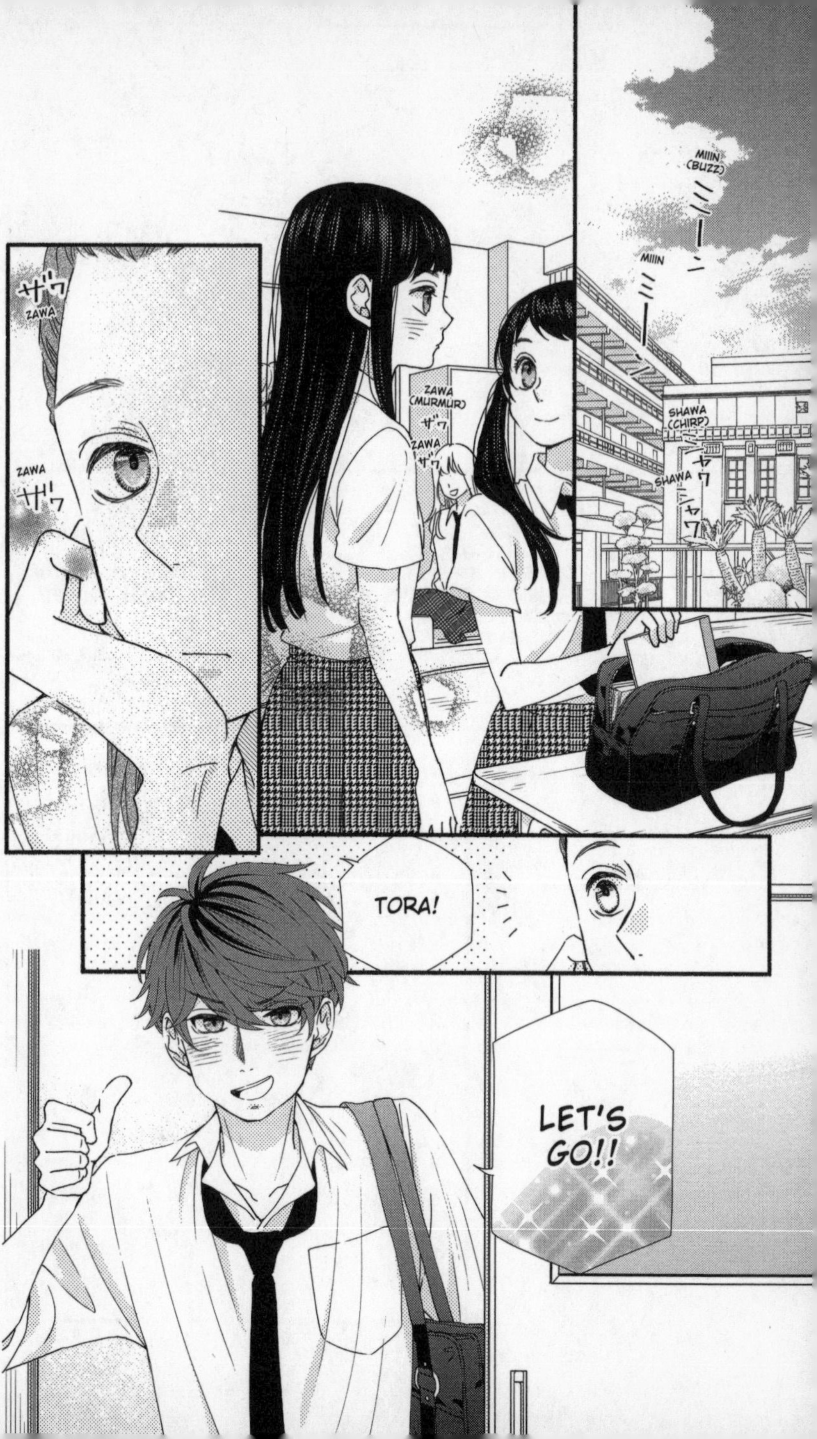

MIIIN (BUZZ)
MIIIN
SHAWA (CHIRP)
SHAWA
ZAWA (MURMUR)
ZAWA
ZAWA
ZAWA
TORA!
LET'S GO!!

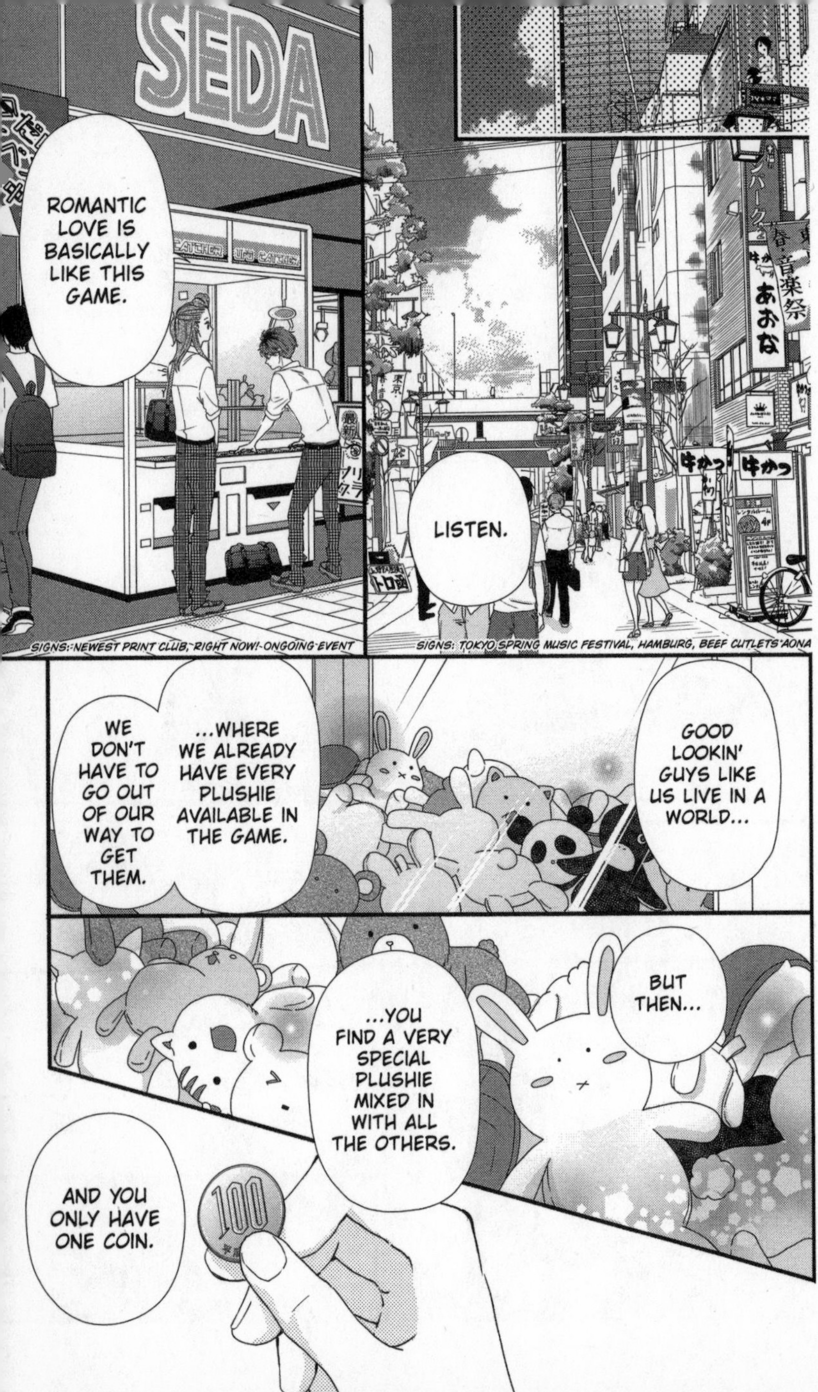
LISTEN.
SIGNS: TOKYO SPRING MUSIC FESTIVAL, HAMBURG, BEEF CUTLETS AONA
牛かつ
牛かつ
あおな
SEDA
ROMANTIC LOVE IS BASICALLY LIKE THIS GAME.
SIGNS: NEWEST PRINT CLUB, RIGHT NOW!-ONGOING EVENT
GOOD LOOKIN' GUYS LIKE US LIVE IN A WORLD...
...WHERE WE ALREADY HAVE EVERY PLUSHIE AVAILABLE IN THE GAME.
WE DON'T HAVE TO GO OUT OF OUR WAY TO GET THEM.
BUT THEN...
...YOU FIND A VERY SPECIAL PLUSHIE MIXED IN WITH ALL THE OTHERS.
AND YOU ONLY HAVE ONE COIN.
100

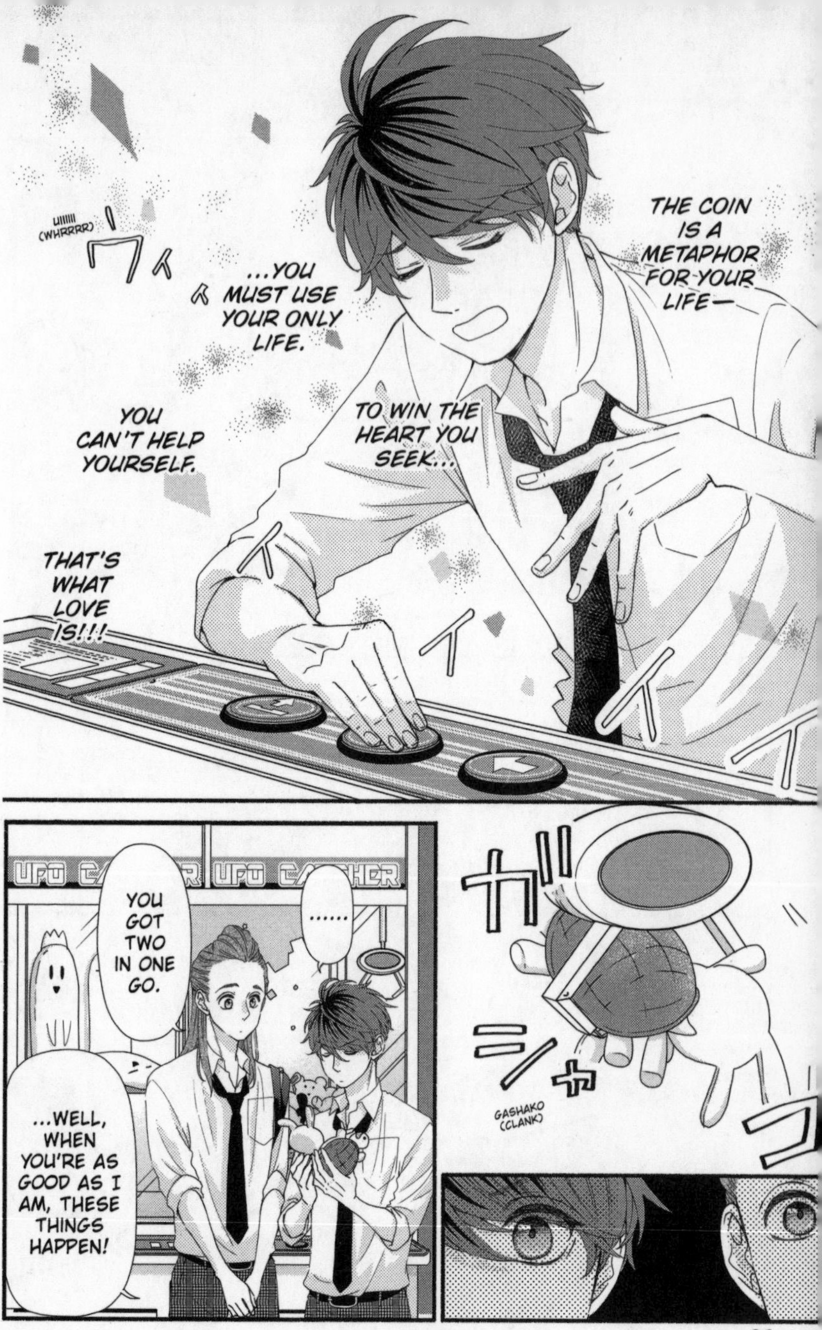
THE COIN IS A METAPHOR FOR YOUR LIFE—
...YOU MUST USE YOUR ONLY LIFE.
UIIIIII (WHRRRR)
TO WIN THE HEART YOU SEEK...
YOU CAN'T HELP YOURSELF.
THAT'S WHAT LOVE IS!!!
GASHAKO (CLANK)
......
YOU GOT TWO IN ONE GO.
...WELL, WHEN YOU'RE AS GOOD AS I AM, THESE THINGS HAPPEN!

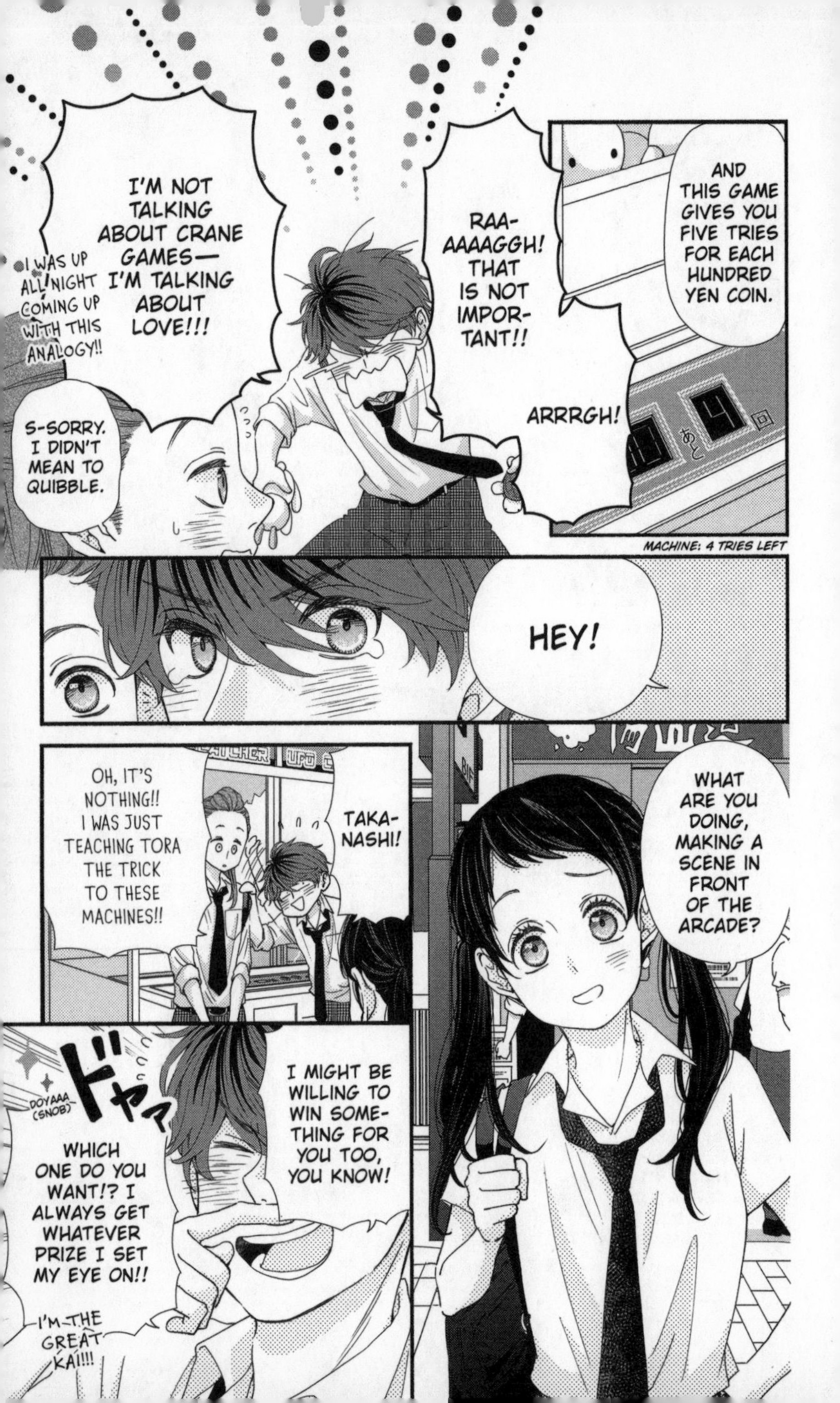
AND THIS GAME GIVES YOU FIVE TRIES FOR EACH HUNDRED YEN COIN.
RAA-AAAAGGH! THAT IS NOT IMPORTANT!!
ARRRGH!
MACHINE: 4 TRIES LEFT
I'M NOT TALKING ABOUT CRANE GAMES—I'M TALKING ABOUT LOVE!!!
I WAS UP ALL NIGHT COMING UP WITH THIS ANALOGY!!
S-SORRY. I DIDN'T MEAN TO QUIBBLE.
HEY!
WHAT ARE YOU DOING, MAKING A SCENE IN FRONT OF THE ARCADE?
TAKA-NASHI!
OH, IT'S NOTHING!! I WAS JUST TEACHING TORA THE TRICK TO THESE MACHINES!!
I MIGHT BE WILLING TO WIN SOMETHING FOR YOU TOO, YOU KNOW!
ドヤァ
DOYAAA (SNOB)
WHICH ONE DO YOU WANT!? I ALWAYS GET WHATEVER PRIZE I SET MY EYE ON!!
I'M THE GREAT KAI!!!

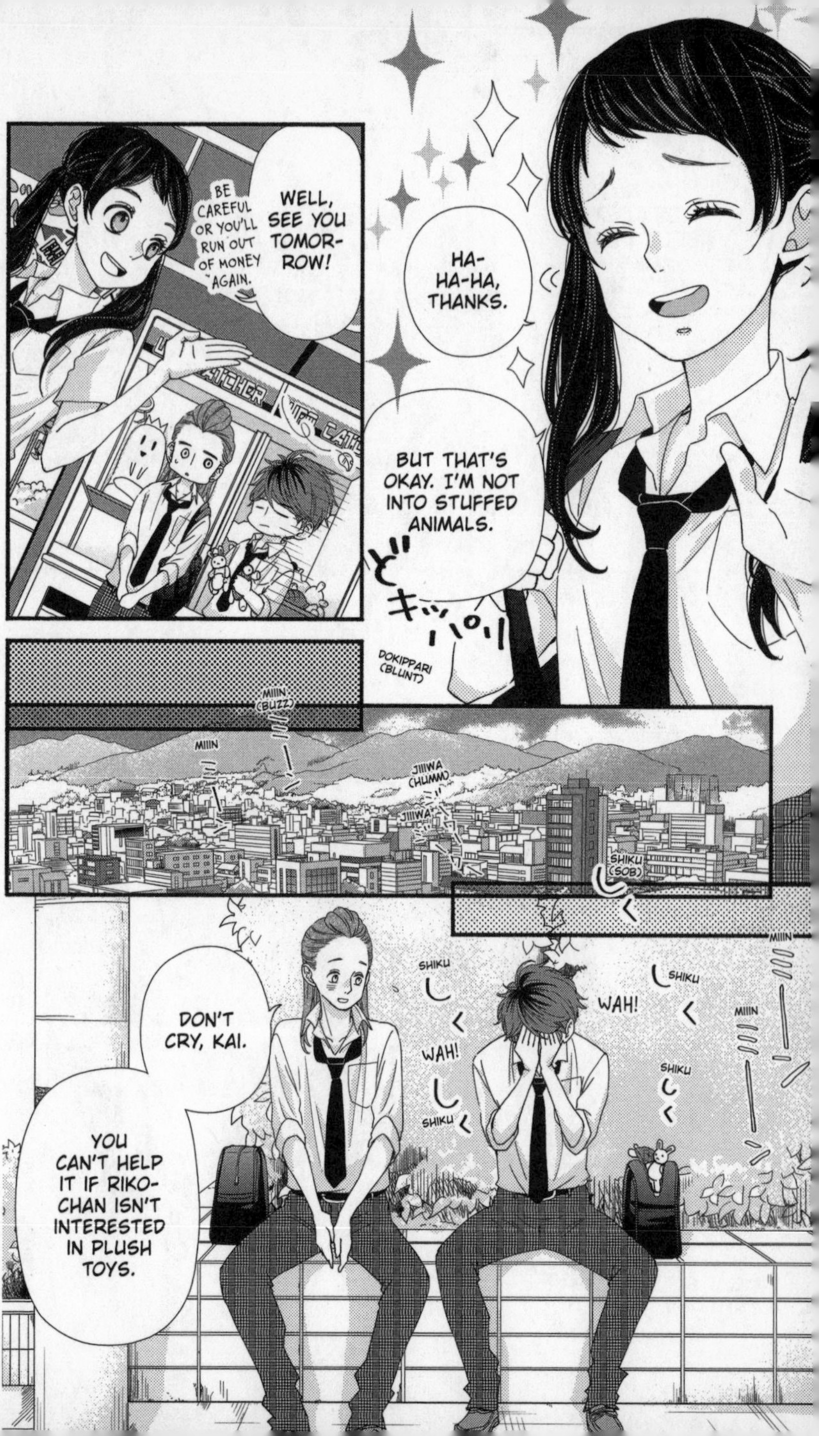
HA-HA-HA, THANKS.
BUT THAT'S OKAY. I'M NOT INTO STUFFED ANIMALS.
DOKIPPARI (BLUNT)
WELL, SEE YOU TOMORROW!
BE CAREFUL OR YOU'LL RUN OUT OF MONEY AGAIN.
MIIIN (BUZZ)
JIIIWA (HUMMM)
JIIIWA
MIIIN
SHIKU (SOB)
MIIIN
MIIIN
SHIKU
SHIKU
WAH!
SHIKU
WAH!
SHIKU
DON'T CRY, KAI.
YOU CAN'T HELP IT IF RIKO-CHAN ISN'T INTERESTED IN PLUSH TOYS.

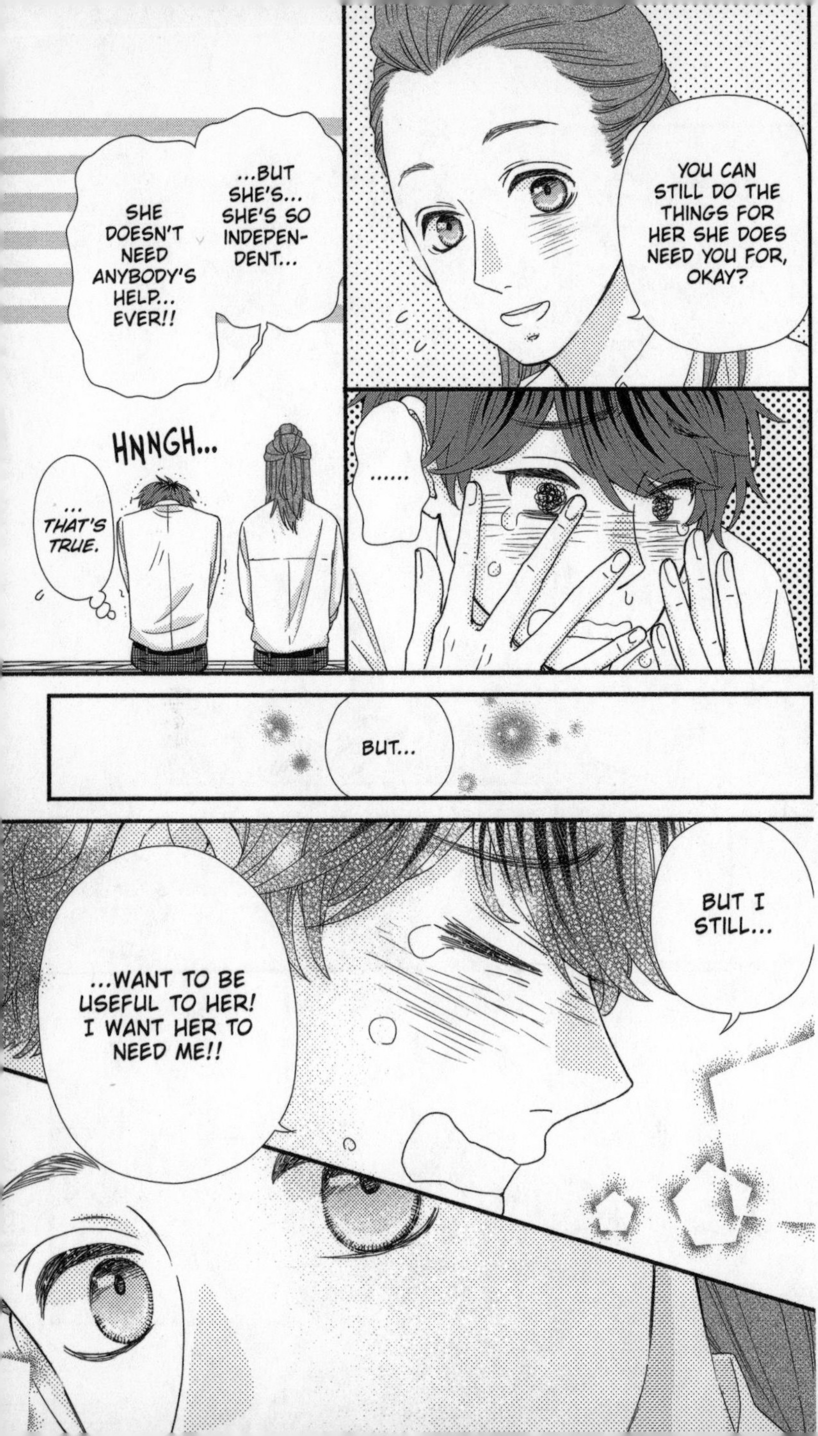
YOU CAN STILL DO THE THINGS FOR HER SHE DOES NEED YOU FOR, OKAY?
......
...BUT SHE'S... SHE'S SO INDEPEN-DENT...
SHE DOESN'T NEED ANYBODY'S HELP... EVER!!
HNNGH...
...THAT'S TRUE.
BUT...
BUT I STILL...
...WANT TO BE USEFUL TO HER! I WANT HER TO NEED ME!!

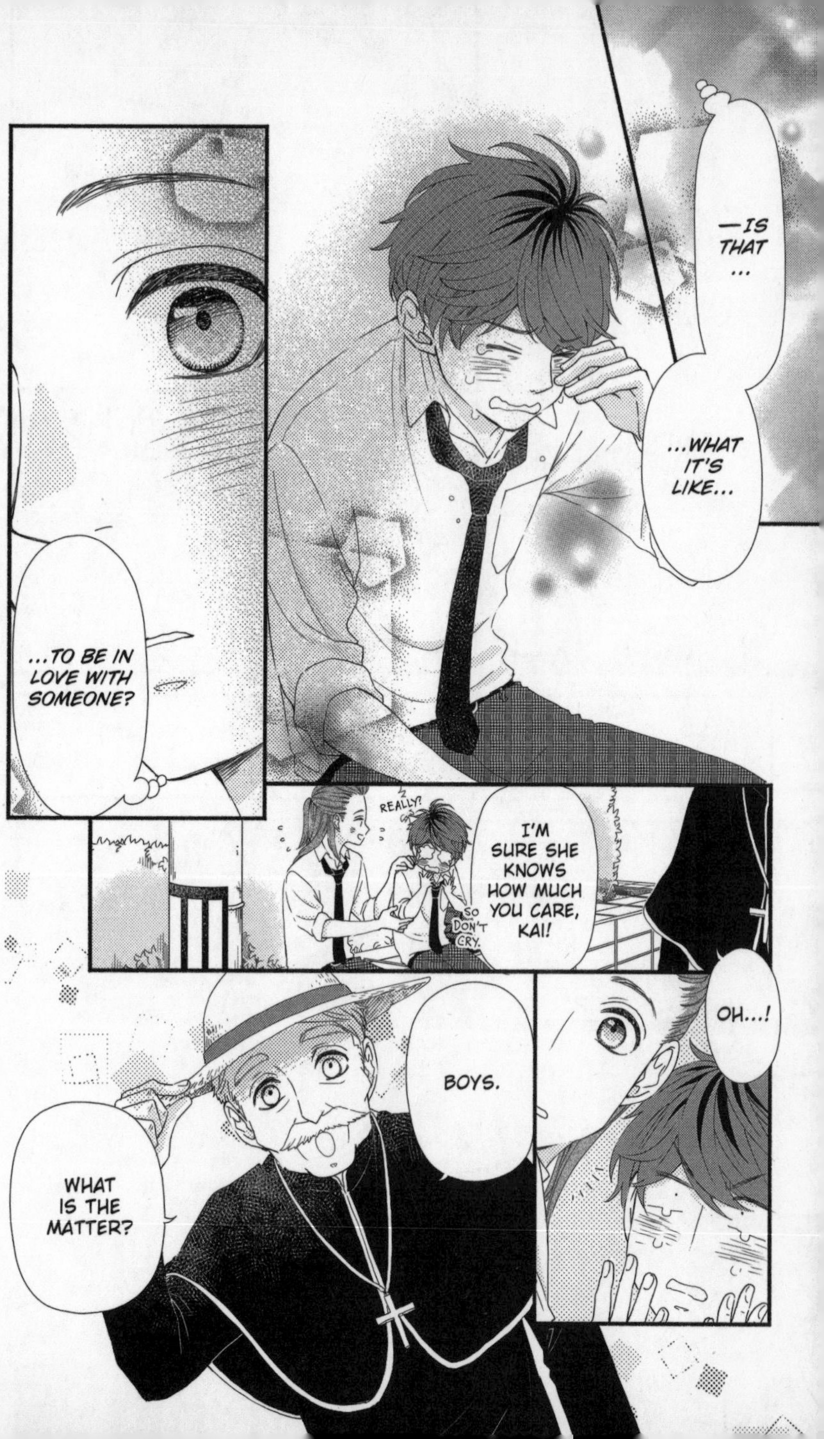
—IS THAT ...
...WHAT IT'S LIKE...
...TO BE IN LOVE WITH SOMEONE?
I'M SURE SHE KNOWS HOW MUCH YOU CARE, KAI!
REALLY?
SO DON'T CRY.
OH...!
BOYS.
WHAT IS THE MATTER?

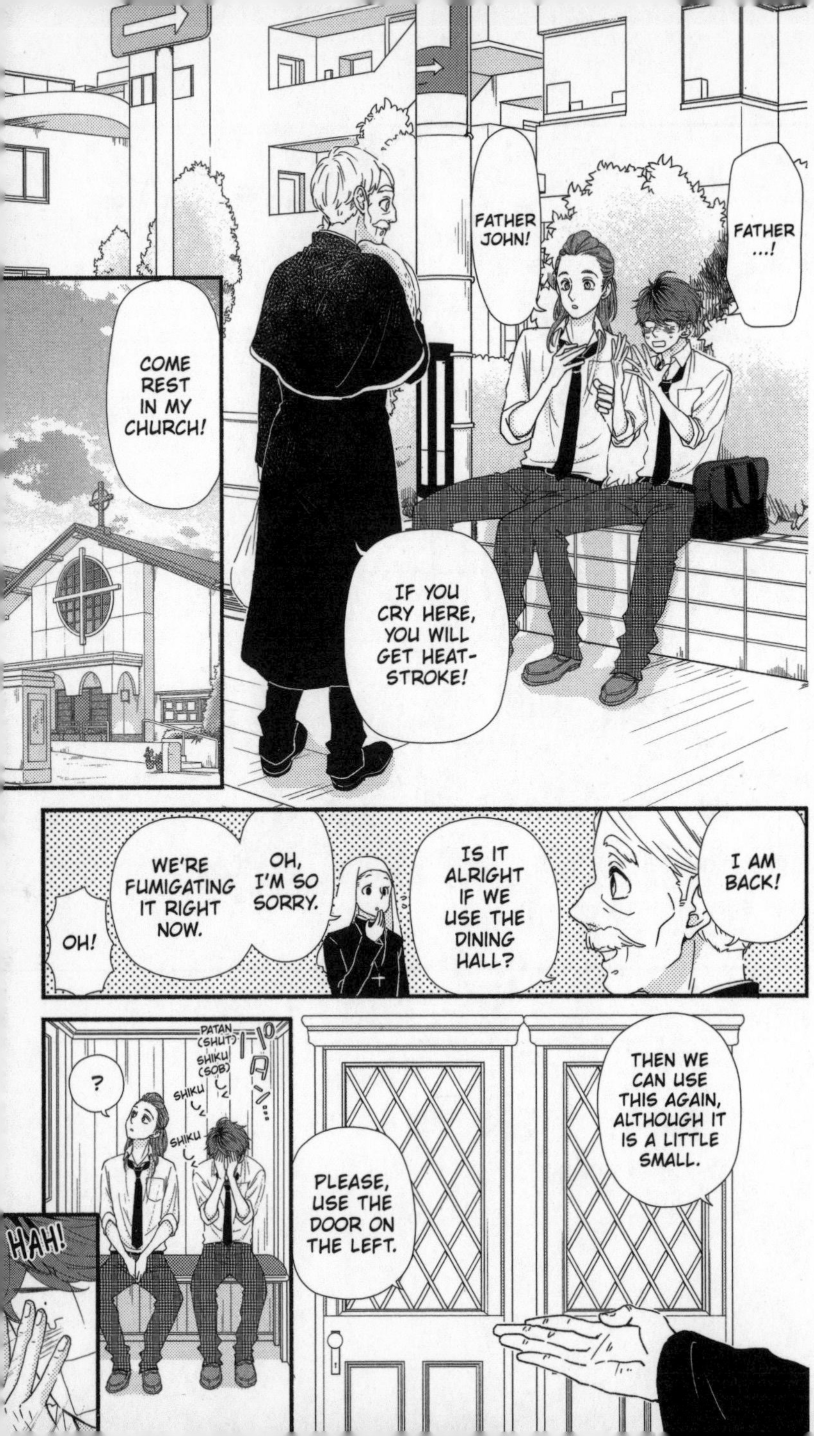
FATHER ...!
FATHER JOHN!
IF YOU CRY HERE, YOU WILL GET HEAT-STROKE!
COME REST IN MY CHURCH!
I AM BACK!
IS IT ALRIGHT IF WE USE THE DINING HALL?
OH, I'M SO SORRY.
WE'RE FUMIGATING IT RIGHT NOW.
OH!
THEN WE CAN USE THIS AGAIN, ALTHOUGH IT IS A LITTLE SMALL.
PLEASE, USE THE DOOR ON THE LEFT.
PATAN (SHUT)
SHIKU (SOB)
SHIKU
SHIKU
?
HAH!

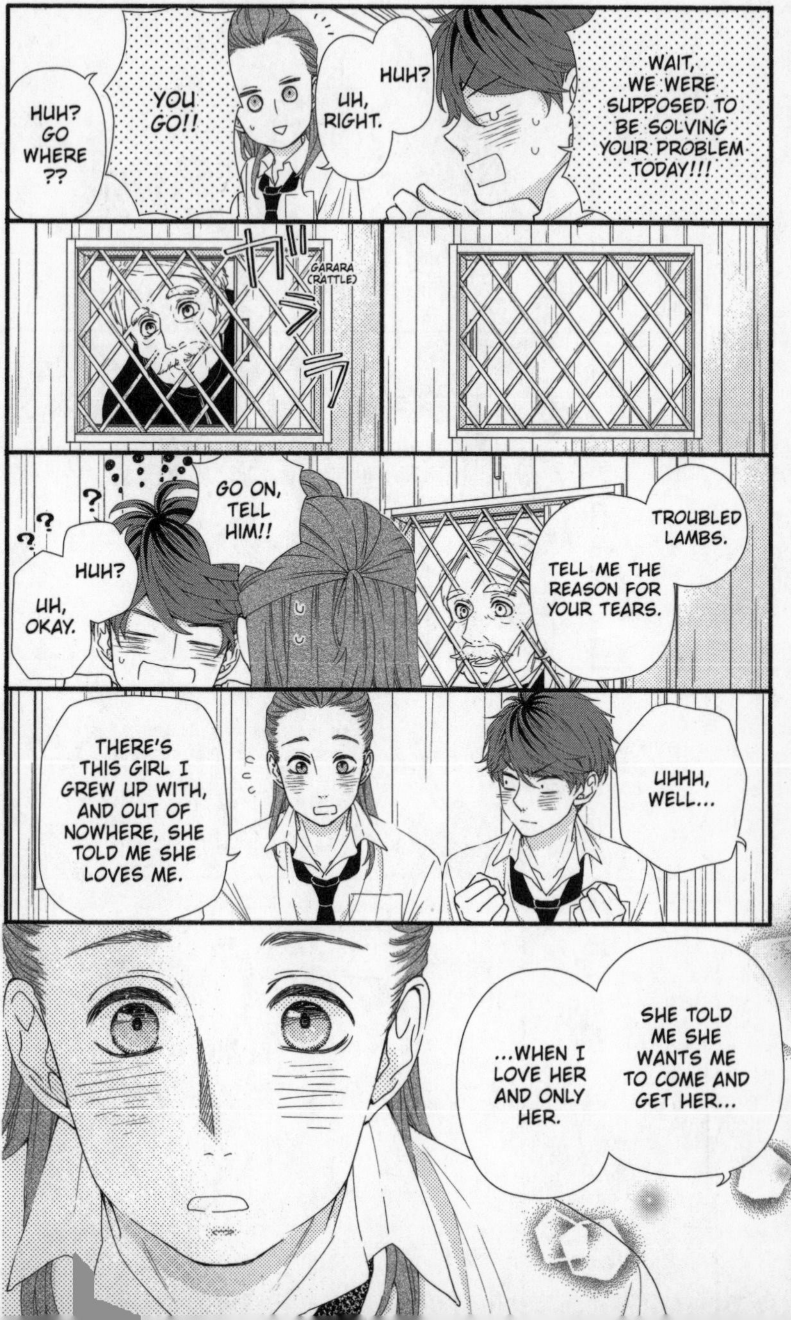
WAIT, WE WERE SUPPOSED TO BE SOLVING YOUR PROBLEM TODAY!!!
HUH?
UH, RIGHT.
YOU GO!!
HUH? GO WHERE ??
GARARA (RATTLE)
TROUBLED LAMBS.
TELL ME THE REASON FOR YOUR TEARS.
GO ON, TELL HIM!!
HUH?
UH, OKAY.
UHHH, WELL...
THERE'S THIS GIRL I GREW UP WITH, AND OUT OF NOWHERE, SHE TOLD ME SHE LOVES ME.
SHE TOLD ME SHE WANTS ME TO COME AND GET HER...
...WHEN I LOVE HER AND ONLY HER.

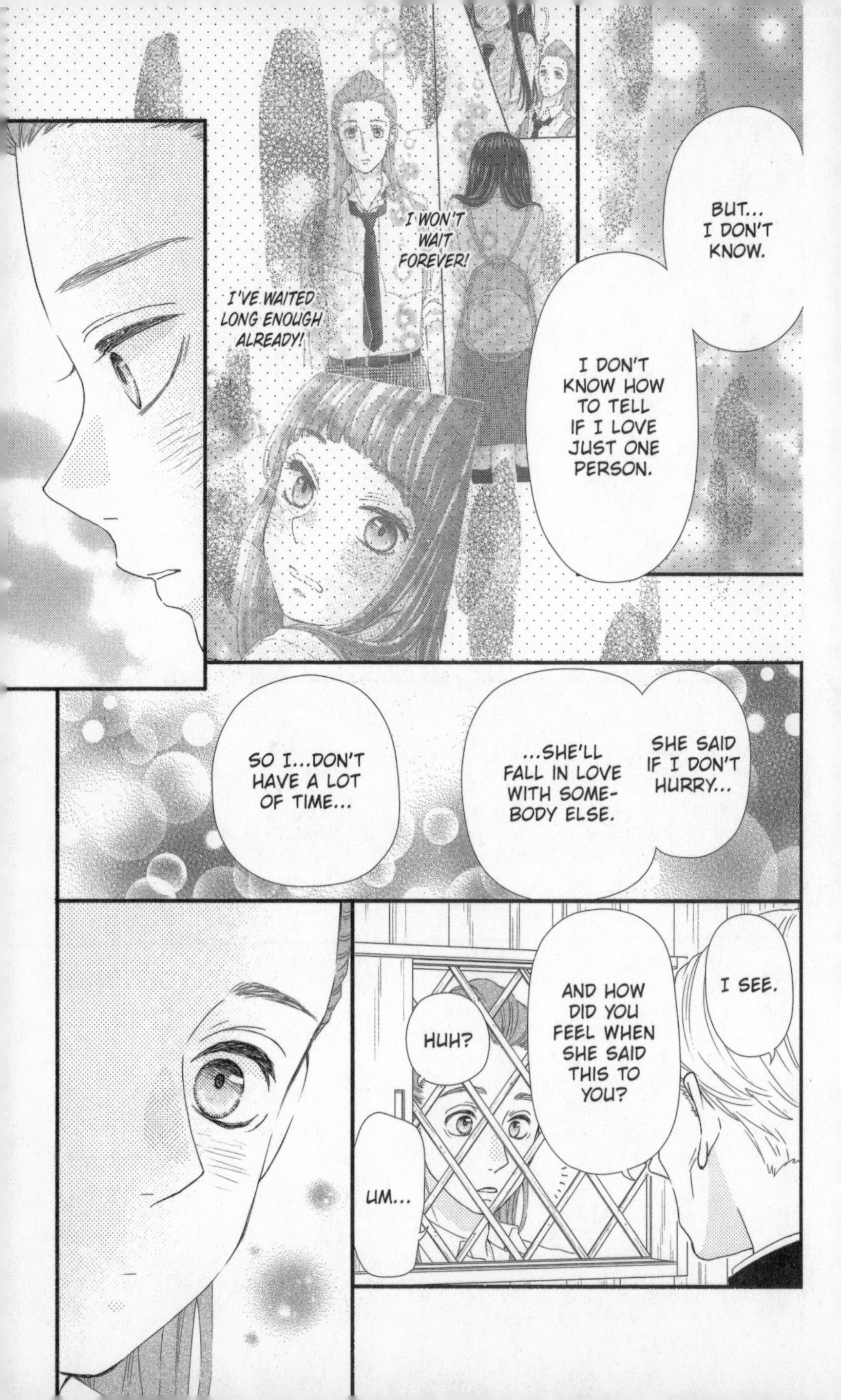
BUT... I DON'T KNOW.
I DON'T KNOW HOW TO TELL IF I LOVE JUST ONE PERSON.
I WON'T WAIT FOREVER!
I'VE WAITED LONG ENOUGH ALREADY!
SHE SAID IF I DON'T HURRY...
...SHE'LL FALL IN LOVE WITH SOME-BODY ELSE.
SO I...DON'T HAVE A LOT OF TIME...
I SEE.
AND HOW DID YOU FEEL WHEN SHE SAID THIS TO YOU?
HUH?
UM...

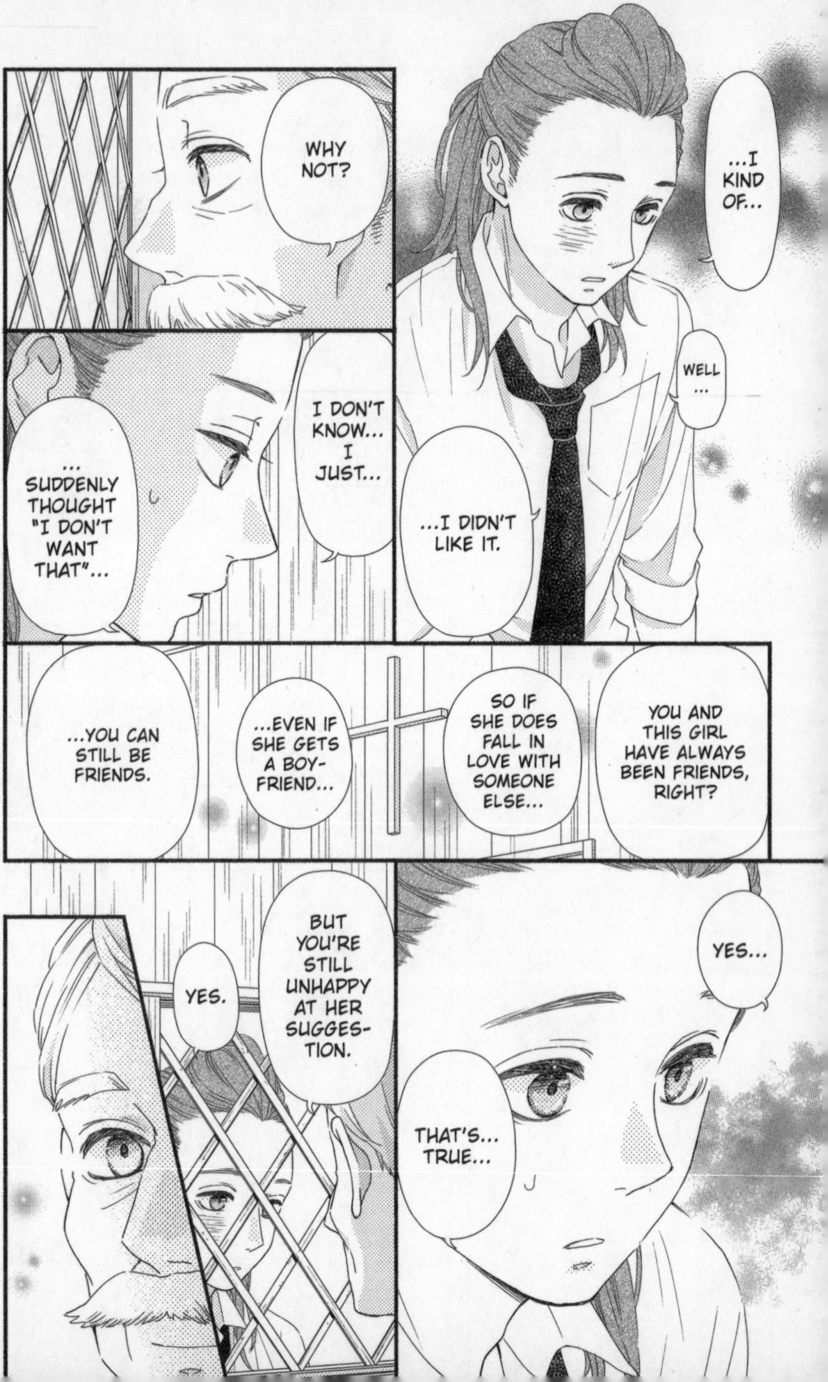
...I KIND OF...
WELL ...
...I DIDN'T LIKE IT.
WHY NOT?
I DON'T KNOW... I JUST...
... SUDDENLY THOUGHT "I DON'T WANT THAT"...
YOU AND THIS GIRL HAVE ALWAYS BEEN FRIENDS, RIGHT?
SO IF SHE DOES FALL IN LOVE WITH SOMEONE ELSE...
...EVEN IF SHE GETS A BOY-FRIEND...
...YOU CAN STILL BE FRIENDS.
YES...
THAT'S... TRUE...
BUT YOU'RE STILL UNHAPPY AT HER SUGGES-TION.
YES.

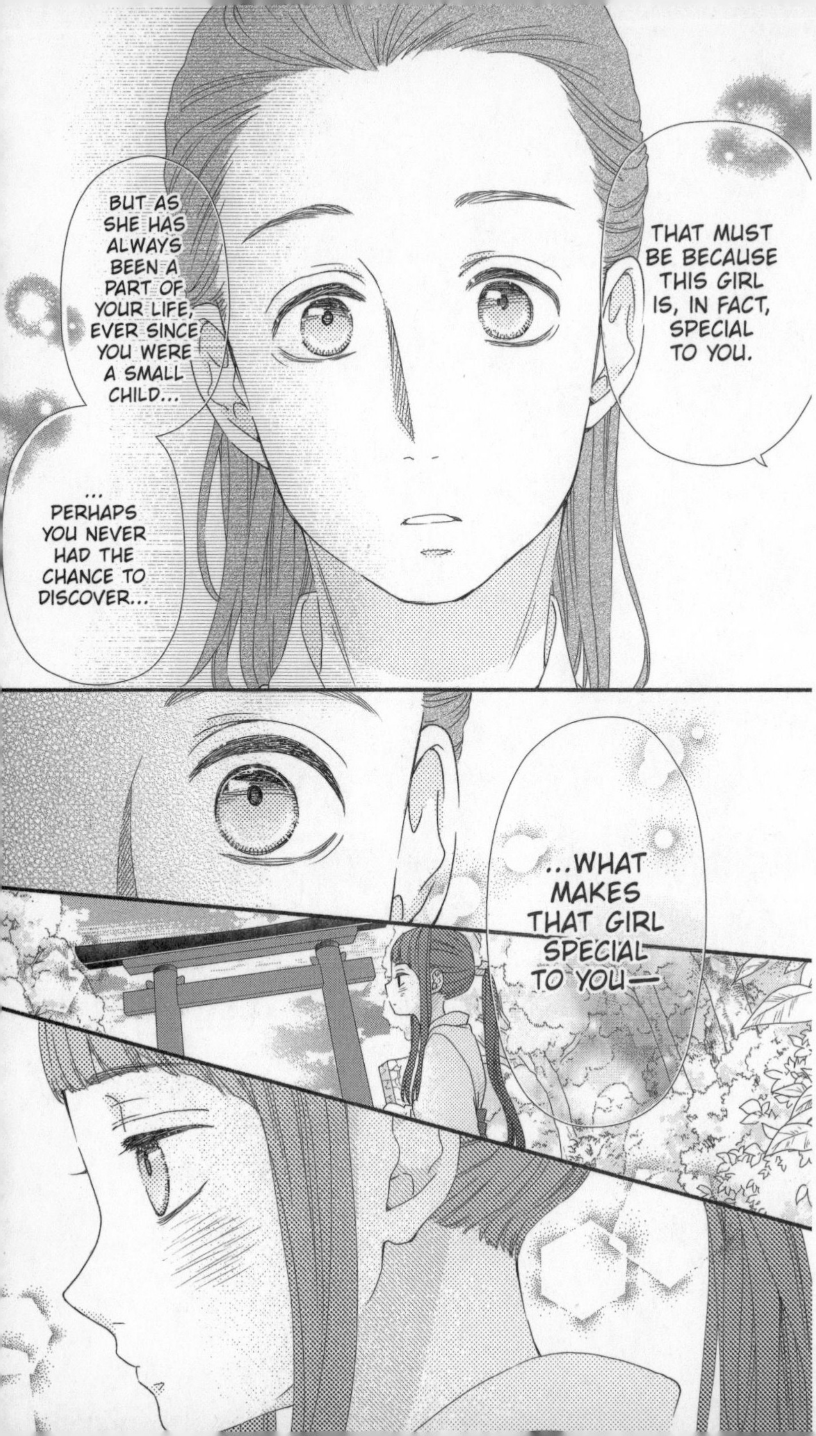
THAT MUST BE BECAUSE THIS GIRL IS, IN FACT, SPECIAL TO YOU.
BUT AS SHE HAS ALWAYS BEEN A PART OF YOUR LIFE, EVER SINCE YOU WERE A SMALL CHILD...
... PERHAPS YOU NEVER HAD THE CHANCE TO DISCOVER...
...WHAT MAKES THAT GIRL SPECIAL TO YOU—

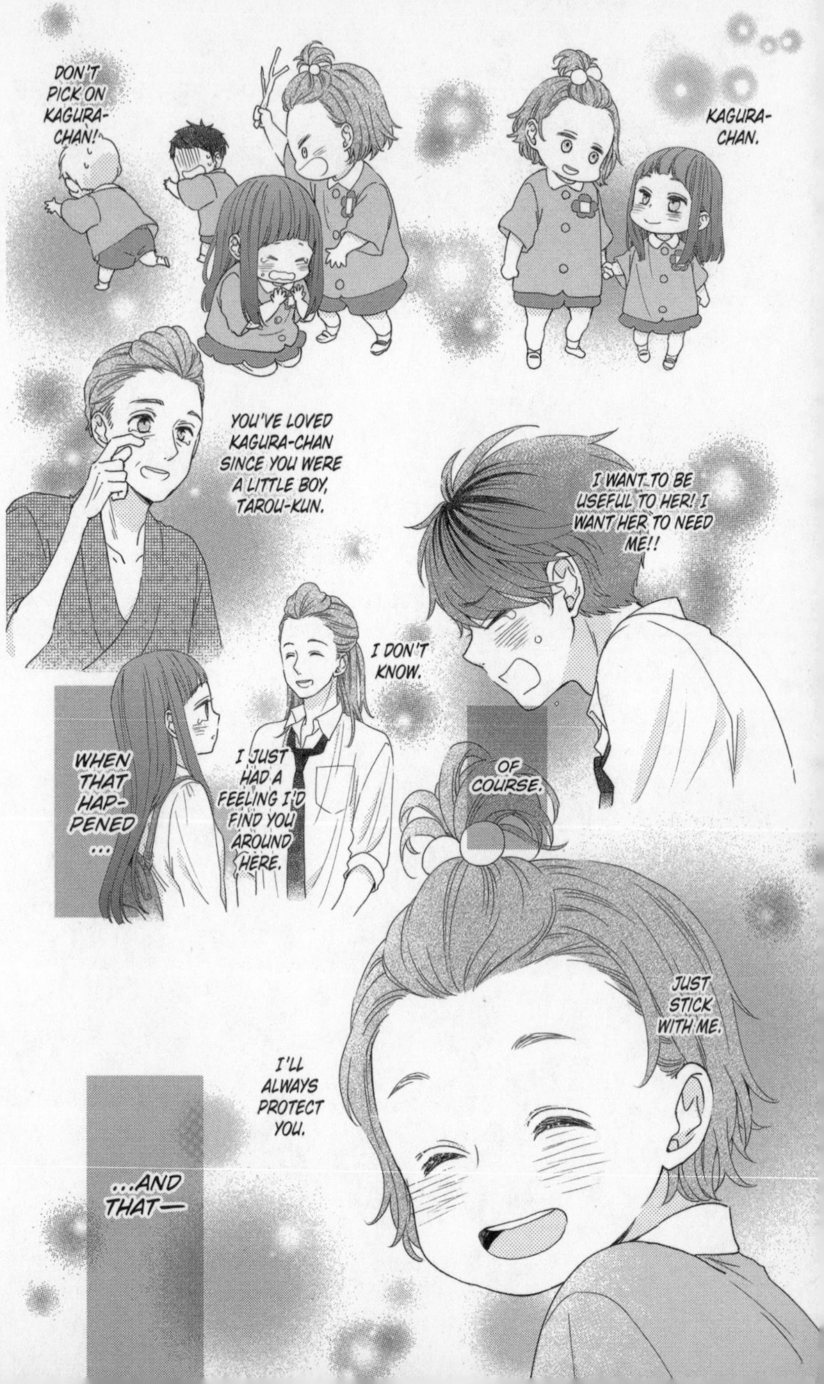
KAGURA-CHAN.
DON'T PICK ON KAGURA-CHAN!
I WANT TO BE USEFUL TO HER! I WANT HER TO NEED ME!!
OF COURSE.
YOU'VE LOVED KAGURA-CHAN SINCE YOU WERE A LITTLE BOY, TAROU-KUN.
I DON'T KNOW.
I JUST HAD A FEELING I'D FIND YOU AROUND HERE.
WHEN THAT HAP-PENED ...
JUST STICK WITH ME.
I'LL ALWAYS PROTECT YOU.
...AND THAT—

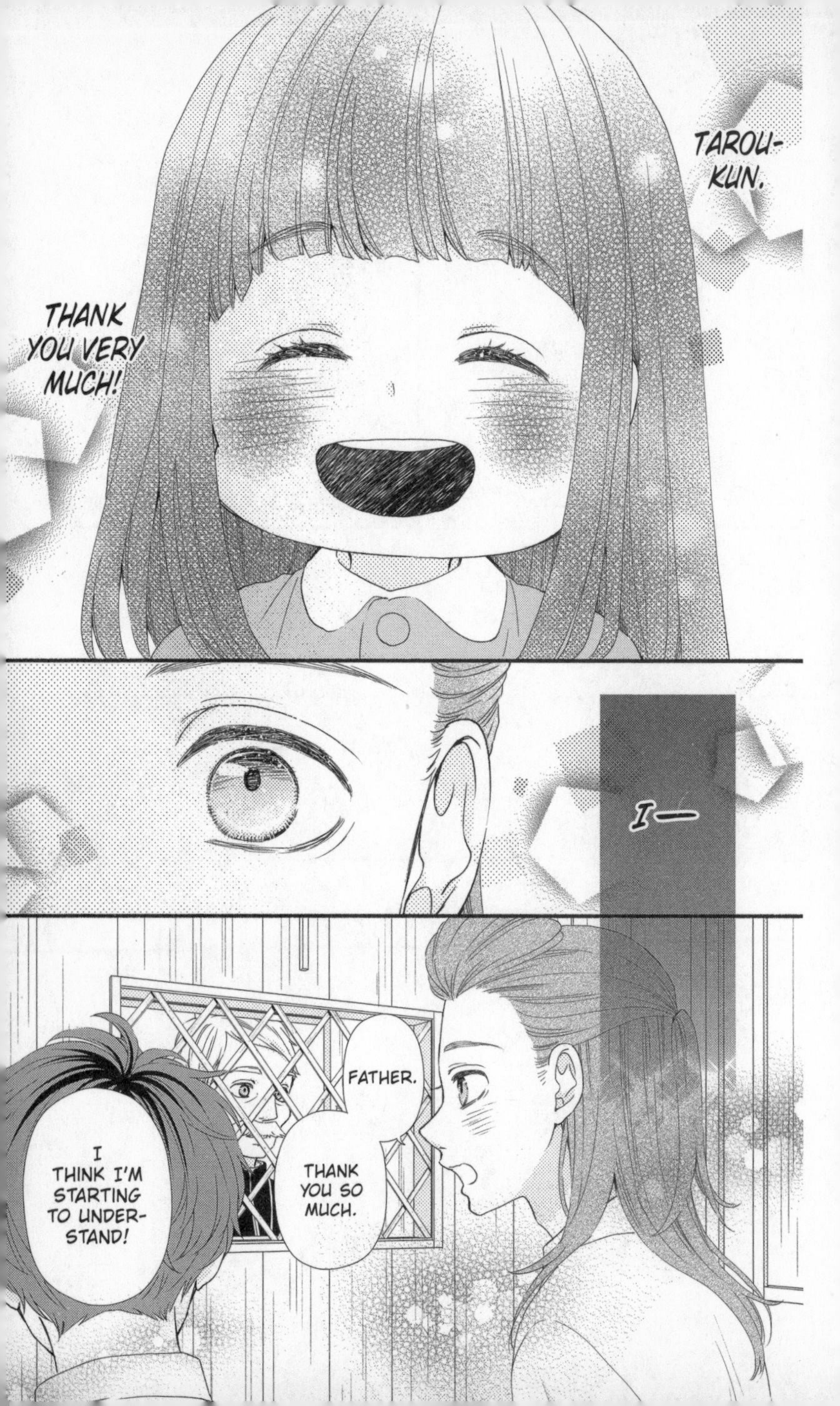
TAROU-KUN.
THANK YOU VERY MUCH!
I—
FATHER.
THANK YOU SO MUCH.
I THINK I'M STARTING TO UNDER-STAND!

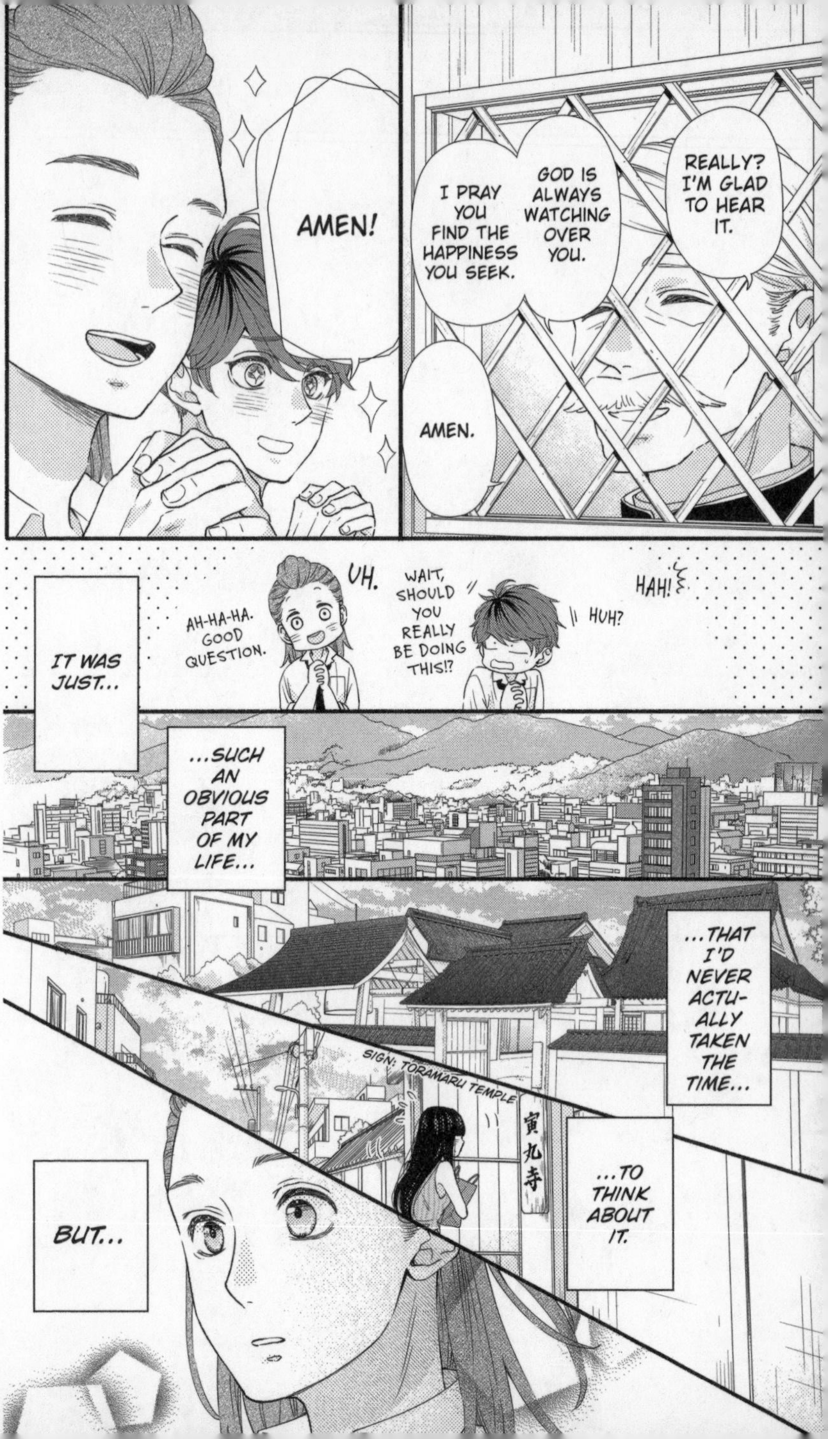
REALLY? I'M GLAD TO HEAR IT.
GOD IS ALWAYS WATCHING OVER YOU.
I PRAY YOU FIND THE HAPPINESS YOU SEEK.
AMEN.
AMEN!
HAH!
HUH?
WAIT, SHOULD YOU REALLY BE DOING THIS!?
UH.
AH-HA-HA. GOOD QUESTION.
IT WAS JUST...
...SUCH AN OBVIOUS PART OF MY LIFE...
...THAT I'D NEVER ACTU-ALLY TAKEN THE TIME...
SIGN: TORAMARU TEMPLE
寅丸寺
...TO THINK ABOUT IT.
BUT...

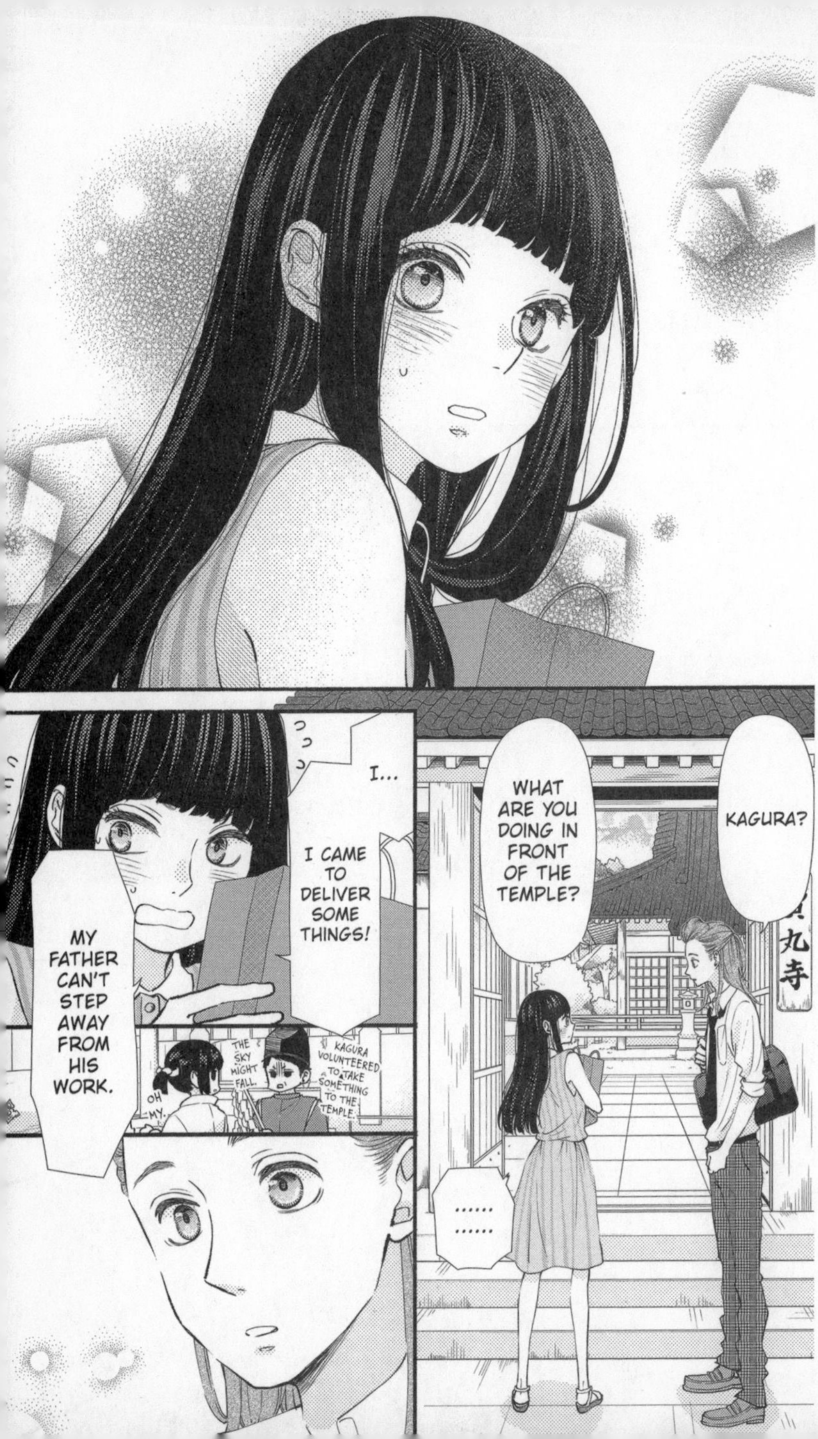
KAGURA?
WHAT ARE YOU DOING IN FRONT OF THE TEMPLE?
......
......
I...
I CAME TO DELIVER SOME THINGS!
MY FATHER CAN'T STEP AWAY FROM HIS WORK.
KAGURA VOLUNTEERED TO TAKE SOMETHING TO THE TEMPLE.
THE SKY MIGHT FALL.
OH MY.

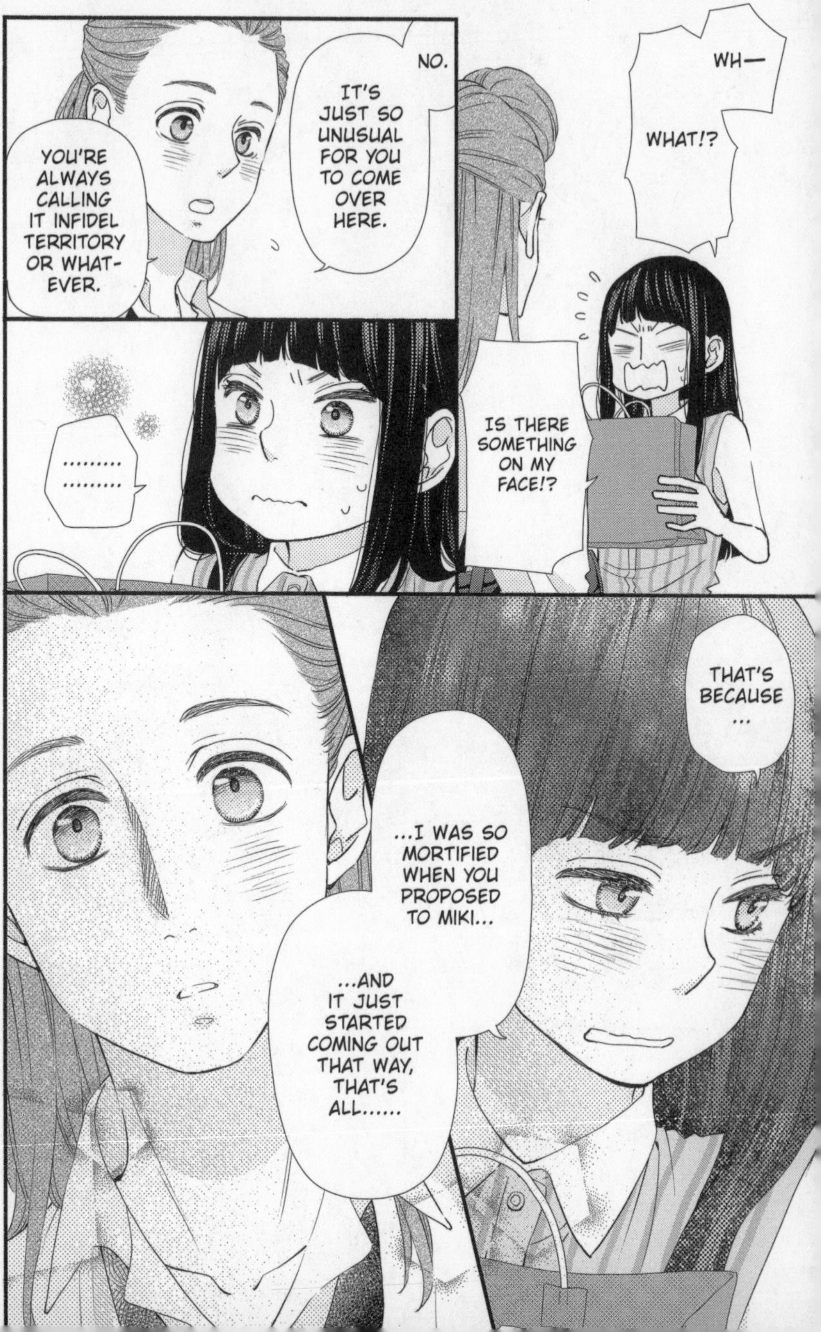
WH—
WHAT!?
IS THERE SOMETHING ON MY FACE!?
NO.
IT'S JUST SO UNUSUAL FOR YOU TO COME OVER HERE.
YOU'RE ALWAYS CALLING IT INFIDEL TERRITORY OR WHAT-EVER.
....
....
THAT'S BECAUSE ...
...I WAS SO MORTIFIED WHEN YOU PROPOSED TO MIKI...
...AND IT JUST STARTED COMING OUT THAT WAY, THAT'S ALL......

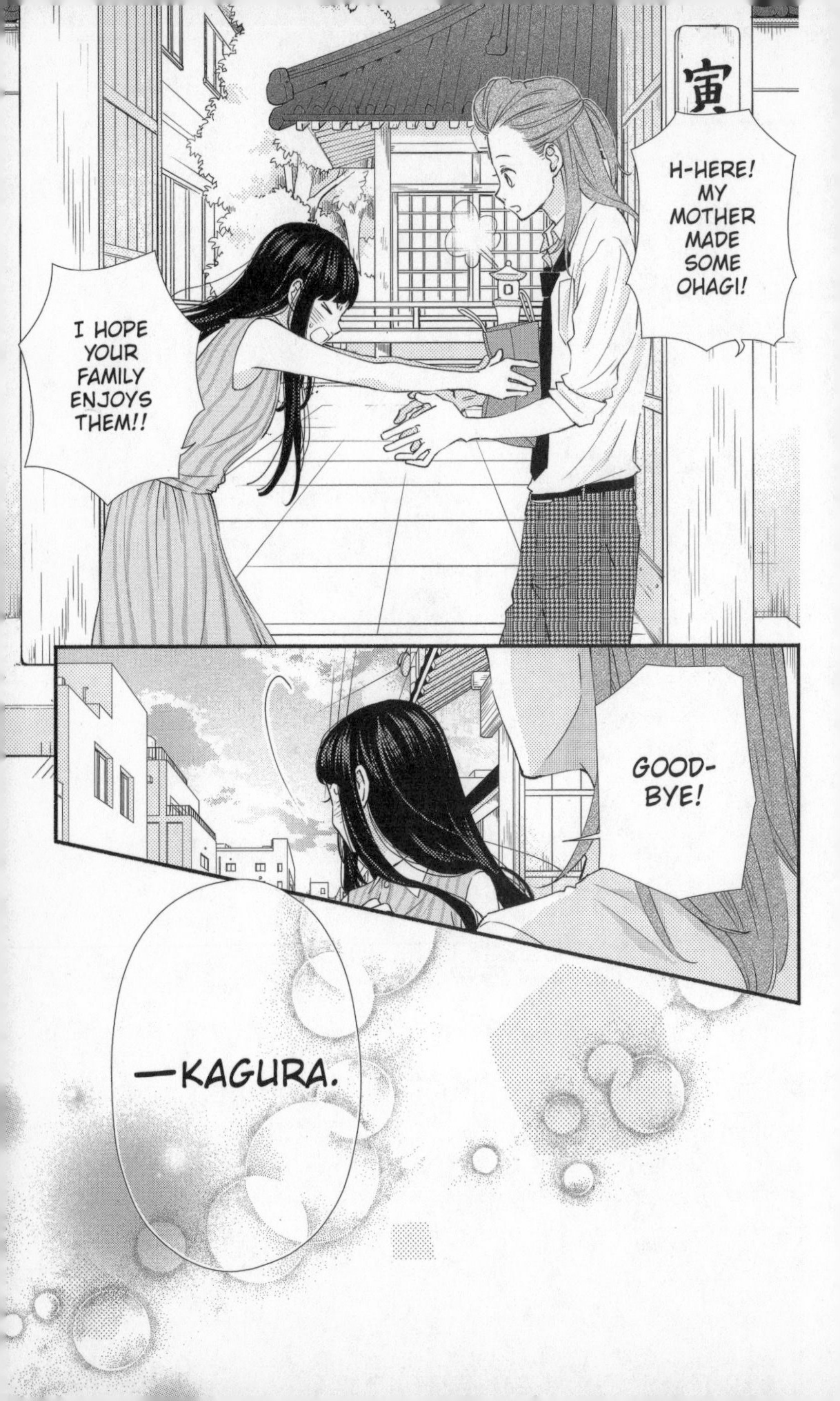
寅
H-HERE! MY MOTHER MADE SOME OHAGI!
I HOPE YOUR FAMILY ENJOYS THEM!!
GOOD-BYE!
—KAGURA.

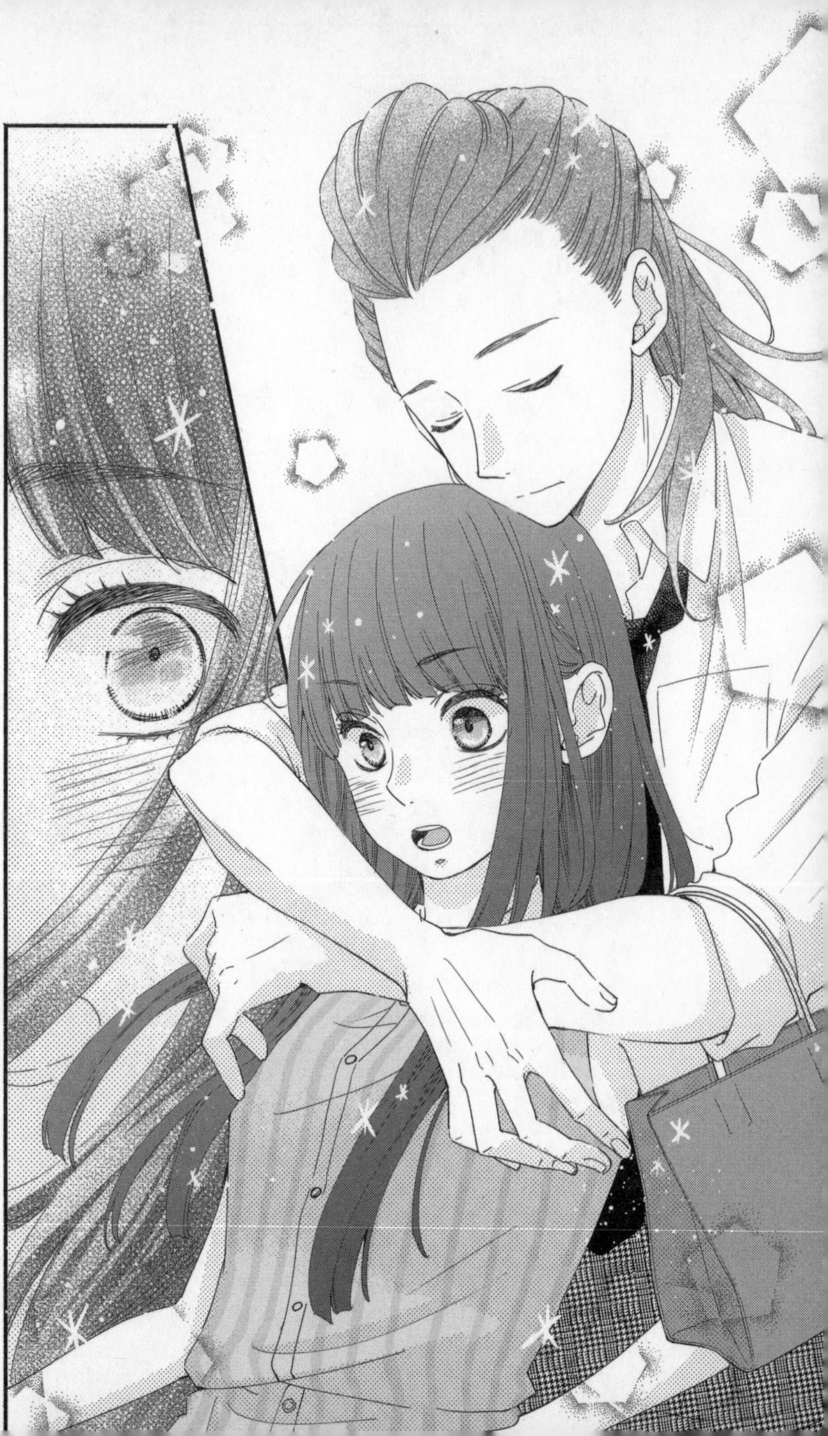

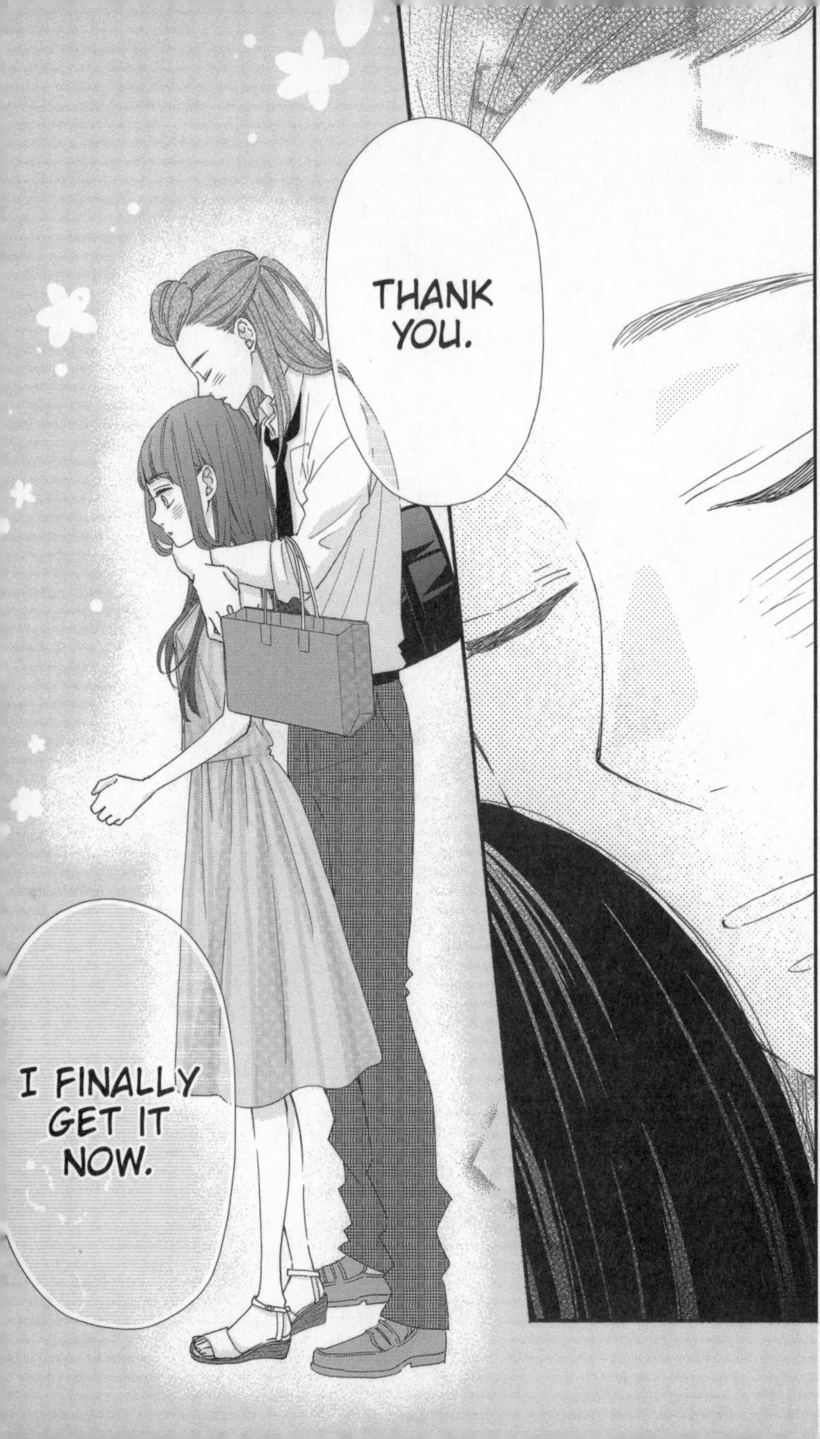
THANK YOU.
I FINALLY GET IT NOW.

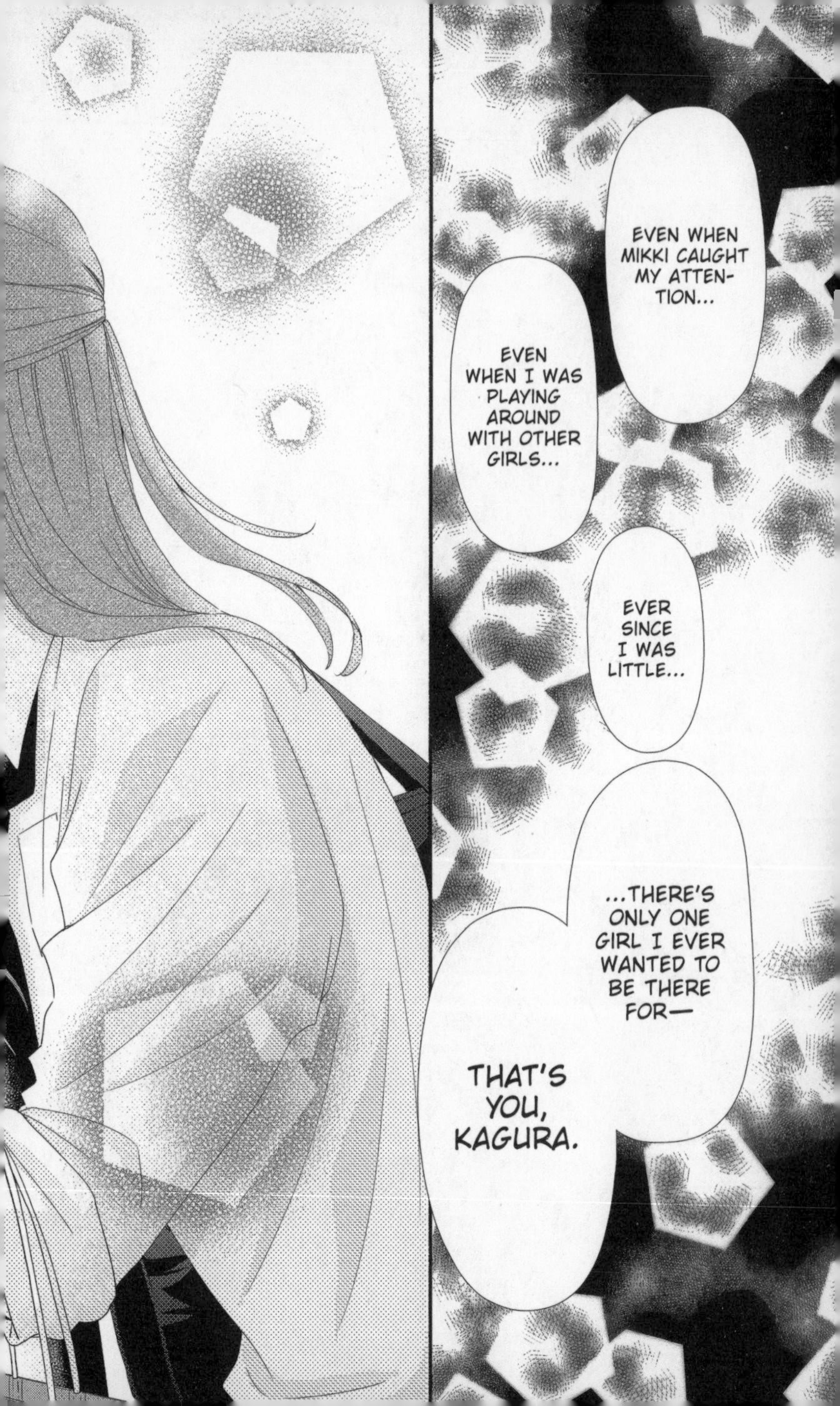
EVEN WHEN MIKKI CAUGHT MY ATTEN- TION...
EVEN WHEN I WAS PLAYING AROUND WITH OTHER GIRLS...
EVER SINCE I WAS LITTLE...
...THERE'S ONLY ONE GIRL I EVER WANTED TO BE THERE FOR—
THAT'S YOU, KAGURA.

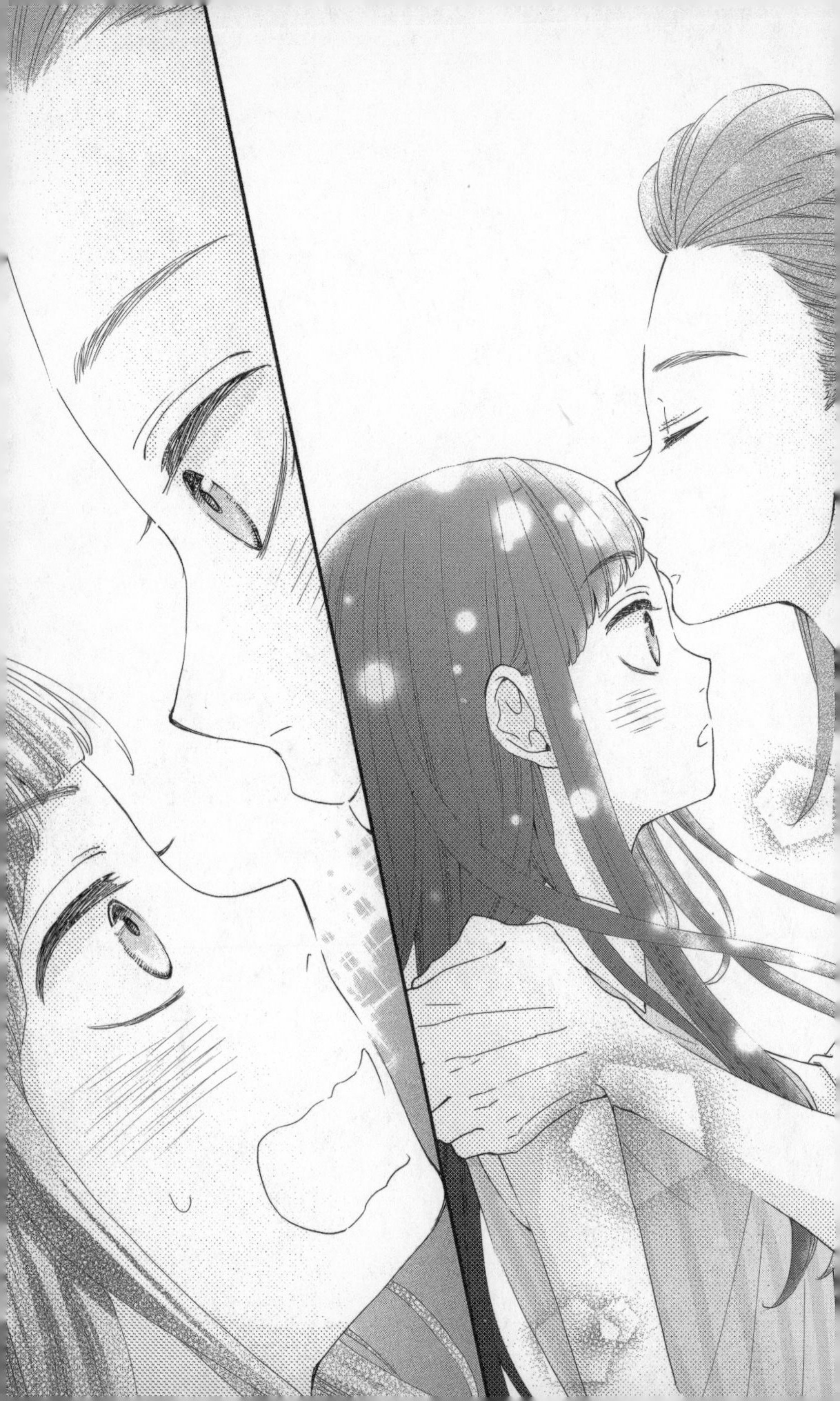

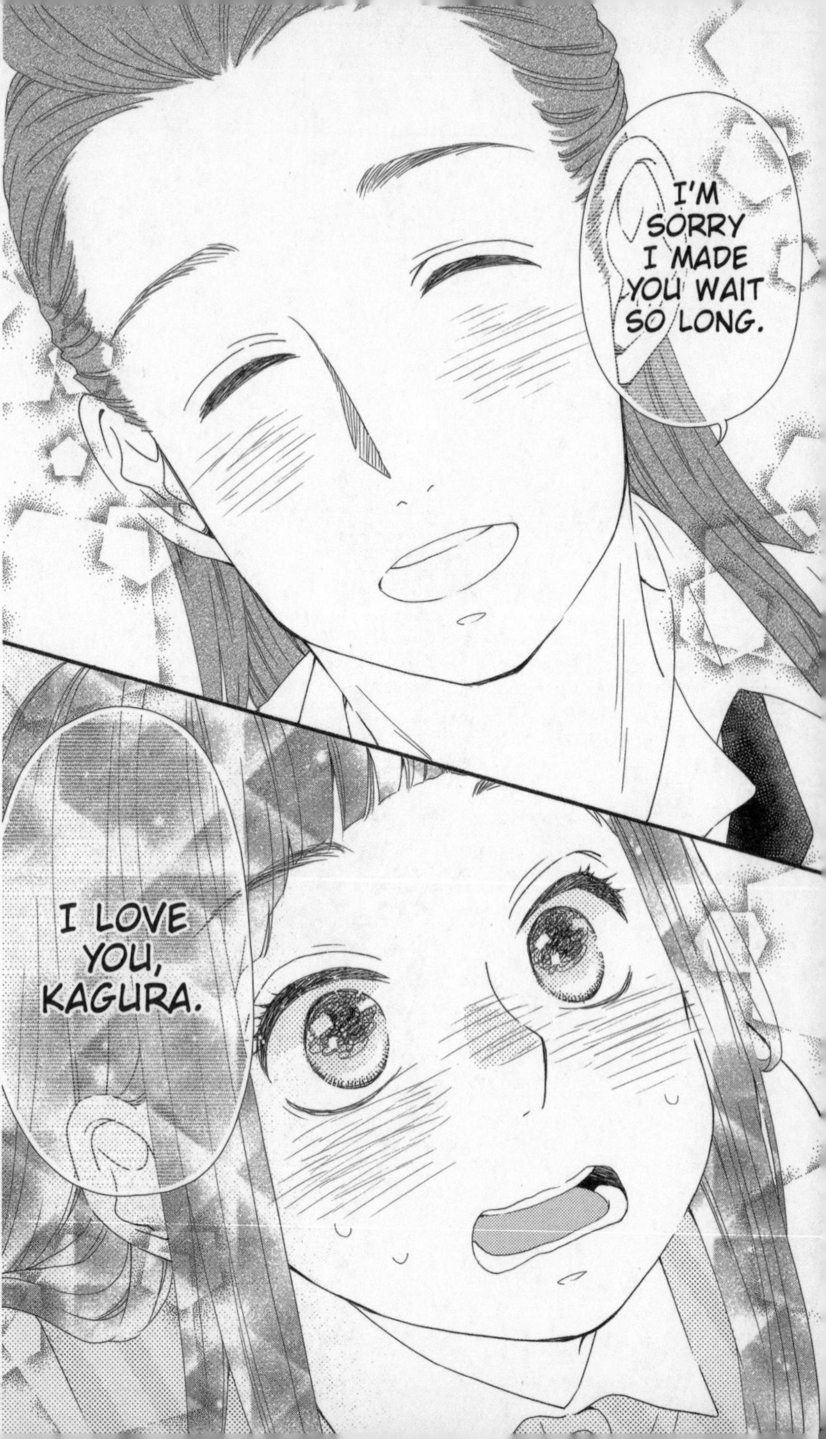
I'M SORRY I MADE YOU WAIT SO LONG.
I LOVE YOU, KAGURA.

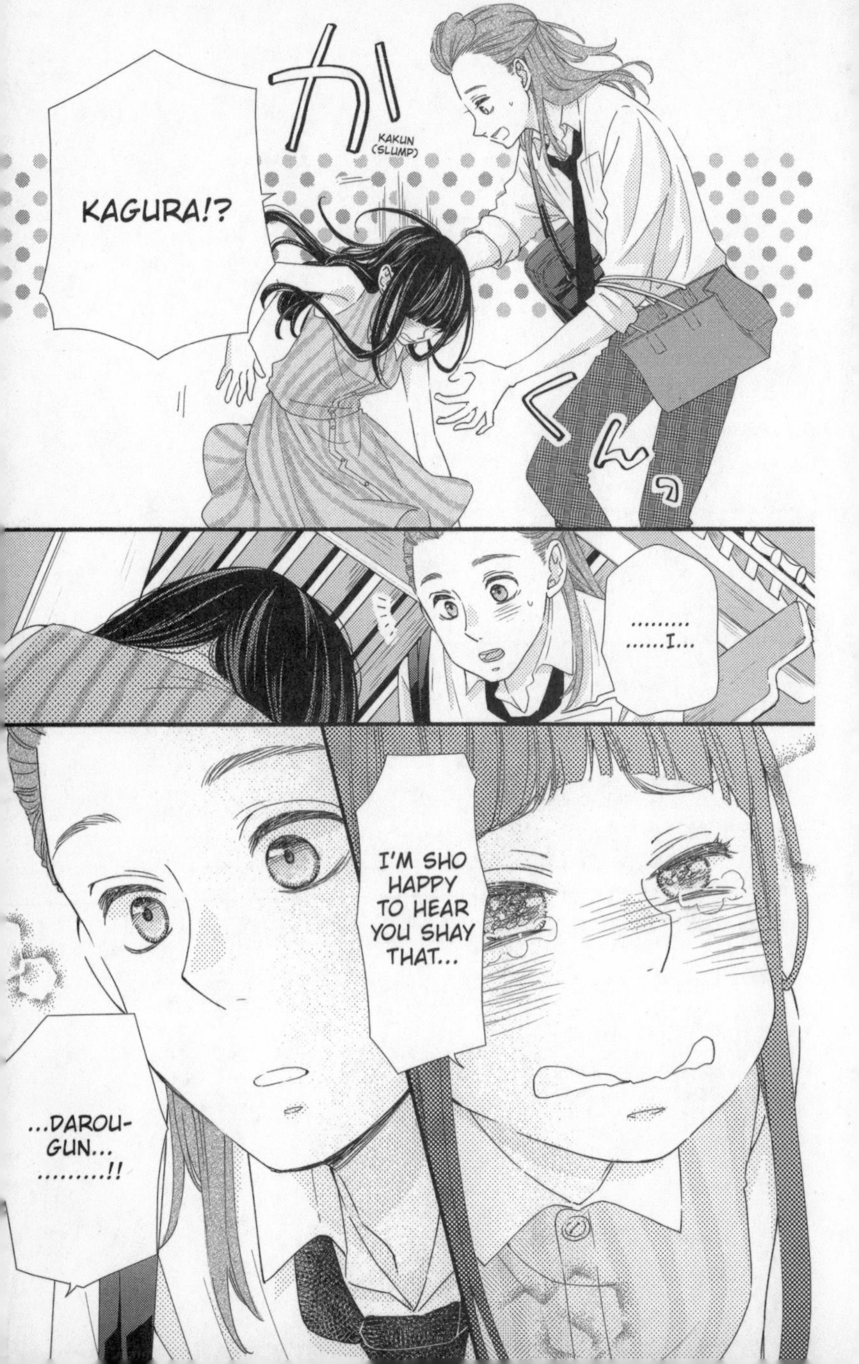
かくん
KAKUN (SLUMP)
KAGURA!?
....
......I...
I'M SHO HAPPY TO HEAR YOU SHAY THAT...
...DAROU-GUN...
.........!!

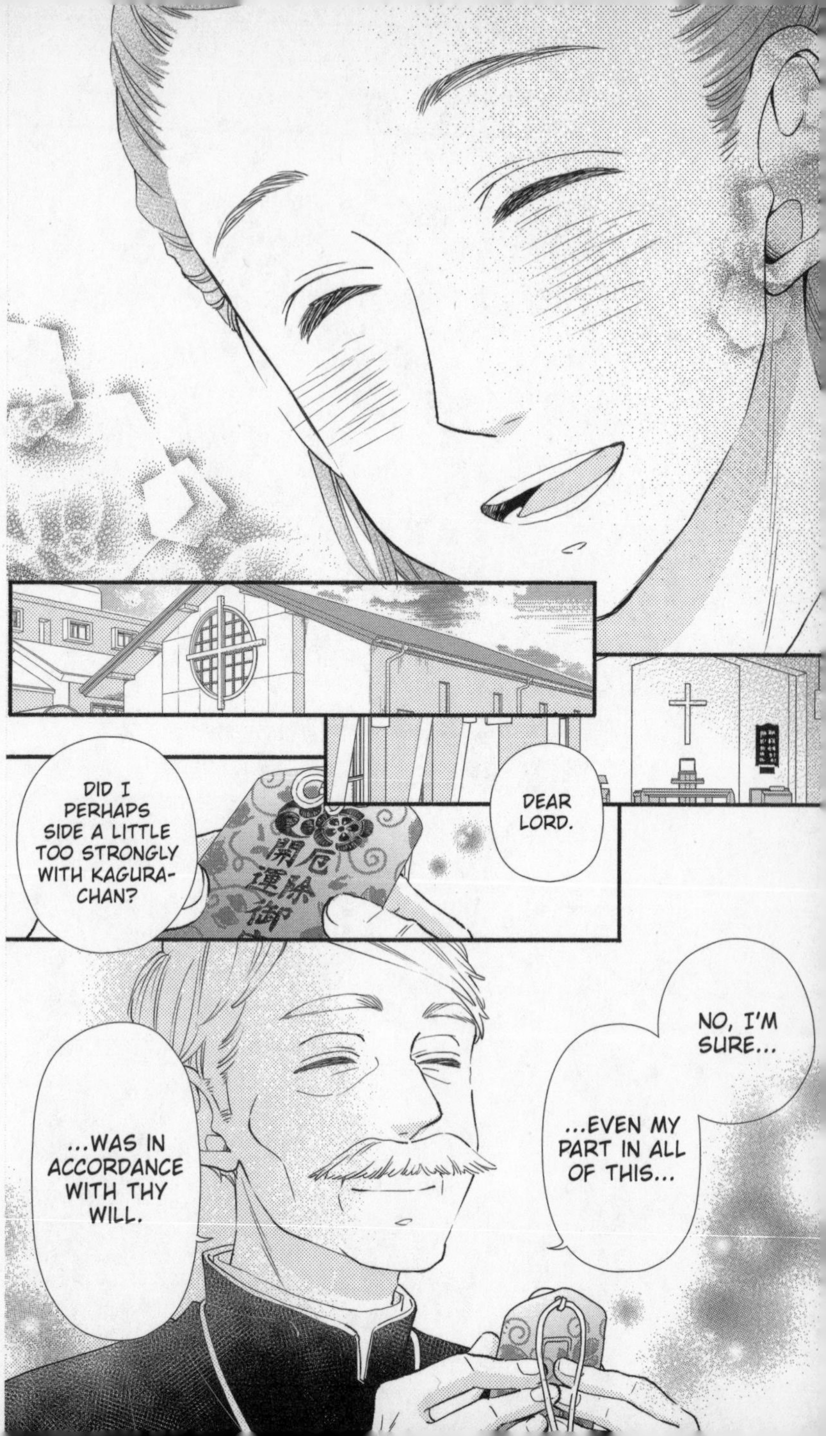
DEAR LORD.
DID I PERHAPS SIDE A LITTLE TOO STRONGLY WITH KAGURA-CHAN?
NO, I'M SURE...
...EVEN MY PART IN ALL OF THIS...
...WAS IN ACCORDANCE WITH THY WILL.

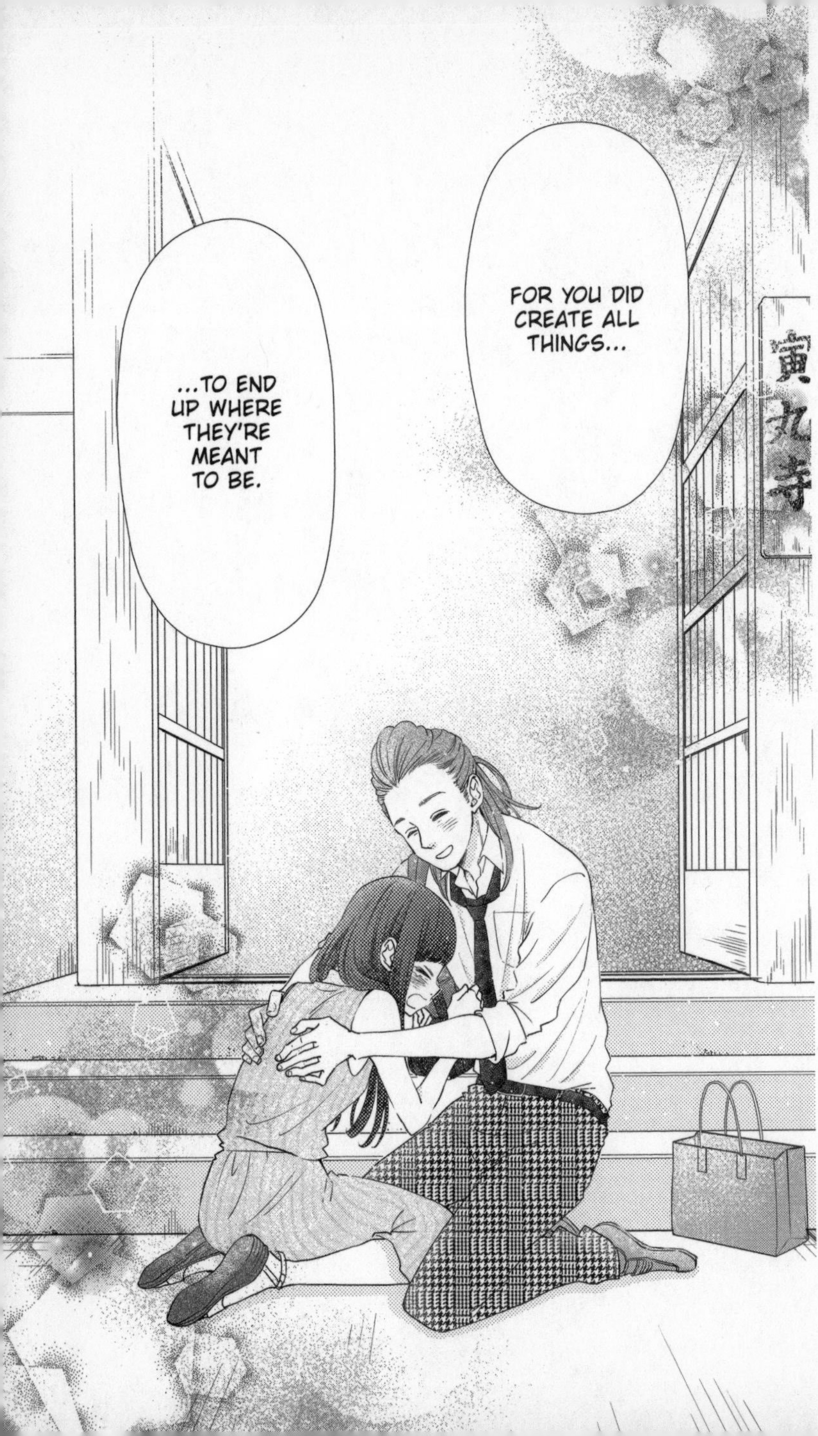
FOR YOU DID CREATE ALL THINGS...
...TO END UP WHERE THEY'RE MEANT TO BE.

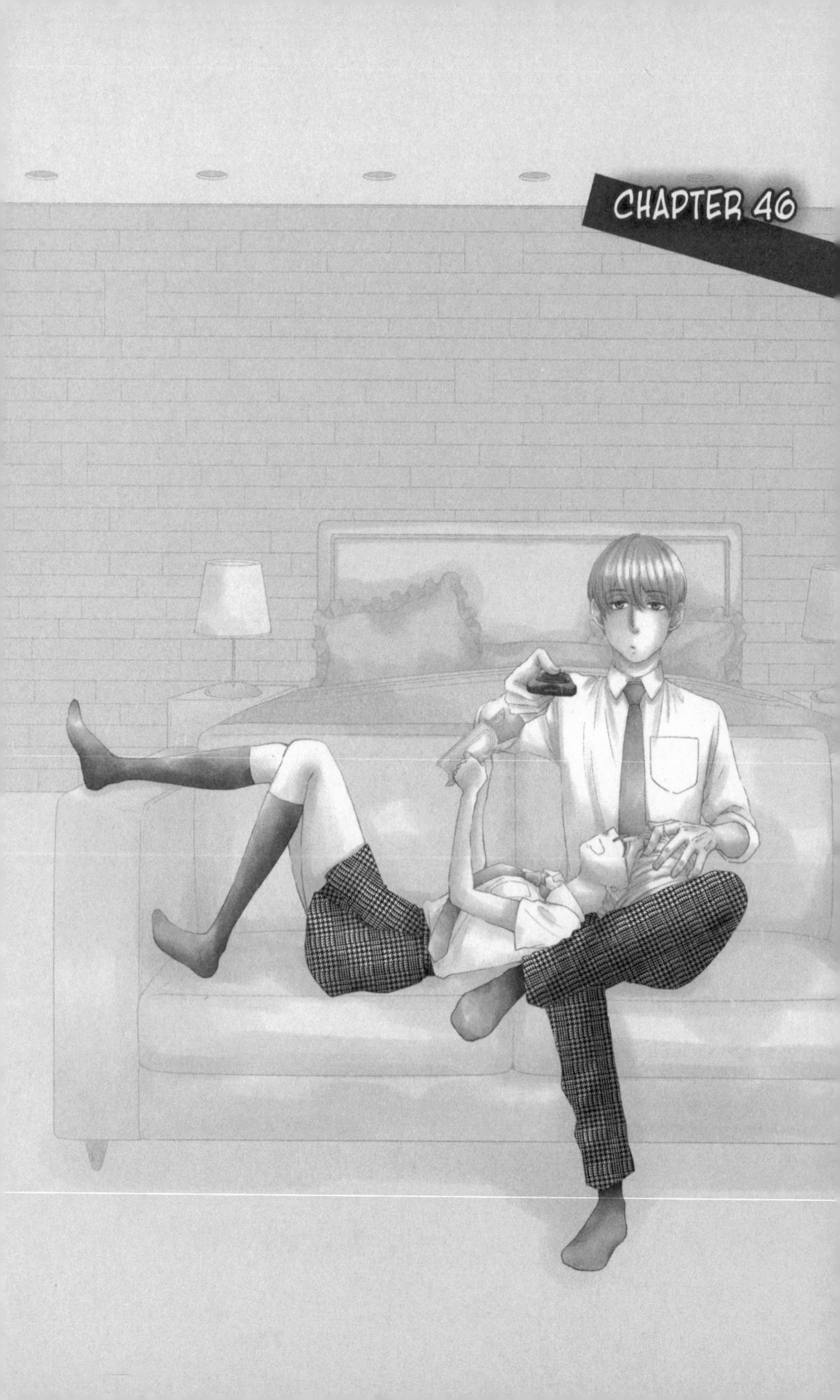
CHAPTER 46

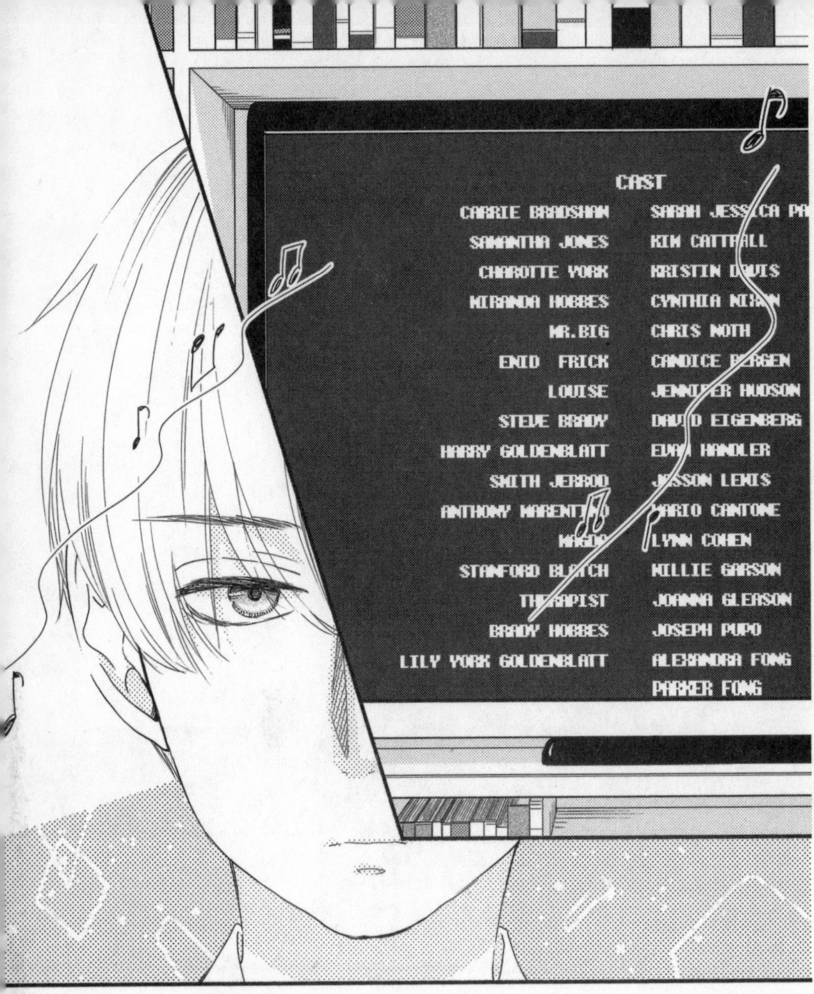
CAST
CARRIE BRADSHAW
SAMANTHA JONES
CHAROTTE YORK
MIRANDA HOBBES
MR.BIG
ENID FRICK
LOUISE
STEVE BRADY
HARRY GOLDENBLATT
SMITH JERROD
BRADY HOBBES
LILY YORK GOLDENBLATT
KIM CATTRALL
KRISTIN DAVIS
CHRIS NOTH
JOSEPH PUPO
ALEXANDRA FONG
PARKER FONG
LYNN COHEN
WILLIE GARSON
JOANNA GLEASON
MARIO CANTONE

hatsu
haru

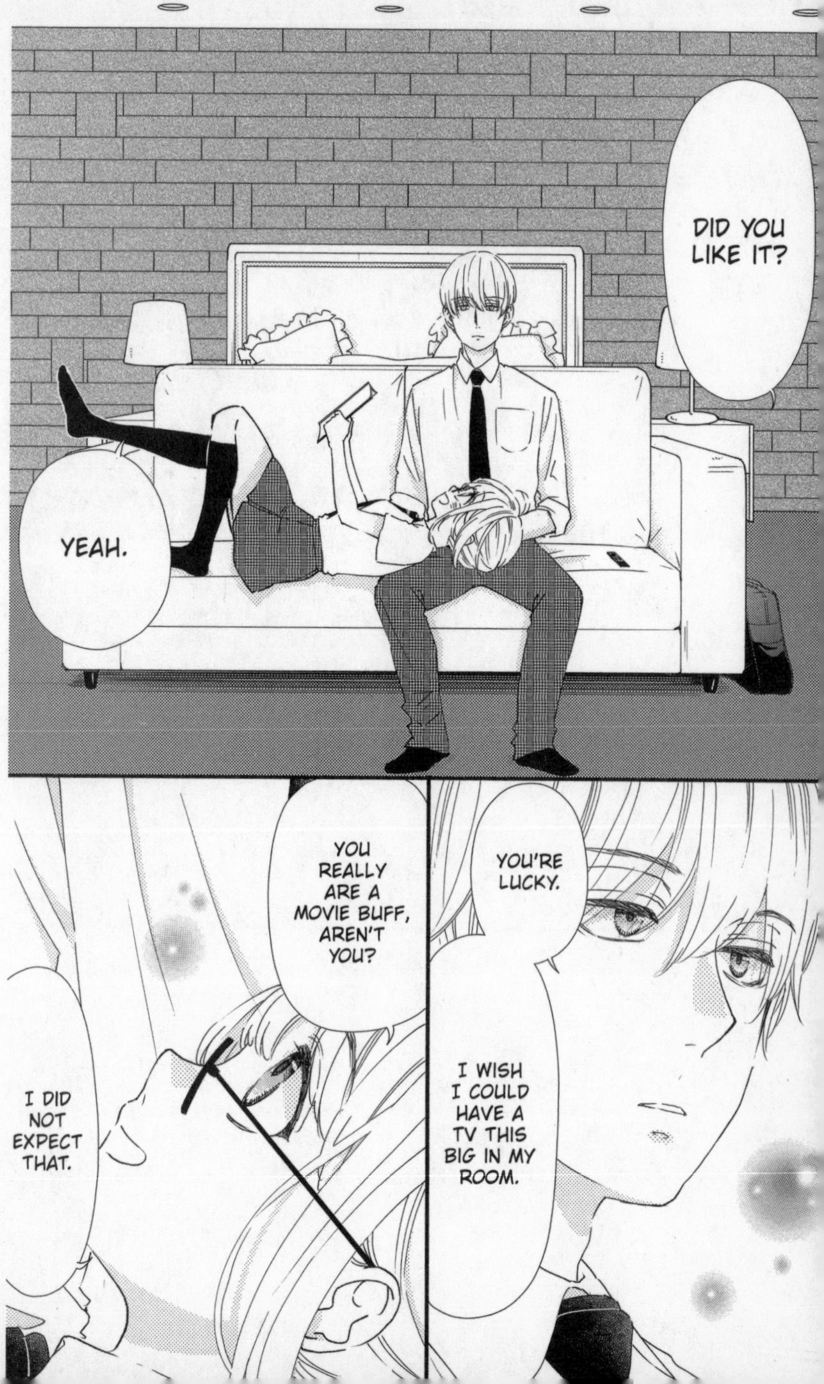
DID YOU LIKE IT?
YEAH.
YOU'RE LUCKY.
I WISH I COULD HAVE A TV THIS BIG IN MY ROOM.
YOU REALLY ARE A MOVIE BUFF, AREN'T YOU?
I DID NOT EXPECT THAT.

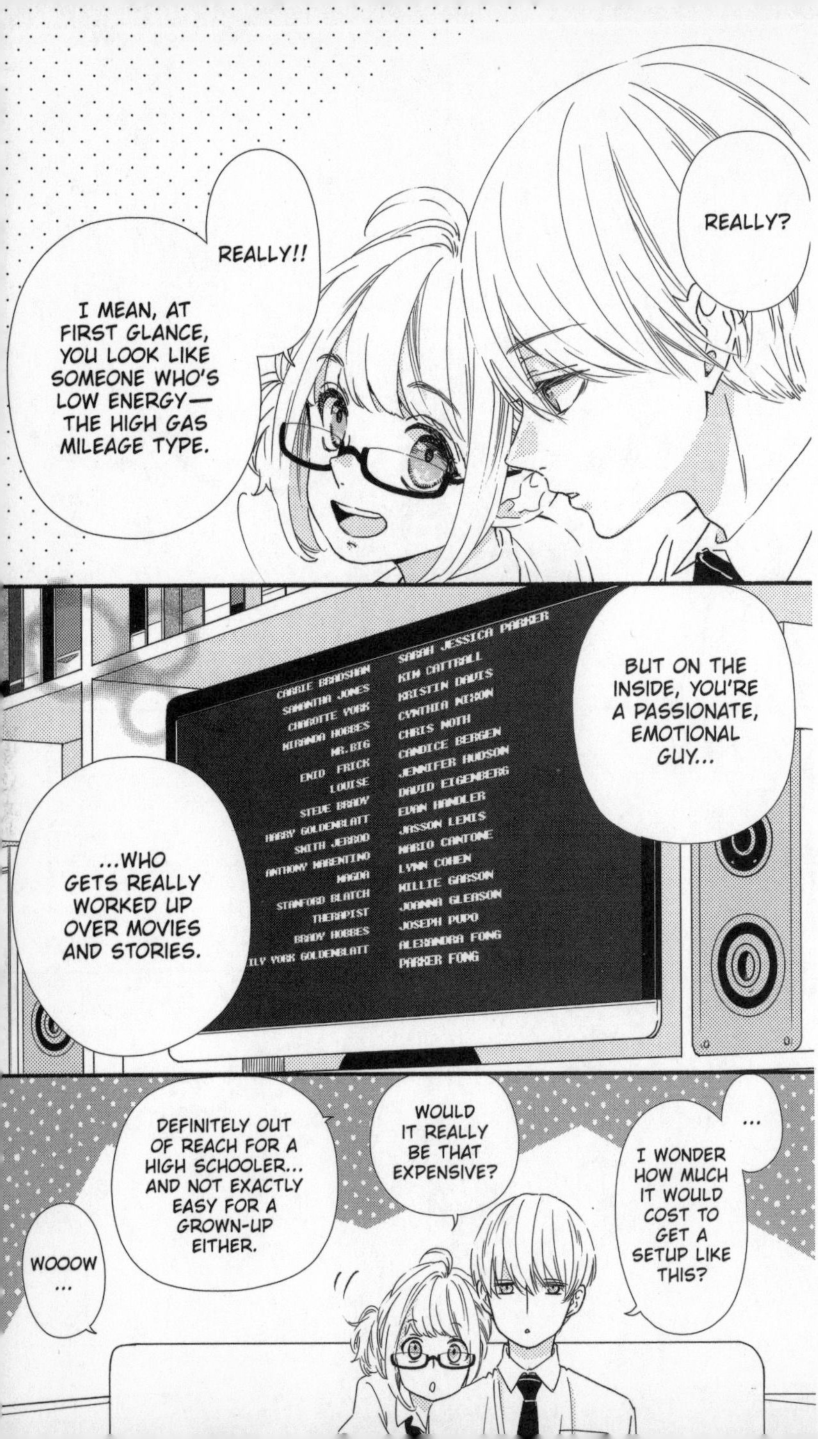
REALLY?
REALLY!!
I MEAN, AT FIRST GLANCE, YOU LOOK LIKE SOMEONE WHO'S LOW ENERGY—THE HIGH GAS MILEAGE TYPE.
BUT ON THE INSIDE, YOU'RE A PASSIONATE, EMOTIONAL GUY...
CARRIE BRADSHAW SARAH JESSICA PARKER
SAMANTHA JONES KIM CATTRALL
CHAROTTE YORK KRISTIN DAVIS
MIRANDA HOBBES CYNTHIA NIXON
MR.BIG CHRIS NOTH
ENID FRICK CANDICE BERGEN
LOUISE JENNIFER HUDSON
STEVE BRADY DAVID EIGENBERG
HARRY GOLDENBLATT EVAN HANDLER
SMITH JERROD JASSON LEWIS
ANTHONY MARENTINO MARIO CANTONE
MAGDA LYNN COHEN
STANFORD BLATCH WILLIE GARSON
THERAPIST JOANNA GLEASON
BRADY HOBBES JOSEPH PUPO
ALEXANDRA FONG
PARKER FONG
...WHO GETS REALLY WORKED UP OVER MOVIES AND STORIES.
...
I WONDER HOW MUCH IT WOULD COST TO GET A SETUP LIKE THIS?
WOULD IT REALLY BE THAT EXPENSIVE?
DEFINITELY OUT OF REACH FOR A HIGH SCHOOLER... AND NOT EXACTLY EASY FOR A GROWN-UP EITHER.
WOOOW ...

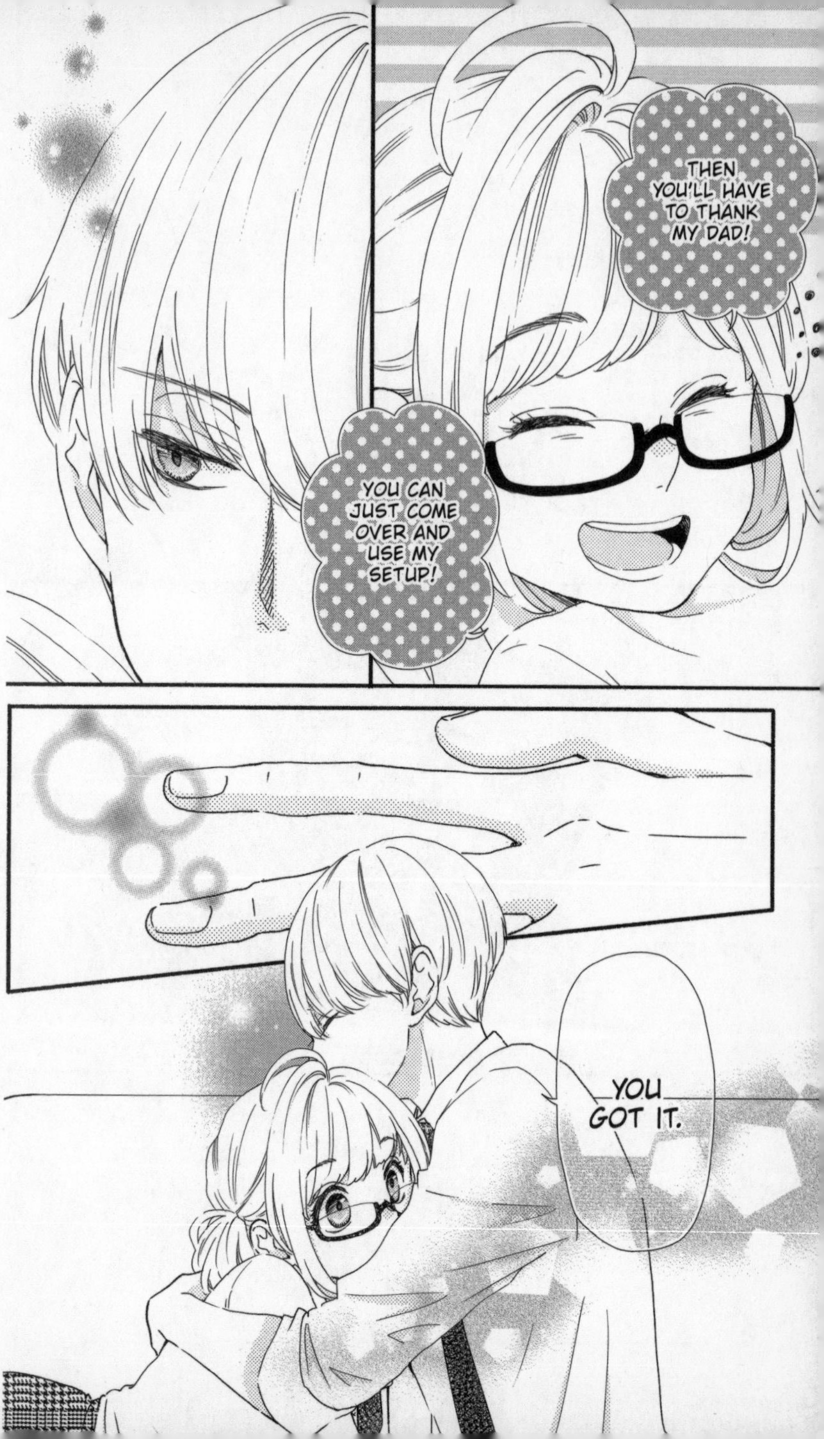
THEN YOU'LL HAVE TO THANK MY DAD!
YOU CAN JUST COME OVER AND USE MY SETUP!
YOU GOT IT.

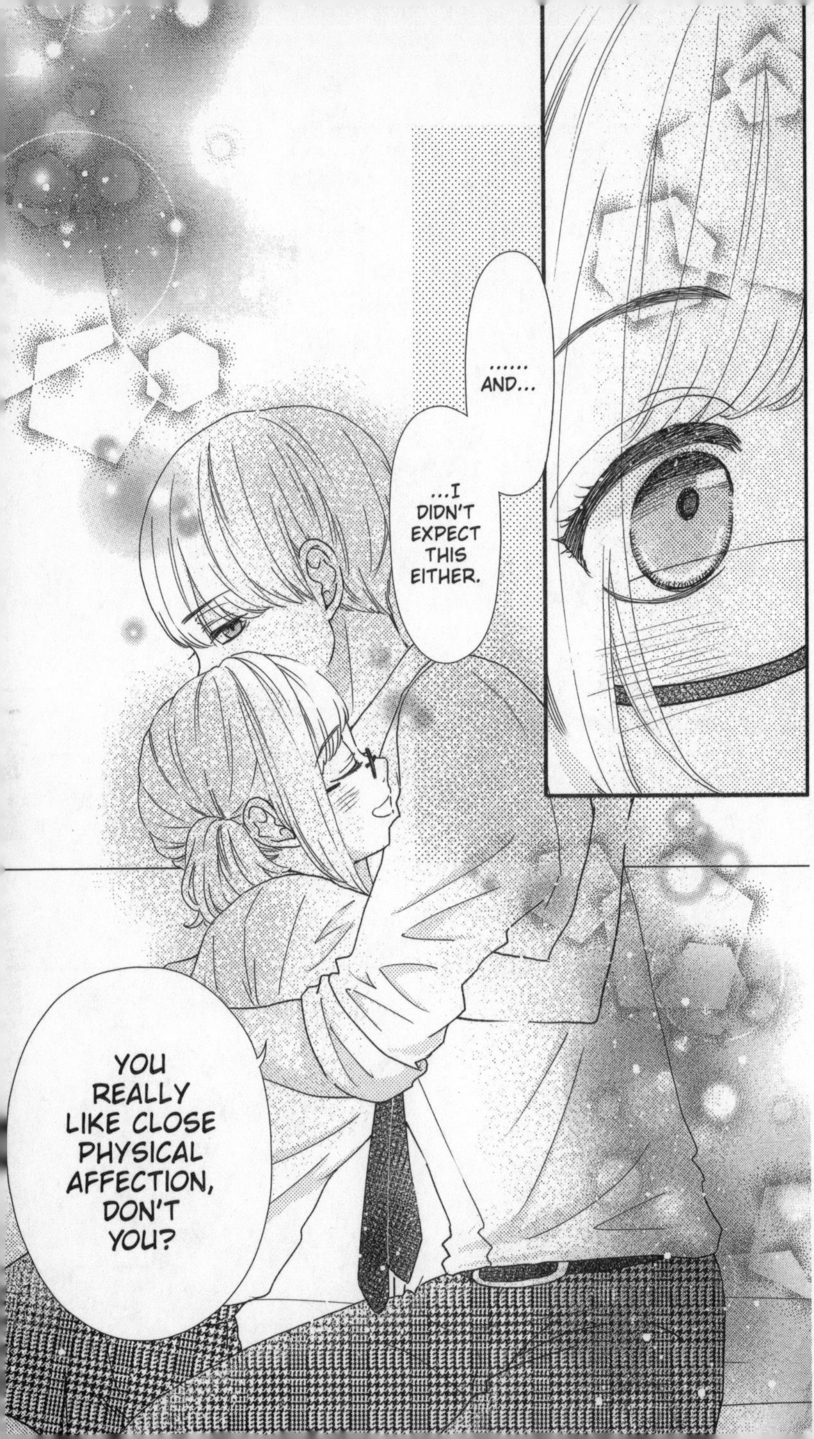
......
AND...
...I DIDN'T EXPECT THIS EITHER.
YOU REALLY LIKE CLOSE PHYSICAL AFFECTION, DON'T YOU?

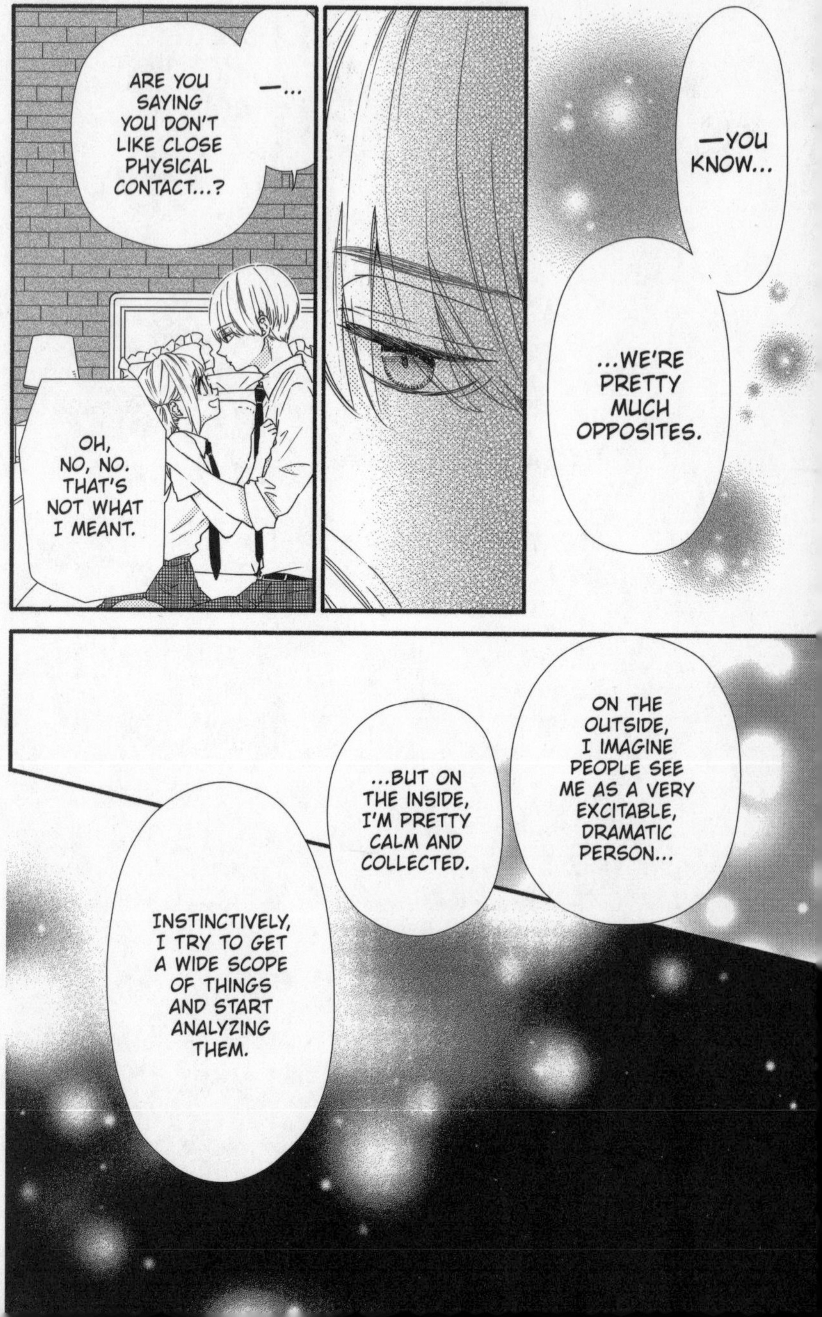
—YOU KNOW...
...WE'RE PRETTY MUCH OPPOSITES.
—...
ARE YOU SAYING YOU DON'T LIKE CLOSE PHYSICAL CONTACT...?
OH, NO, NO. THAT'S NOT WHAT I MEANT.
ON THE OUTSIDE, I IMAGINE PEOPLE SEE ME AS A VERY EXCITABLE, DRAMATIC PERSON...
...BUT ON THE INSIDE, I'M PRETTY CALM AND COLLECTED.
INSTINCTIVELY, I TRY TO GET A WIDE SCOPE OF THINGS AND START ANALYZING THEM.

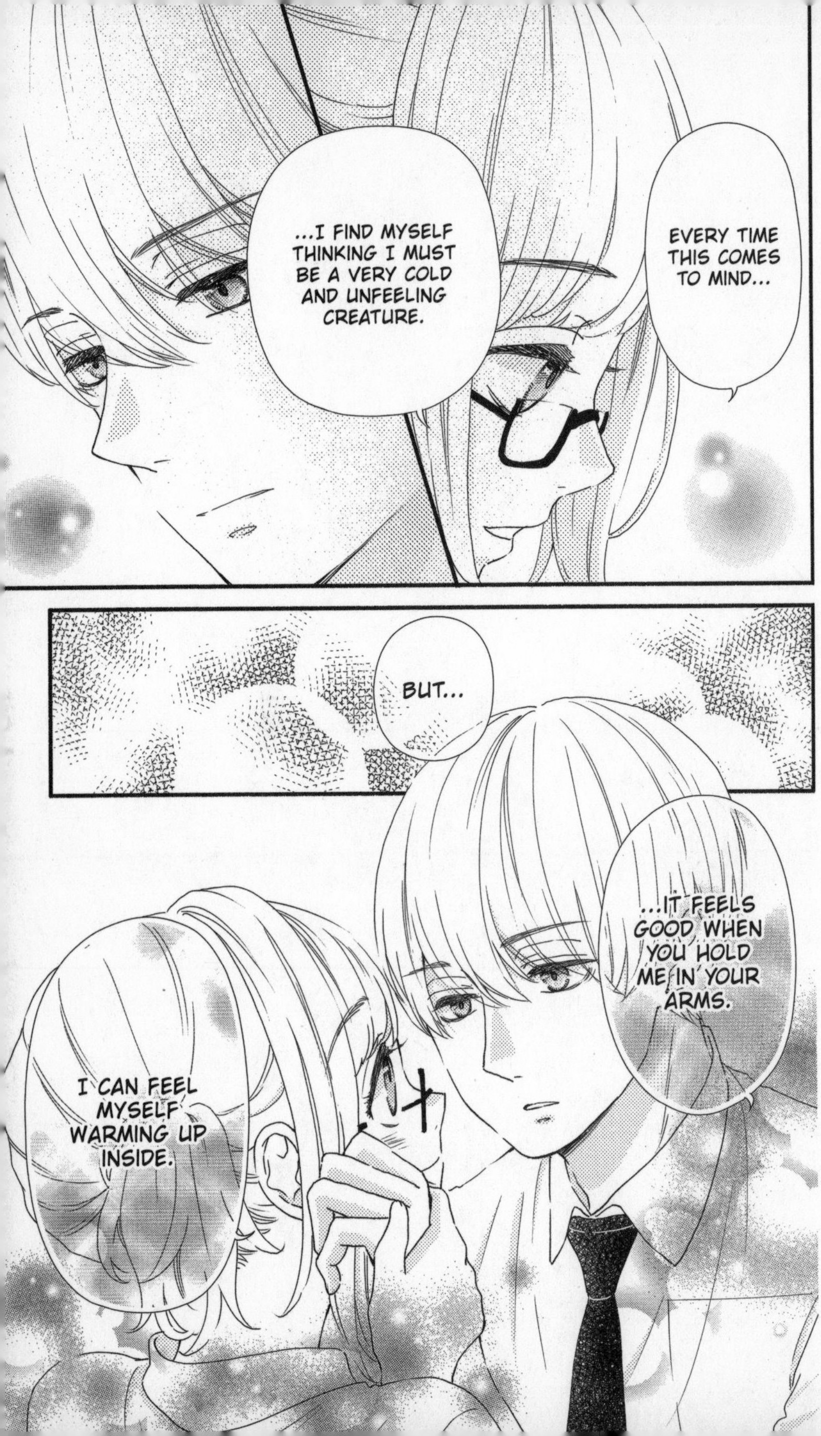
EVERY TIME THIS COMES TO MIND...
...I FIND MYSELF THINKING I MUST BE A VERY COLD AND UNFEELING CREATURE.
BUT...
...IT FEELS GOOD WHEN YOU HOLD ME IN YOUR ARMS.
I CAN FEEL MYSELF WARMING UP INSIDE.

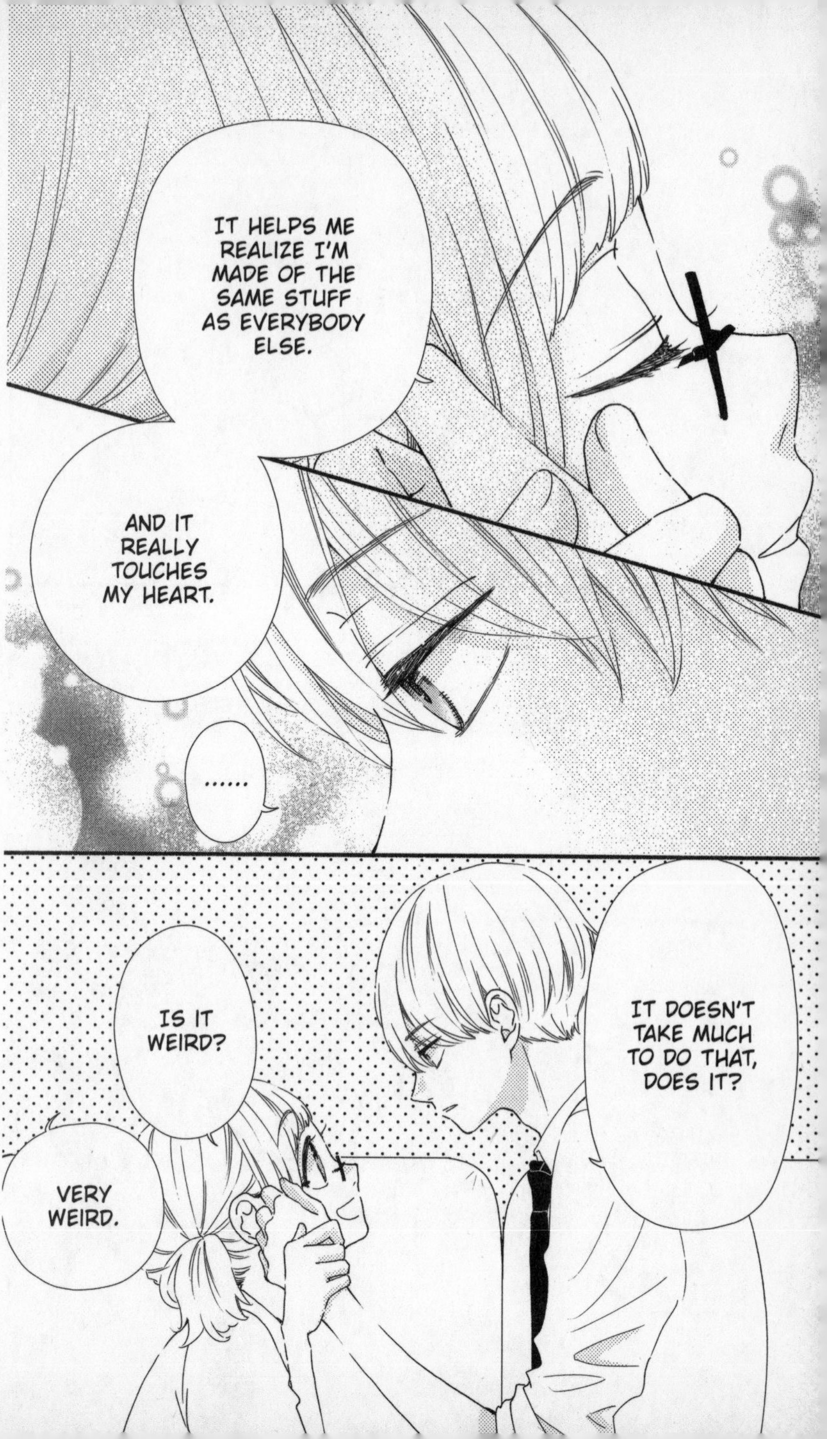
IT HELPS ME REALIZE I'M MADE OF THE SAME STUFF AS EVERYBODY ELSE.
AND IT REALLY TOUCHES MY HEART.
......
IT DOESN'T TAKE MUCH TO DO THAT, DOES IT?
IS IT WEIRD?
VERY WEIRD.

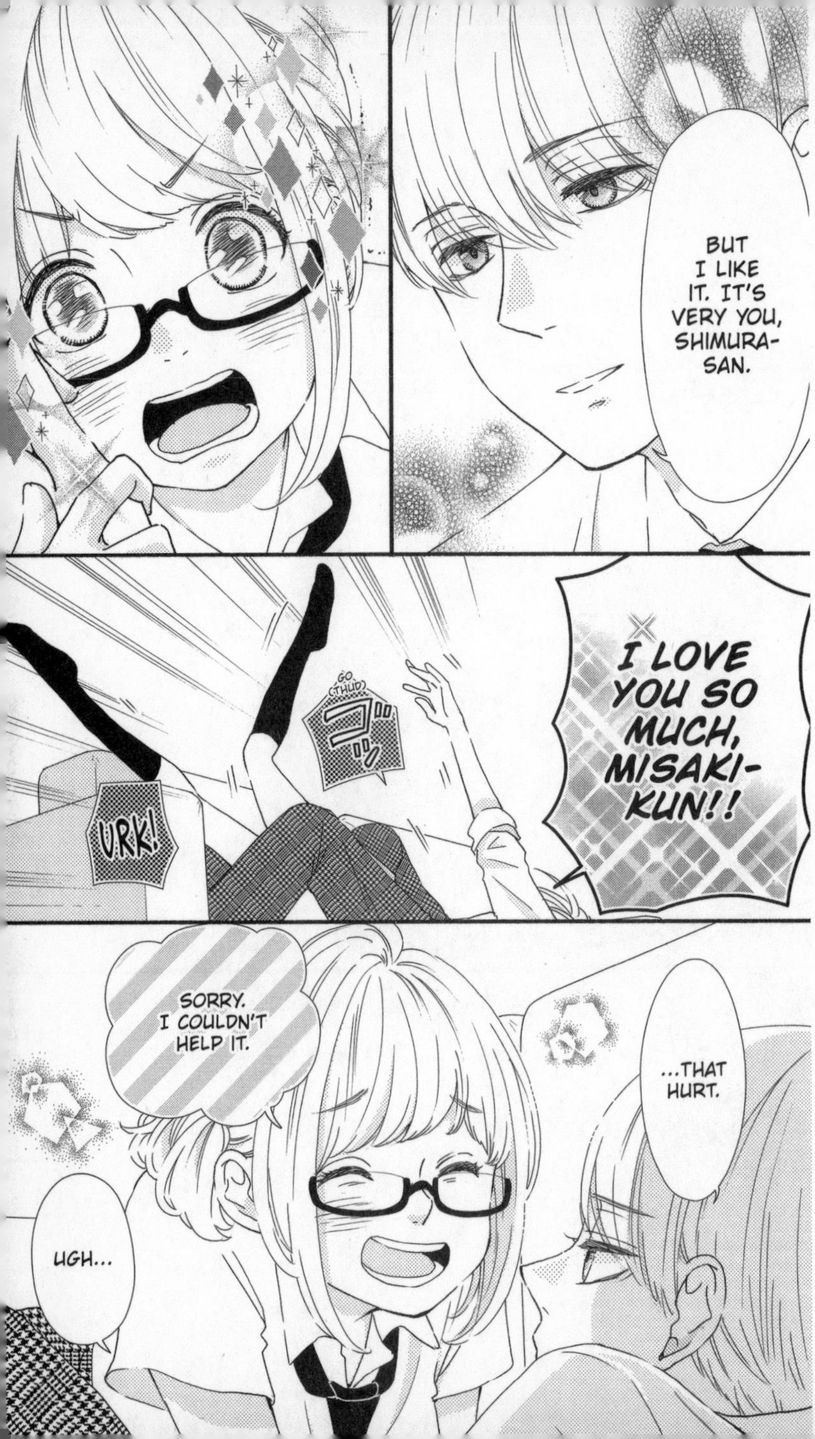
BUT I LIKE IT. IT'S VERY YOU, SHIMURA-SAN.
I LOVE YOU SO MUCH, MISAKI-KUN!!
GO (THUD)
URK!
...THAT HURT.
SORRY. I COULDN'T HELP IT.
UGH...

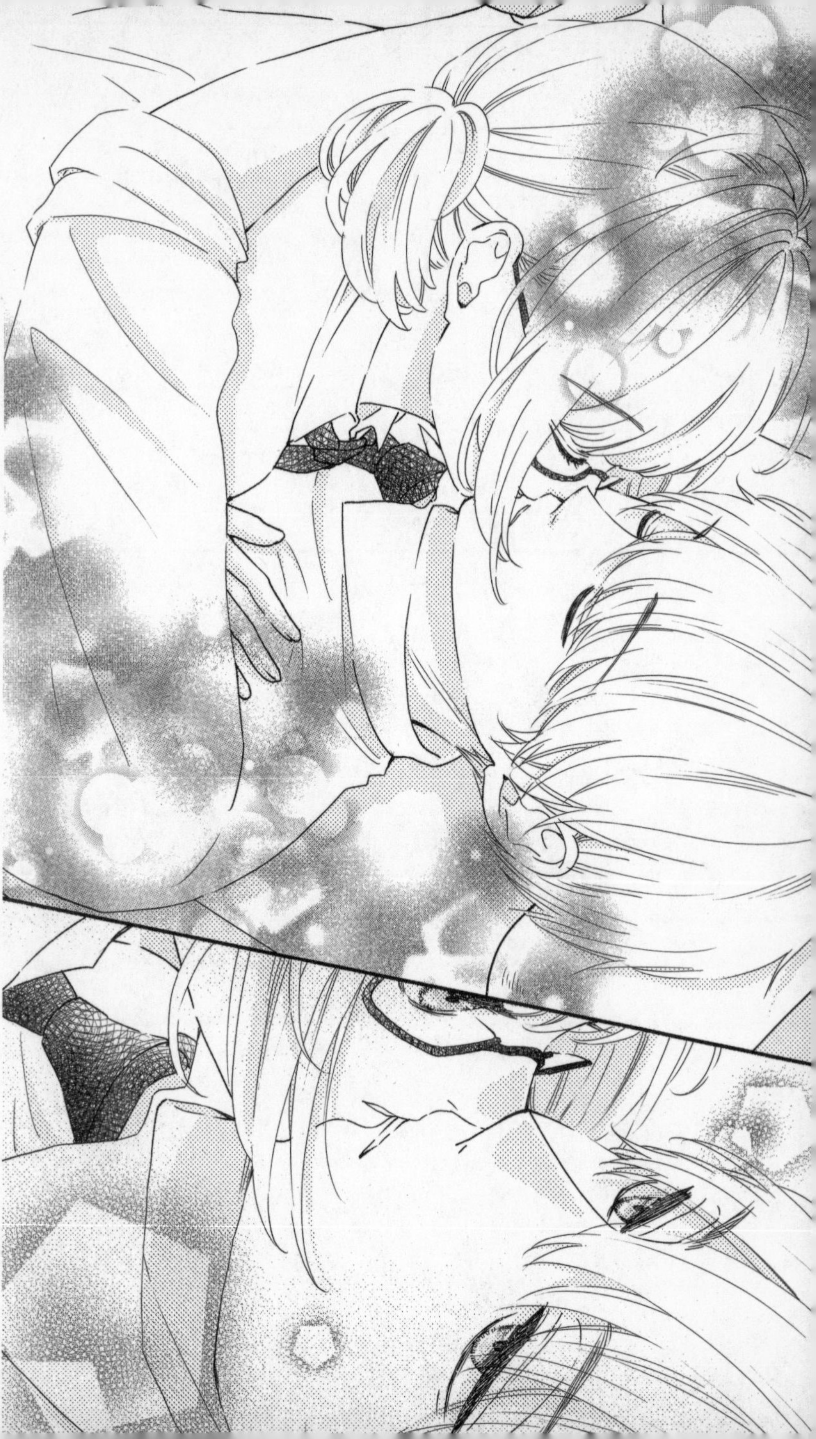

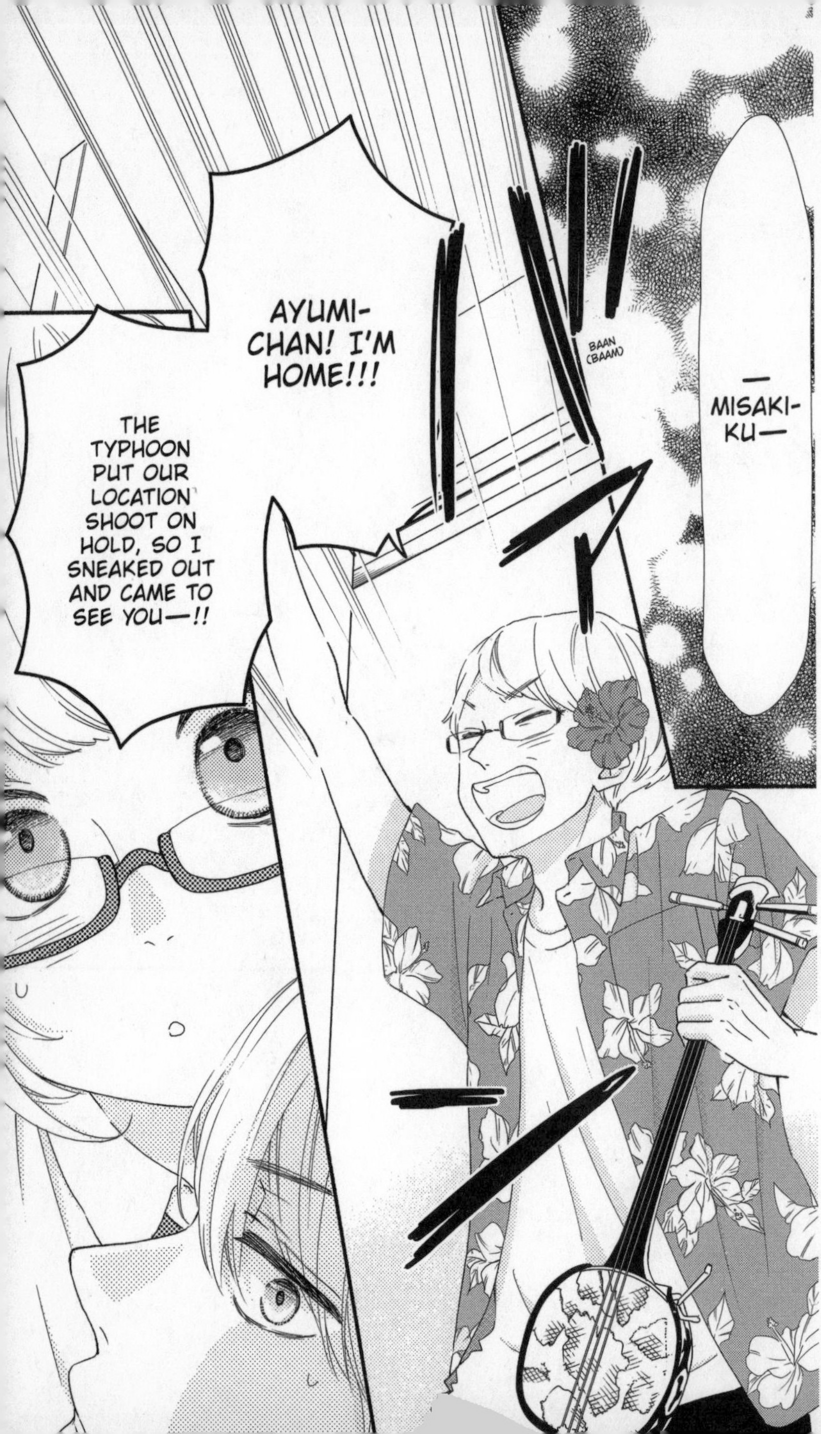
—MISAKI-KU—
AYUMI-CHAN! I'M HOME!!!
BAAN (BAAM)
THE TYPHOON PUT OUR LOCATION SHOOT ON HOLD, SO I SNEAKED OUT AND CAME TO SEE YOU—!!

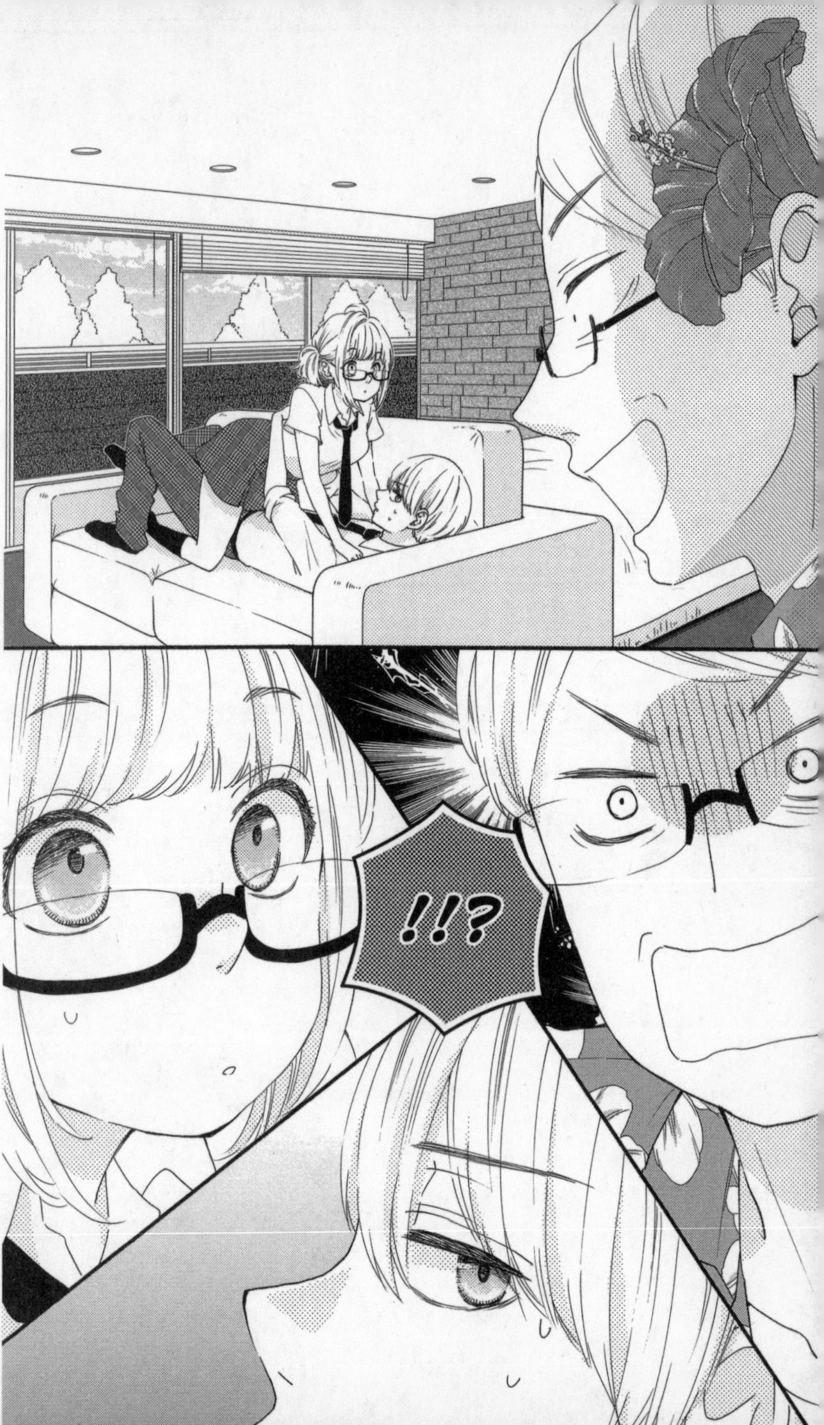
!!?

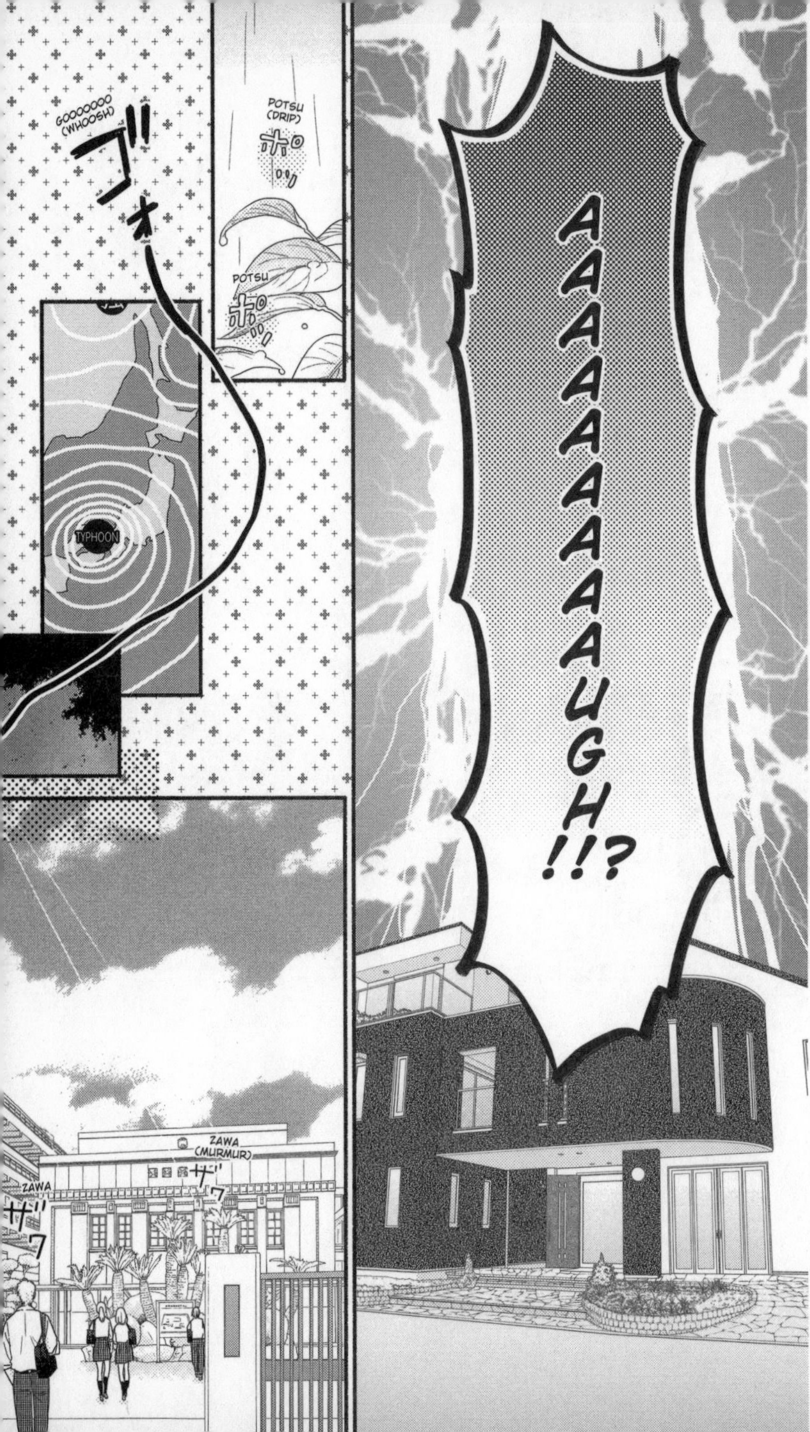
AAAAAAAAAAUGH!!?
POTSU (DRIP)
POTSU
GOOOOOOO (WHOOSH)
TYPHOON
ZAWA (MURMUR)
ZAWA

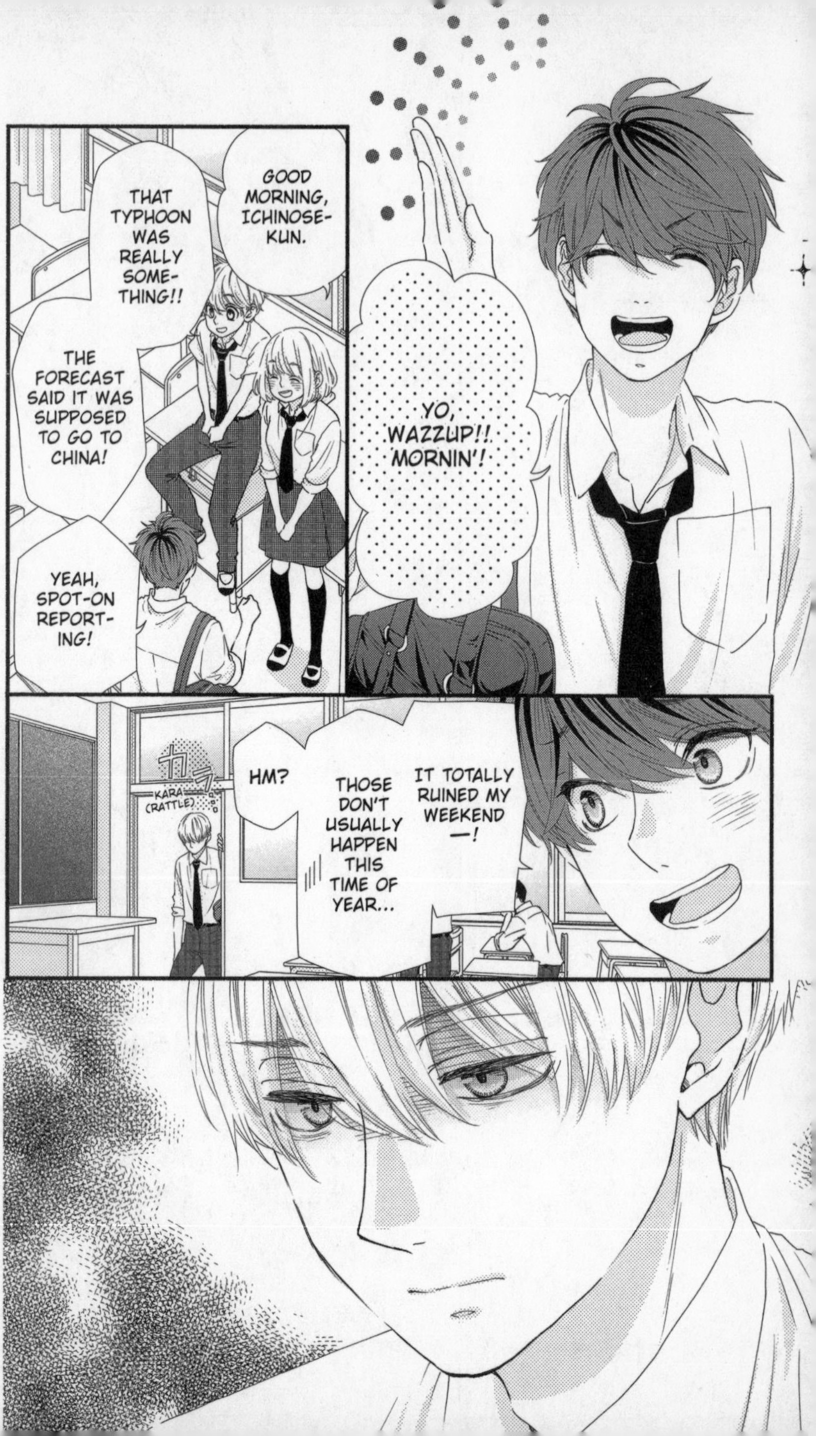
YO, WAZZUP!! MORNIN'!
GOOD MORNING, ICHINOSE-KUN.
THAT TYPHOON WAS REALLY SOME-THING!!
THE FORECAST SAID IT WAS SUPPOSED TO GO TO CHINA!
YEAH, SPOT-ON REPORT-ING!
IT TOTALLY RUINED MY WEEKEND—!
THOSE DON'T USUALLY HAPPEN THIS TIME OF YEAR...
HM?
カラ
KARA (RATTLE)

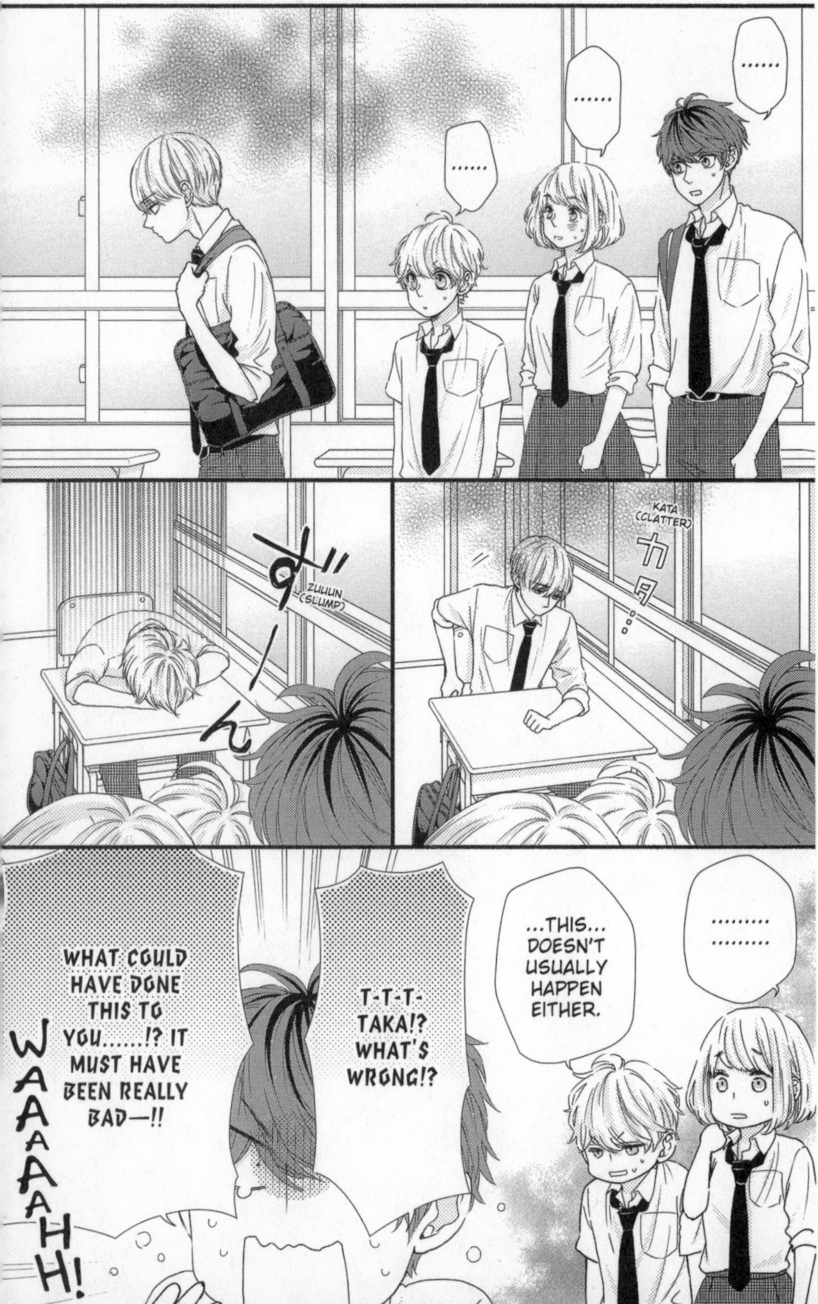

......
......
......
KATA (CLATTER)
カタ
ZUUUN (SLUMP)
ずーん
....
...THIS... DOESN'T USUALLY HAPPEN EITHER.
T-T-T-TAKA!? WHAT'S WRONG!?
WHAT COULD HAVE DONE THIS TO YOU......!? IT MUST HAVE BEEN REALLY BAD—!!
WAAAAAAH!

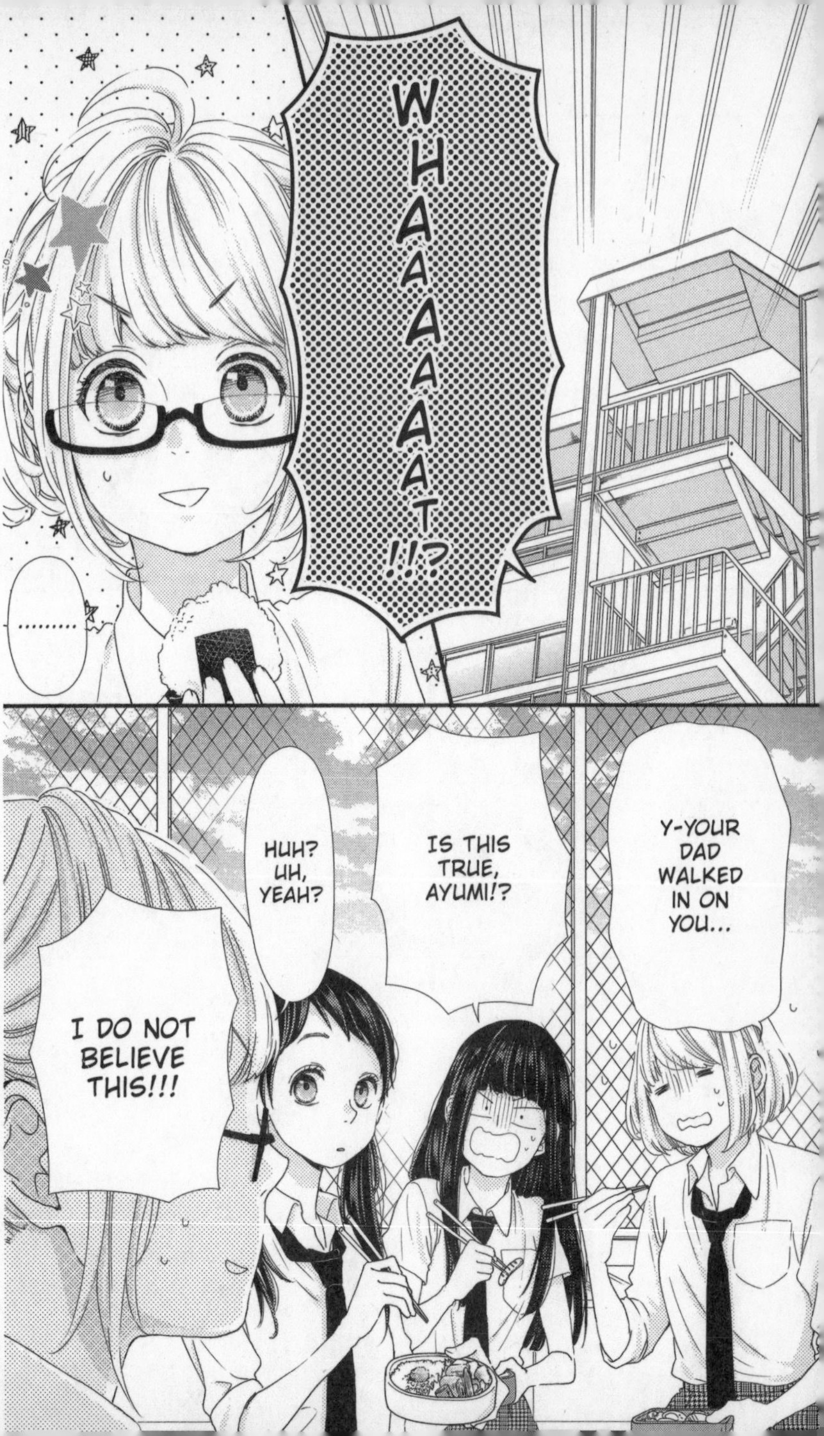
WHAAAAAAT!!?
....
Y-YOUR DAD WALKED IN ON YOU...
IS THIS TRUE, AYUMI!?
HUH? UH, YEAH?
I DO NOT BELIEVE THIS!!!

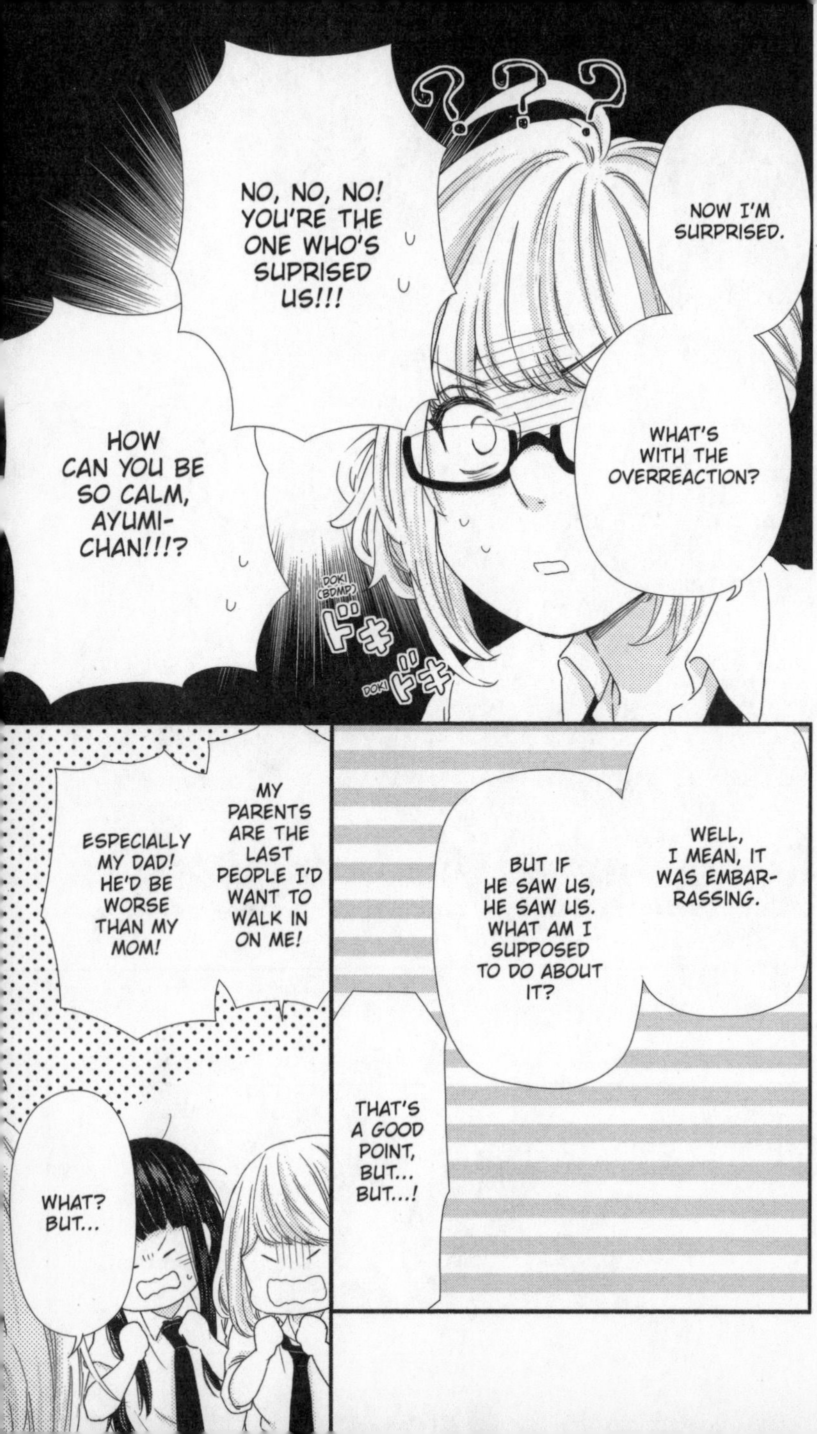
NOW I'M SURPRISED.
WHAT'S WITH THE OVERREACTION?
NO, NO, NO! YOU'RE THE ONE WHO'S SUPRISED US!!!
HOW CAN YOU BE SO CALM, AYUMI-CHAN!!!?
DOKI (BDMP)
DOKI
WELL, I MEAN, IT WAS EMBAR-RASSING.
BUT IF HE SAW US, HE SAW US. WHAT AM I SUPPOSED TO DO ABOUT IT?
THAT'S A GOOD POINT, BUT... BUT...!
MY PARENTS ARE THE LAST PEOPLE I'D WANT TO WALK IN ON ME!
ESPECIALLY MY DAD! HE'D BE WORSE THAN MY MOM!
WHAT? BUT...

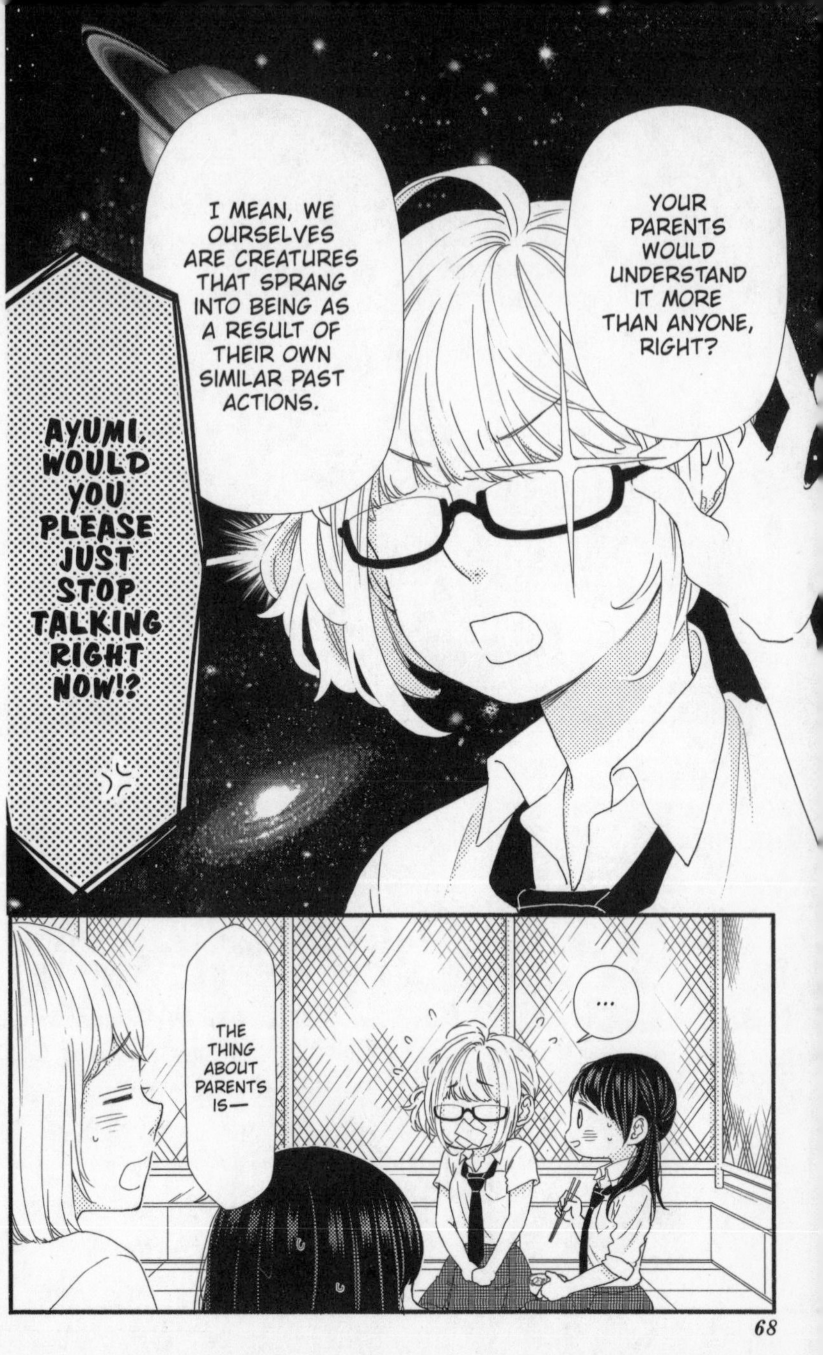
YOUR PARENTS WOULD UNDERSTAND IT MORE THAN ANYONE, RIGHT?
I MEAN, WE OURSELVES ARE CREATURES THAT SPRANG INTO BEING AS A RESULT OF THEIR OWN SIMILAR PAST ACTIONS.
AYUMI, WOULD YOU PLEASE JUST STOP TALKING RIGHT NOW!?
...
THE THING ABOUT PARENTS IS—

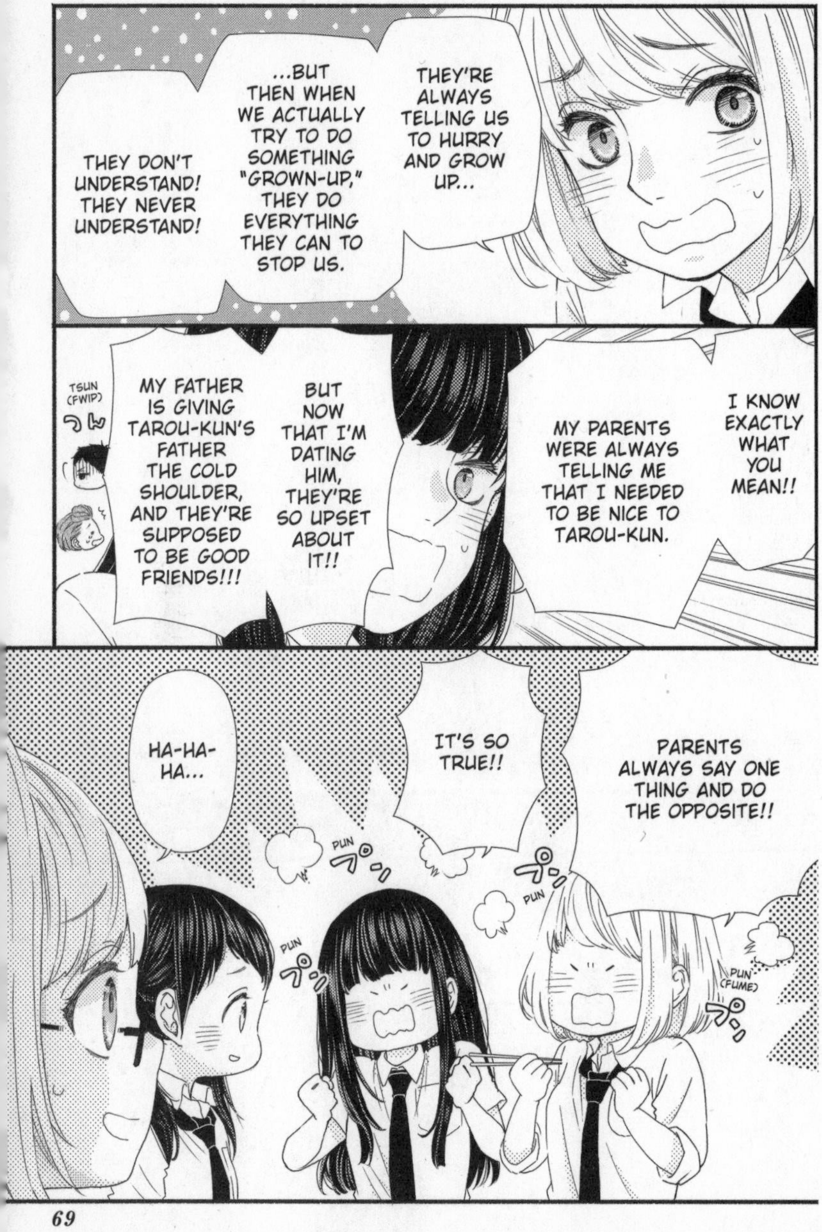

THEY'RE ALWAYS TELLING US TO HURRY AND GROW UP...
...BUT THEN WHEN WE ACTUALLY TRY TO DO SOMETHING "GROWN-UP," THEY DO EVERYTHING THEY CAN TO STOP US.
THEY DON'T UNDERSTAND! THEY NEVER UNDERSTAND!
I KNOW EXACTLY WHAT YOU MEAN!!
MY PARENTS WERE ALWAYS TELLING ME THAT I NEEDED TO BE NICE TO TAROU-KUN.
BUT NOW THAT I'M DATING HIM, THEY'RE SO UPSET ABOUT IT!!
MY FATHER IS GIVING TAROU-KUN'S FATHER THE COLD SHOULDER, AND THEY'RE SUPPOSED TO BE GOOD FRIENDS!!!
TSUN (FWIP)
つん
PARENTS ALWAYS SAY ONE THING AND DO THE OPPOSITE!!
IT'S SO TRUE!!
PUN (FUME)
PUN
PUN
PUN
HA-HA-HA...

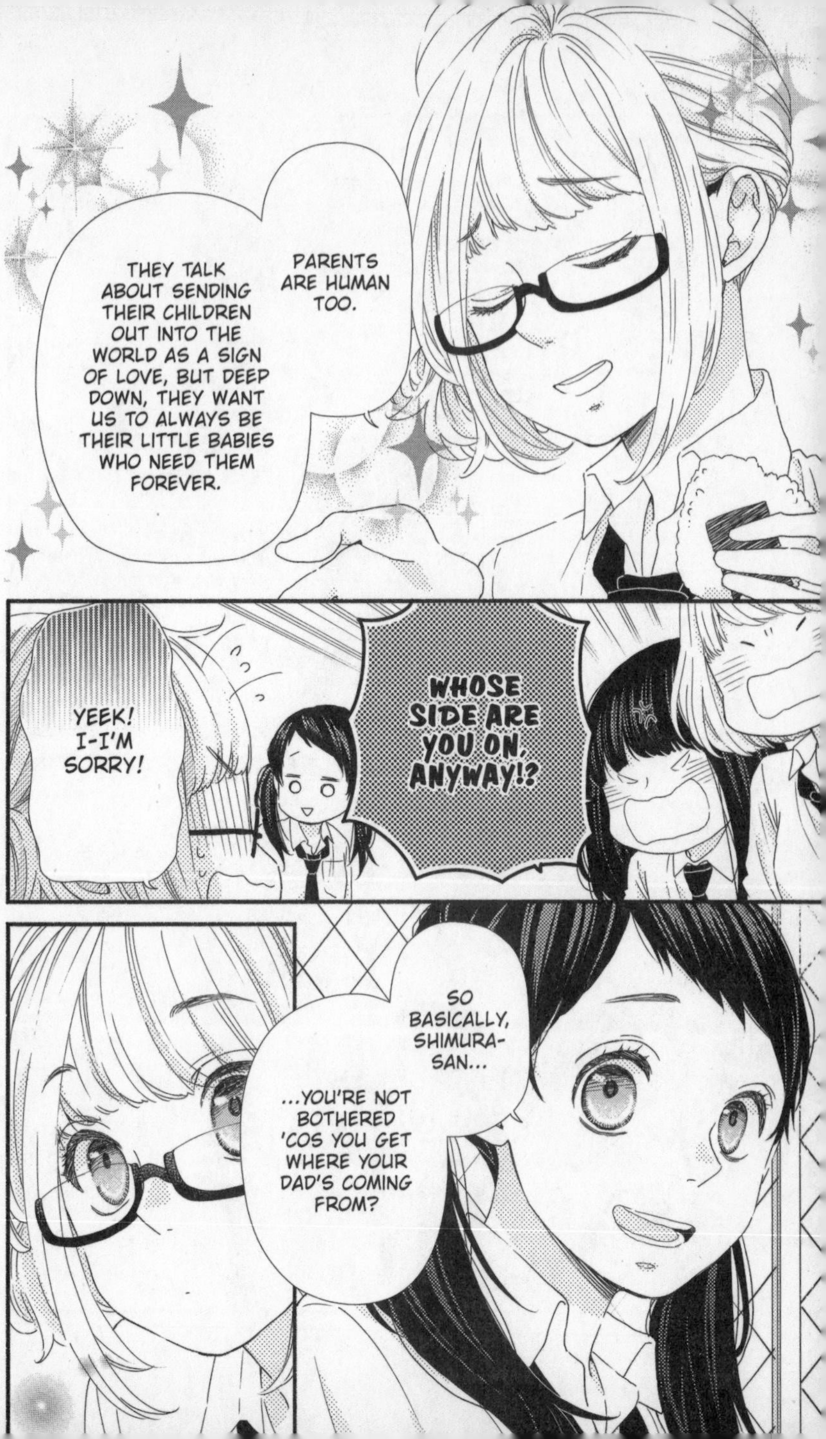
PARENTS ARE HUMAN TOO.
THEY TALK ABOUT SENDING THEIR CHILDREN OUT INTO THE WORLD AS A SIGN OF LOVE, BUT DEEP DOWN, THEY WANT US TO ALWAYS BE THEIR LITTLE BABIES WHO NEED THEM FOREVER.
WHOSE SIDE ARE YOU ON, ANYWAY!?
YEEK! I-I'M SORRY!
SO BASICALLY, SHIMURA-SAN...
...YOU'RE NOT BOTHERED 'COS YOU GET WHERE YOUR DAD'S COMING FROM?

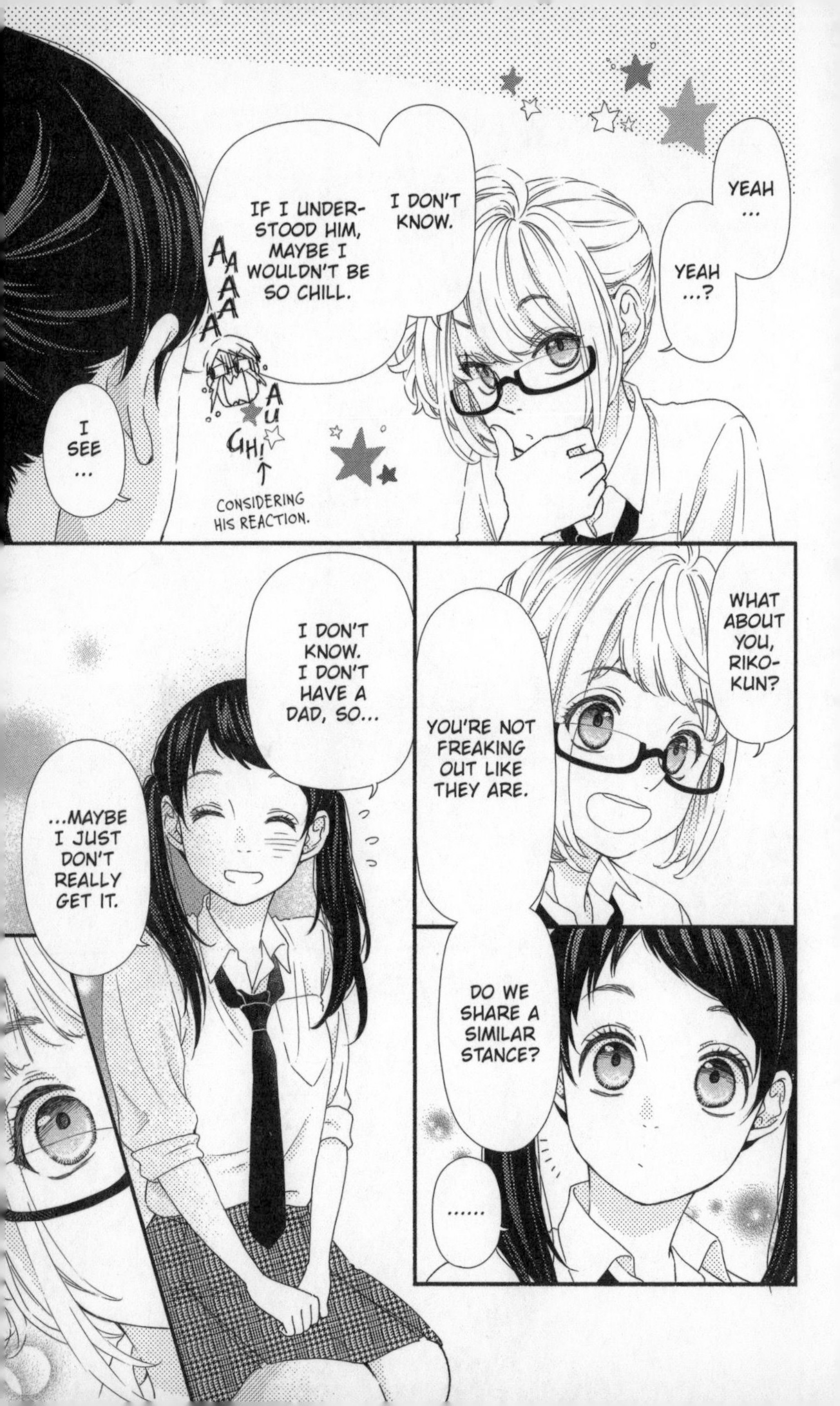
YEAH...
YEAH...?
I DON'T KNOW.
IF I UNDER-STOOD HIM, MAYBE I WOULDN'T BE SO CHILL.
AAAAAAUGH!
CONSIDERING HIS REACTION.
I SEE...
WHAT ABOUT YOU, RIKO-KUN?
YOU'RE NOT FREAKING OUT LIKE THEY ARE.
DO WE SHARE A SIMILAR STANCE?
......
I DON'T KNOW. I DON'T HAVE A DAD, SO...
...MAYBE I JUST DON'T REALLY GET IT.

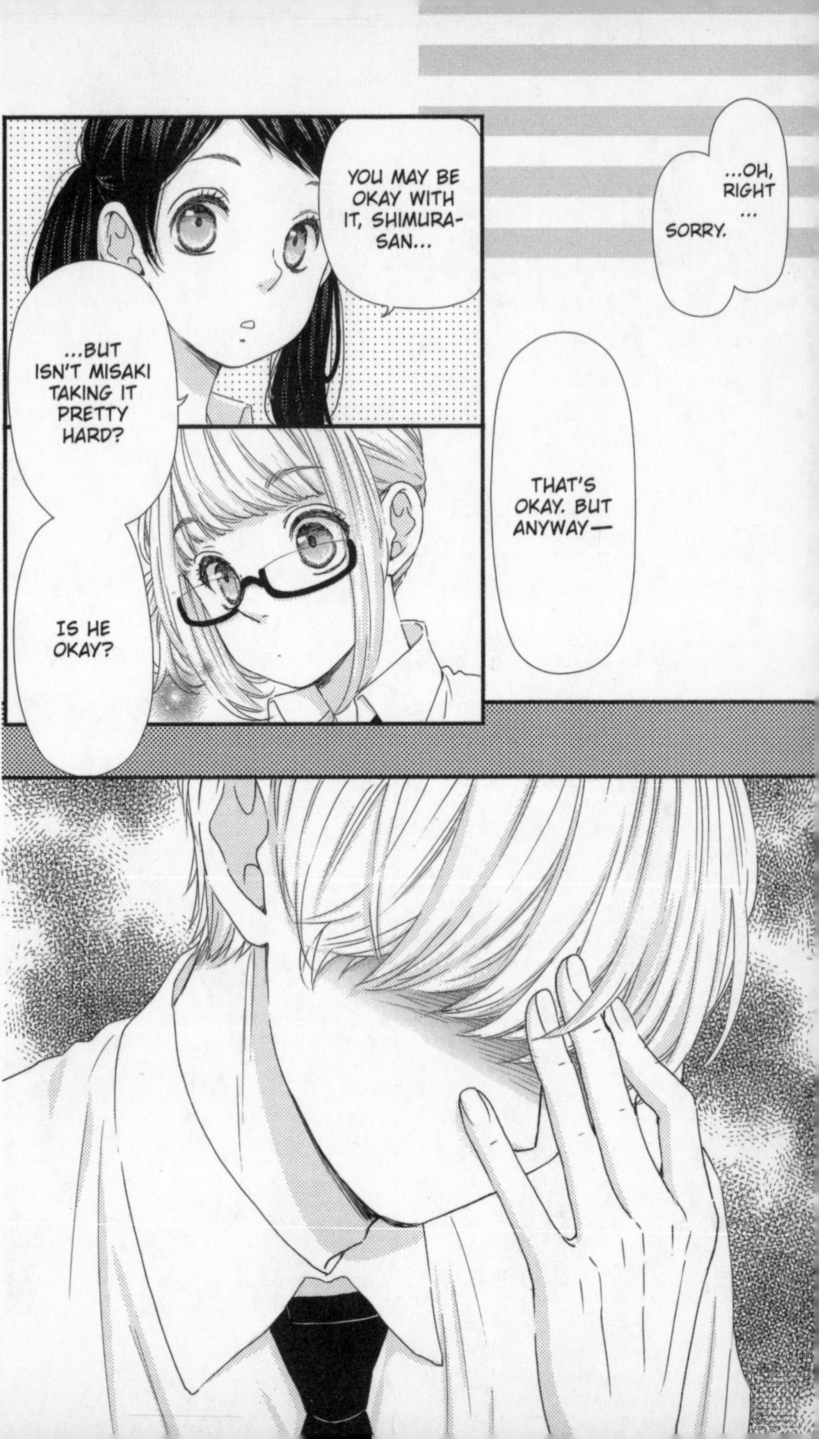
...OH, RIGHT ... SORRY.
THAT'S OKAY. BUT ANYWAY—
YOU MAY BE OKAY WITH IT, SHIMURA-SAN...
...BUT ISN'T MISAKI TAKING IT PRETTY HARD?
IS HE OKAY?

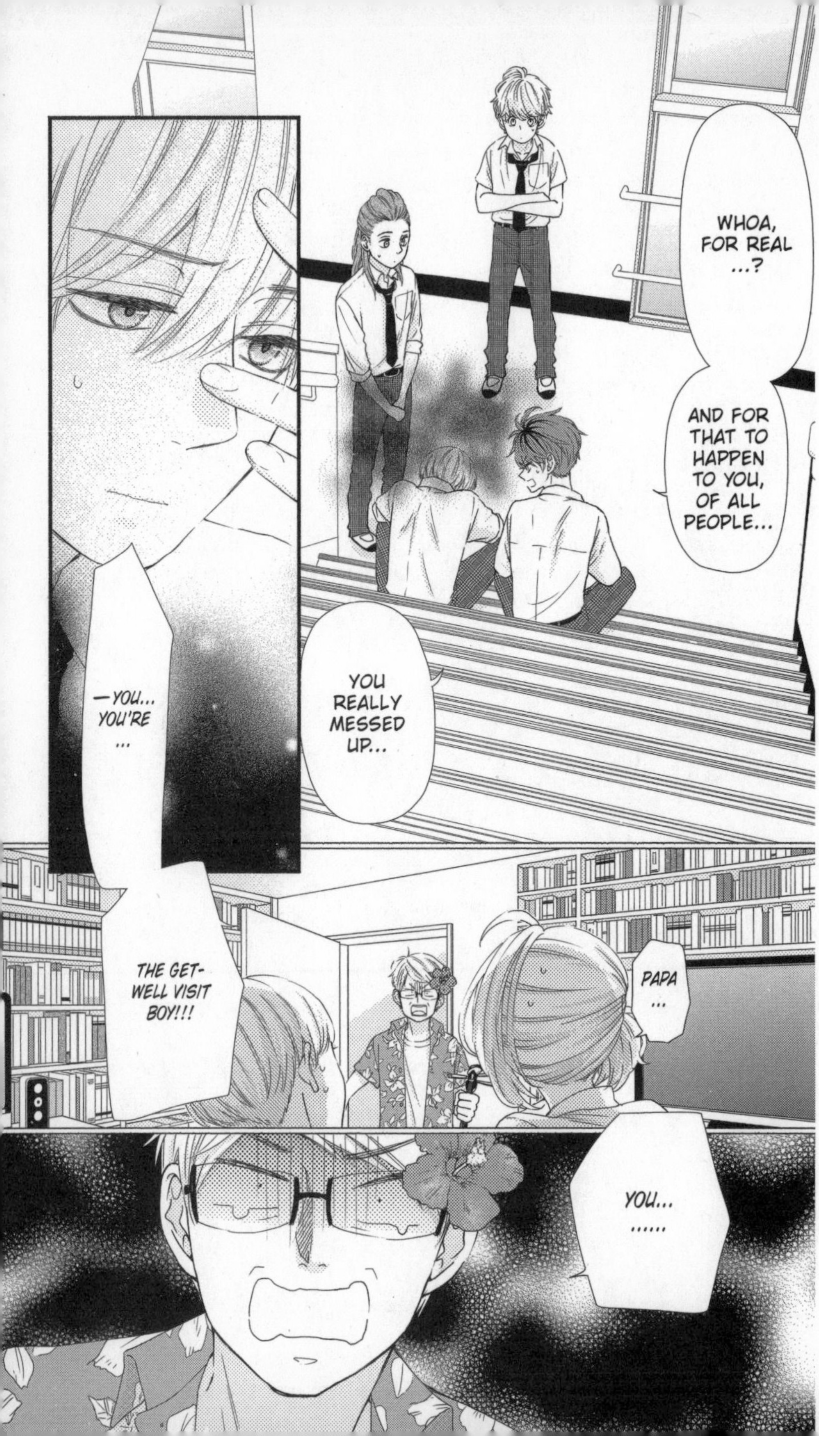
WHOA, FOR REAL ...?
AND FOR THAT TO HAPPEN TO YOU, OF ALL PEOPLE...
YOU REALLY MESSED UP...
—YOU... YOU'RE ... THE GET-WELL VISIT BOY!!!
PAPA ...
YOU... ......

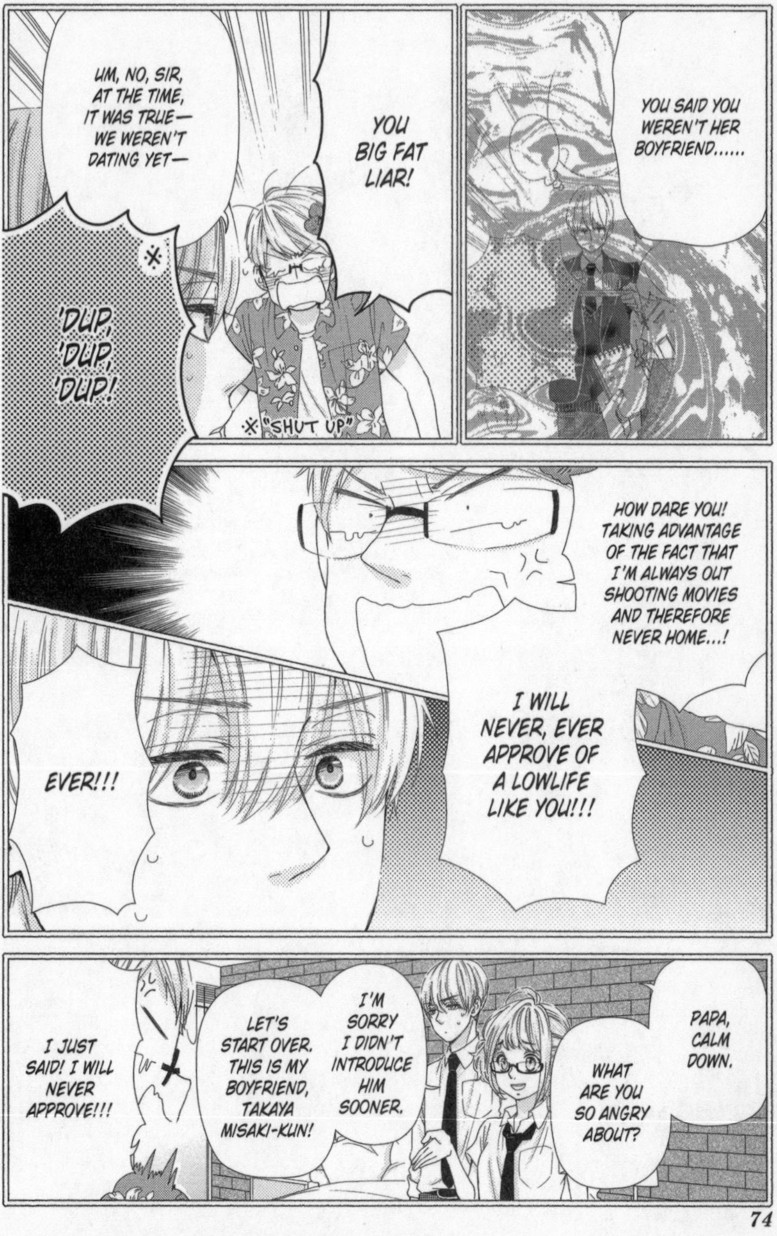
YOU SAID YOU WEREN'T HER BOYFRIEND......
YOU BIG FAT LIAR!
UM, NO, SIR, AT THE TIME, IT WAS TRUE— WE WEREN'T DATING YET—
※ 'DUP, 'DUP, 'DUP!
※ "SHUT UP"
HOW DARE YOU! TAKING ADVANTAGE OF THE FACT THAT I'M ALWAYS OUT SHOOTING MOVIES AND THEREFORE NEVER HOME...!
I WILL NEVER, EVER APPROVE OF A LOWLIFE LIKE YOU!!!
EVER!!!
PAPA, CALM DOWN.
WHAT ARE YOU SO ANGRY ABOUT?
I'M SORRY I DIDN'T INTRODUCE HIM SOONER.
LET'S START OVER. THIS IS MY BOYFRIEND, TAKAYA MISAKI-KUN!
I JUST SAID! I WILL NEVER APPROVE!!!

? WHAT ARE YOU TALKING ABOUT, PAPA?
HE'S NOT DATING YOU. HE'S DATING ME.
YOU AND I MAY BE FATHER AND DAUGHTER, BUT WE ARE OUR OWN PEOPLE WITH DIFFERENT PERSONALITIES.
....
ERGO, I AM THE ONLY ONE WHO HAS THE RIGHT TO DETERMINE WHAT KIND OF RELATIONSHIP I'M WILLING TO HAVE WITH MISAKI-KUN.
IN OTHER WORDS, WE DON'T NEED YOUR APPROVAL.
...!! 'DUP, 'DUP, 'DUUUP!!!
I SAID I DON'T APPROVE, AND I DON'T!
DID YOU LISTEN TO ANYTHING I JUST SAID, PAPA?
I'LL SAY IT AGAIN.
...SHIMURA-SAN...... I'M JUST GONNA GO...
....
SHIMURA, YOU IDIOT!
SHE WASN'T WRONG, THOUGH ......
IT'S STILL JUST PUTTING OIL ON THE FIRE.

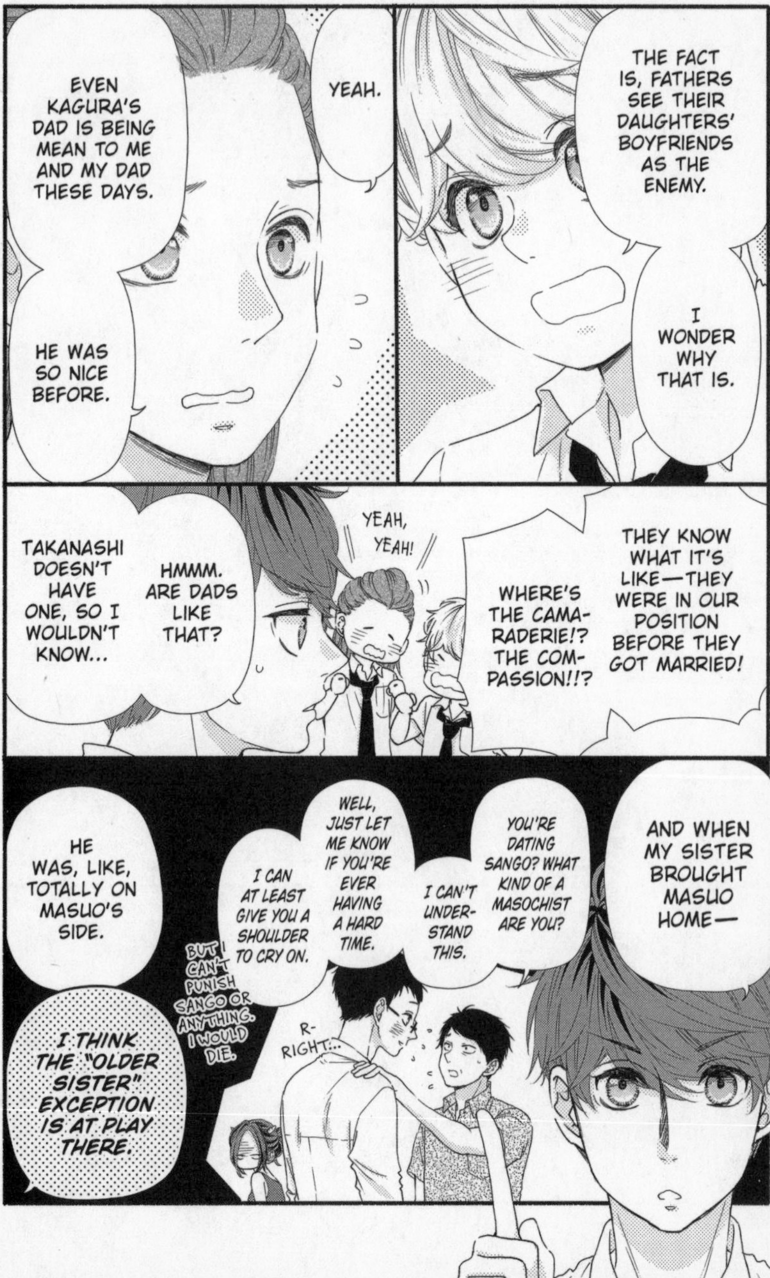
THE FACT IS, FATHERS SEE THEIR DAUGHTERS' BOYFRIENDS AS THE ENEMY.
I WONDER WHY THAT IS.
YEAH.
EVEN KAGURA'S DAD IS BEING MEAN TO ME AND MY DAD THESE DAYS.
HE WAS SO NICE BEFORE.
THEY KNOW WHAT IT'S LIKE—THEY WERE IN OUR POSITION BEFORE THEY GOT MARRIED!
WHERE'S THE CAMA-RADERIE!? THE COM-PASSION!!?
YEAH, YEAH!
HMMM. ARE DADS LIKE THAT?
TAKANASHI DOESN'T HAVE ONE, SO I WOULDN'T KNOW...
AND WHEN MY SISTER BROUGHT MASUO HOME—
YOU'RE DATING SANGO? WHAT KIND OF A MASOCHIST ARE YOU?
I CAN'T UNDER-STAND THIS.
WELL, JUST LET ME KNOW IF YOU'RE EVER HAVING A HARD TIME.
I CAN AT LEAST GIVE YOU A SHOULDER TO CRY ON.
BUT I CAN'T PUNISH SANGO OR ANYTHING. I WOULD DIE.
R-RIGHT...
HE WAS, LIKE, TOTALLY ON MASUO'S SIDE.
I THINK THE "OLDER SISTER" EXCEPTION IS AT PLAY THERE.

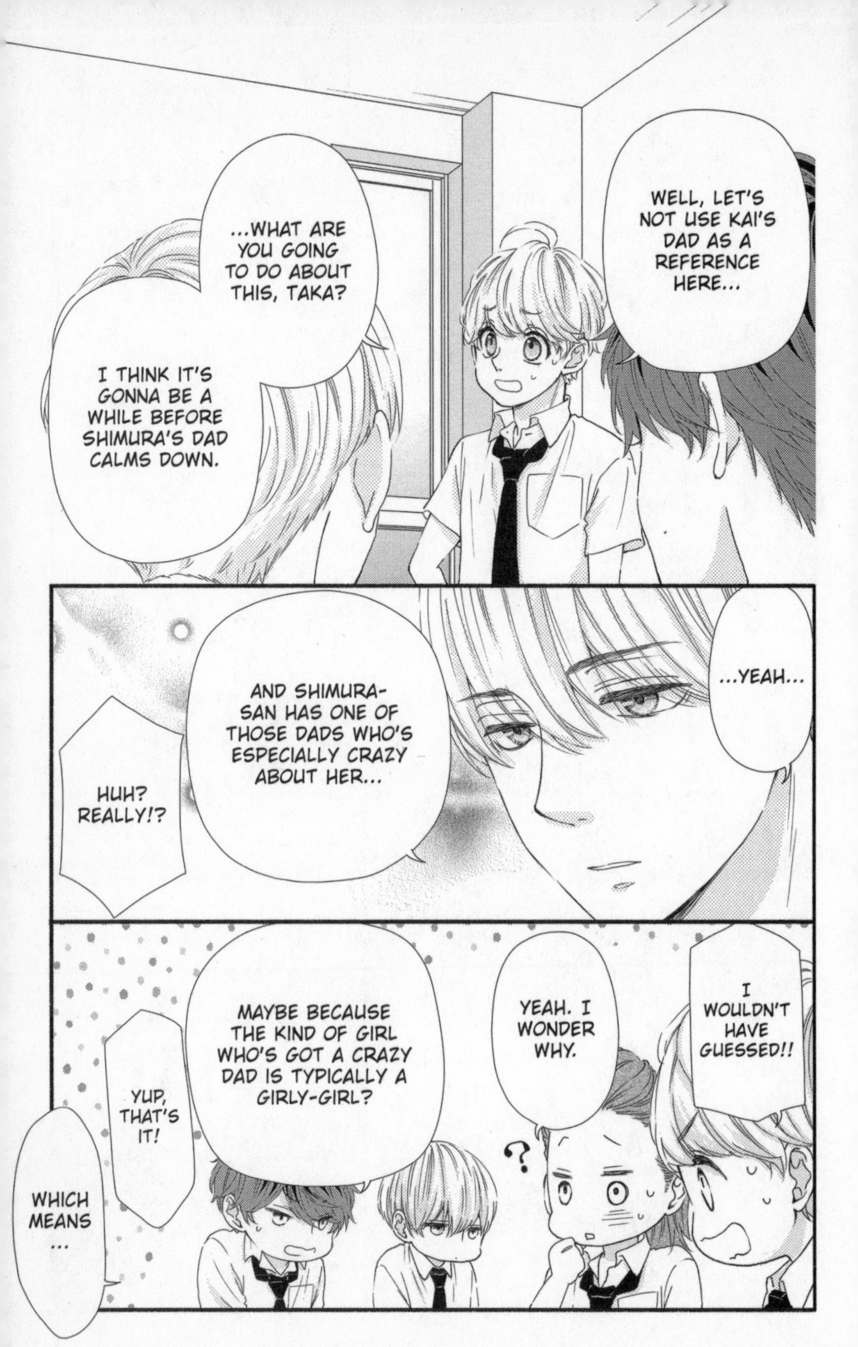
WELL, LET'S NOT USE KAI'S DAD AS A REFERENCE HERE...
...WHAT ARE YOU GOING TO DO ABOUT THIS, TAKA?
I THINK IT'S GONNA BE A WHILE BEFORE SHIMURA'S DAD CALMS DOWN.
...YEAH...
AND SHIMURA-SAN HAS ONE OF THOSE DADS WHO'S ESPECIALLY CRAZY ABOUT HER...
HUH? REALLY!?
I WOULDN'T HAVE GUESSED!!
YEAH. I WONDER WHY.
MAYBE BECAUSE THE KIND OF GIRL WHO'S GOT A CRAZY DAD IS TYPICALLY A GIRLY-GIRL?
YUP, THAT'S IT!
WHICH MEANS ...

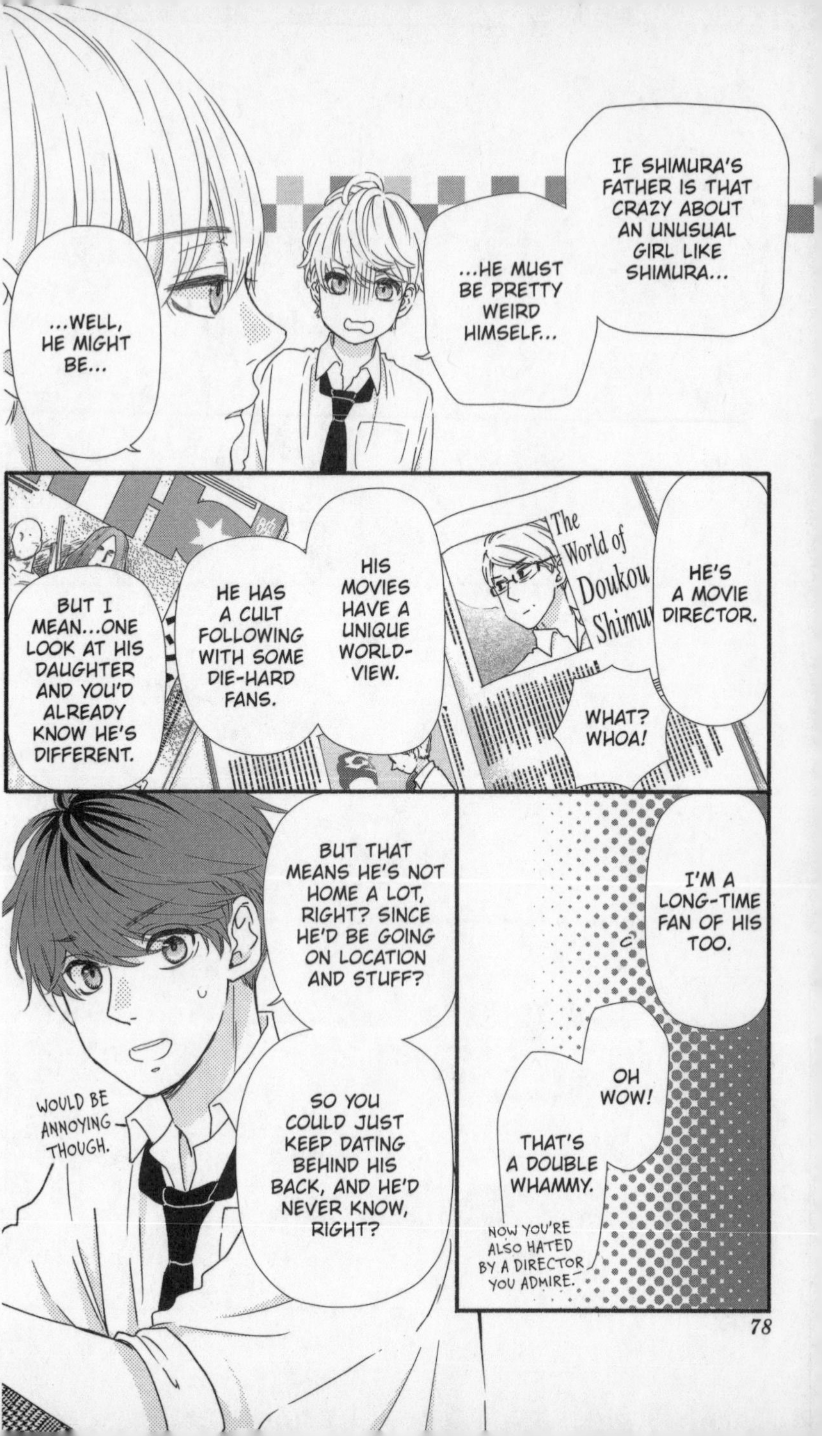
IF SHIMURA'S FATHER IS THAT CRAZY ABOUT AN UNUSUAL GIRL LIKE SHIMURA...
...HE MUST BE PRETTY WEIRD HIMSELF...
...WELL, HE MIGHT BE...
HE'S A MOVIE DIRECTOR.
WHAT? WHOA!
The World of Doukou Shimu
HIS MOVIES HAVE A UNIQUE WORLD-VIEW.
HE HAS A CULT FOLLOWING WITH SOME DIE-HARD FANS.
BUT I MEAN...ONE LOOK AT HIS DAUGHTER AND YOU'D ALREADY KNOW HE'S DIFFERENT.
I'M A LONG-TIME FAN OF HIS TOO.
OH WOW!
THAT'S A DOUBLE WHAMMY.
NOW YOU'RE ALSO HATED BY A DIRECTOR YOU ADMIRE.
BUT THAT MEANS HE'S NOT HOME A LOT, RIGHT? SINCE HE'D BE GOING ON LOCATION AND STUFF?
SO YOU COULD JUST KEEP DATING BEHIND HIS BACK, AND HE'D NEVER KNOW, RIGHT?
WOULD BE ANNOYING THOUGH.

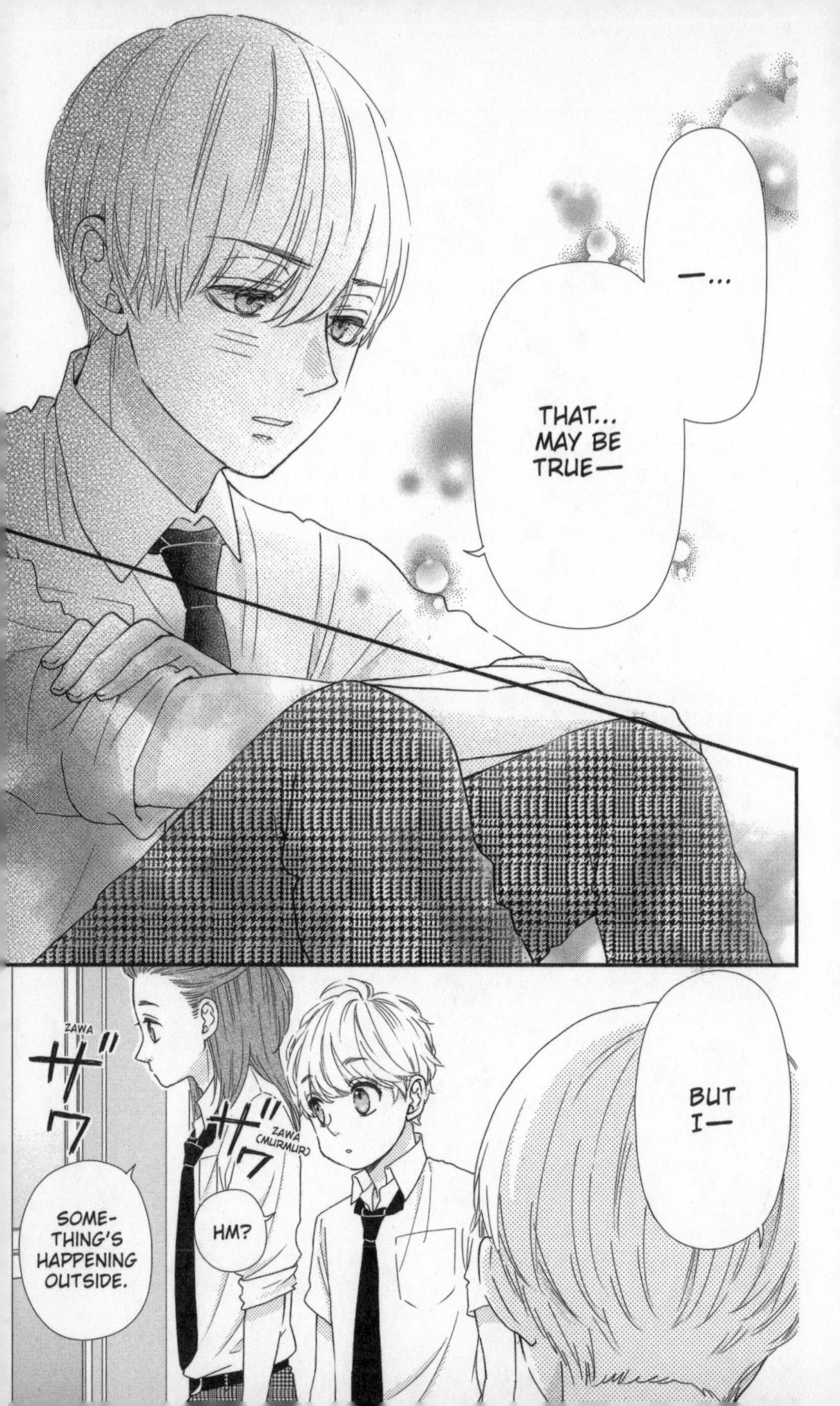
—...
THAT... MAY BE TRUE—
BUT I—
ZAWA (MURMUR)
HM?
ZAWA
SOME-THING'S HAPPENING OUTSIDE.

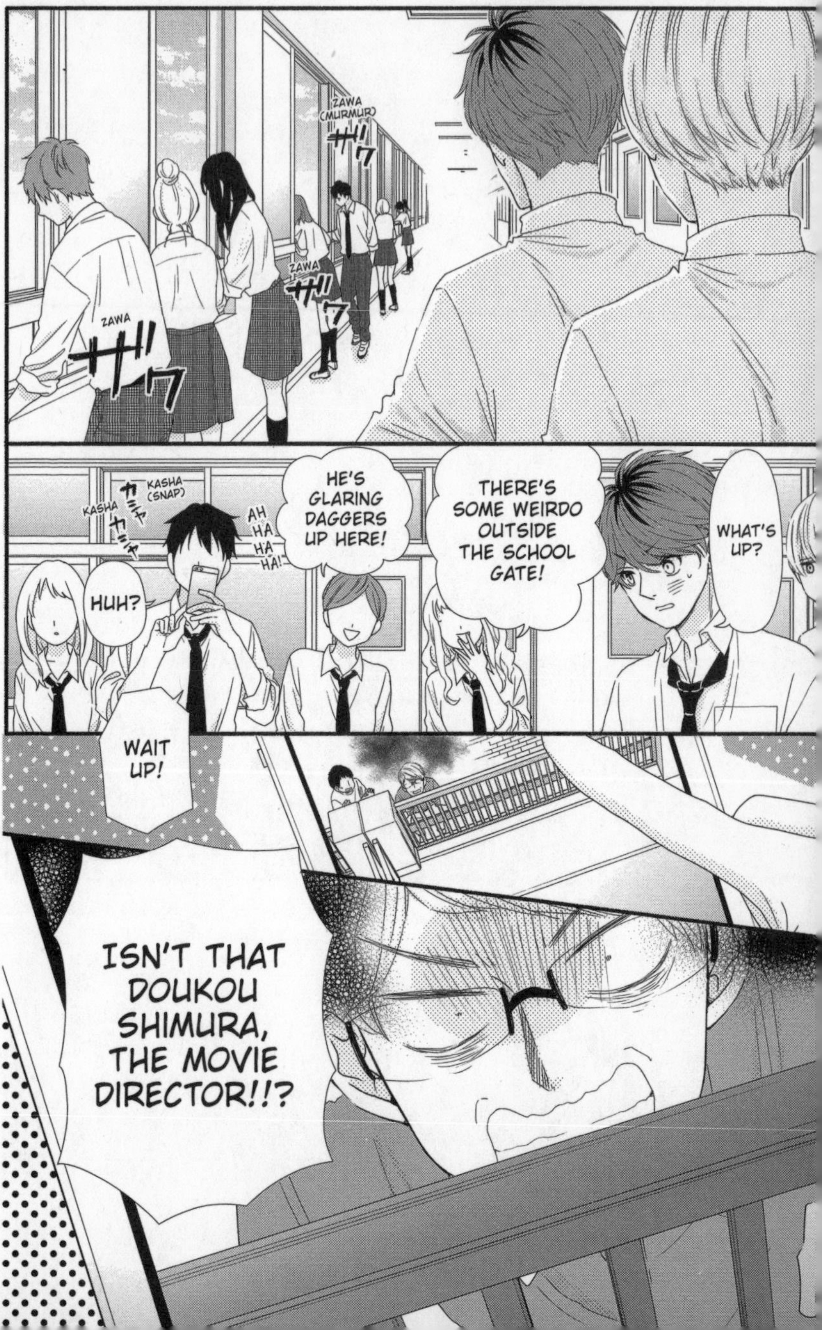
ZAWA (MURMUR)
ザワ
ZAWA
ザワ
ZAWA
ザワ
WHAT'S UP?
THERE'S SOME WEIRDO OUTSIDE THE SCHOOL GATE!
HE'S GLARING DAGGERS UP HERE!
AH HA HA HA!
KASHA (SNAP)
カシャ
KASHA
カシャ
HUH?
WAIT UP!
ISN'T THAT DOUKOU SHIMURA, THE MOVIE DIRECTOR!!?

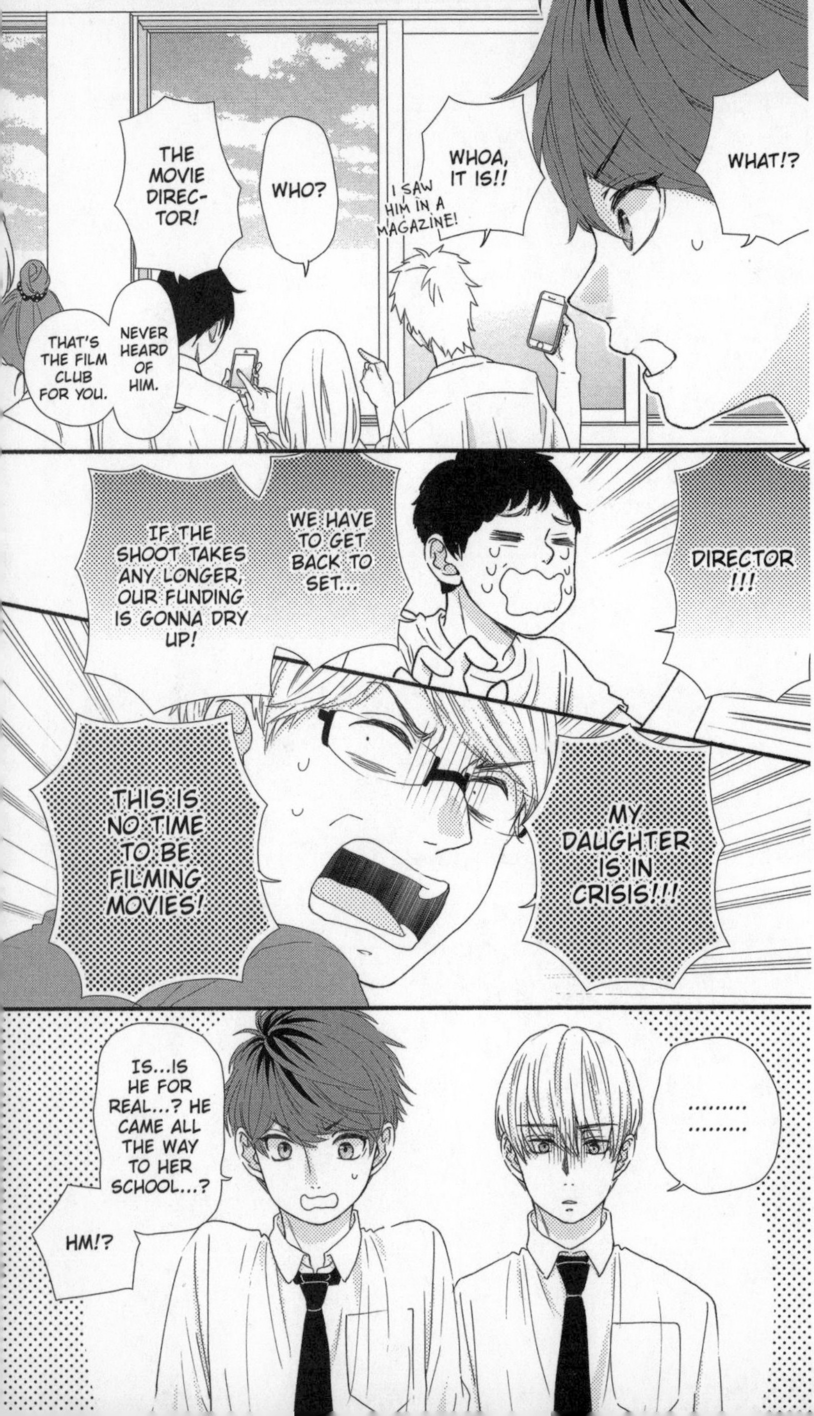

WHAT!?
WHOA, IT IS!!
I SAW HIM IN A MAGAZINE!
WHO?
THE MOVIE DIRECTOR!
NEVER HEARD OF HIM.
THAT'S THE FILM CLUB FOR YOU.
DIRECTOR!!!
WE HAVE TO GET BACK TO SET...
IF THE SHOOT TAKES ANY LONGER, OUR FUNDING IS GONNA DRY UP!
MY DAUGHTER IS IN CRISIS!!!
THIS IS NO TIME TO BE FILMING MOVIES!
....
IS...IS HE FOR REAL...? HE CAME ALL THE WAY TO HER SCHOOL...?
HM!?

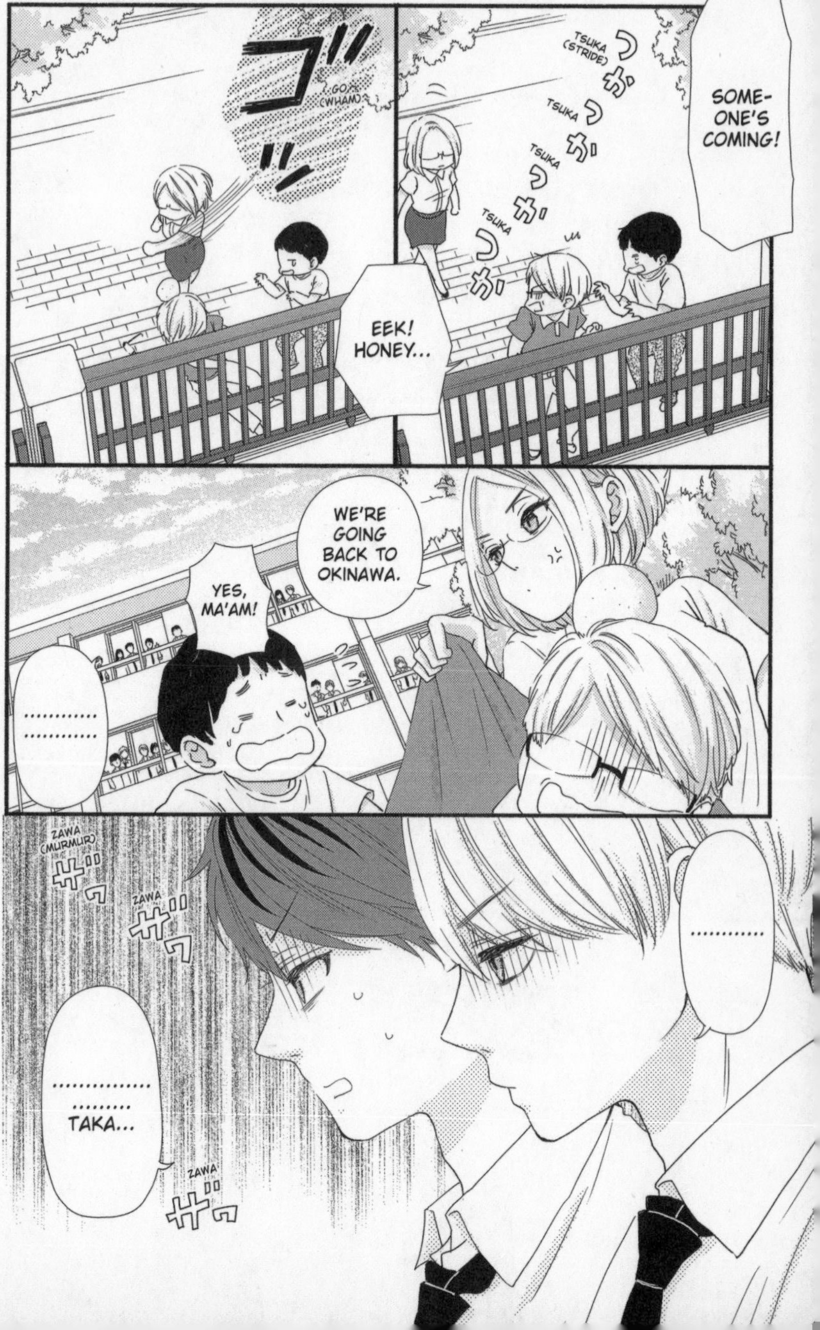
SOME-ONE'S COMING!
TSUKA (STRIDE)
TSUKA
TSUKA
TSUKA
EEK! HONEY...
GO (WHAM)
WE'RE GOING BACK TO OKINAWA.
YES, MA'AM!
....
....
ZAWA (MURMUR)
ZAWA
....
TAKA...
ZAWA

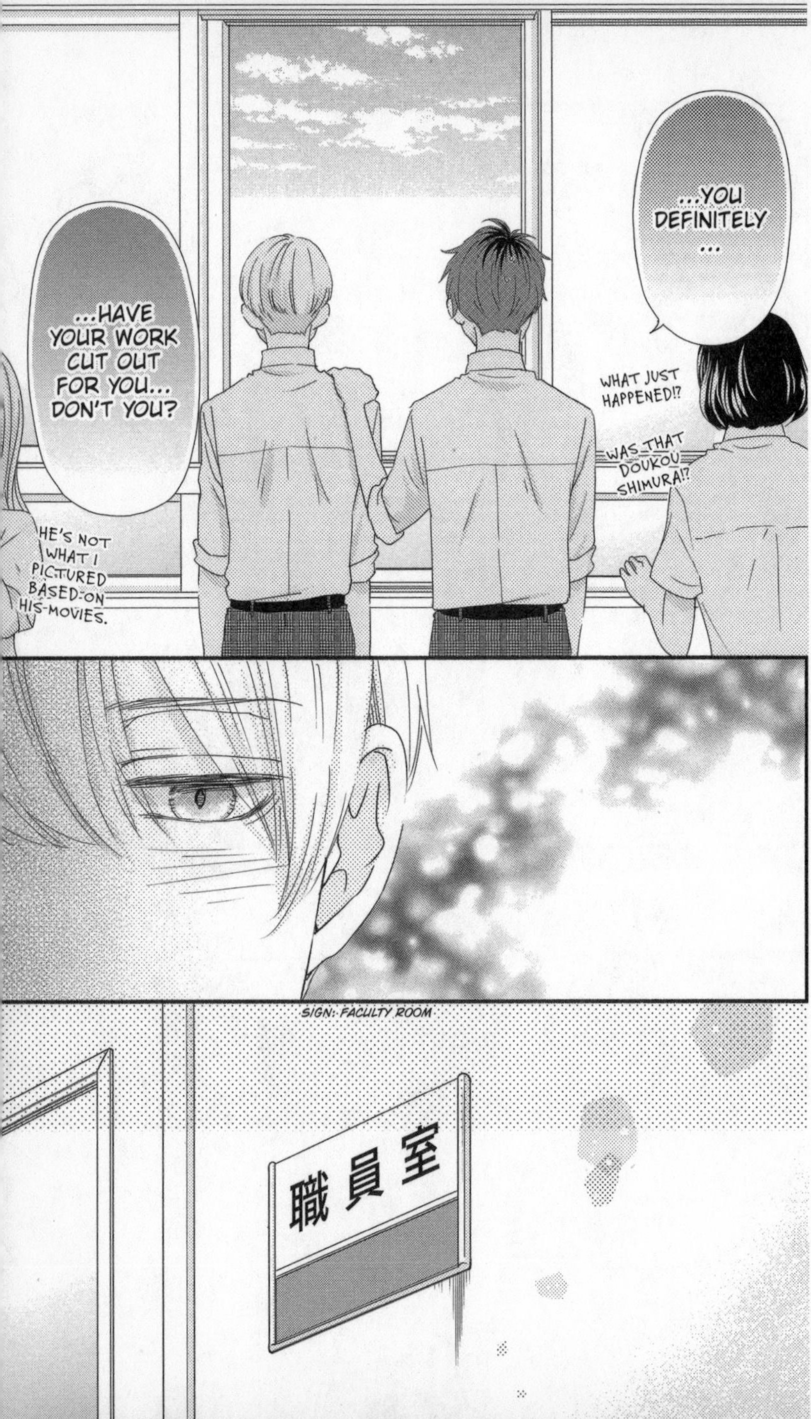
...YOU DEFINITELY ...
...HAVE YOUR WORK CUT OUT FOR YOU... DON'T YOU?
WHAT JUST HAPPENED!?
WAS THAT DOUKOU SHIMURA!?
HE'S NOT WHAT I PICTURED BASED ON HIS MOVIES.
SIGN: FACULTY ROOM
職員室

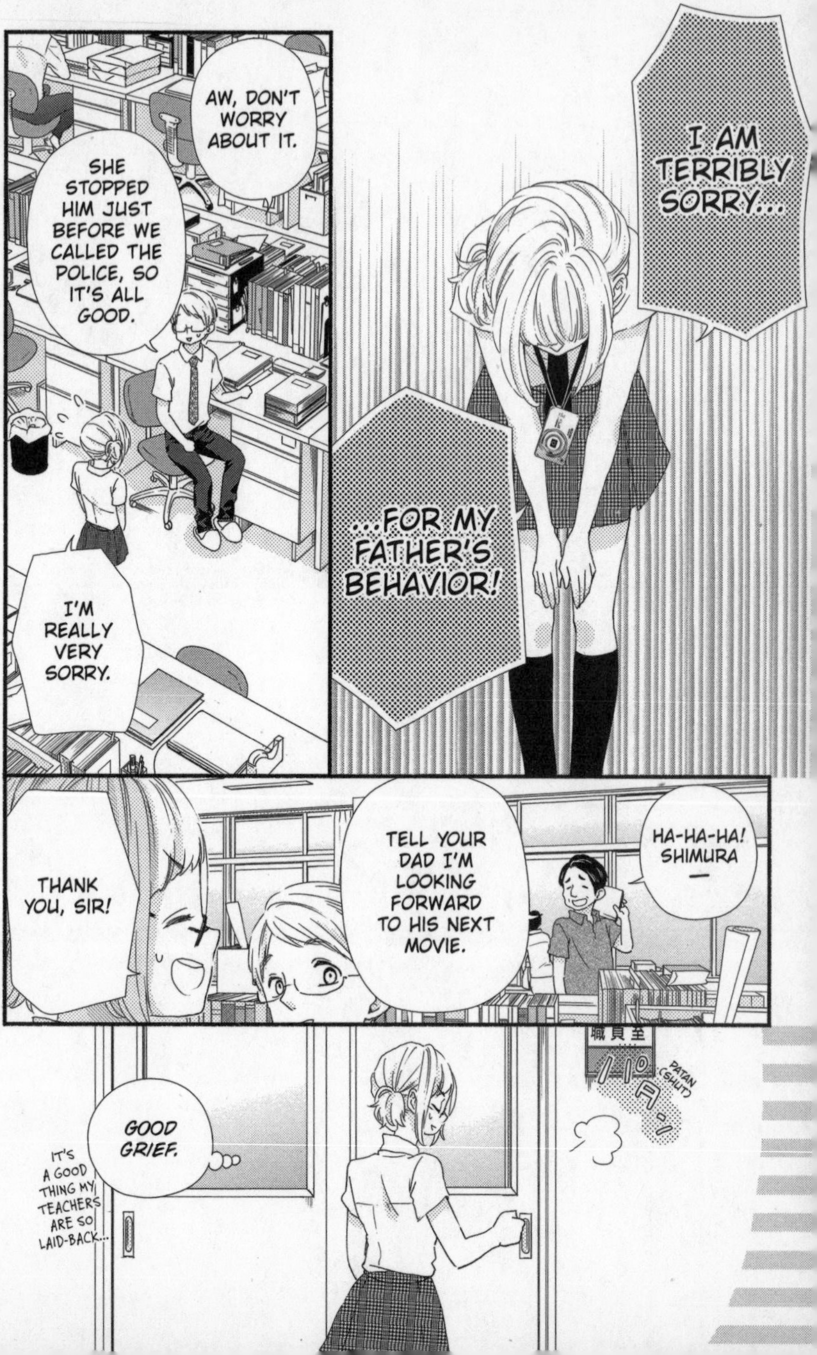
I AM TERRIBLY SORRY...
...FOR MY FATHER'S BEHAVIOR!
AW, DON'T WORRY ABOUT IT.
SHE STOPPED HIM JUST BEFORE WE CALLED THE POLICE, SO IT'S ALL GOOD.
I'M REALLY VERY SORRY.
HA-HA-HA! SHIMURA—
TELL YOUR DAD I'M LOOKING FORWARD TO HIS NEXT MOVIE.
THANK YOU, SIR!
職員室
PATAN (SHUT)
GOOD GRIEF.
IT'S A GOOD THING MY TEACHERS ARE SO LAID-BACK...

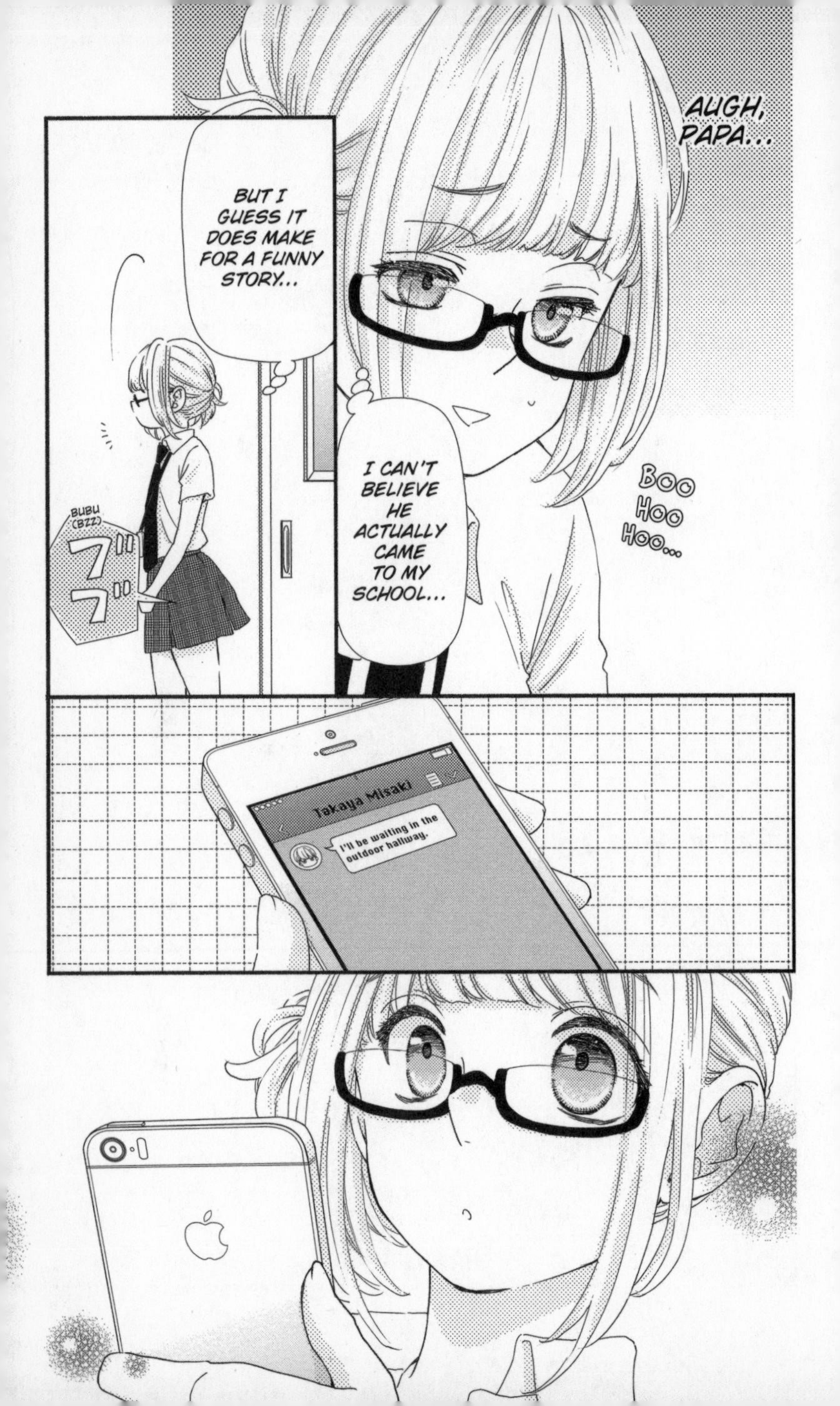
AUGH, PAPA...
BOO HOO HOO...
I CAN'T BELIEVE HE ACTUALLY CAME TO MY SCHOOL...
BUT I GUESS IT DOES MAKE FOR A FUNNY STORY...
BUBU (BZZ)
Takaya Misaki
I'll be waiting in the outdoor hallway.

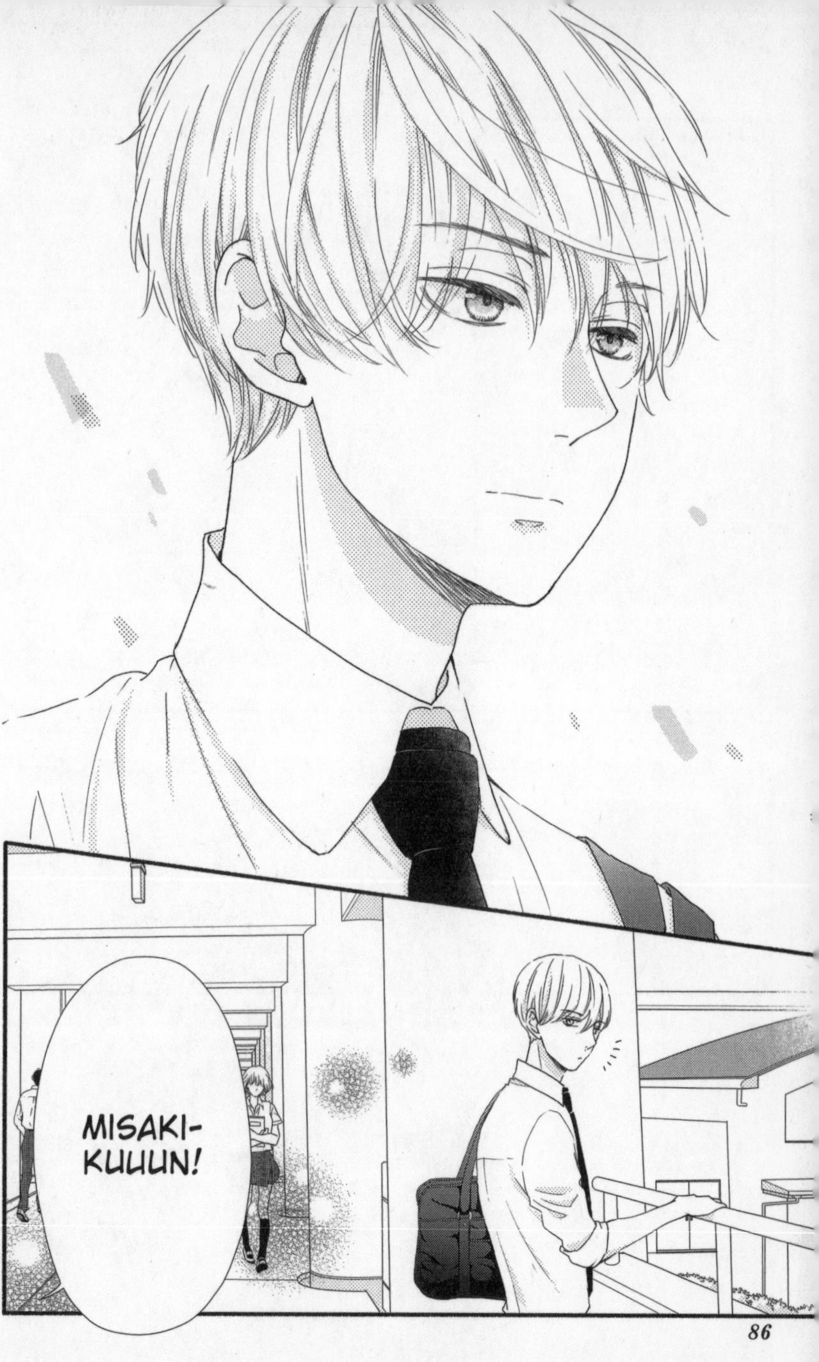
MISAKI-
KUUUN!

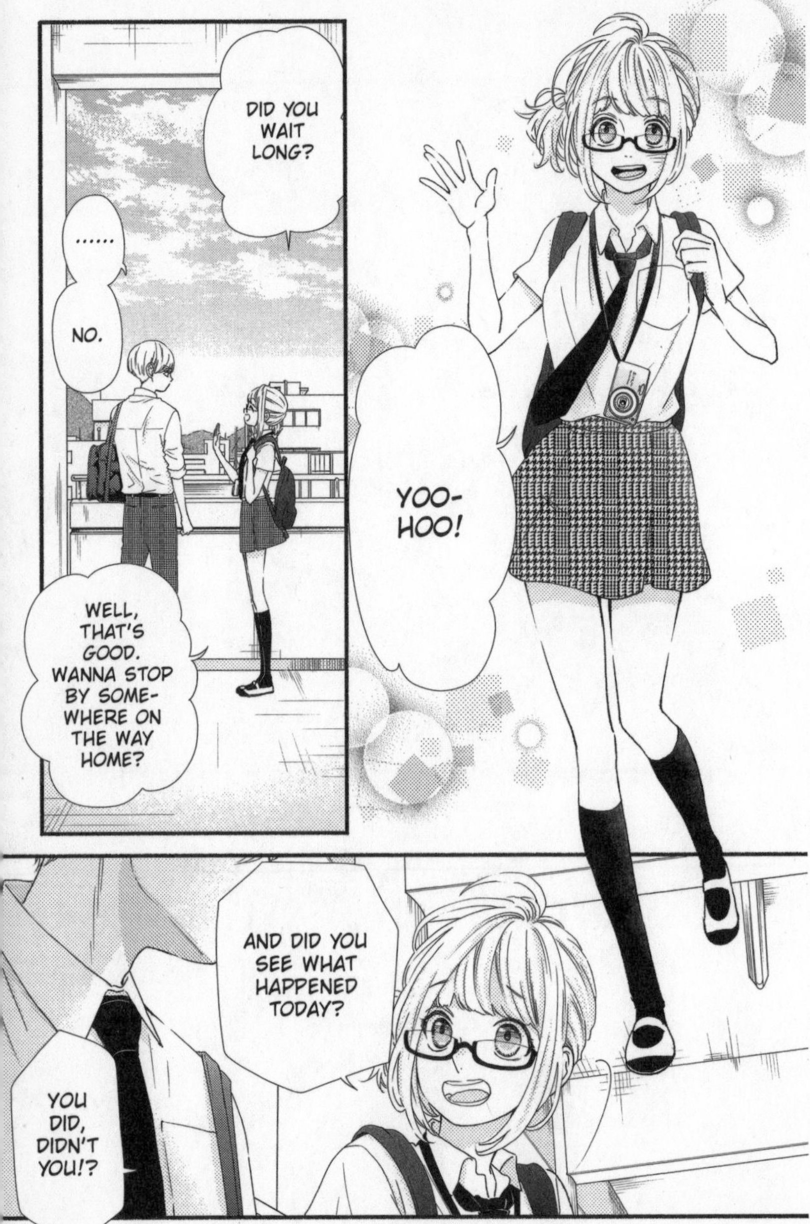
YOO-HOO!
DID YOU WAIT LONG?
......
NO.
WELL, THAT'S GOOD. WANNA STOP BY SOME-WHERE ON THE WAY HOME?
AND DID YOU SEE WHAT HAPPENED TODAY?
YOU DID, DIDN'T YOU!?

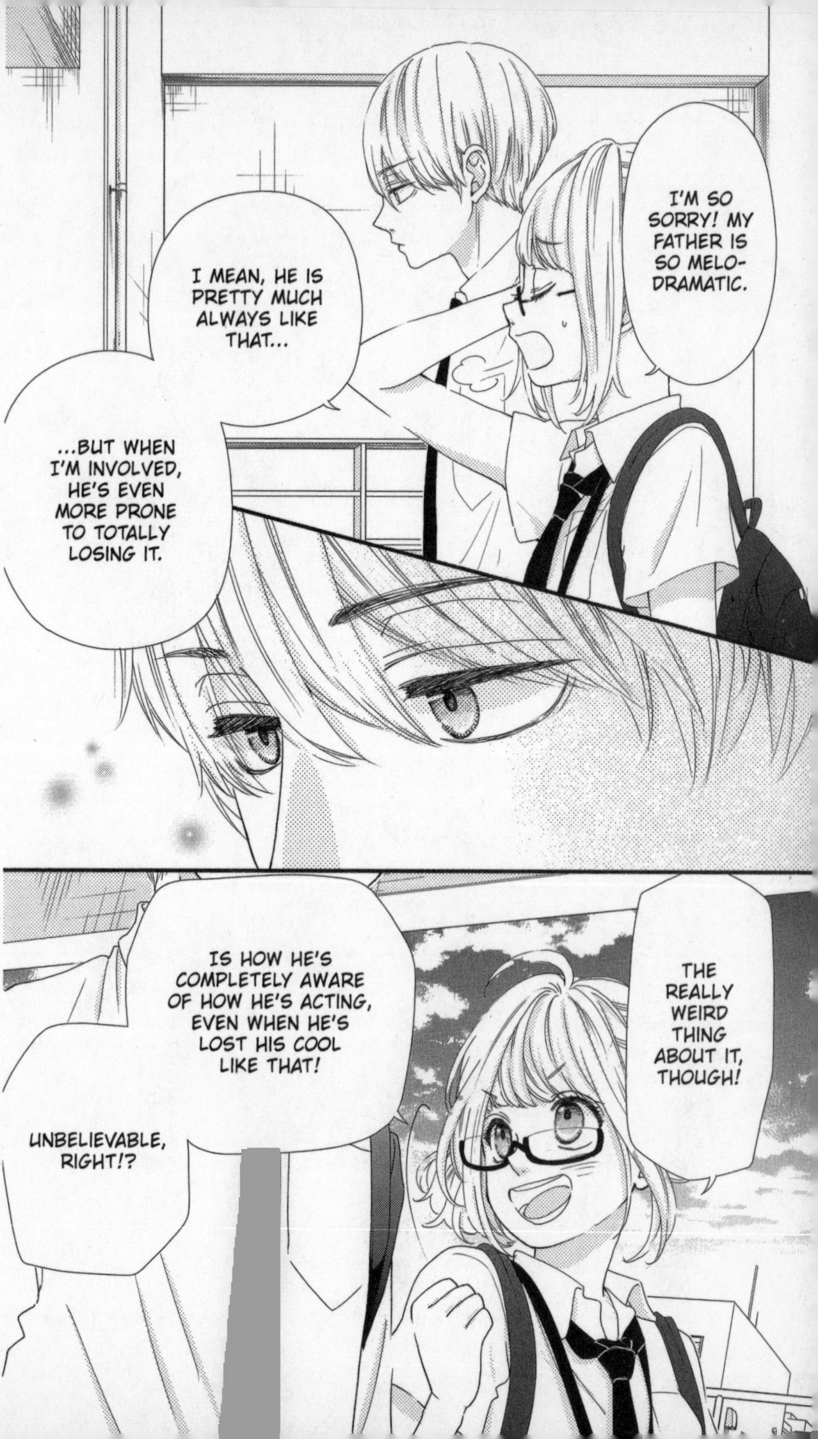
I'M SO SORRY! MY FATHER IS SO MELO-DRAMATIC.
I MEAN, HE IS PRETTY MUCH ALWAYS LIKE THAT...
...BUT WHEN I'M INVOLVED, HE'S EVEN MORE PRONE TO TOTALLY LOSING IT.
THE REALLY WEIRD THING ABOUT IT, THOUGH!
IS HOW HE'S COMPLETELY AWARE OF HOW HE'S ACTING, EVEN WHEN HE'S LOST HIS COOL LIKE THAT!
UNBELIEVABLE, RIGHT!?

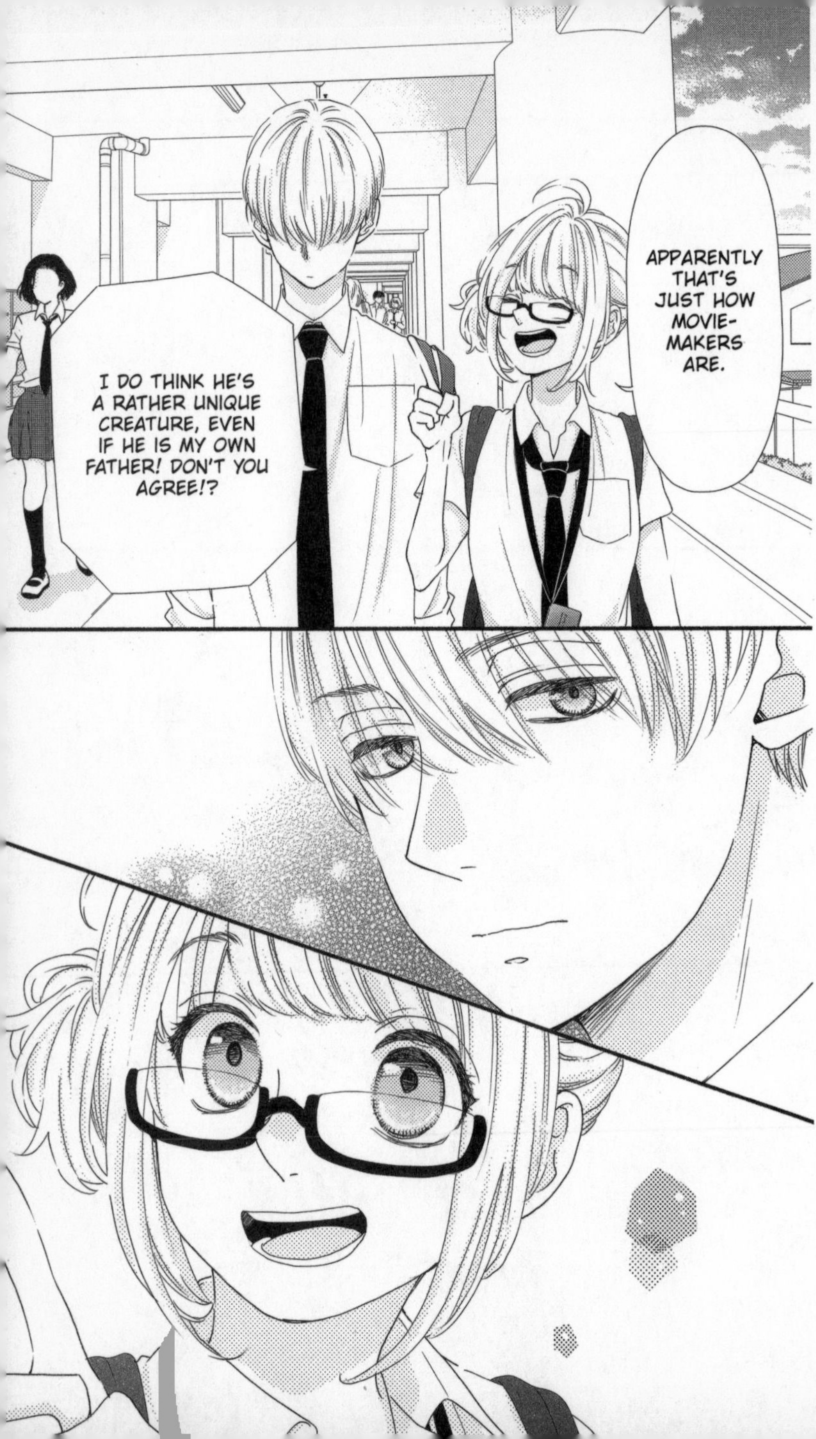
APPARENTLY THAT'S JUST HOW MOVIE-MAKERS ARE.
I DO THINK HE'S A RATHER UNIQUE CREATURE, EVEN IF HE IS MY OWN FATHER! DON'T YOU AGREE!?

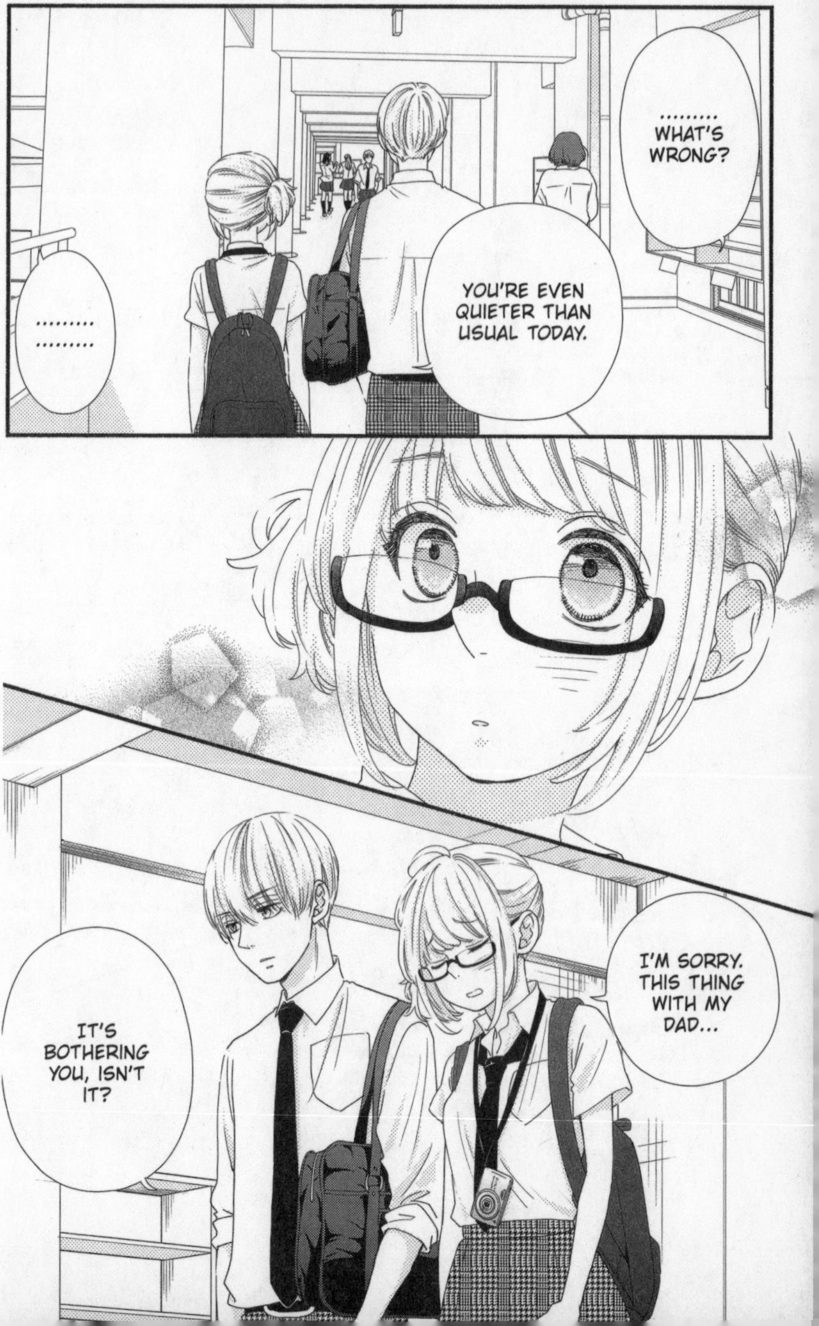
....
WHAT'S WRONG?
YOU'RE EVEN QUIETER THAN USUAL TODAY.
....
....
I'M SORRY. THIS THING WITH MY DAD...
IT'S BOTHERING YOU, ISN'T IT?

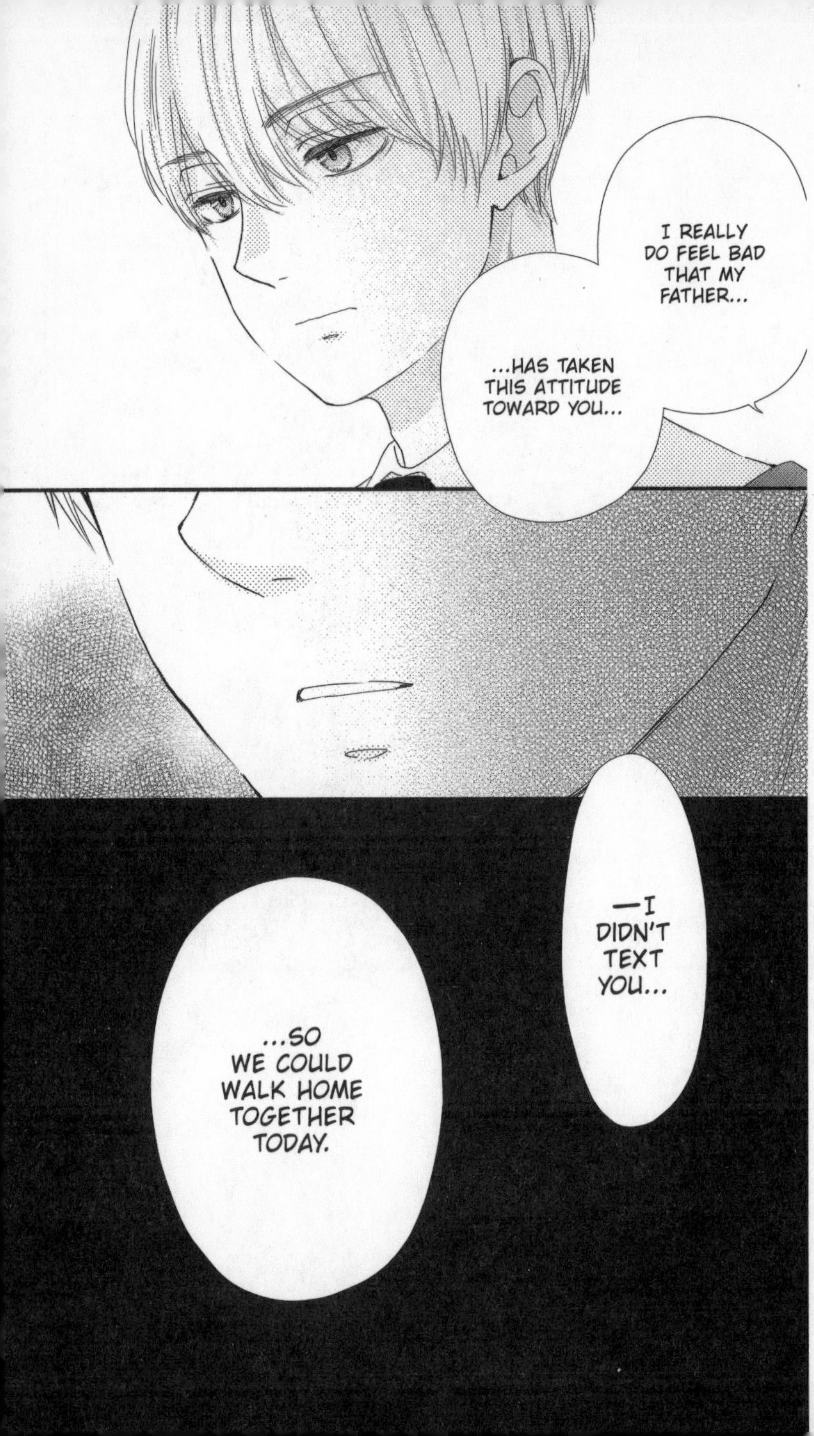
I REALLY DO FEEL BAD THAT MY FATHER...
...HAS TAKEN THIS ATTITUDE TOWARD YOU...
—I DIDN'T TEXT YOU...
...SO WE COULD WALK HOME TOGETHER TODAY.

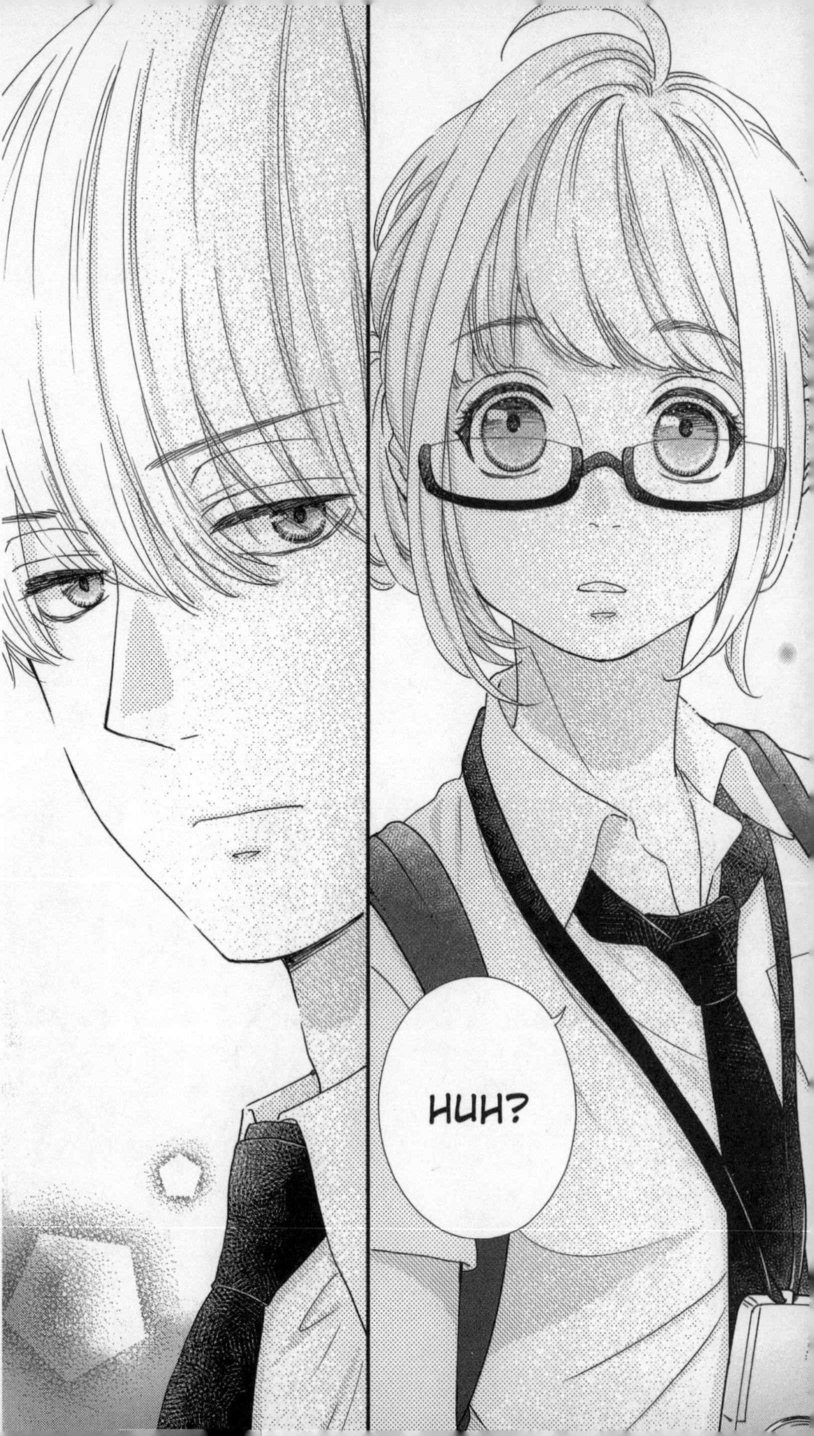
HUH?

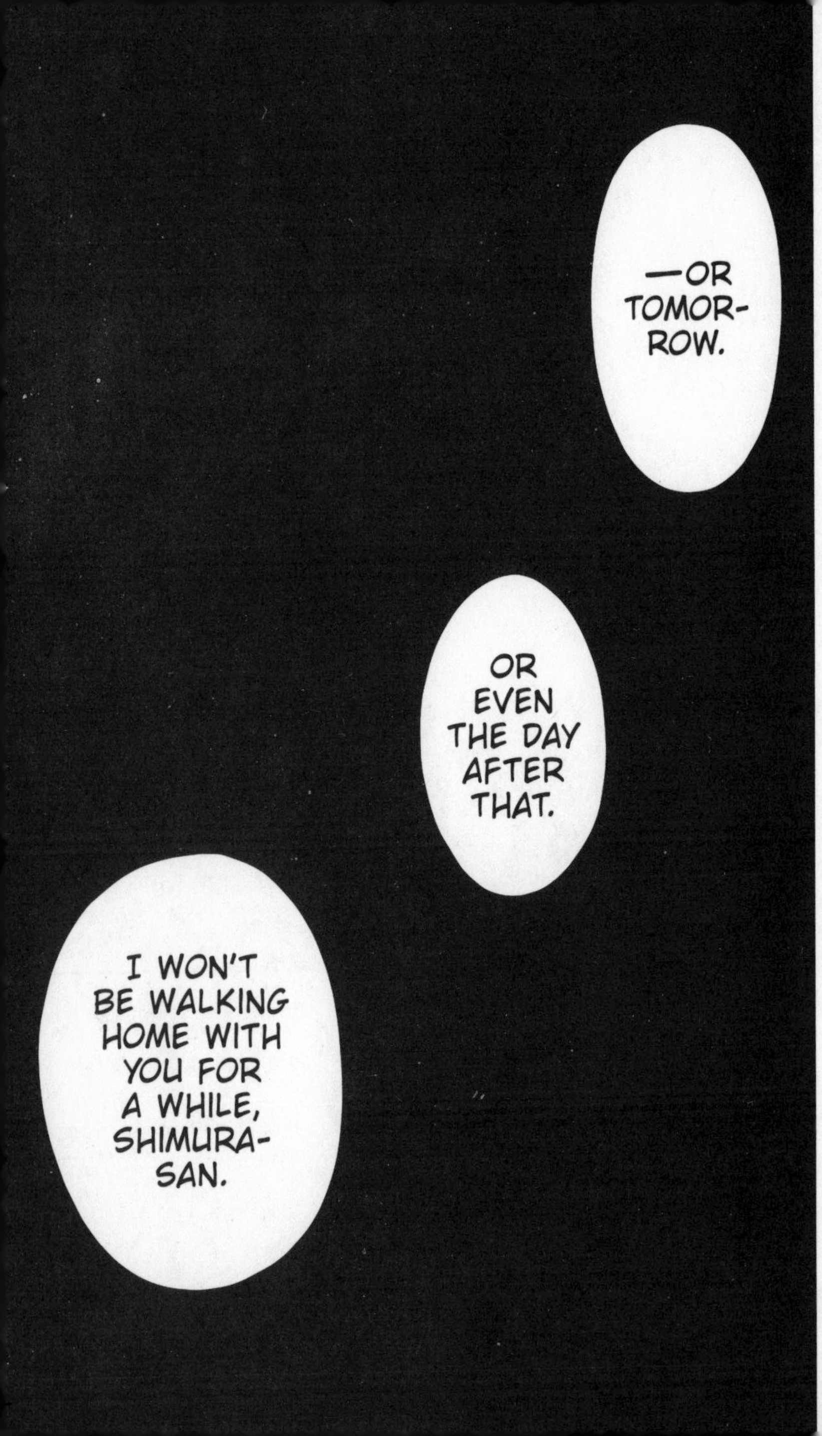
—OR TOMORROW.
OR EVEN THE DAY AFTER THAT.
I WON'T BE WALKING HOME WITH YOU FOR A WHILE, SHIMURA-SAN.

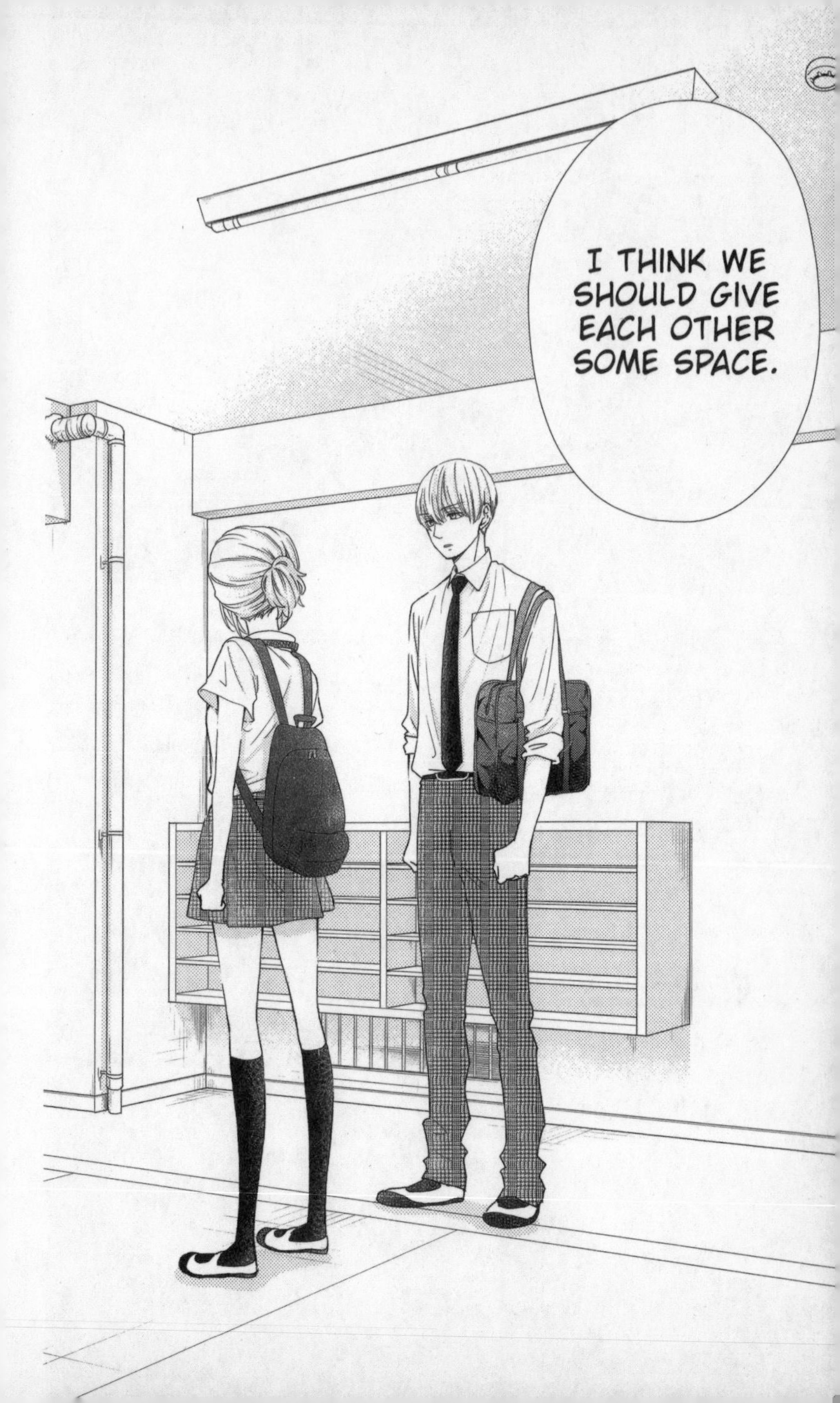
I THINK WE SHOULD GIVE EACH OTHER SOME SPACE.

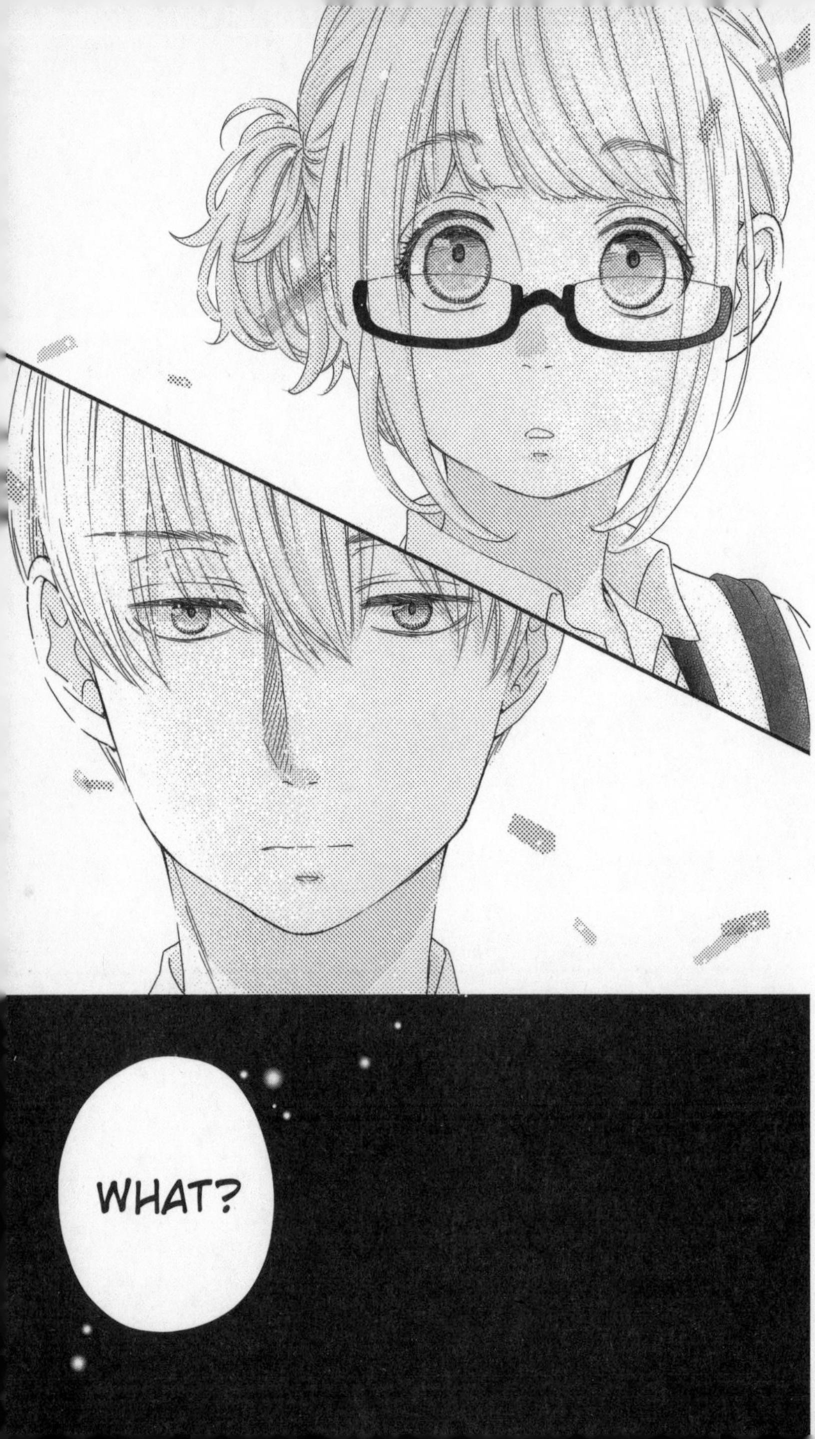
WHAT?

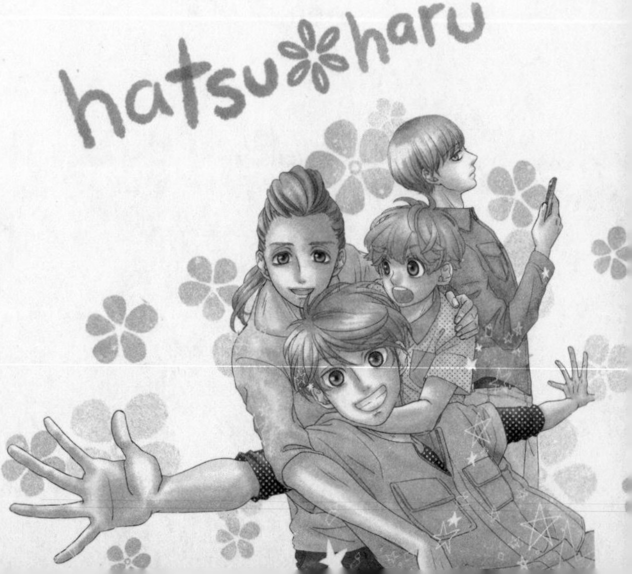
hatsu haru

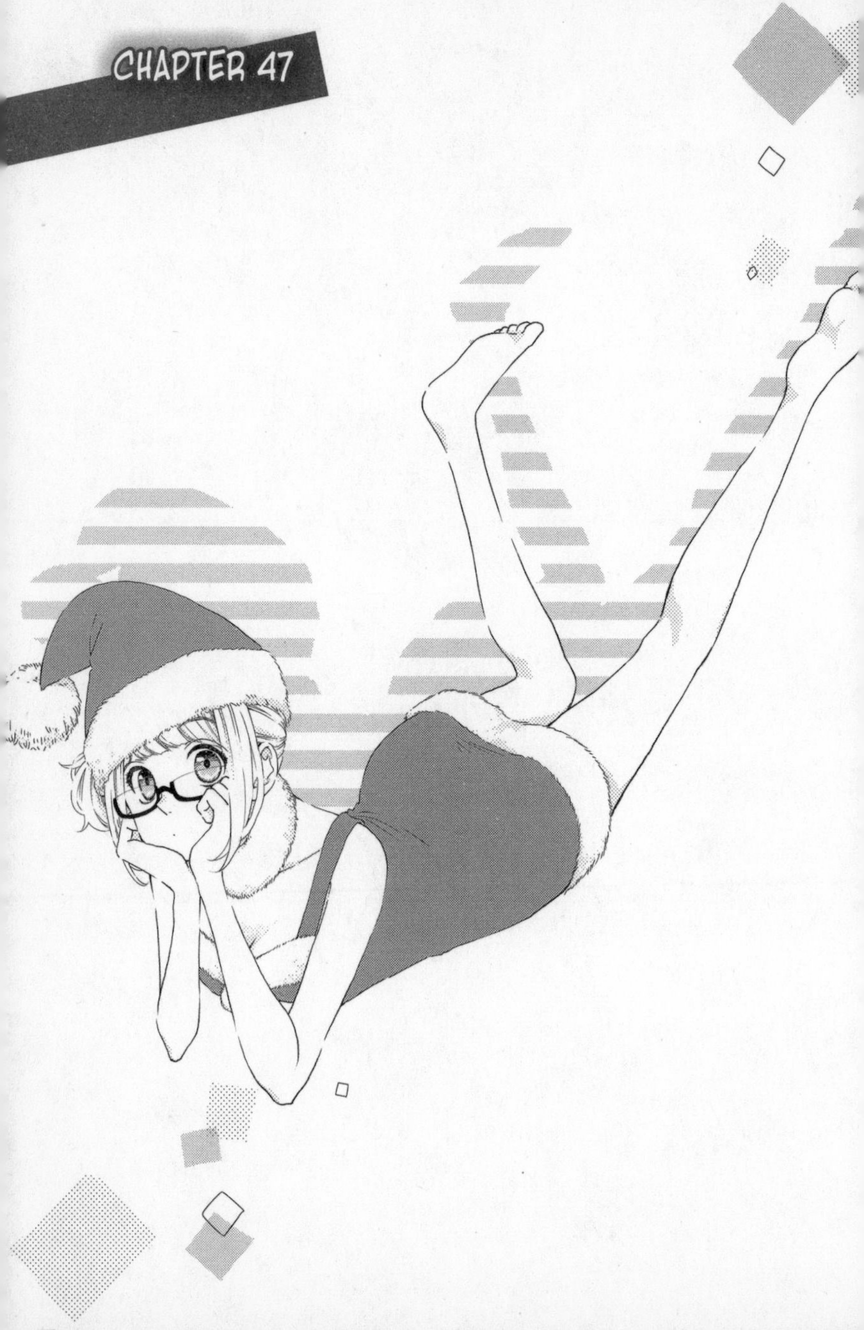
CHAPTER 47

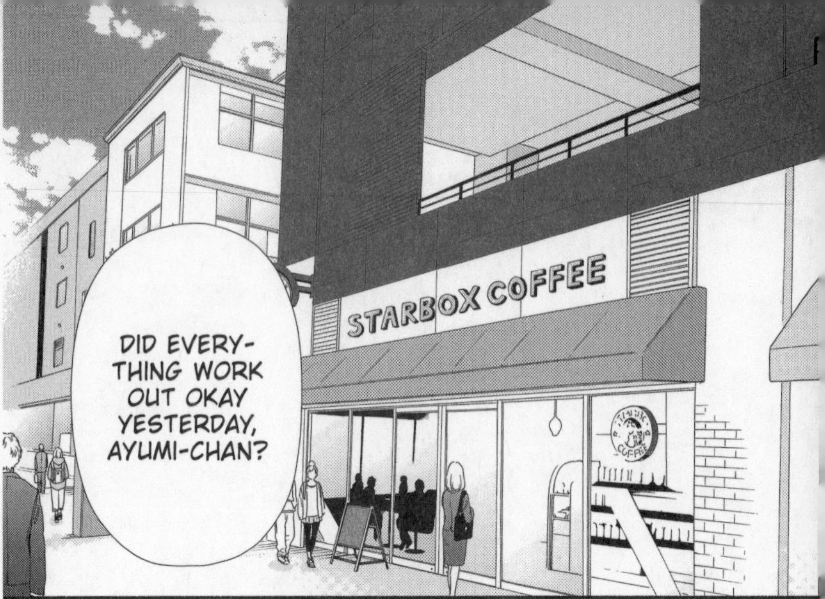
STARBOX COFFEE
DID EVERYTHING WORK OUT OKAY YESTERDAY, AYUMI-CHAN?

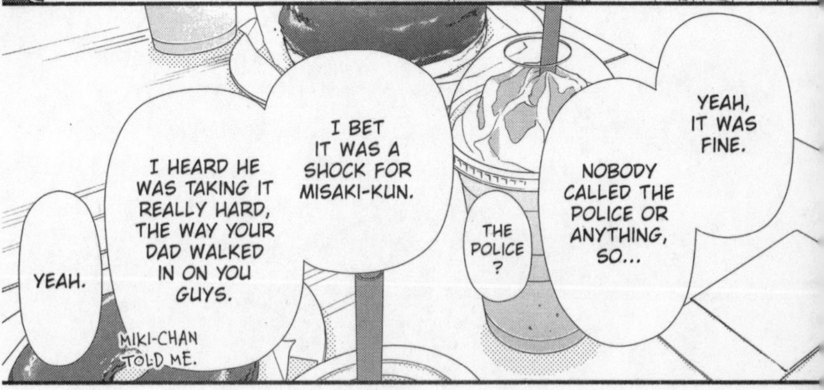
YEAH, IT WAS FINE.
NOBODY CALLED THE POLICE OR ANYTHING, SO...
THE POLICE?
I BET IT WAS A SHOCK FOR MISAKI-KUN.
I HEARD HE WAS TAKING IT REALLY HARD, THE WAY YOUR DAD WALKED IN ON YOU GUYS.
MIKI-CHAN TOLD ME.
YEAH.

hatsu haru

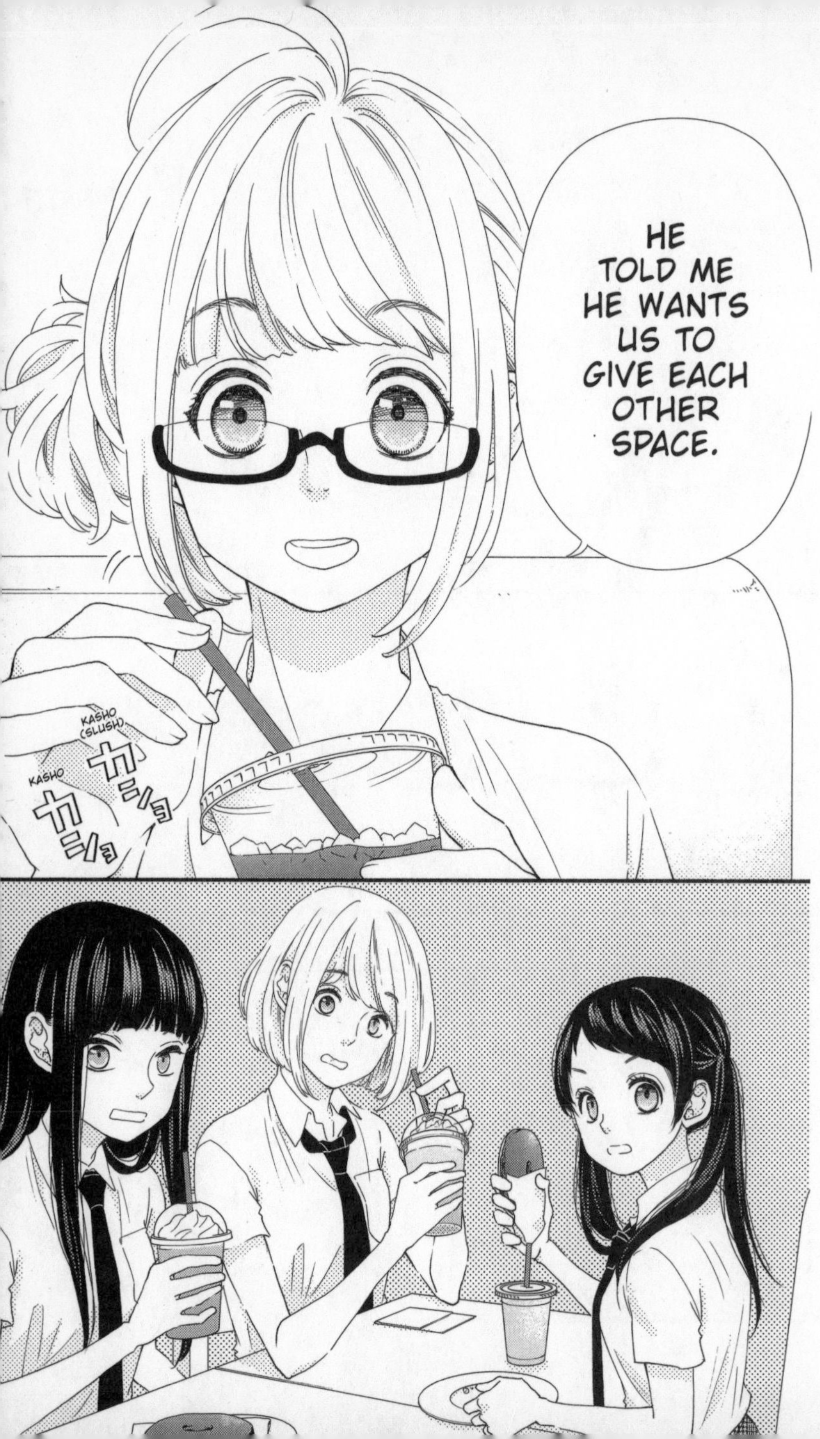
HE TOLD ME HE WANTS US TO GIVE EACH OTHER SPACE.
KASHO (SLUSH)
カショ
KASHO
カショ

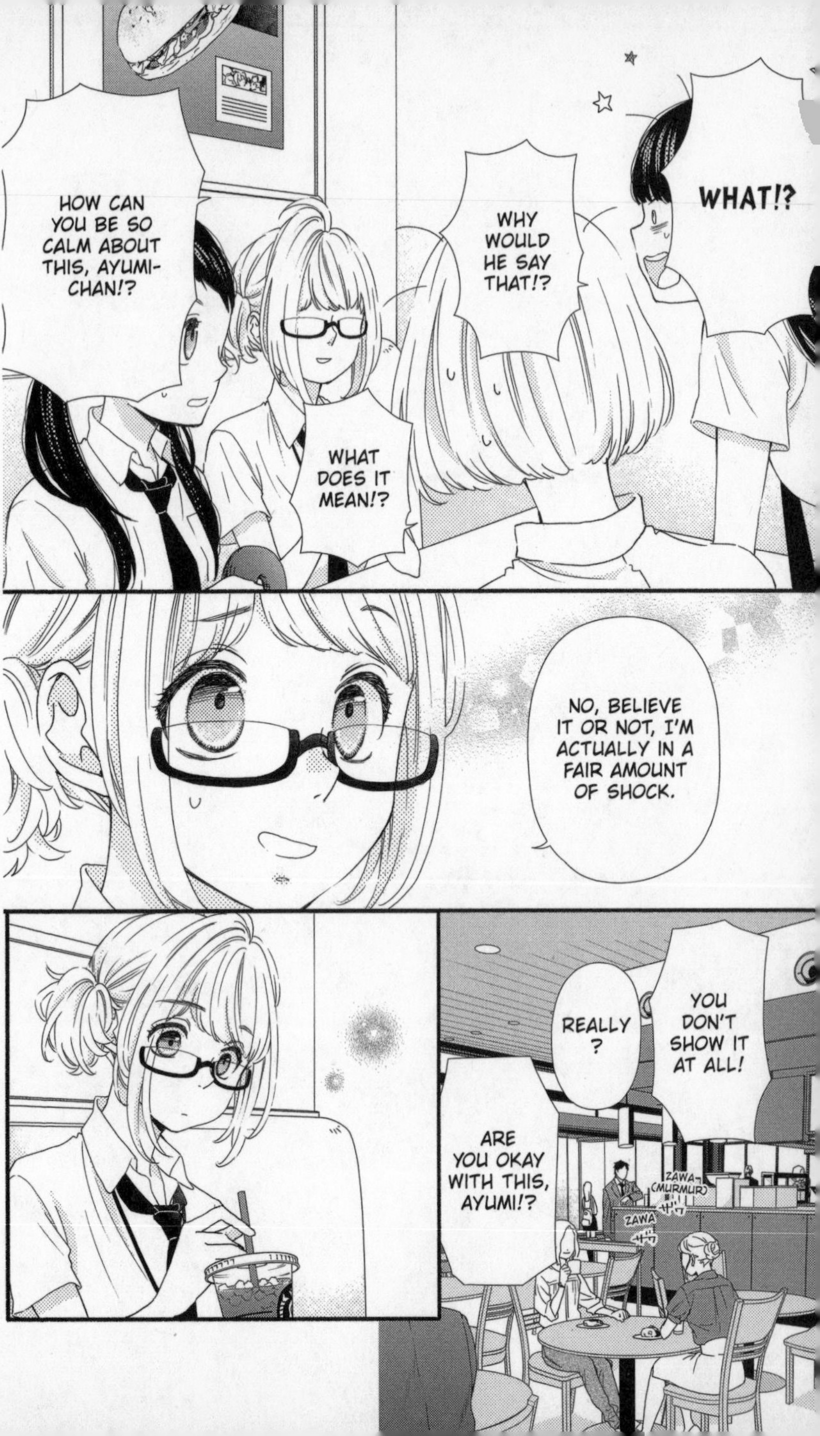
WHAT!?
WHY WOULD HE SAY THAT!?
WHAT DOES IT MEAN!?
HOW CAN YOU BE SO CALM ABOUT THIS, AYUMI-CHAN!?
NO, BELIEVE IT OR NOT, I'M ACTUALLY IN A FAIR AMOUNT OF SHOCK.
YOU DON'T SHOW IT AT ALL!
REALLY?
ARE YOU OKAY WITH THIS, AYUMI!?
ZAWA (MURMUR)
ザワ
ZAWA
ザワ

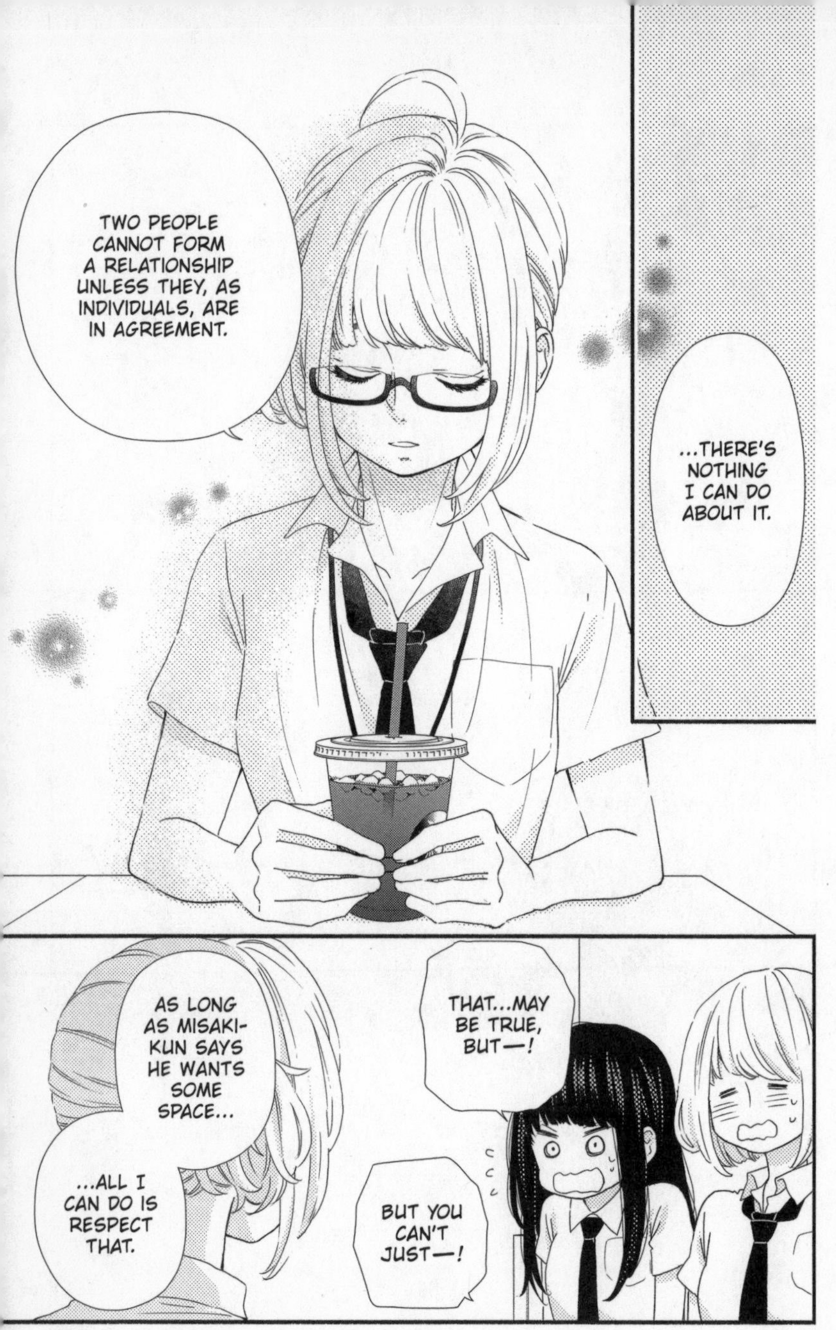
...THERE'S NOTHING I CAN DO ABOUT IT.
TWO PEOPLE CANNOT FORM A RELATIONSHIP UNLESS THEY, AS INDIVIDUALS, ARE IN AGREEMENT.
THAT...MAY BE TRUE, BUT—!
BUT YOU CAN'T JUST—!
AS LONG AS MISAKI-KUN SAYS HE WANTS SOME SPACE...
...ALL I CAN DO IS RESPECT THAT.

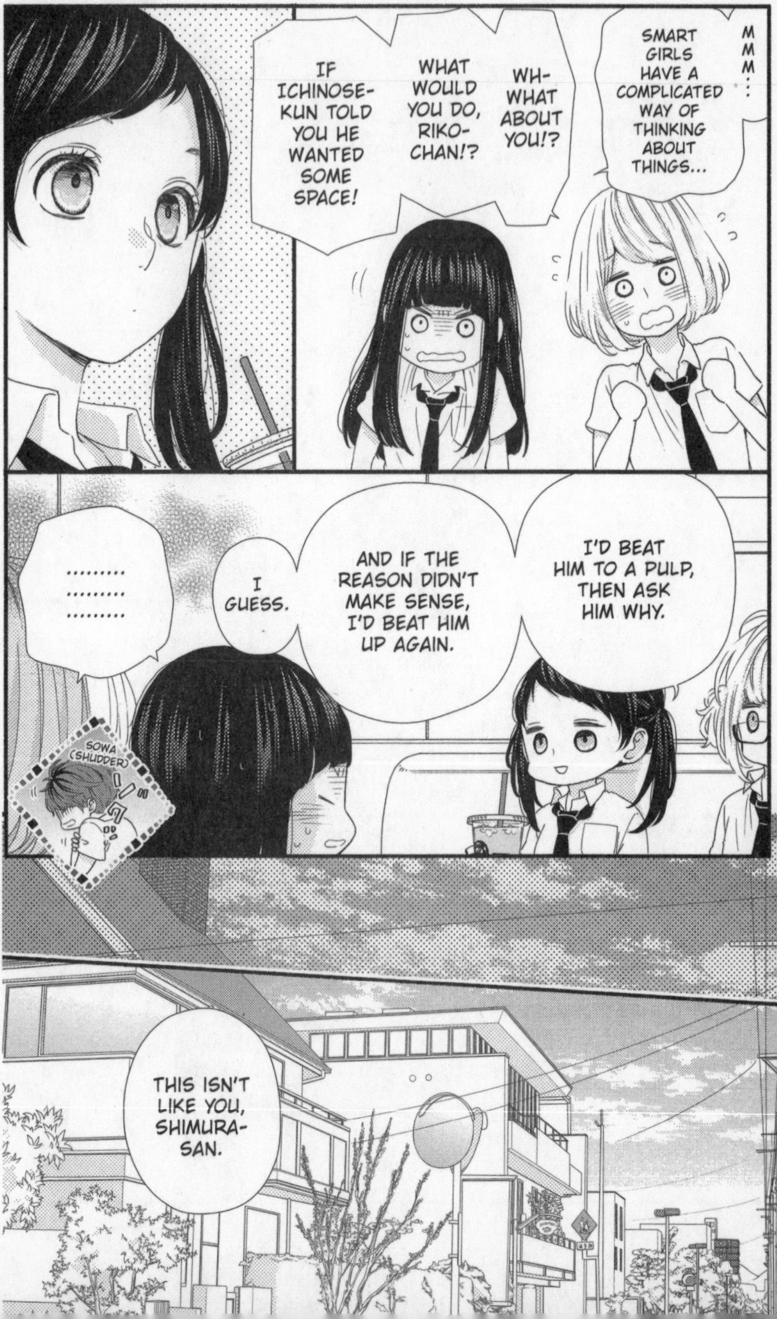
MMM...
SMART GIRLS HAVE A COMPLICATED WAY OF THINKING ABOUT THINGS...
WH- WHAT ABOUT YOU!?
WHAT WOULD YOU DO, RIKO-CHAN!?
IF ICHINOSE-KUN TOLD YOU HE WANTED SOME SPACE!
I'D BEAT HIM TO A PULP, THEN ASK HIM WHY.
AND IF THE REASON DIDN'T MAKE SENSE, I'D BEAT HIM UP AGAIN.
I GUESS.
....
....
....
SOWA (SHUDDER)
THIS ISN'T LIKE YOU, SHIMURA-SAN.

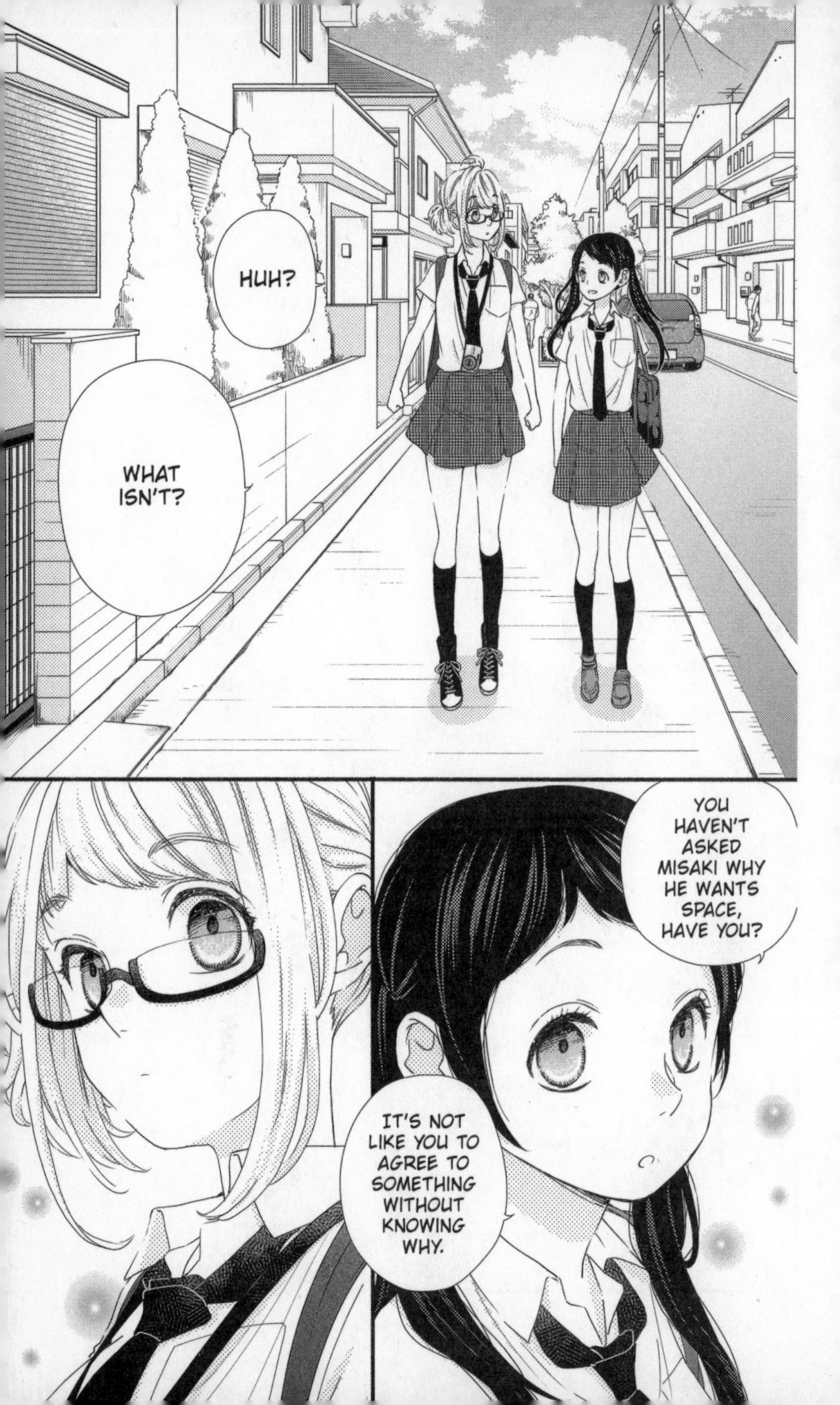
HUH?
WHAT ISN'T?
YOU HAVEN'T ASKED MISAKI WHY HE WANTS SPACE, HAVE YOU?
IT'S NOT LIKE YOU TO AGREE TO SOMETHING WITHOUT KNOWING WHY.

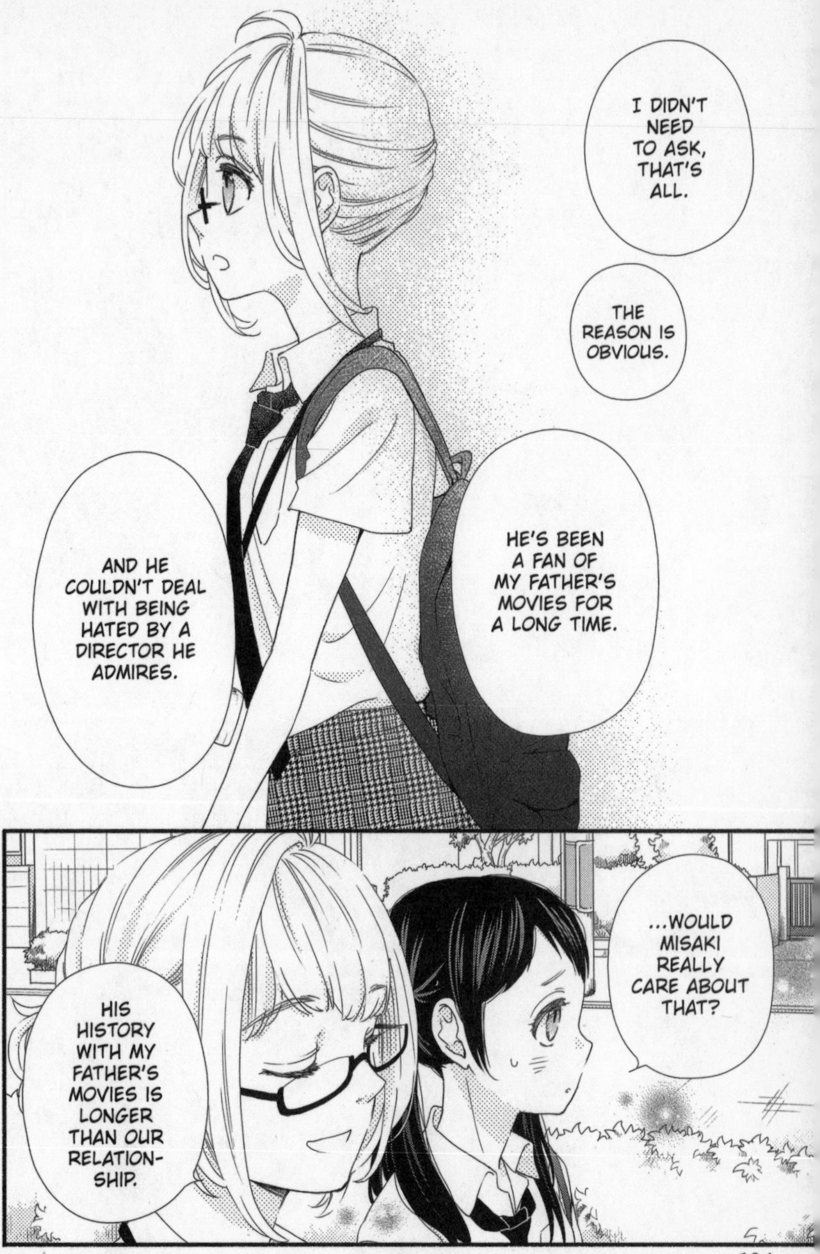
I DIDN'T NEED TO ASK, THAT'S ALL.
THE REASON IS OBVIOUS.
HE'S BEEN A FAN OF MY FATHER'S MOVIES FOR A LONG TIME.
AND HE COULDN'T DEAL WITH BEING HATED BY A DIRECTOR HE ADMIRES.
...WOULD MISAKI REALLY CARE ABOUT THAT?
HIS HISTORY WITH MY FATHER'S MOVIES IS LONGER THAN OUR RELATION-SHIP.

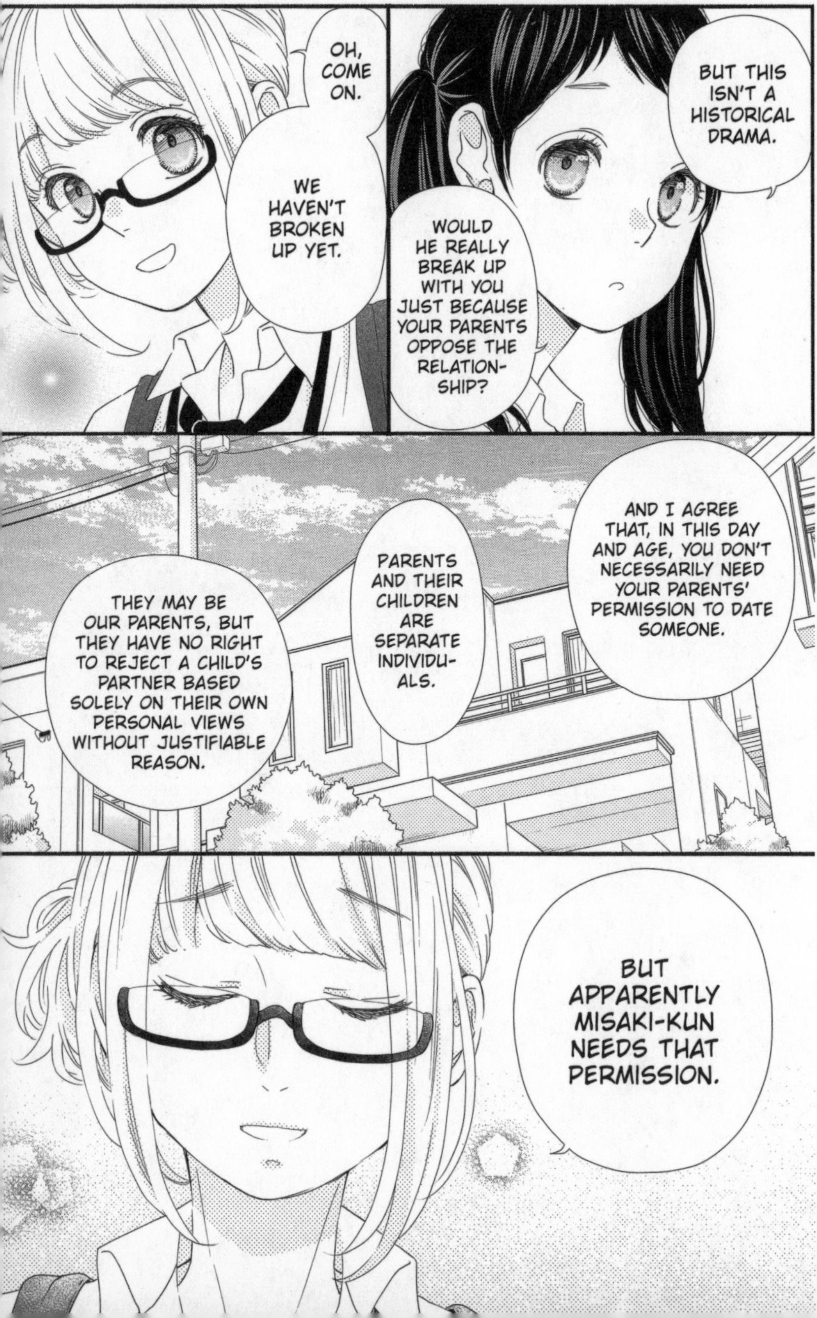
BUT THIS ISN'T A HISTORICAL DRAMA.
WOULD HE REALLY BREAK UP WITH YOU JUST BECAUSE YOUR PARENTS OPPOSE THE RELATIONSHIP?
OH, COME ON.
WE HAVEN'T BROKEN UP YET.
AND I AGREE THAT, IN THIS DAY AND AGE, YOU DON'T NECESSARILY NEED YOUR PARENTS' PERMISSION TO DATE SOMEONE.
PARENTS AND THEIR CHILDREN ARE SEPARATE INDIVIDUALS.
THEY MAY BE OUR PARENTS, BUT THEY HAVE NO RIGHT TO REJECT A CHILD'S PARTNER BASED SOLELY ON THEIR OWN PERSONAL VIEWS WITHOUT JUSTIFIABLE REASON.
BUT APPARENTLY MISAKI-KUN NEEDS THAT PERMISSION.

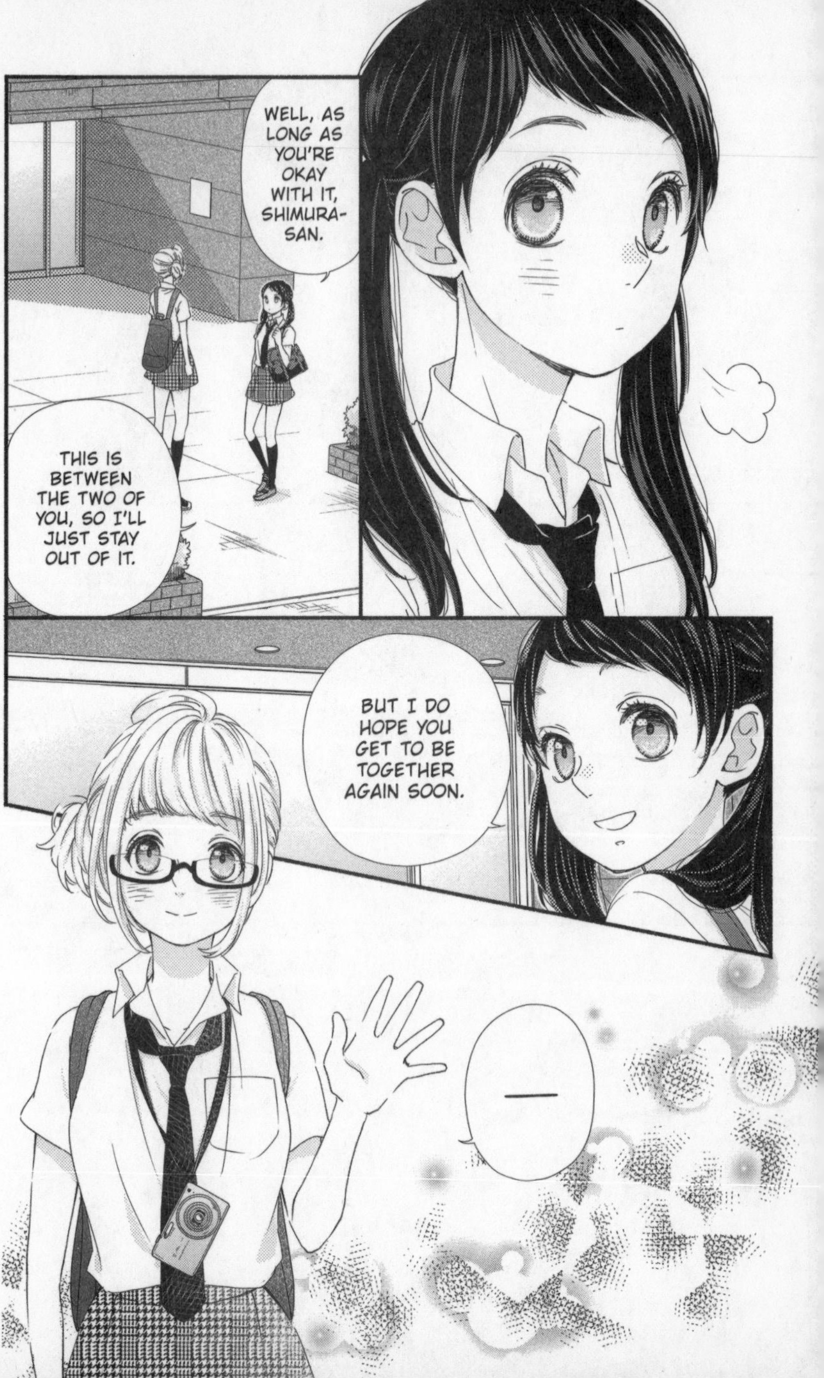
WELL, AS LONG AS YOU'RE OKAY WITH IT, SHIMURA-SAN.
THIS IS BETWEEN THE TWO OF YOU, SO I'LL JUST STAY OUT OF IT.
BUT I DO HOPE YOU GET TO BE TOGETHER AGAIN SOON.
—

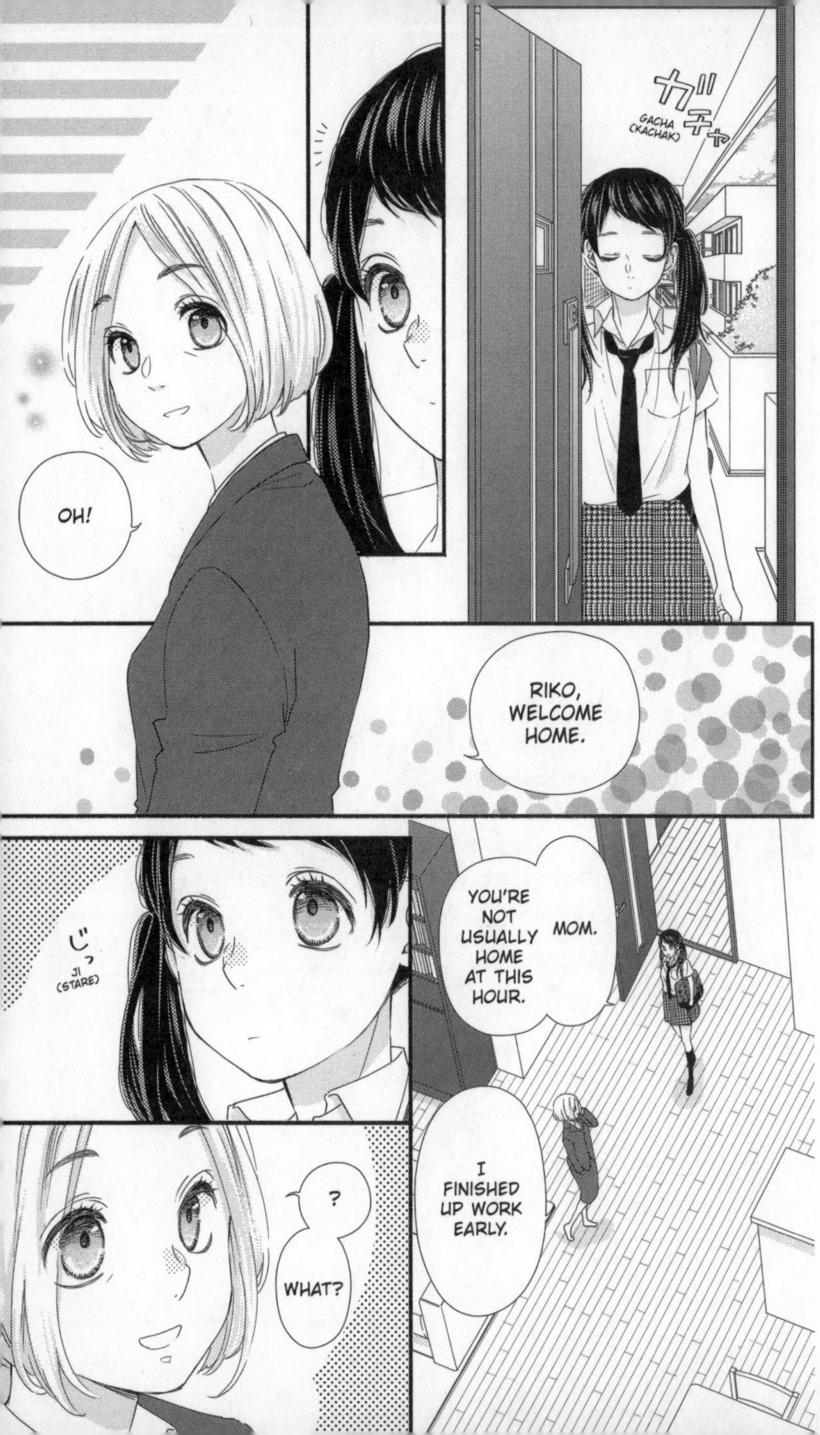
ガチャ
GACHA (KACHAK)
OH!
RIKO, WELCOME HOME.
YOU'RE NOT USUALLY HOME AT THIS HOUR.
MOM.
I FINISHED UP WORK EARLY.
じっ
JI (STARE)
?
WHAT?

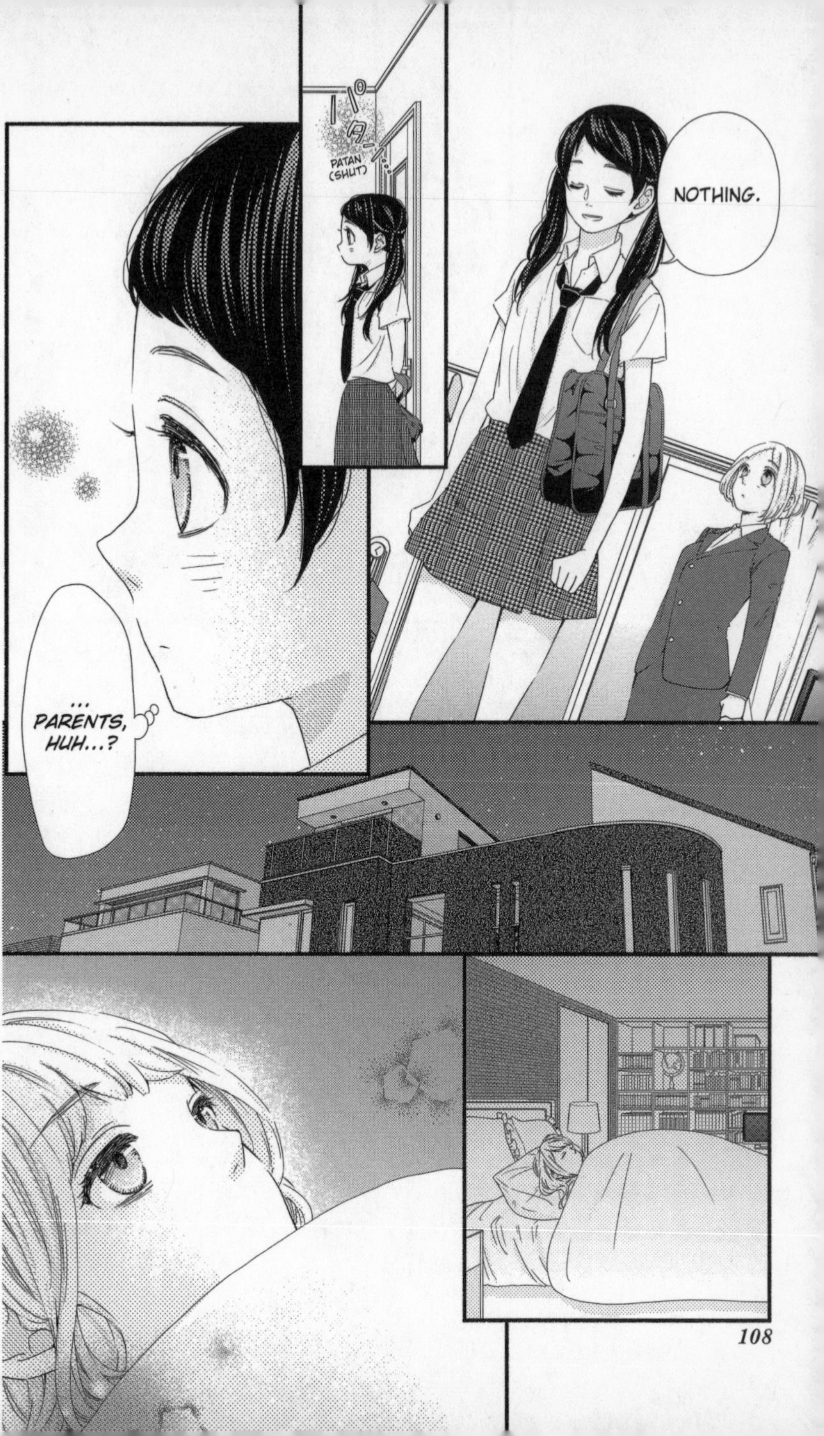
NOTHING.
PATAN (SHUT)
... PARENTS, HUH...?

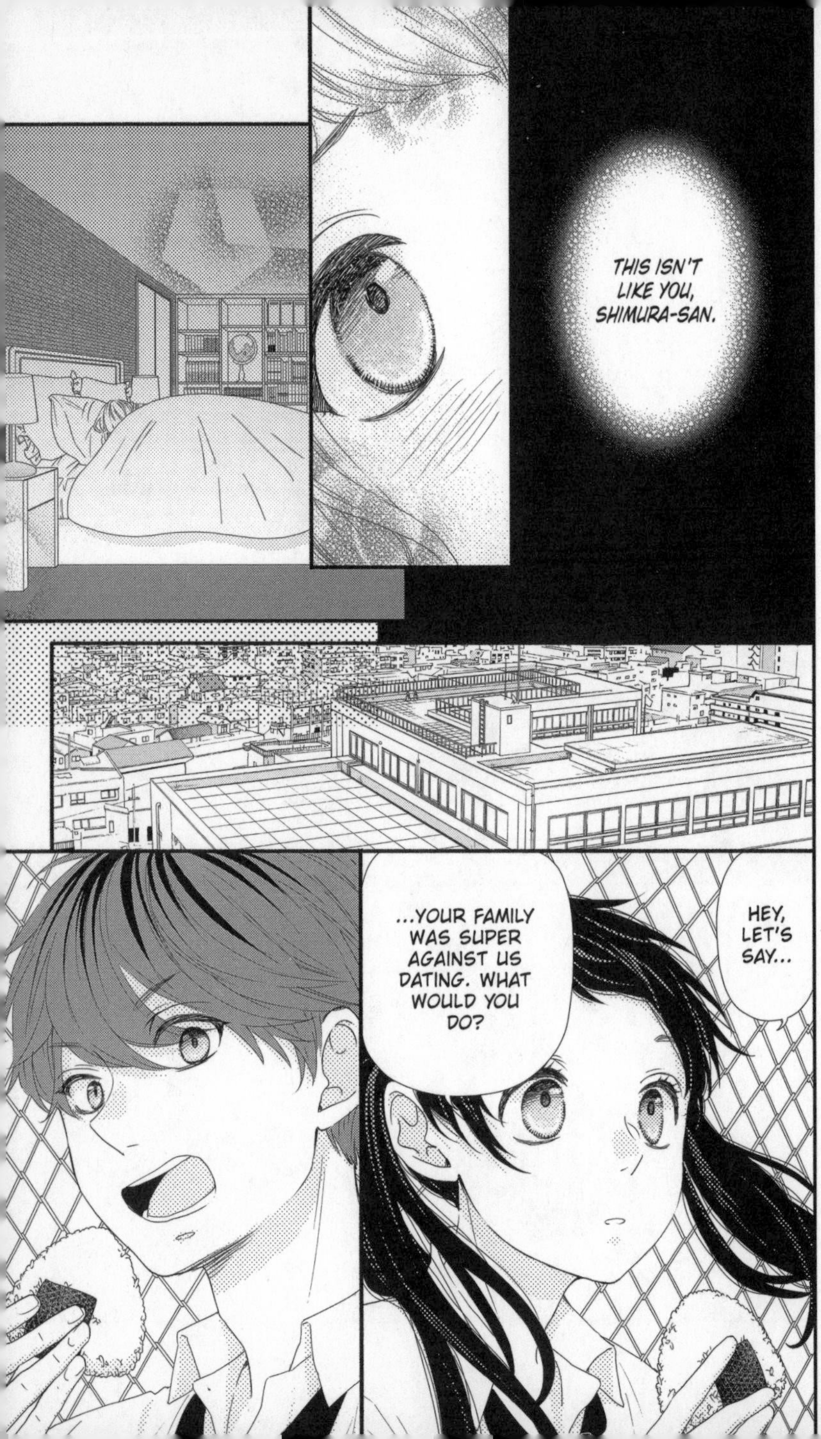
THIS ISN'T LIKE YOU, SHIMURA-SAN.
HEY, LET'S SAY...
...YOUR FAMILY WAS SUPER AGAINST US DATING. WHAT WOULD YOU DO?

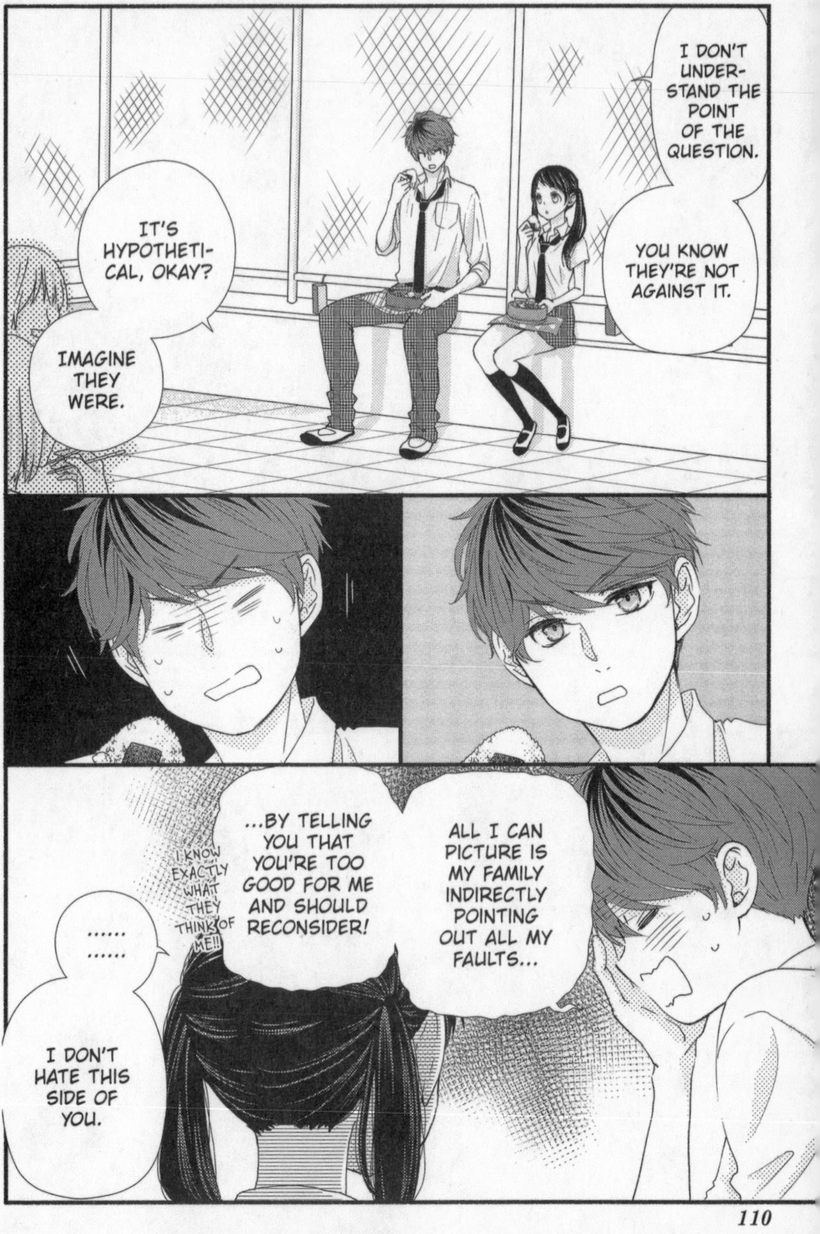
I DON'T UNDER-STAND THE POINT OF THE QUESTION.
YOU KNOW THEY'RE NOT AGAINST IT.
IT'S HYPOTHETI-CAL, OKAY?
IMAGINE THEY WERE.
ALL I CAN PICTURE IS MY FAMILY INDIRECTLY POINTING OUT ALL MY FAULTS...
...BY TELLING YOU THAT YOU'RE TOO GOOD FOR ME AND SHOULD RECONSIDER!
I KNOW EXACTLY WHAT THEY THINK OF ME!!
....
I DON'T HATE THIS SIDE OF YOU.

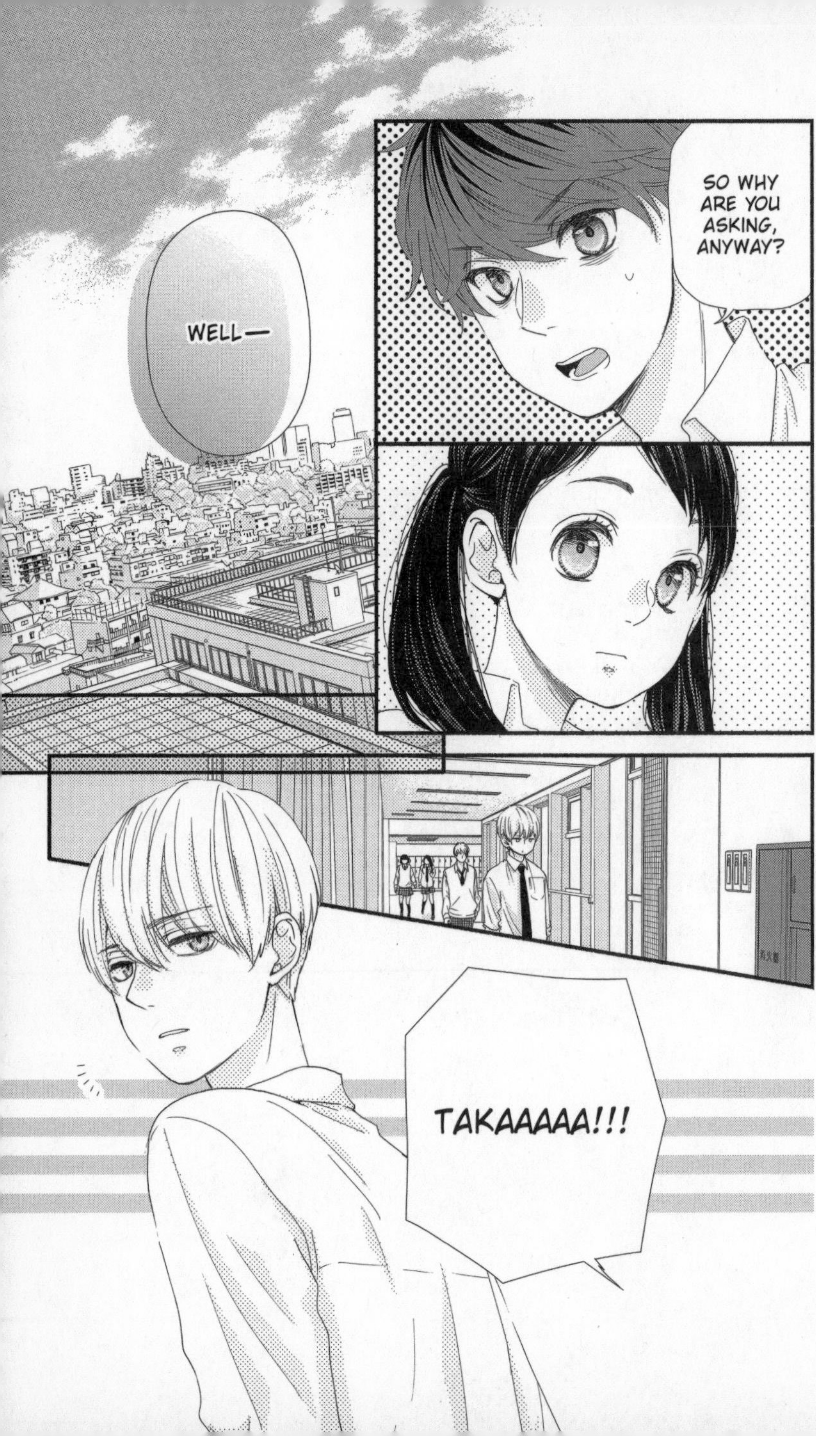
SO WHY ARE YOU ASKING, ANYWAY?
WELL—
TAKAAAAA!!!

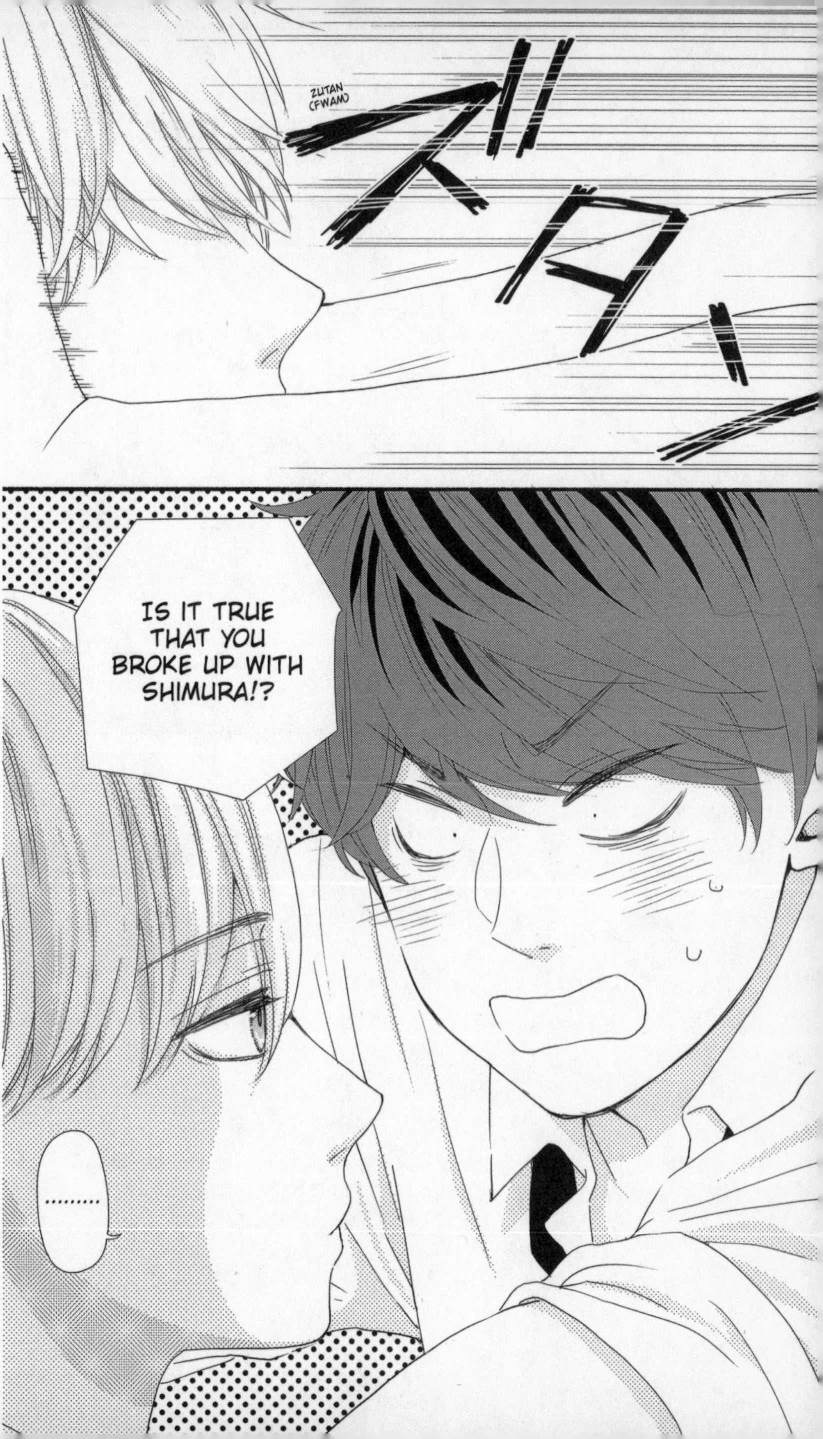
ZUTAN (FWAM)
IS IT TRUE THAT YOU BROKE UP WITH SHIMURA!?
....

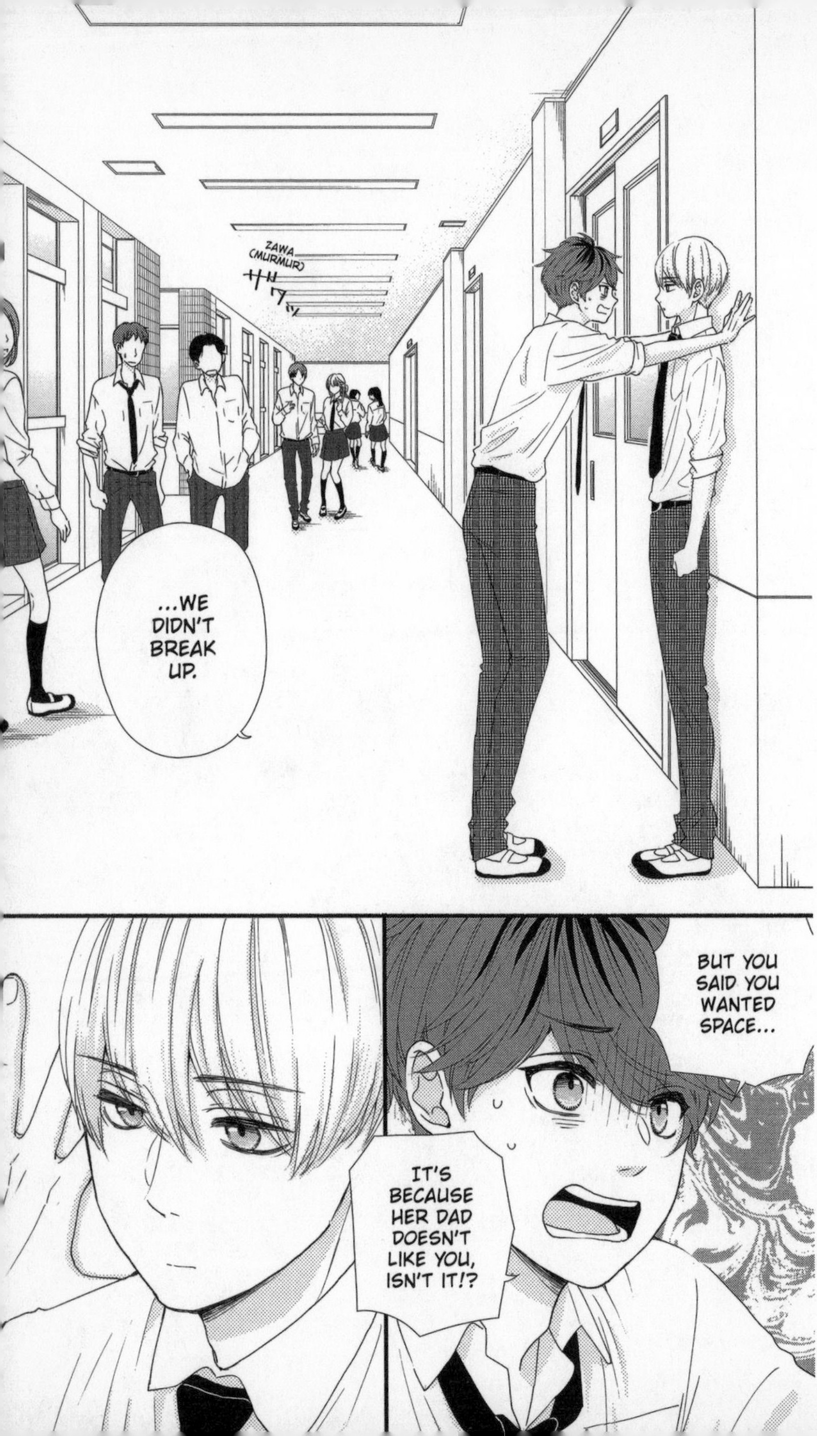
ZAWA (MURMUR)
...WE DIDN'T BREAK UP.
BUT YOU SAID YOU WANTED SPACE...
IT'S BECAUSE HER DAD DOESN'T LIKE YOU, ISN'T IT!?

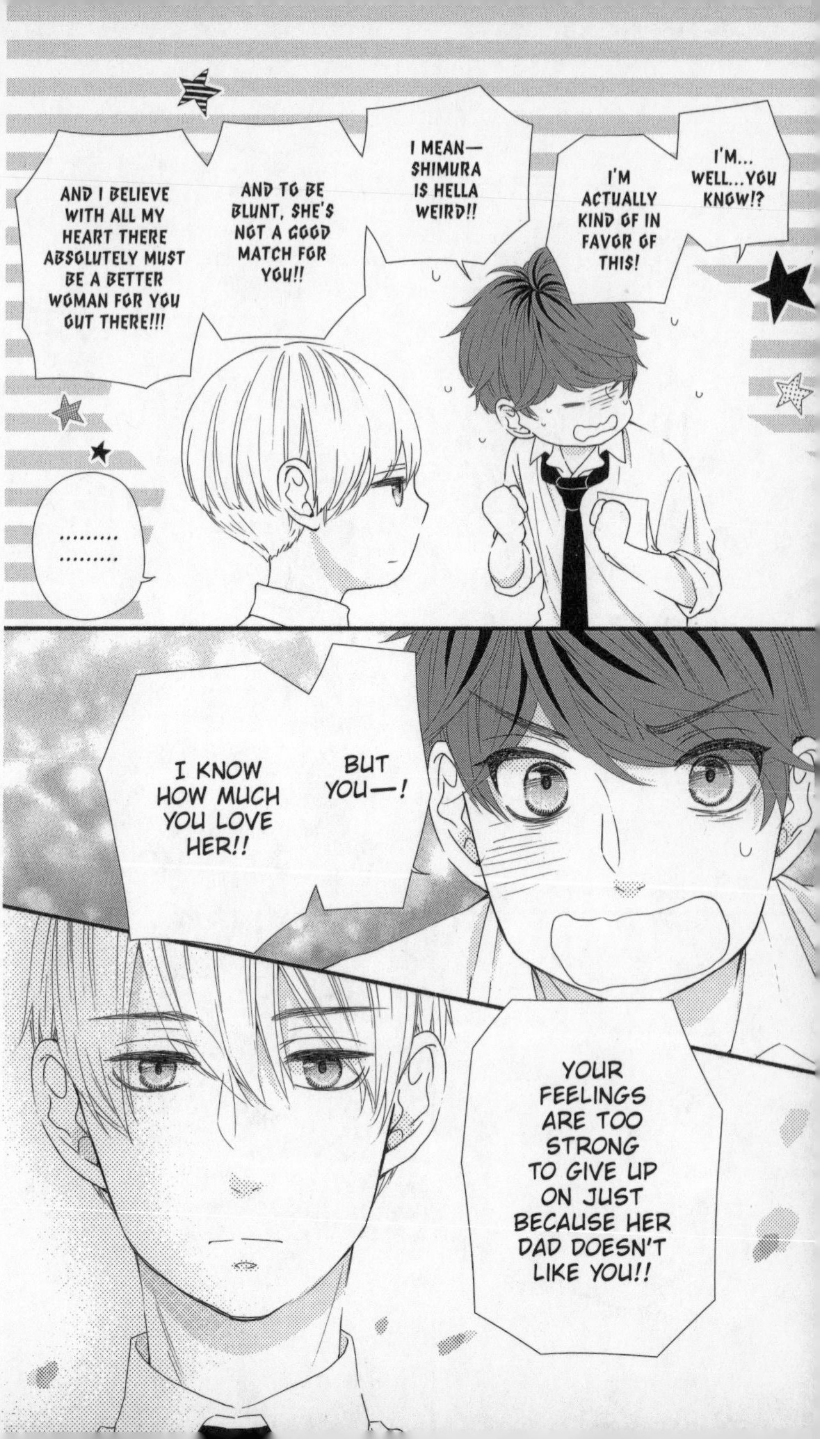
I'M... WELL...YOU KNOW!?
I'M ACTUALLY KIND OF IN FAVOR OF THIS!
I MEAN— SHIMURA IS HELLA WEIRD!!
AND TO BE BLUNT, SHE'S NOT A GOOD MATCH FOR YOU!!
AND I BELIEVE WITH ALL MY HEART THERE ABSOLUTELY MUST BE A BETTER WOMAN FOR YOU OUT THERE!!!
....
....
BUT YOU—!
I KNOW HOW MUCH YOU LOVE HER!!
YOUR FEELINGS ARE TOO STRONG TO GIVE UP ON JUST BECAUSE HER DAD DOESN'T LIKE YOU!!

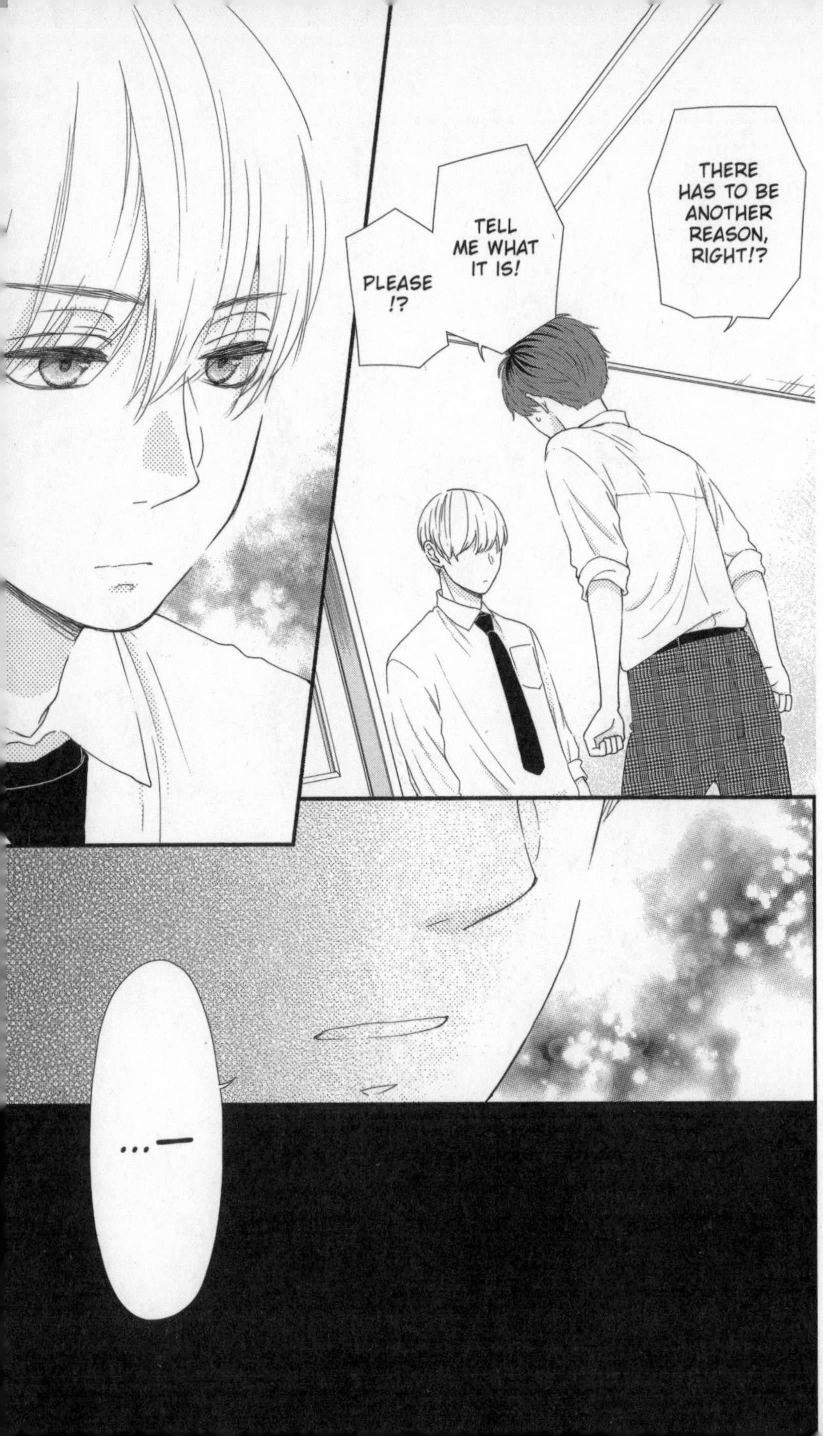
THERE HAS TO BE ANOTHER REASON, RIGHT!?
TELL ME WHAT IT IS!
PLEASE !?
...—

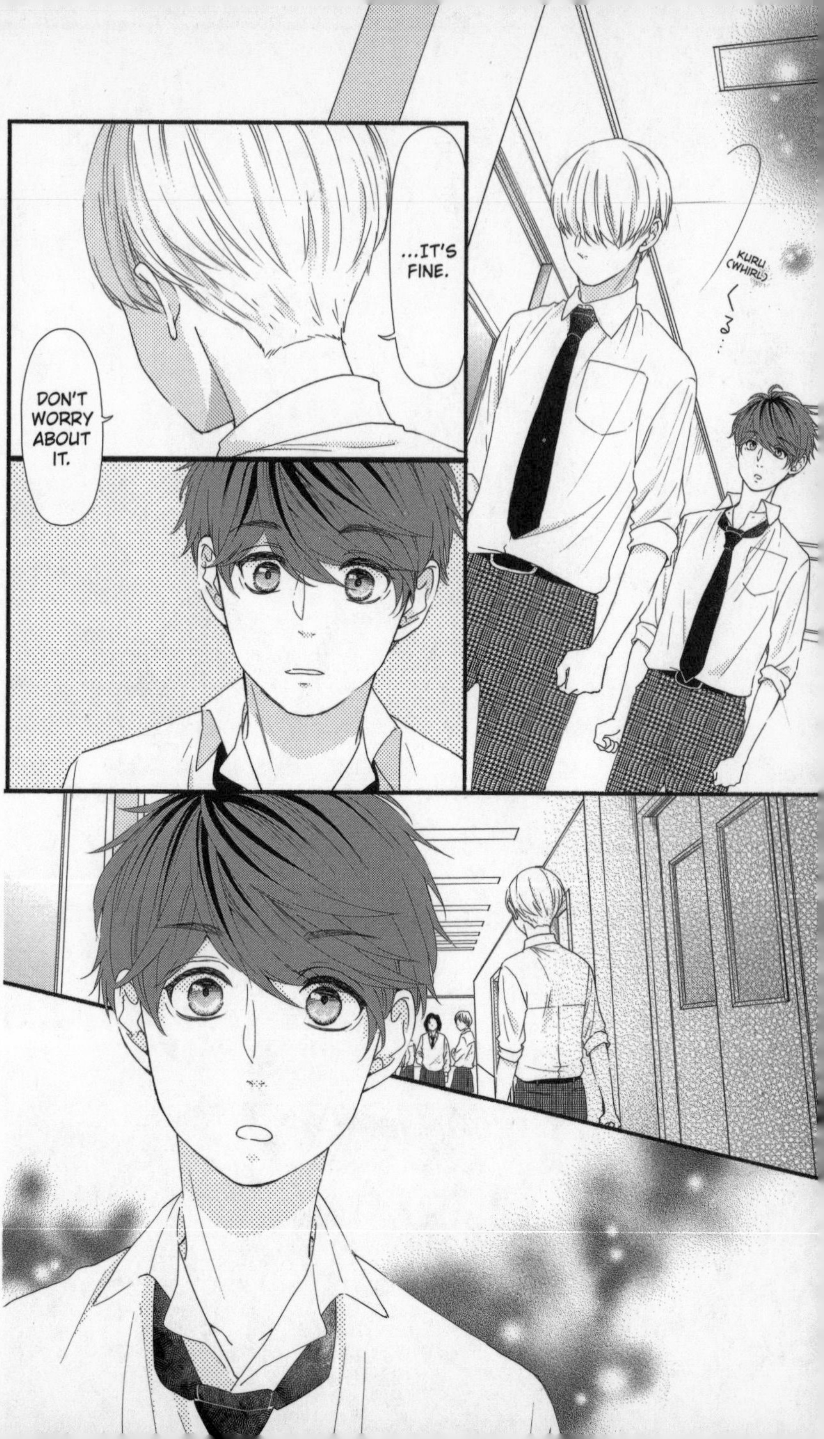
KURU (WHIRL)
...IT'S FINE.
DON'T WORRY ABOUT IT.

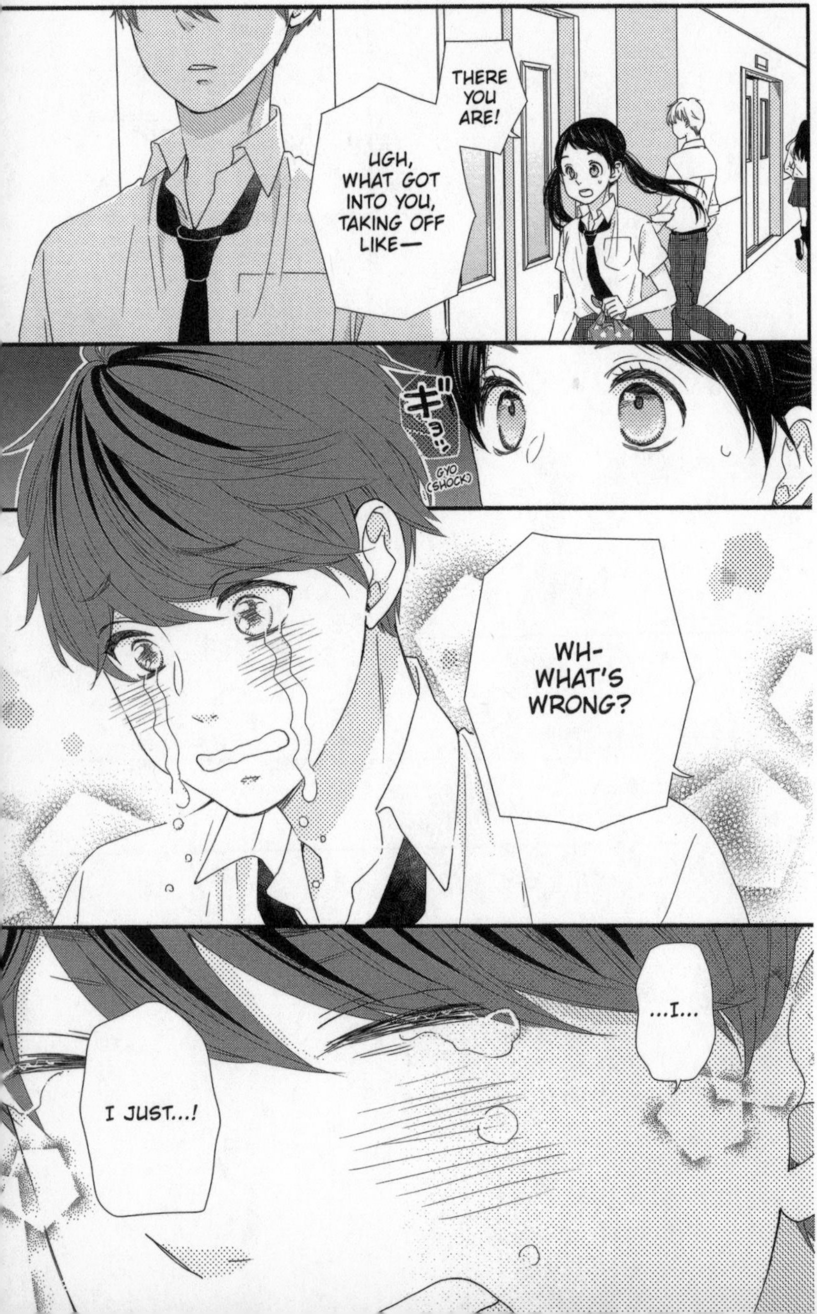
THERE YOU ARE!
UGH, WHAT GOT INTO YOU, TAKING OFF LIKE—
ギョ
GYO (SHOCK)
WH-WHAT'S WRONG?
...I...
I JUST...!

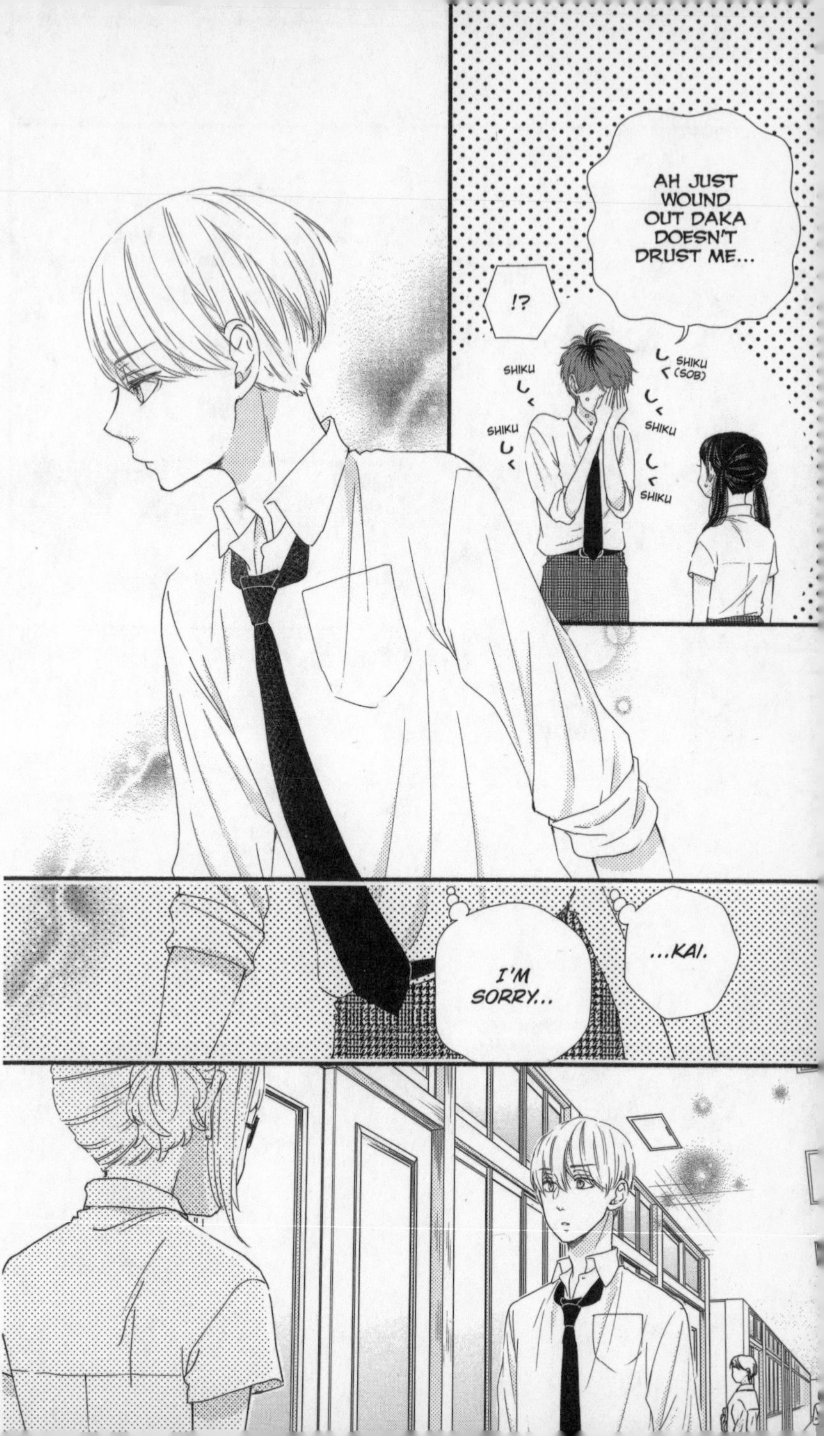
AH JUST WOUND OUT DAKA DOESN'T DRUST ME...
!?
SHIKU (SOB)
SHIKU
SHIKU
SHIKU
SHIKU
...KAI.
I'M SORRY...

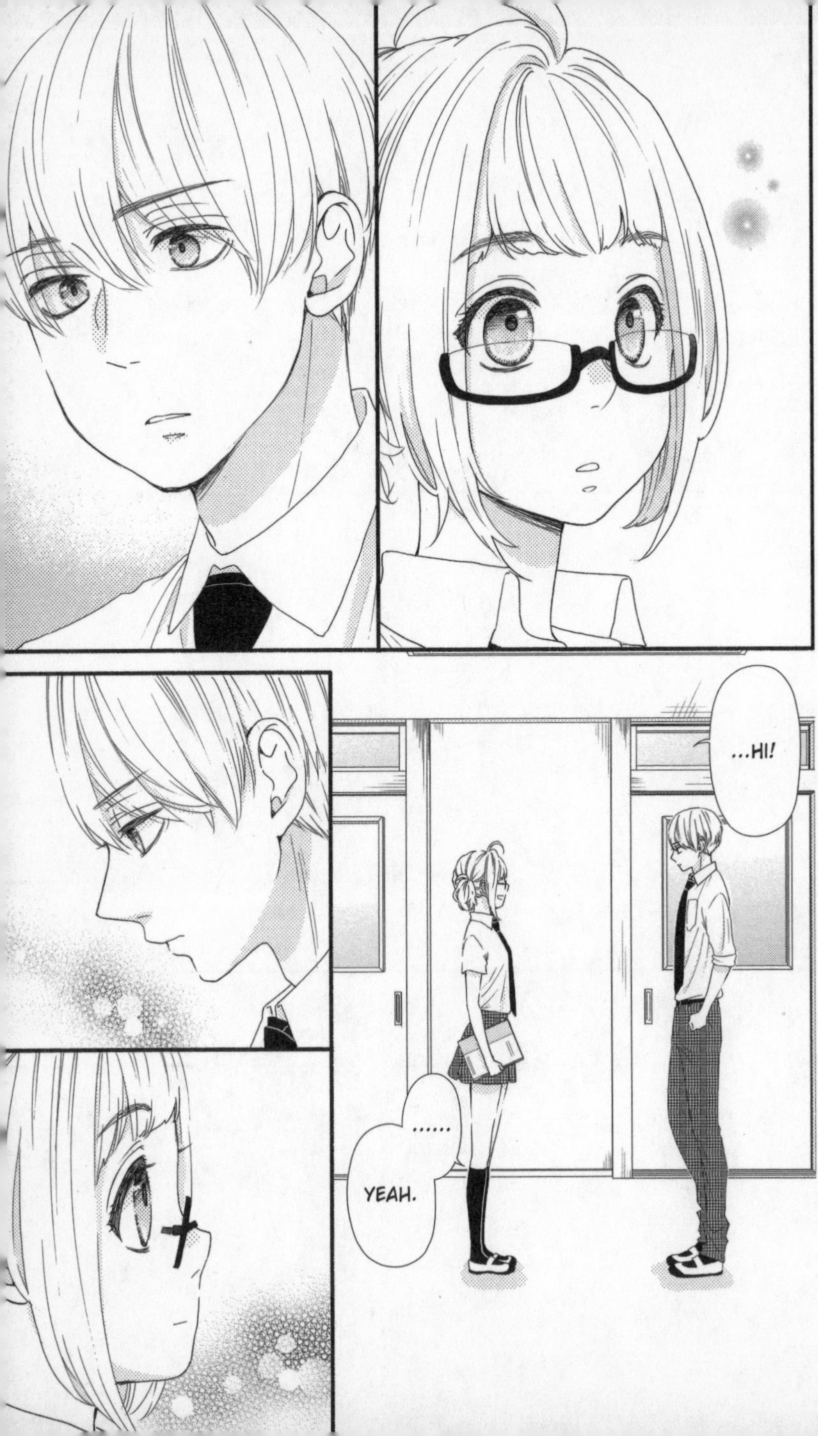
...HI!
......
YEAH.

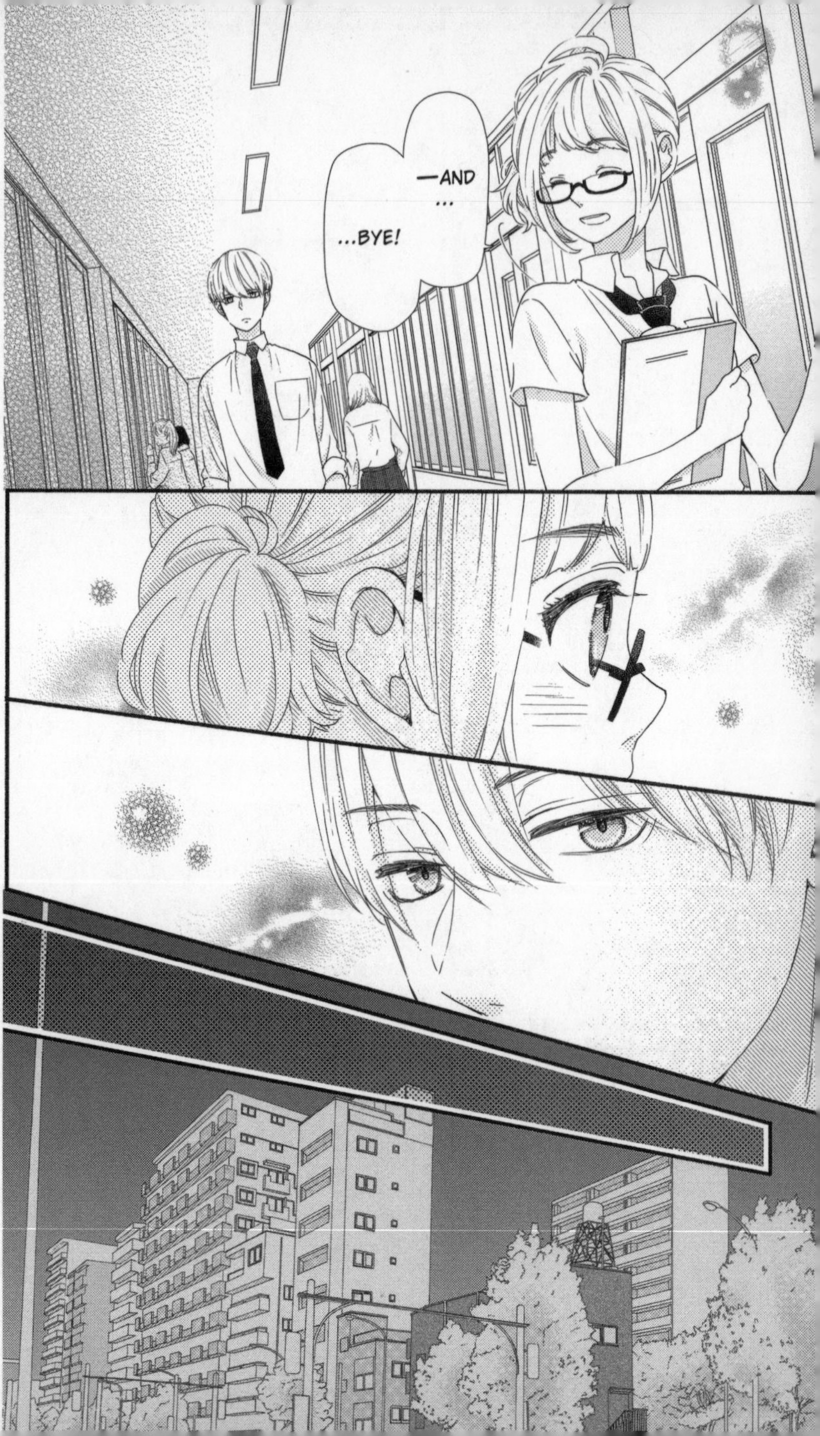
—AND
...
...BYE!

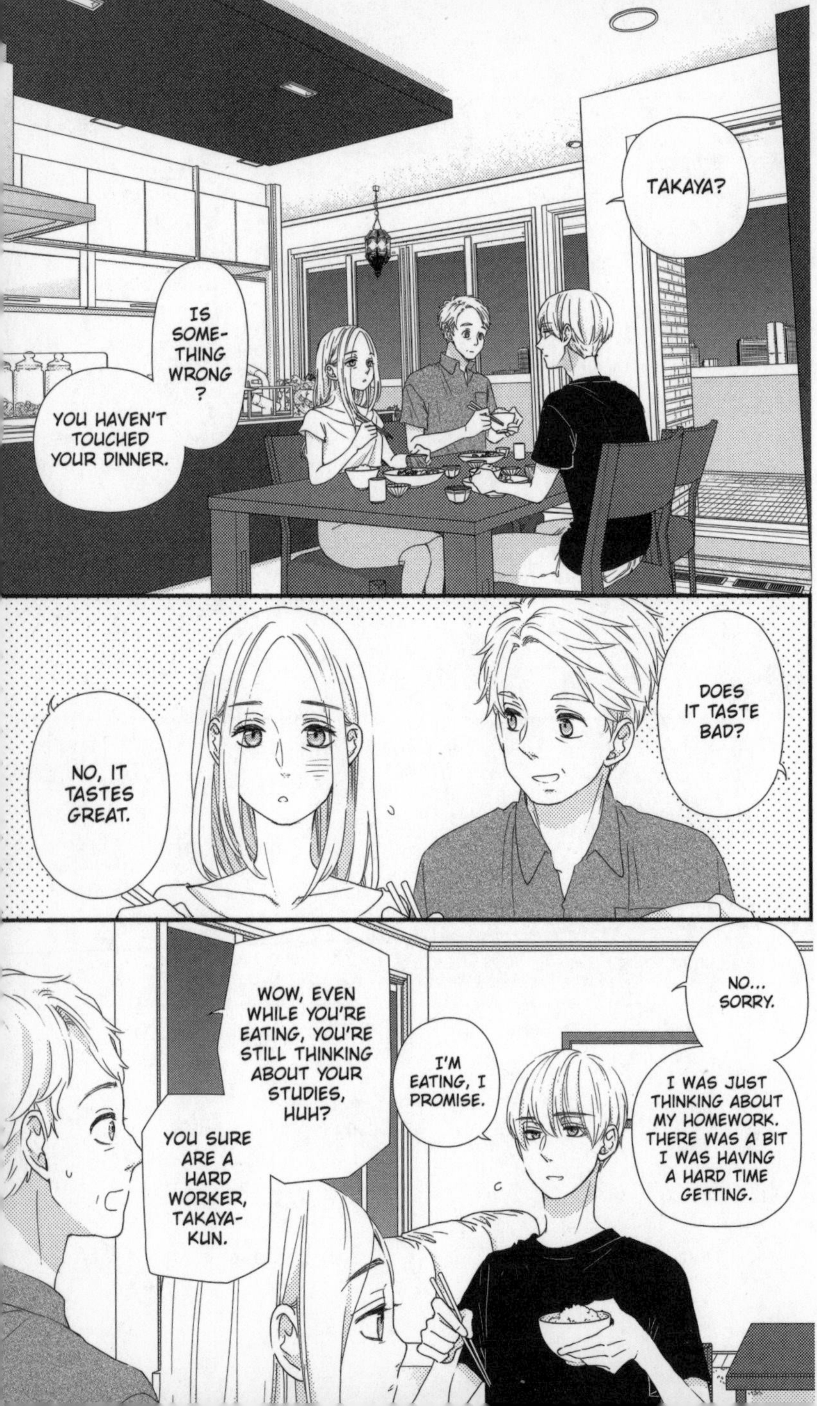
TAKAYA?
IS SOME-THING WRONG?
YOU HAVEN'T TOUCHED YOUR DINNER.
DOES IT TASTE BAD?
NO, IT TASTES GREAT.
NO... SORRY.
I WAS JUST THINKING ABOUT MY HOMEWORK. THERE WAS A BIT I WAS HAVING A HARD TIME GETTING.
I'M EATING, I PROMISE.
WOW, EVEN WHILE YOU'RE EATING, YOU'RE STILL THINKING ABOUT YOUR STUDIES, HUH?
YOU SURE ARE A HARD WORKER, TAKAYA-KUN.

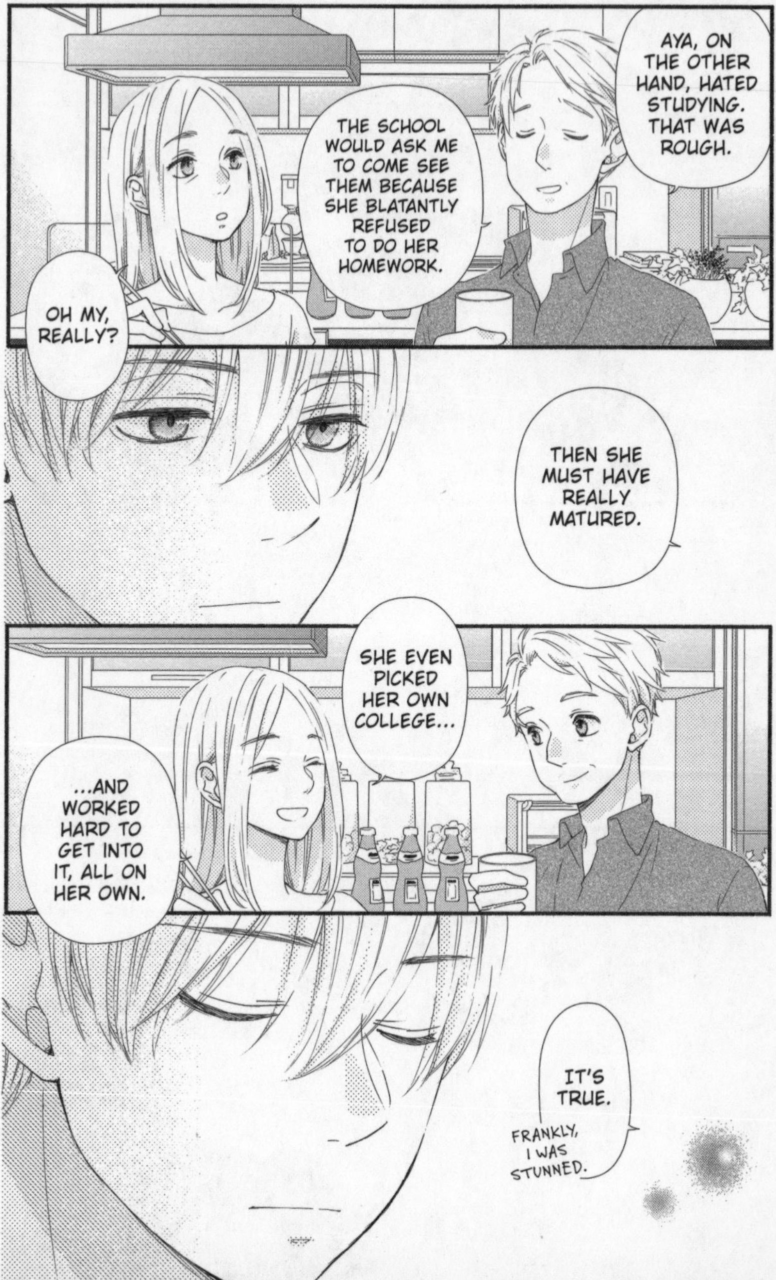
AYA, ON THE OTHER HAND, HATED STUDYING. THAT WAS ROUGH.
THE SCHOOL WOULD ASK ME TO COME SEE THEM BECAUSE SHE BLATANTLY REFUSED TO DO HER HOMEWORK.
OH MY, REALLY?
THEN SHE MUST HAVE REALLY MATURED.
SHE EVEN PICKED HER OWN COLLEGE...
...AND WORKED HARD TO GET INTO IT, ALL ON HER OWN.
IT'S TRUE.
FRANKLY, I WAS STUNNED.

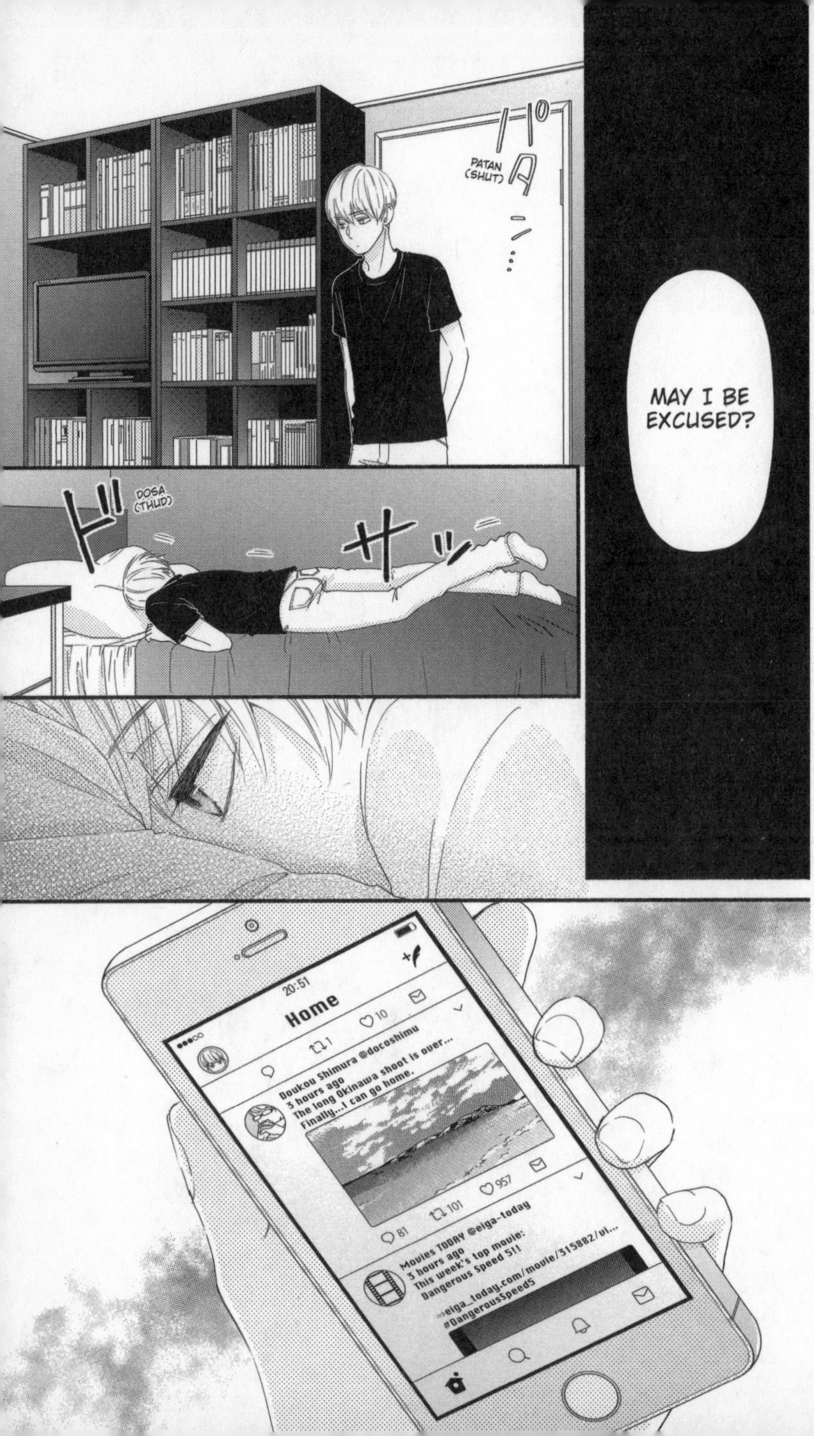
MAY I BE EXCUSED?
PATAN (SHUT)
...
DOSA (THUD)
20:51
Home
Doukou Shimura @docoshimu
3 hours ago
The long Okinawa shoot is over... Finally...I can go home.
81
101
957
10
1
Movies TODAY @eiga-today
3 hours ago
This week's top movie: Dangerous Speed 5!!
⇒eiga_today.com/movie/315882/vi...
#DangerousSpeed5

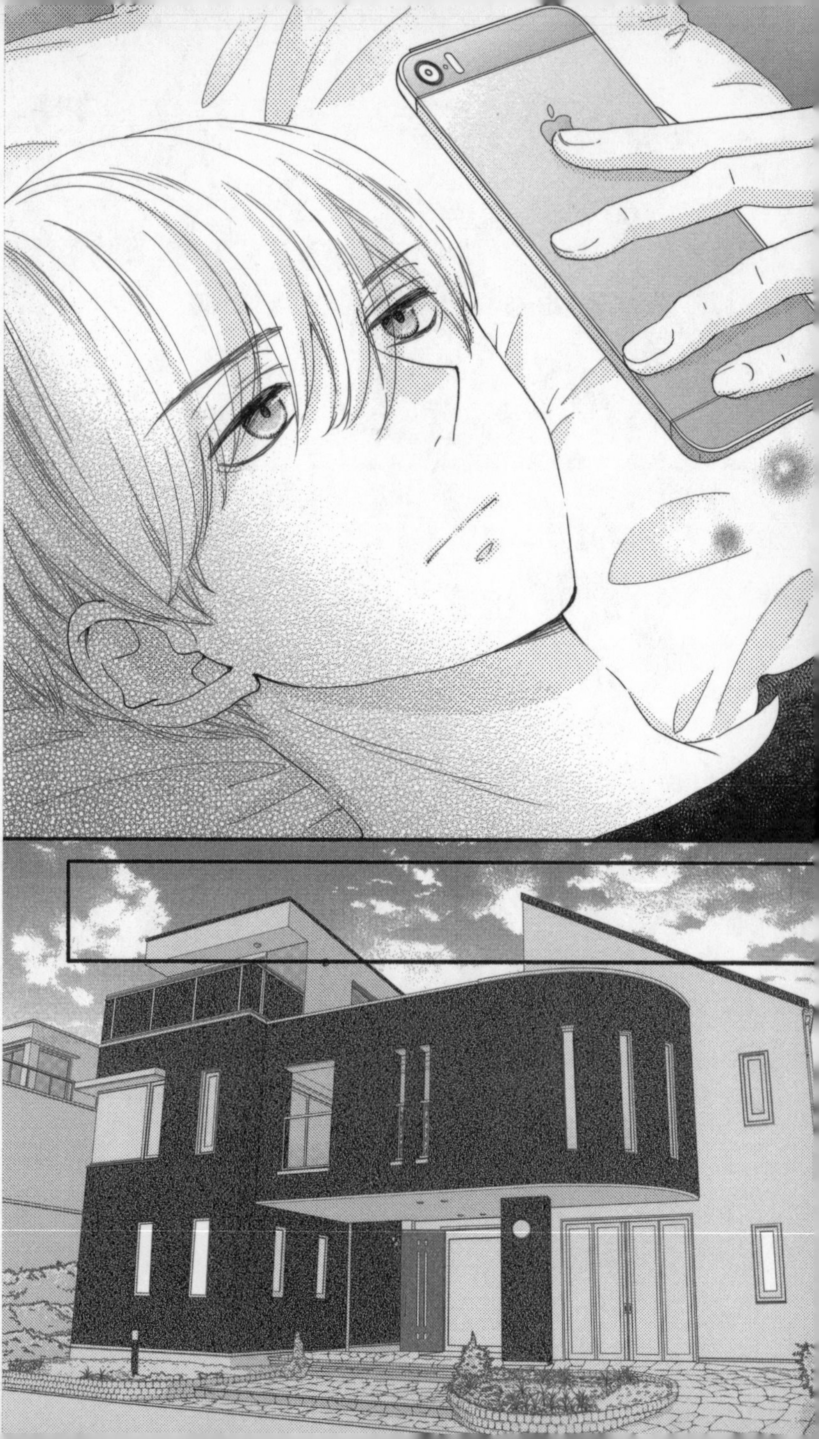

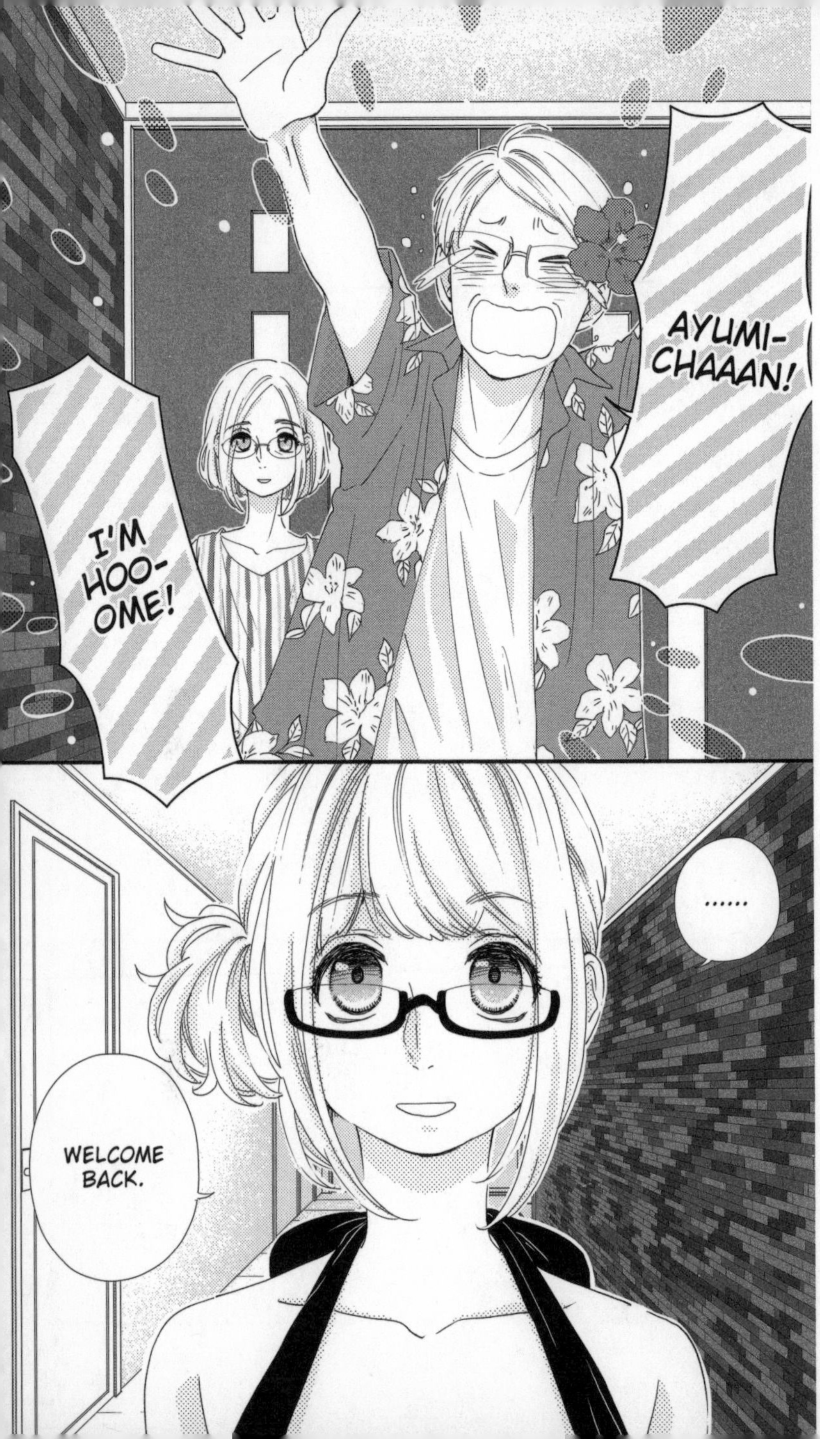
AYUMI-CHAAAN!
I'M HOO-OME!
......
WELCOME BACK.

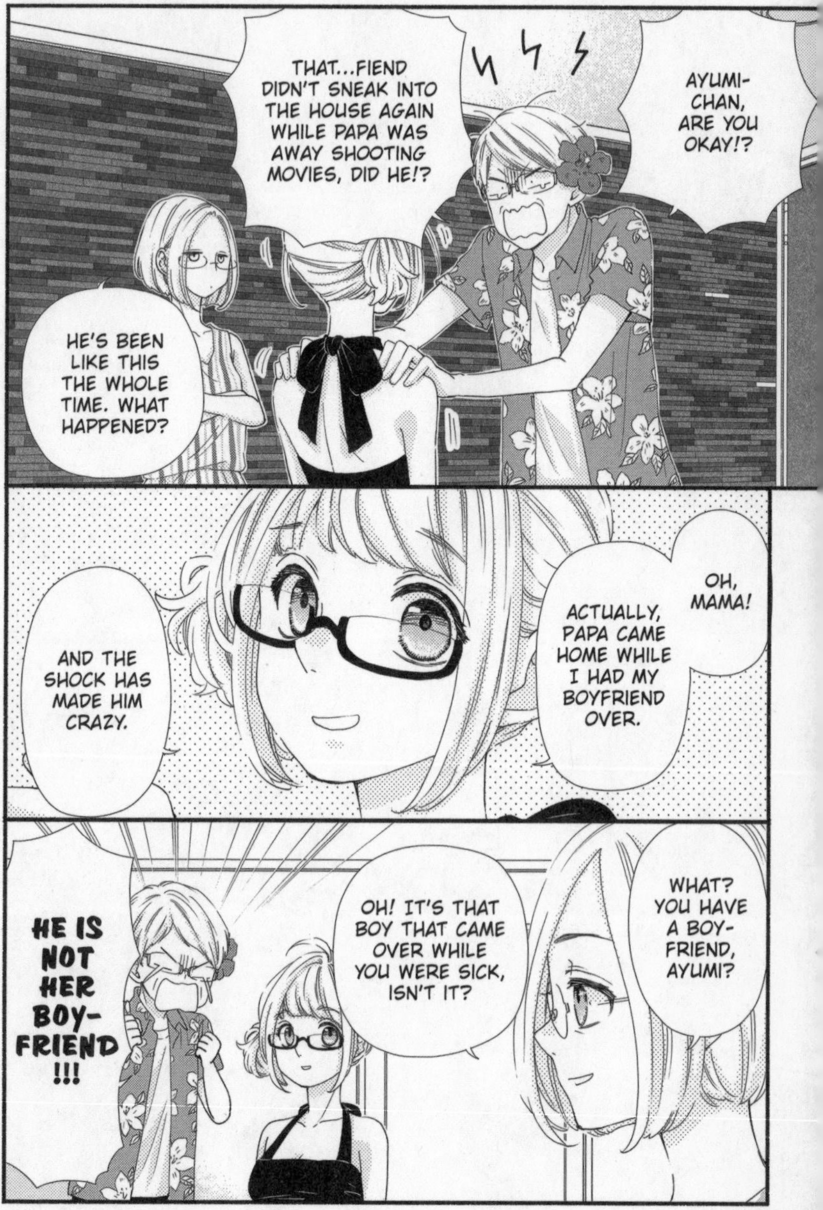
AYUMI-CHAN, ARE YOU OKAY!?
THAT...FIEND DIDN'T SNEAK INTO THE HOUSE AGAIN WHILE PAPA WAS AWAY SHOOTING MOVIES, DID HE!?
HE'S BEEN LIKE THIS THE WHOLE TIME. WHAT HAPPENED?
OH, MAMA!
ACTUALLY, PAPA CAME HOME WHILE I HAD MY BOYFRIEND OVER.
AND THE SHOCK HAS MADE HIM CRAZY.
WHAT? YOU HAVE A BOY-FRIEND, AYUMI?
OH! IT'S THAT BOY THAT CAME OVER WHILE YOU WERE SICK, ISN'T IT?
HE IS NOT HER BOY-FRIEND!!!

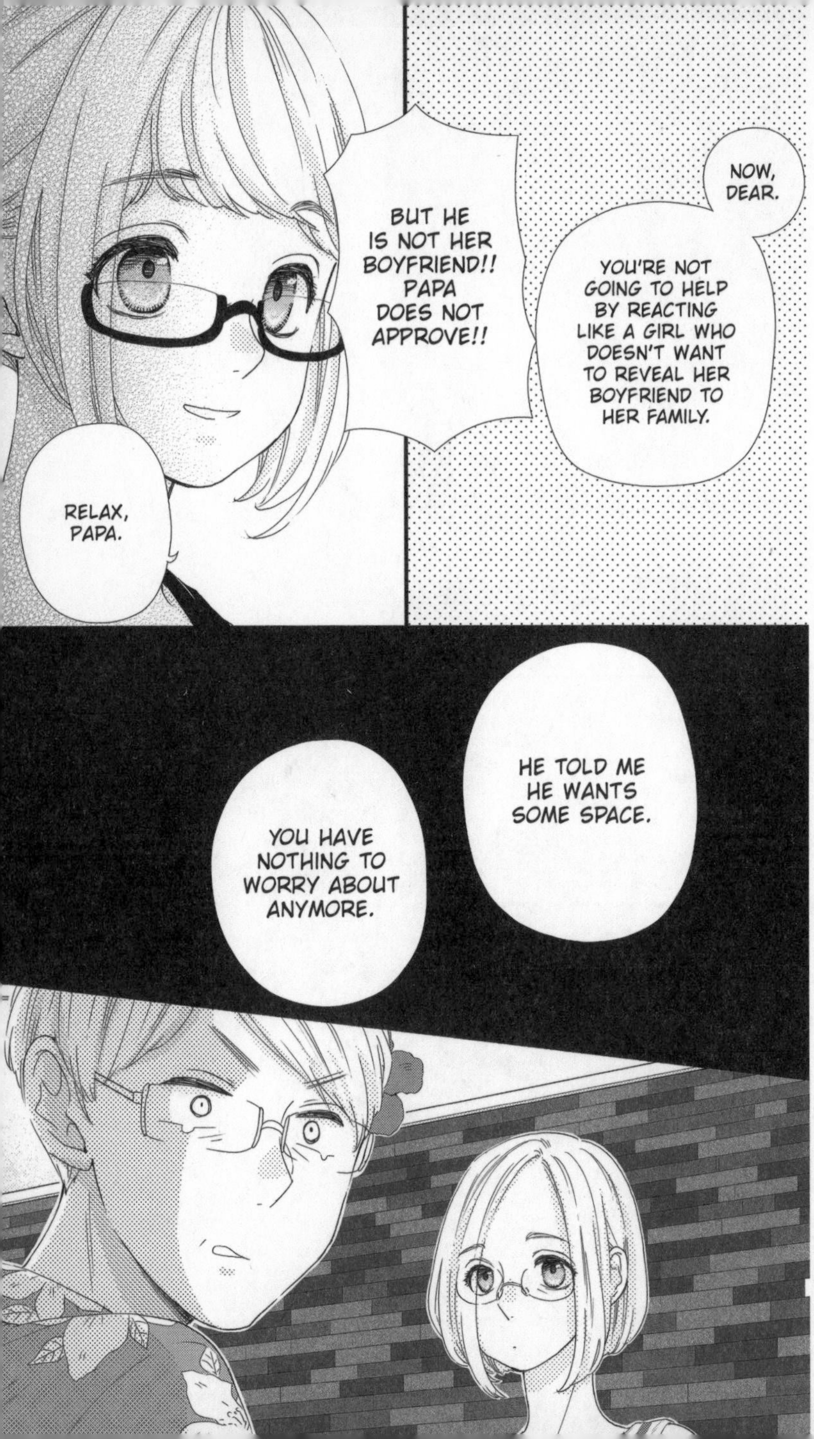
NOW, DEAR.
YOU'RE NOT GOING TO HELP BY REACTING LIKE A GIRL WHO DOESN'T WANT TO REVEAL HER BOYFRIEND TO HER FAMILY.
BUT HE IS NOT HER BOYFRIEND!! PAPA DOES NOT APPROVE!!
RELAX, PAPA.
HE TOLD ME HE WANTS SOME SPACE.
YOU HAVE NOTHING TO WORRY ABOUT ANYMORE.

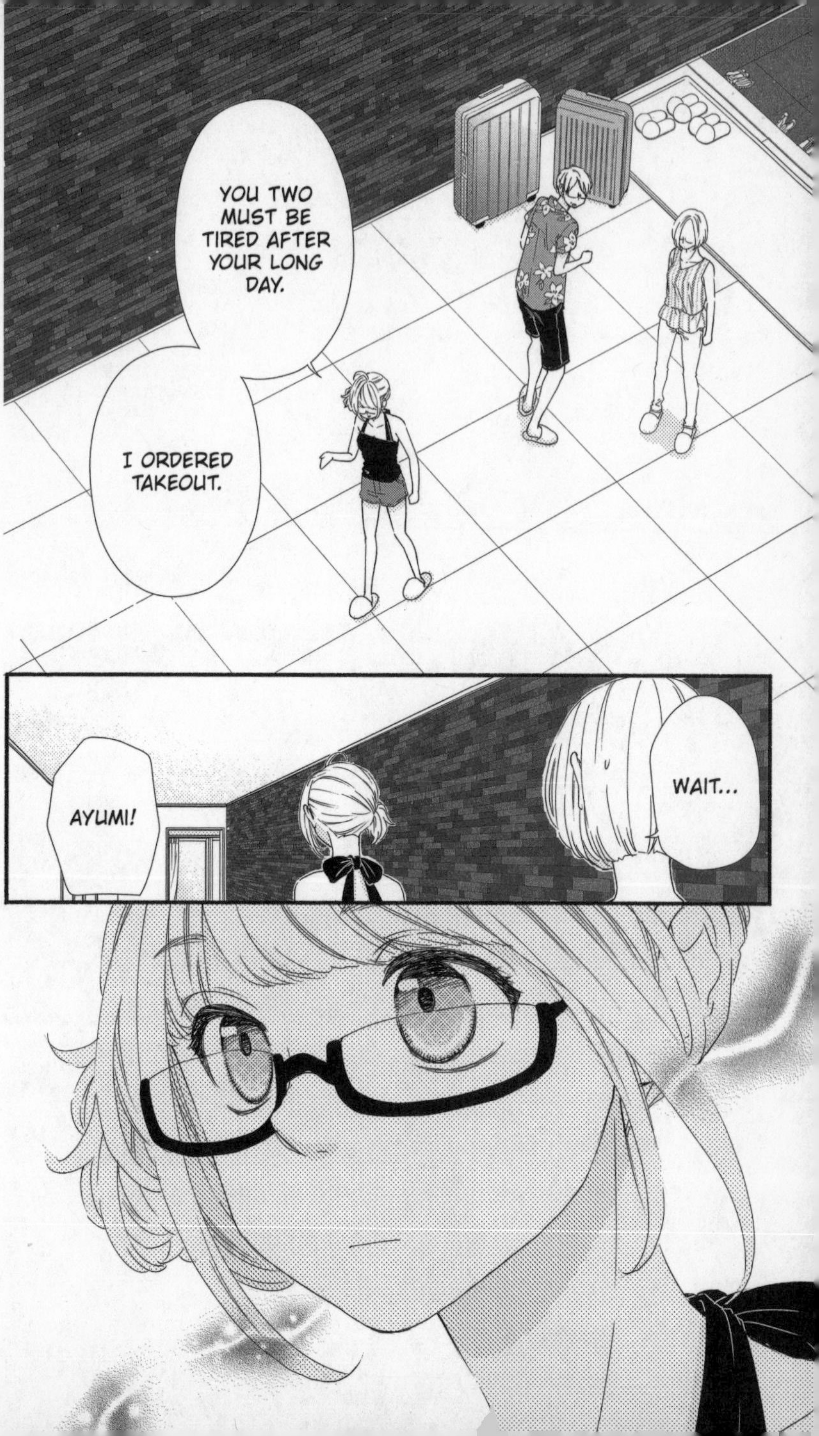
YOU TWO MUST BE TIRED AFTER YOUR LONG DAY.
I ORDERED TAKEOUT.
WAIT...
AYUMI!

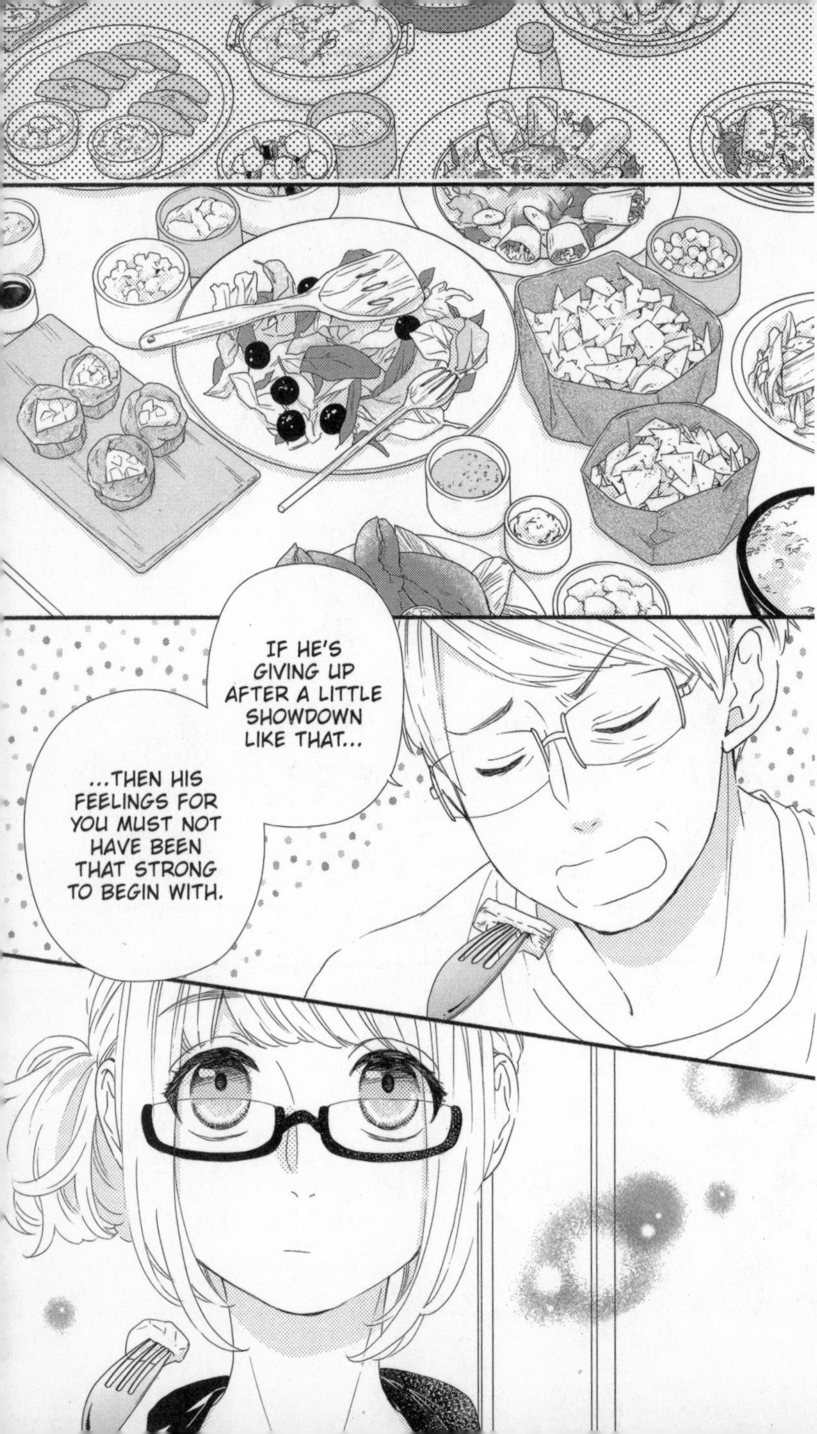
IF HE'S GIVING UP AFTER A LITTLE SHOWDOWN LIKE THAT...
...THEN HIS FEELINGS FOR YOU MUST NOT HAVE BEEN THAT STRONG TO BEGIN WITH.

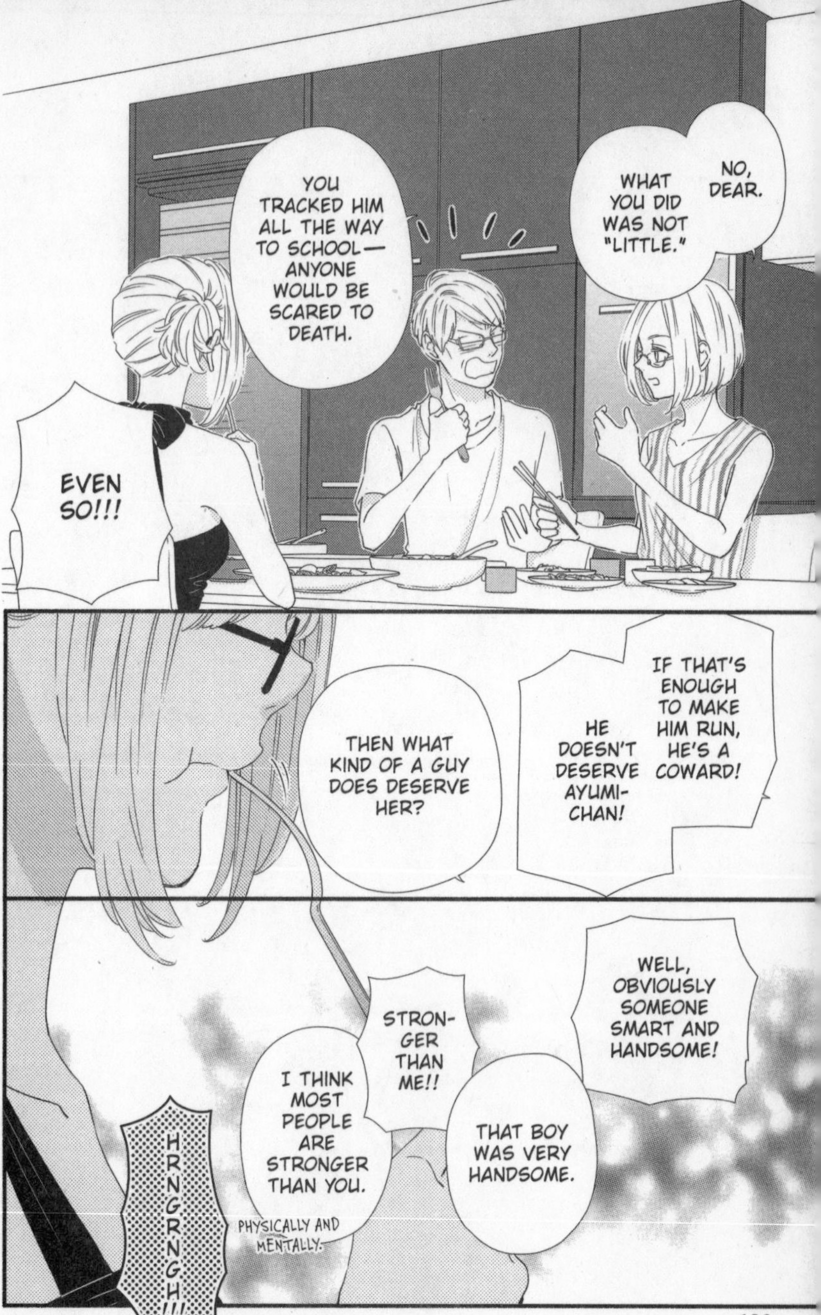
NO, DEAR. WHAT YOU DID WAS NOT "LITTLE."
YOU TRACKED HIM ALL THE WAY TO SCHOOL—ANYONE WOULD BE SCARED TO DEATH.
EVEN SO!!!
IF THAT'S ENOUGH TO MAKE HIM RUN, HE'S A COWARD! HE DOESN'T DESERVE AYUMI-CHAN!
THEN WHAT KIND OF A GUY DOES DESERVE HER?
WELL, OBVIOUSLY SOMEONE SMART AND HANDSOME!
STRONGER THAN ME!!
THAT BOY WAS VERY HANDSOME.
I THINK MOST PEOPLE ARE STRONGER THAN YOU.
PHYSICALLY AND MENTALLY.
HRNGRNGH!!!

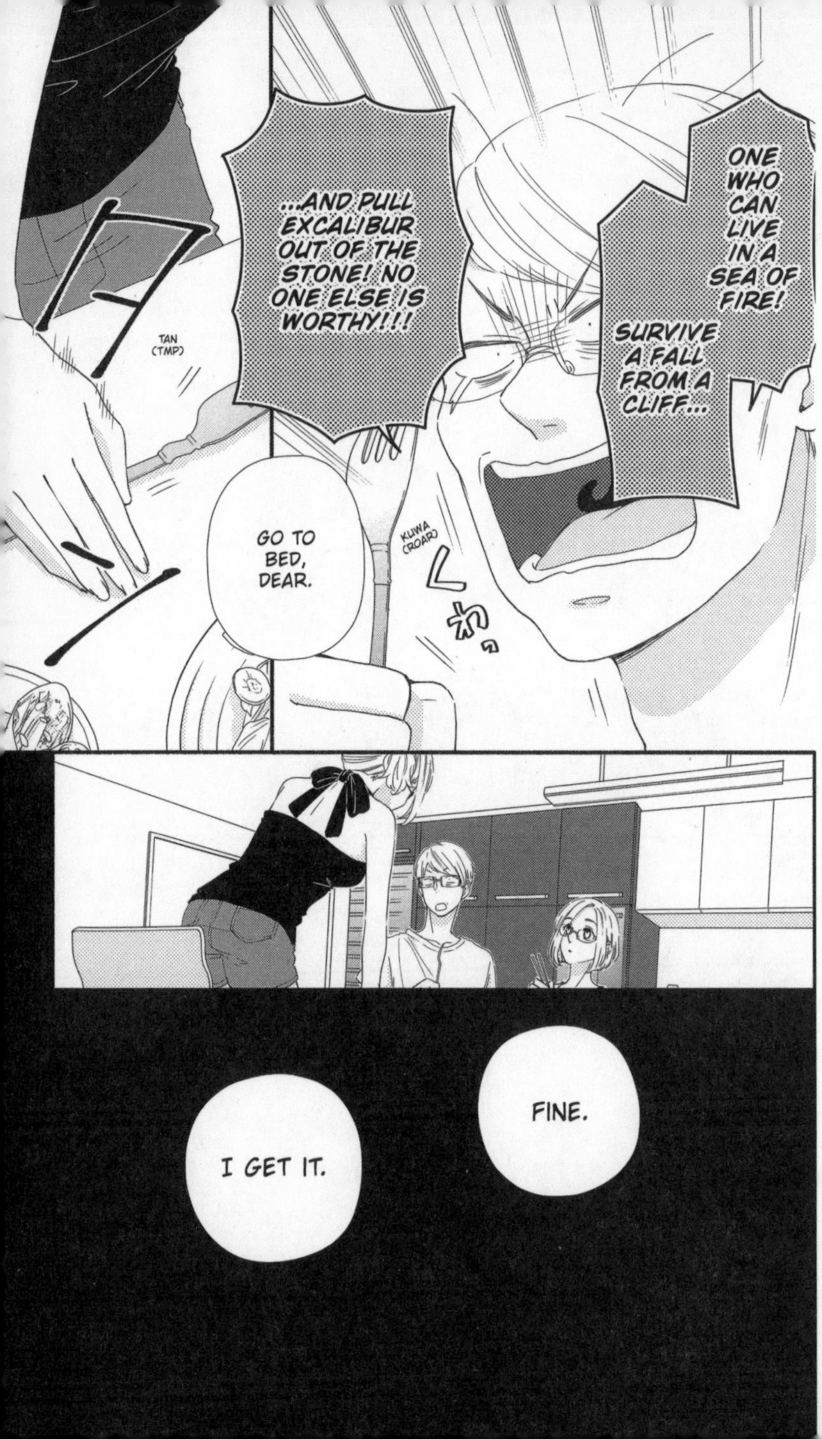
ONE WHO CAN LIVE IN A SEA OF FIRE!
SURVIVE A FALL FROM A CLIFF...
...AND PULL EXCALIBUR OUT OF THE STONE! NO ONE ELSE IS WORTHY!!!
KUWA (ROAR)
TAN (TMP)
GO TO BED, DEAR.
FINE.
I GET IT.

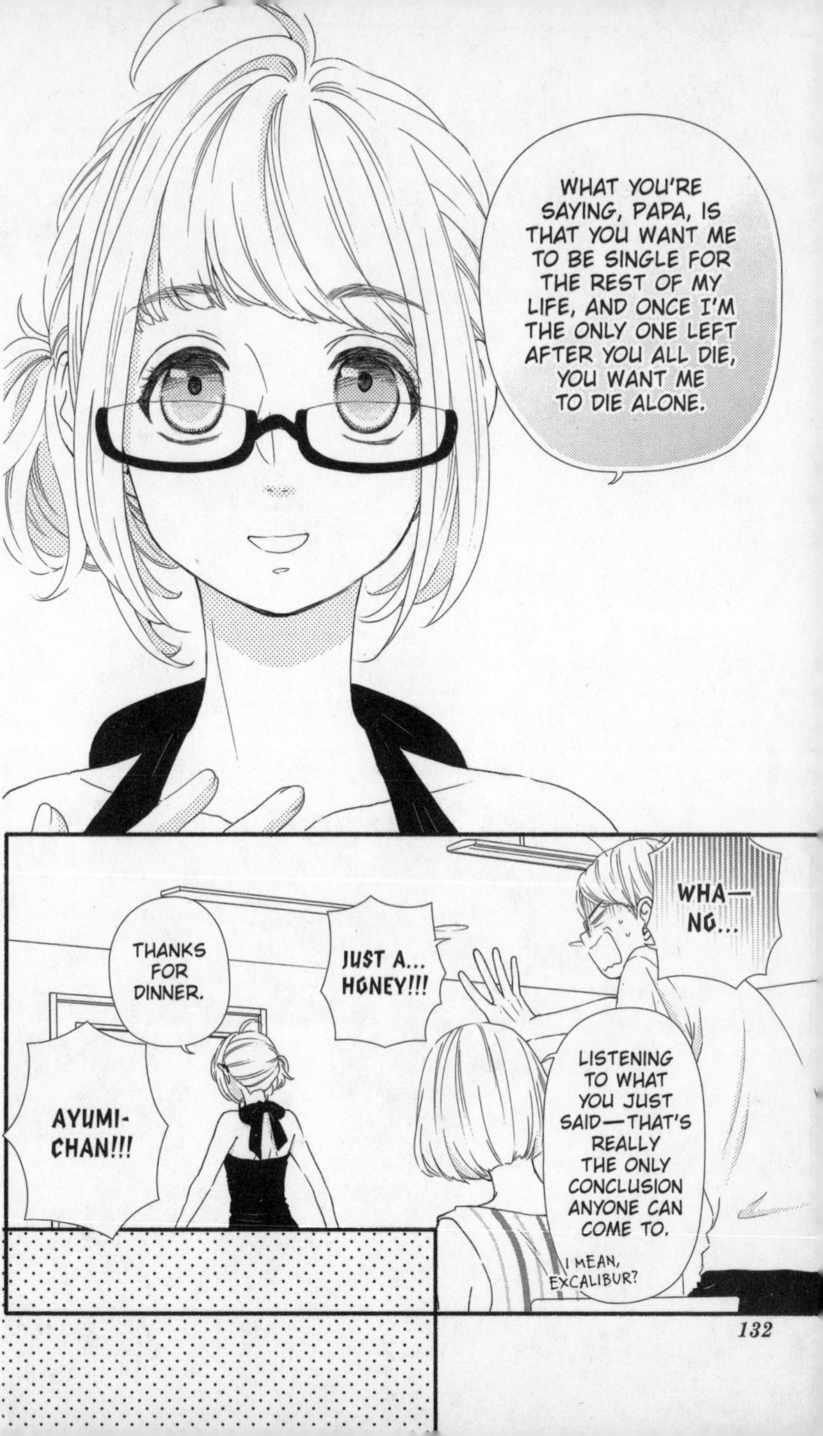
WHAT YOU'RE SAYING, PAPA, IS THAT YOU WANT ME TO BE SINGLE FOR THE REST OF MY LIFE, AND ONCE I'M THE ONLY ONE LEFT AFTER YOU ALL DIE, YOU WANT ME TO DIE ALONE.
WHA— NG...
JUST A... HONEY!!!
THANKS FOR DINNER.
LISTENING TO WHAT YOU JUST SAID—THAT'S REALLY THE ONLY CONCLUSION ANYONE CAN COME TO.
I MEAN, EXCALIBUR?
AYUMI-CHAN!!!

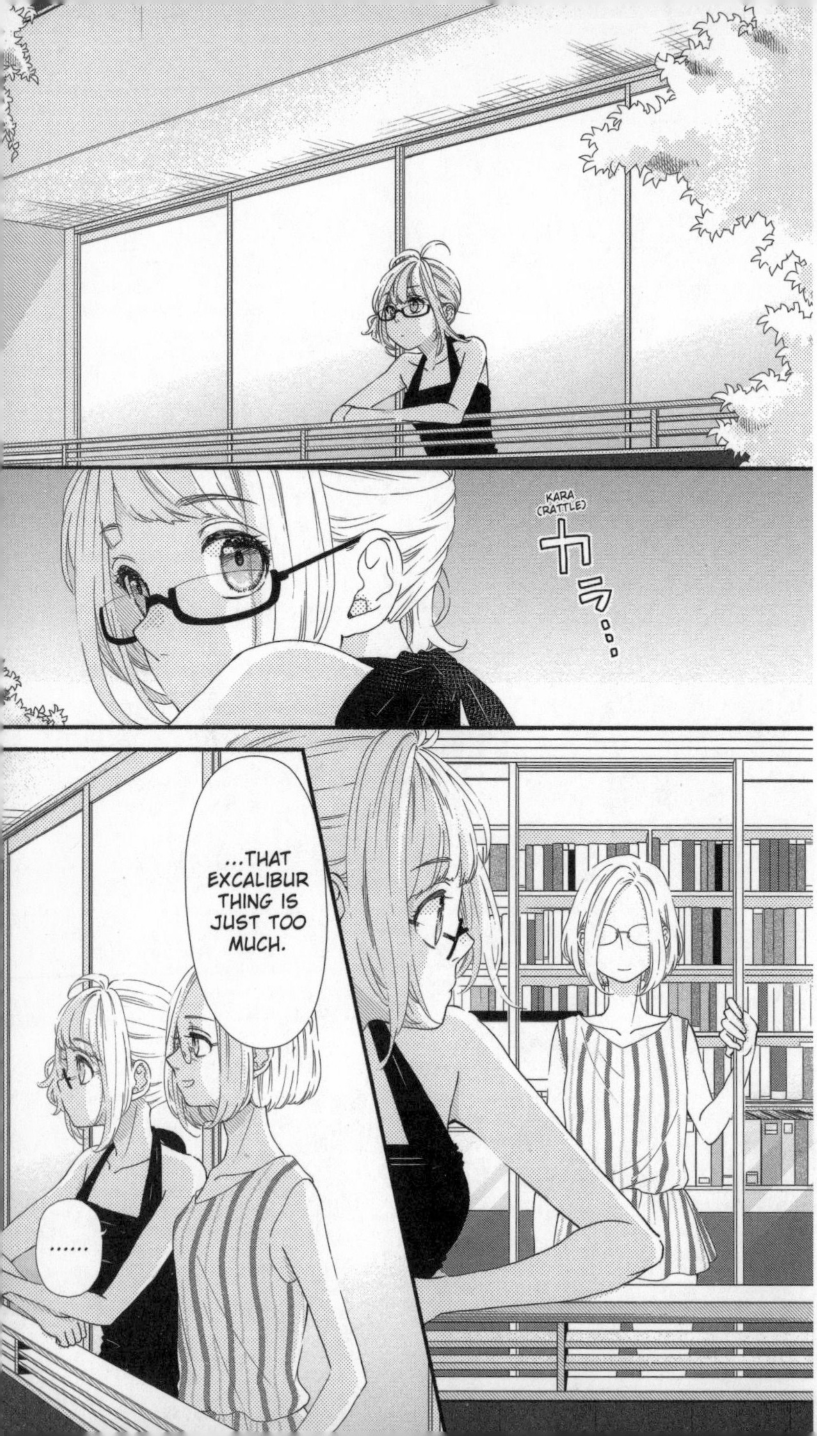
KARA (RATTLE)
カラ...
...THAT EXCALIBUR THING IS JUST TOO MUCH.
......

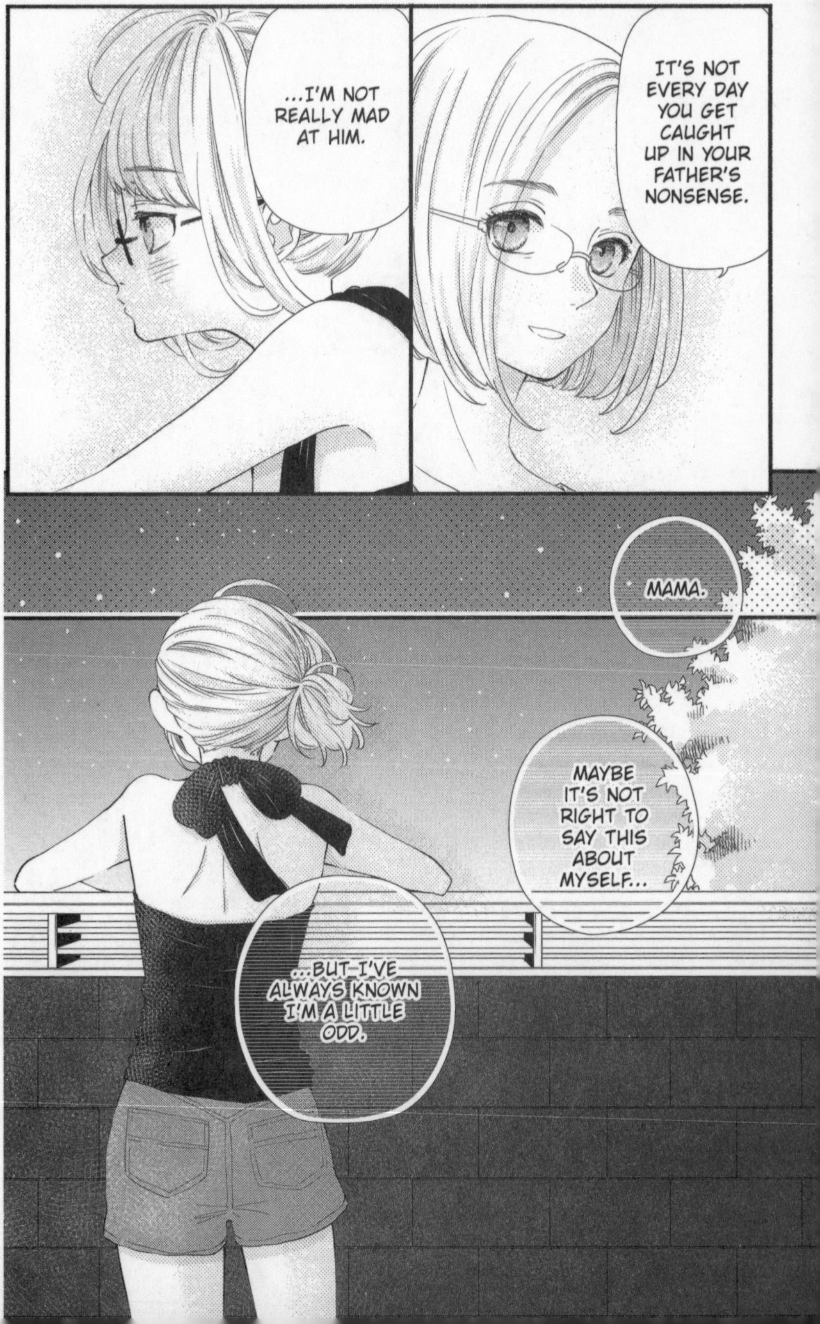
IT'S NOT EVERY DAY YOU GET CAUGHT UP IN YOUR FATHER'S NONSENSE.
...I'M NOT REALLY MAD AT HIM.
MAMA.
MAYBE IT'S NOT RIGHT TO SAY THIS ABOUT MYSELF...
...BUT I'VE ALWAYS KNOWN I'M A LITTLE ODD.

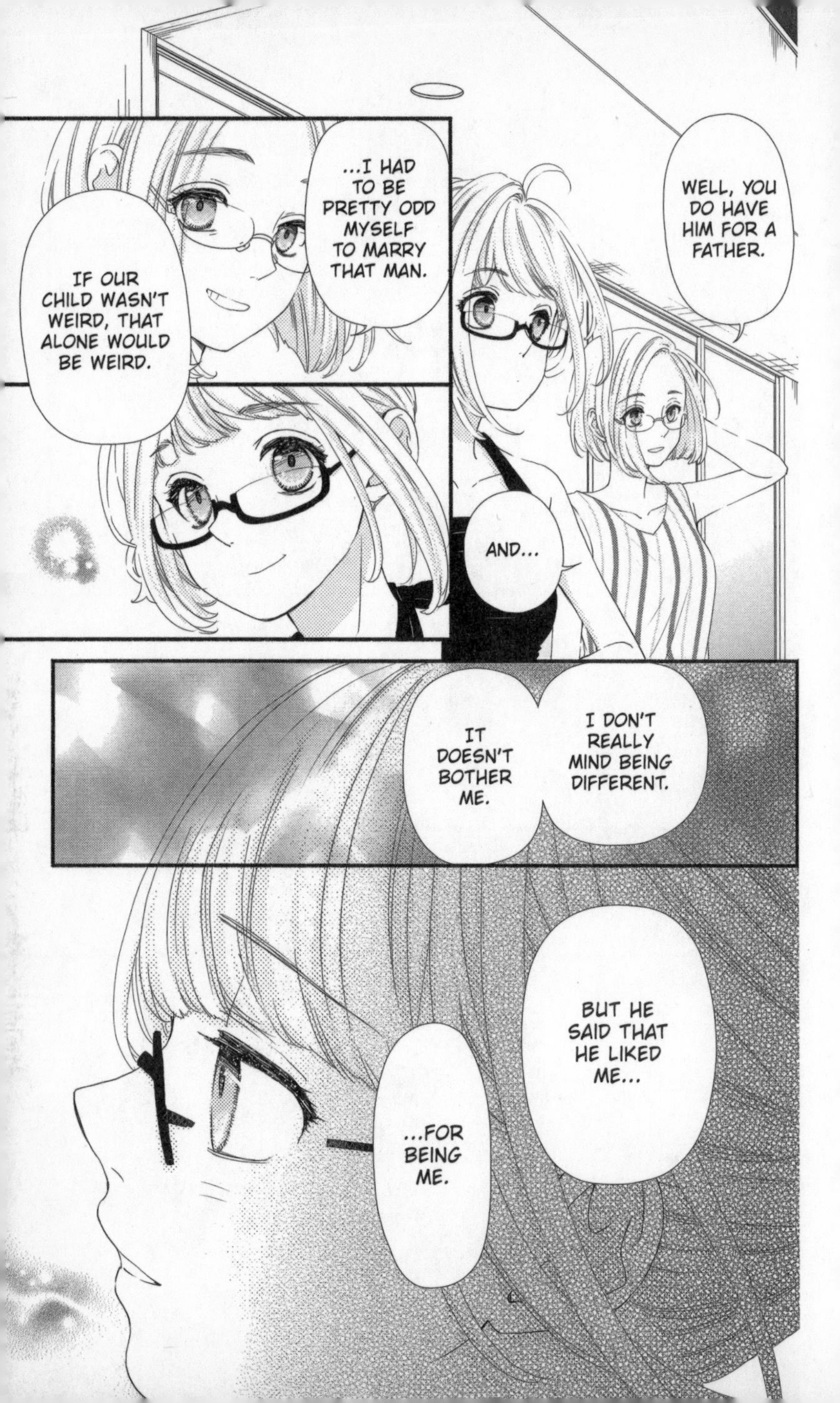
WELL, YOU DO HAVE HIM FOR A FATHER.
...I HAD TO BE PRETTY ODD MYSELF TO MARRY THAT MAN.
IF OUR CHILD WASN'T WEIRD, THAT ALONE WOULD BE WEIRD.
AND...
I DON'T REALLY MIND BEING DIFFERENT.
IT DOESN'T BOTHER ME.
BUT HE SAID THAT HE LIKED ME...
...FOR BEING ME.

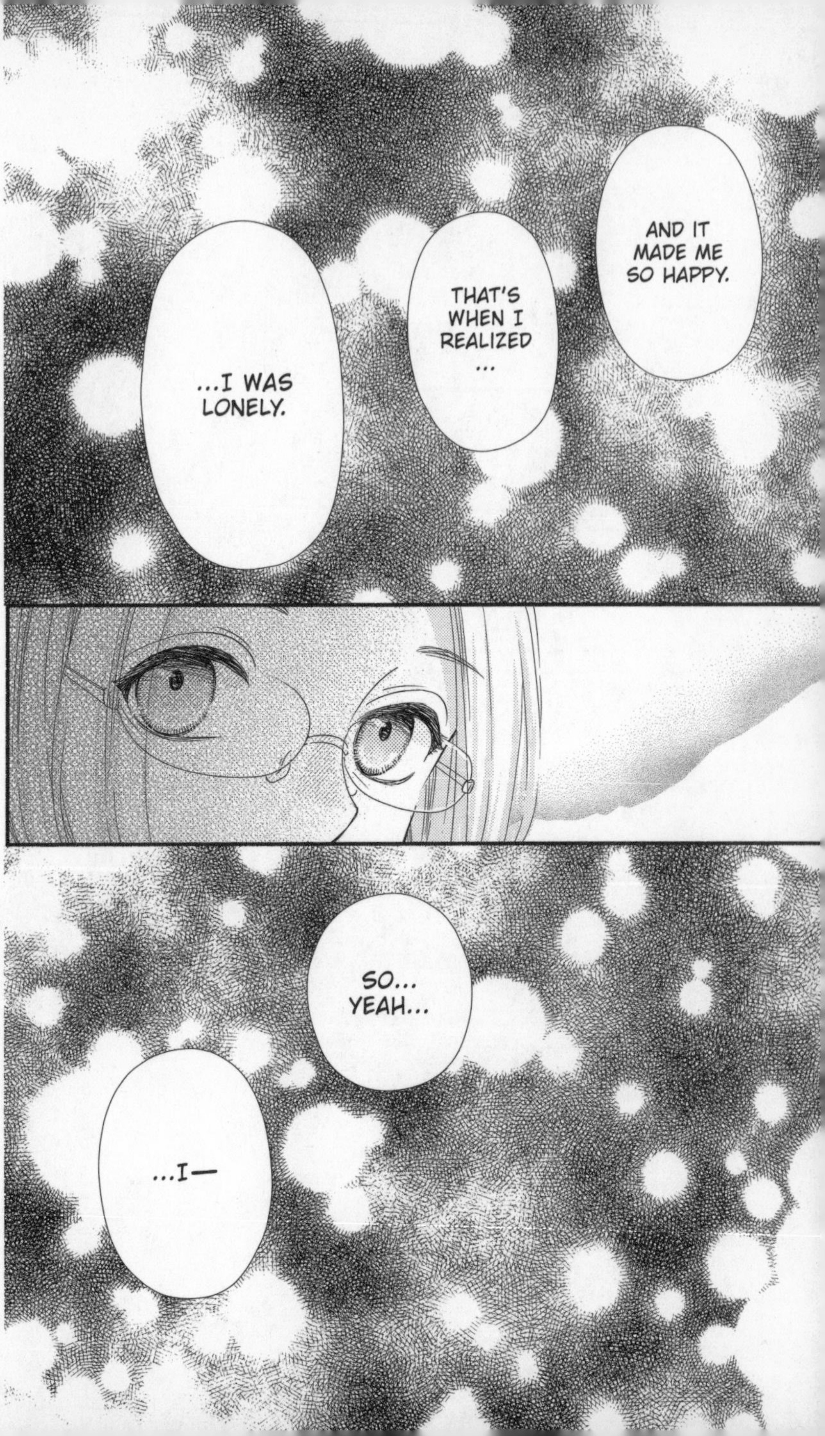
AND IT MADE ME SO HAPPY.
THAT'S WHEN I REALIZED ...
...I WAS LONELY.
SO... YEAH...
...I—

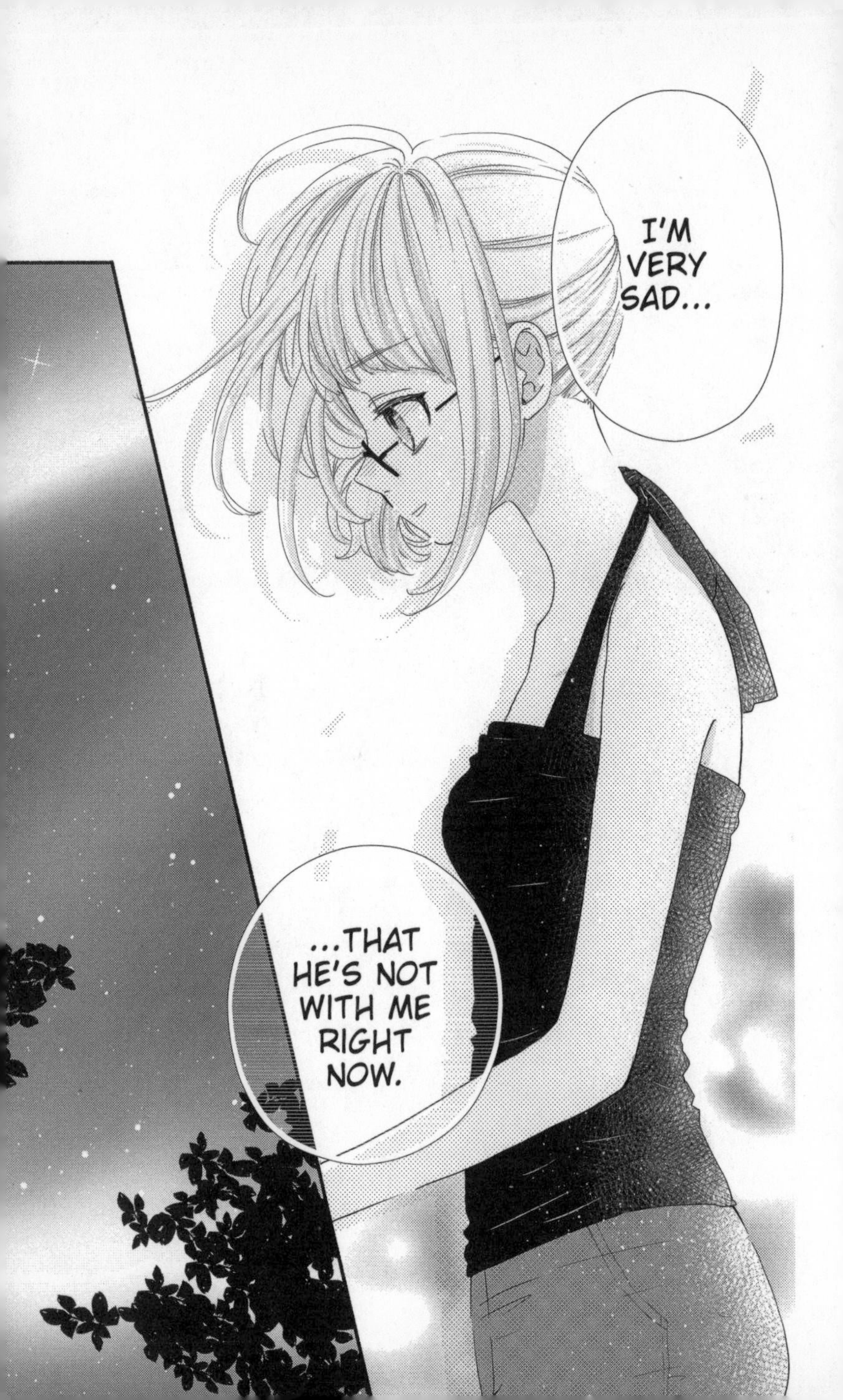
I'M VERY SAD...
...THAT HE'S NOT WITH ME RIGHT NOW.

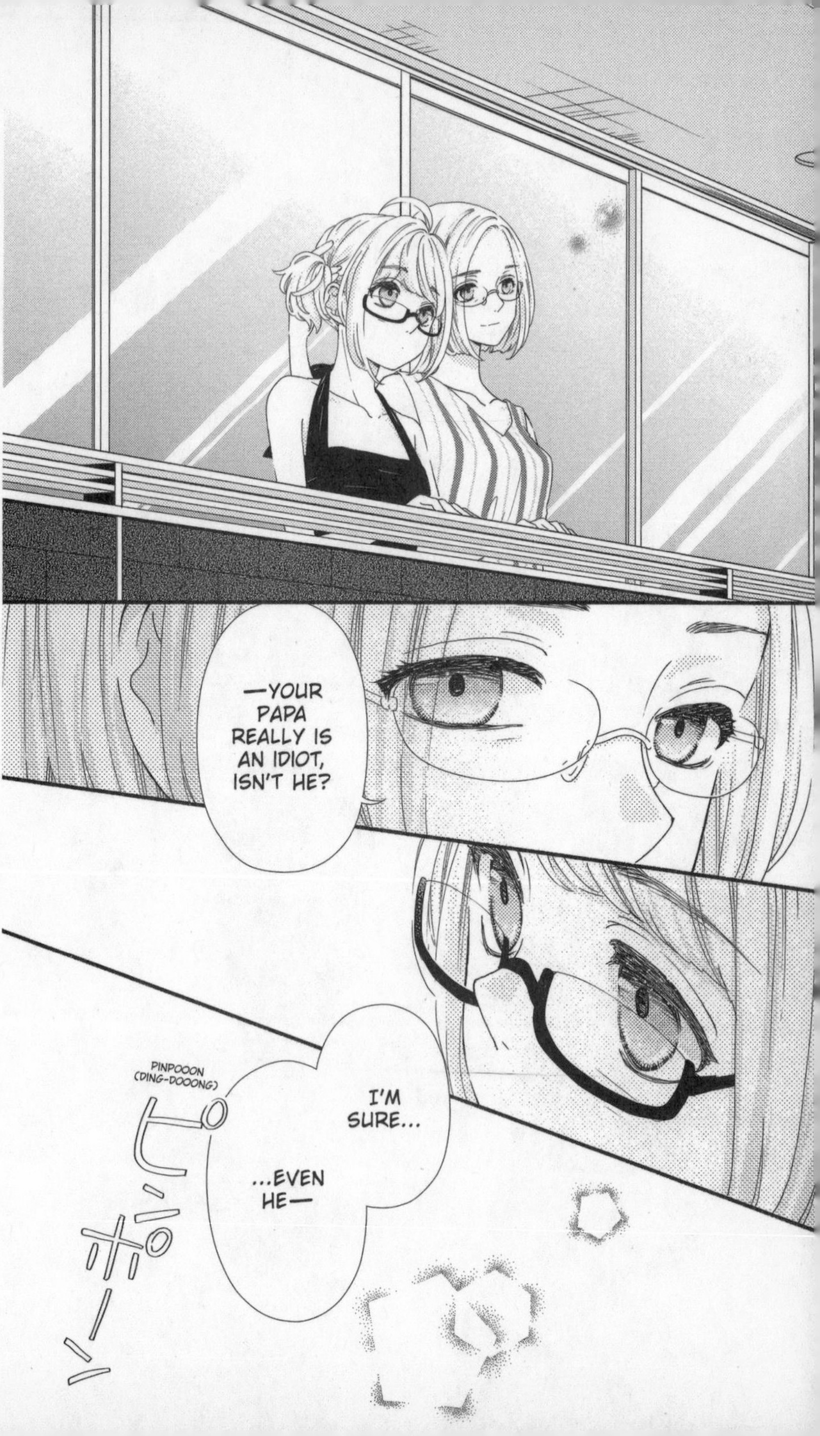
—YOUR PAPA REALLY IS AN IDIOT, ISN'T HE?
I'M SURE...
...EVEN HE—
PINPOOON (DING-DOOONG)

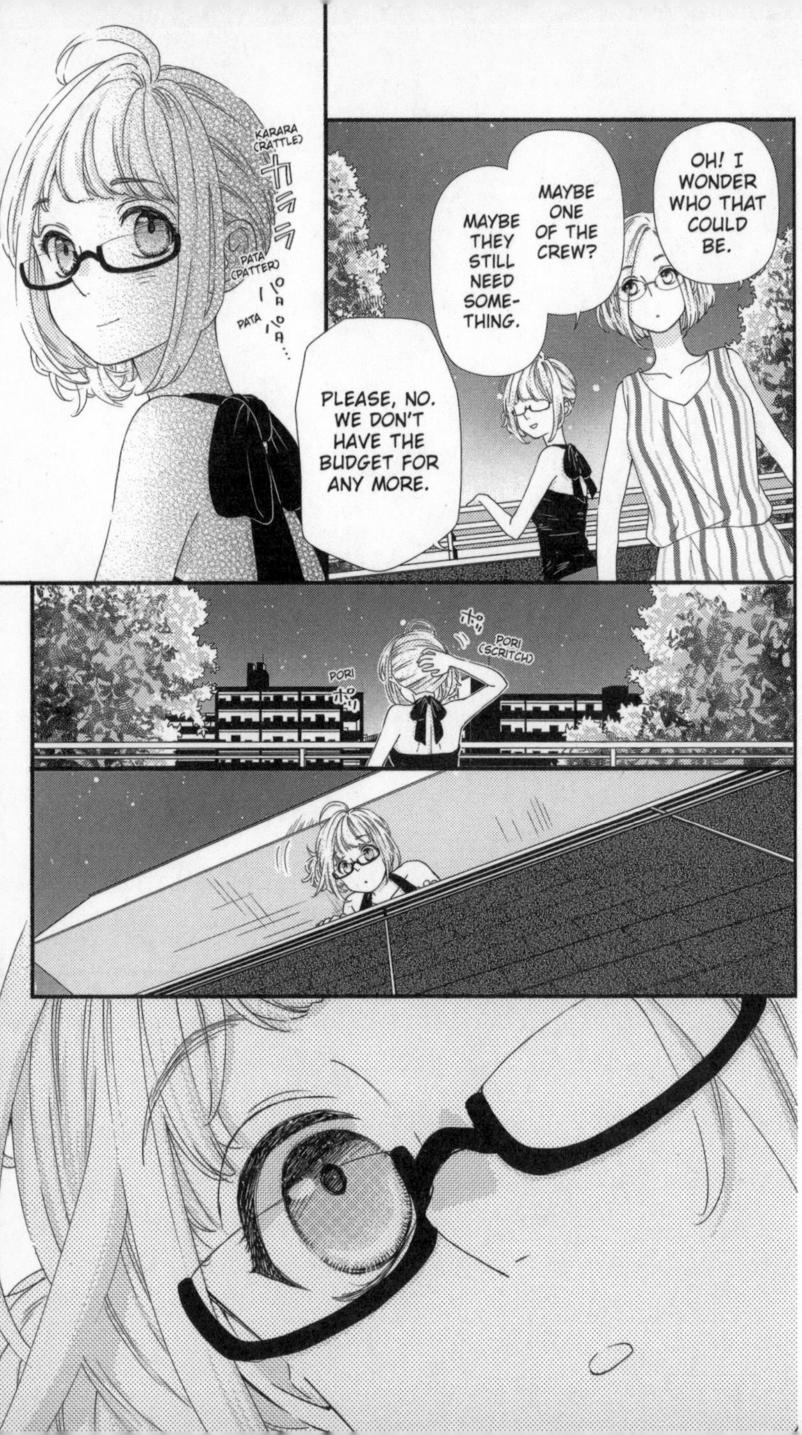

OH! I WONDER WHO THAT COULD BE.
MAYBE ONE OF THE CREW?
MAYBE THEY STILL NEED SOMETHING.
PLEASE, NO. WE DON'T HAVE THE BUDGET FOR ANY MORE.
KARARA (RATTLE)
PATA (PATTER)
PATA
PORI (SCRITCH)
PORI

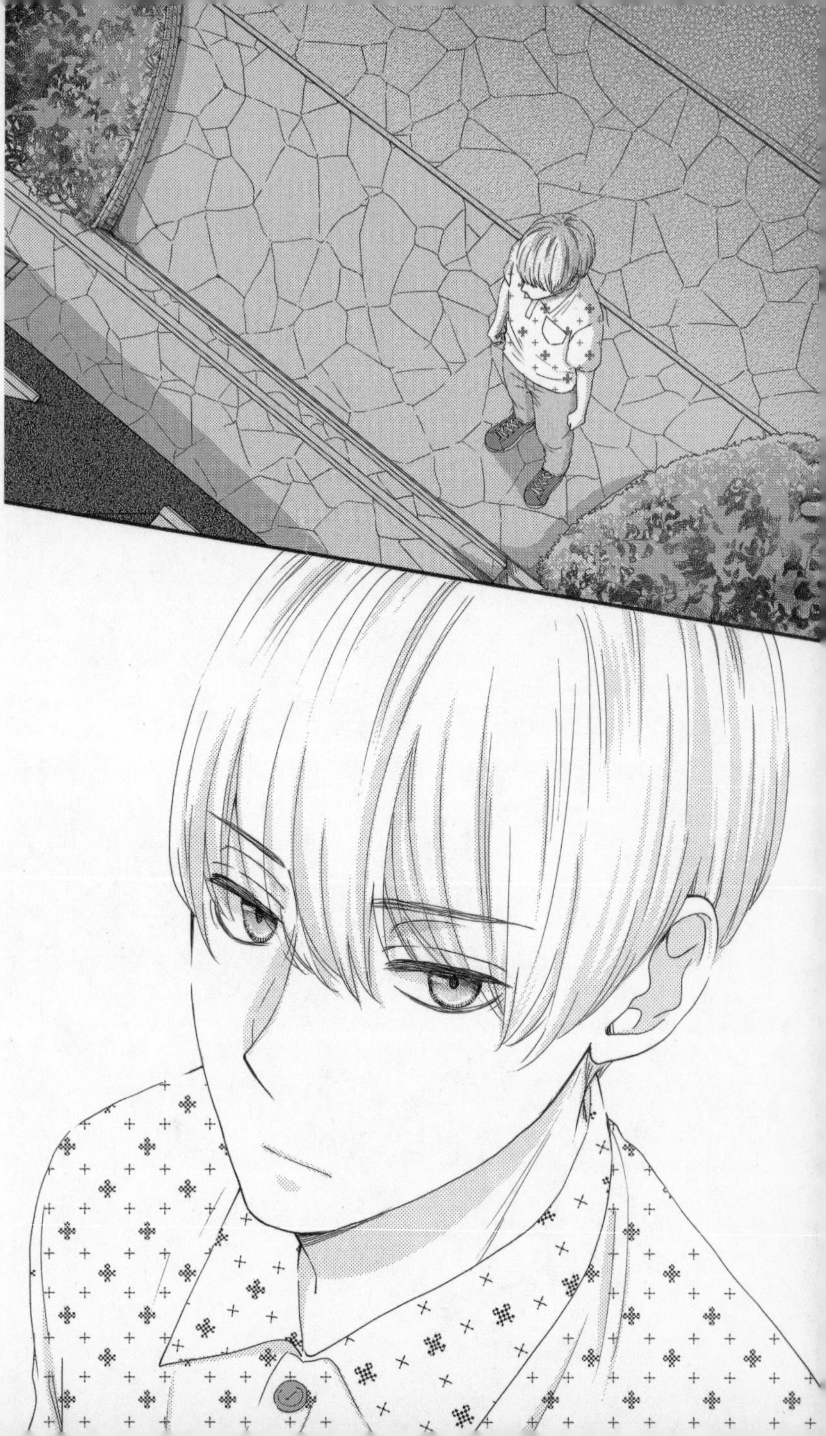

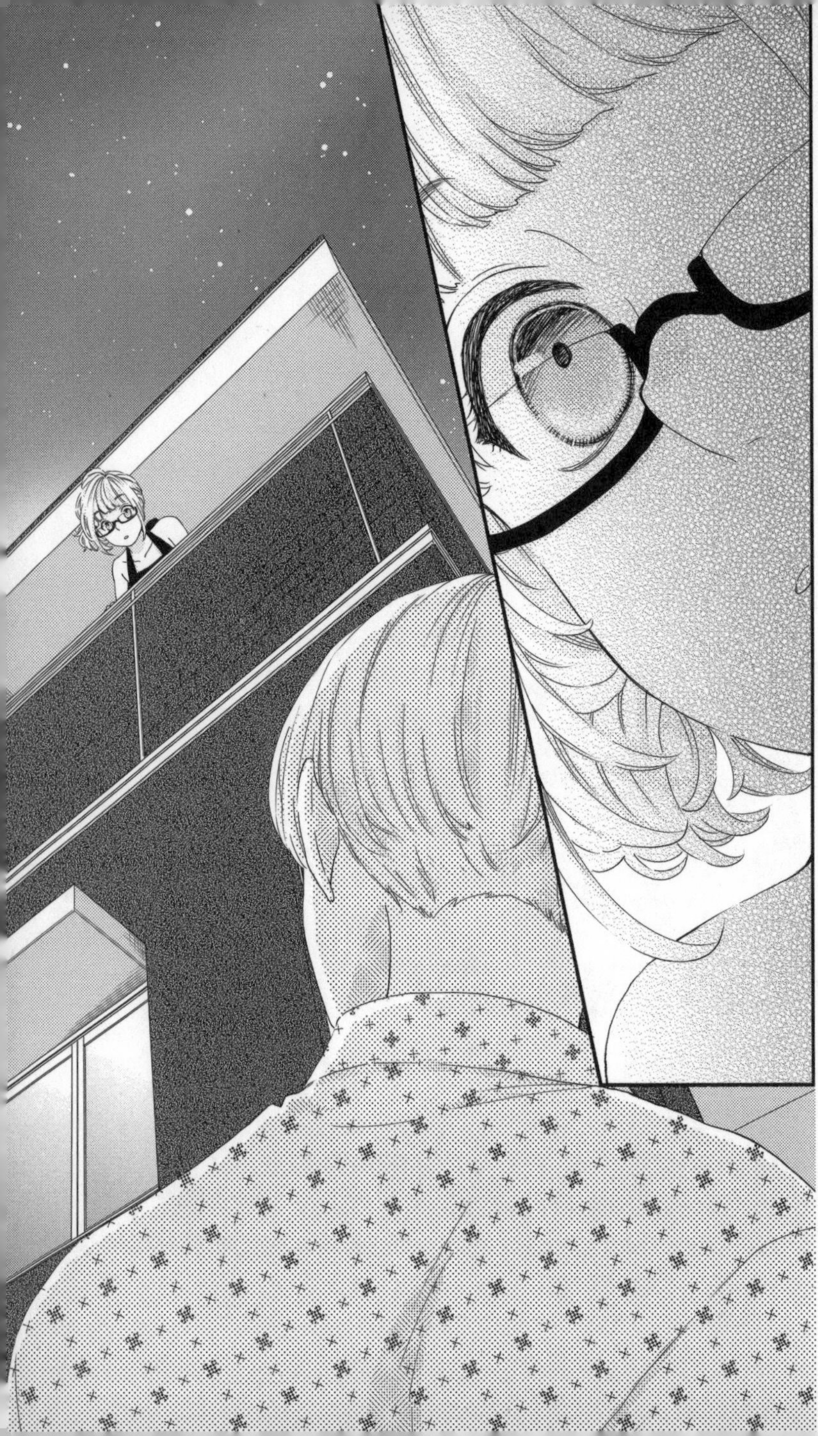

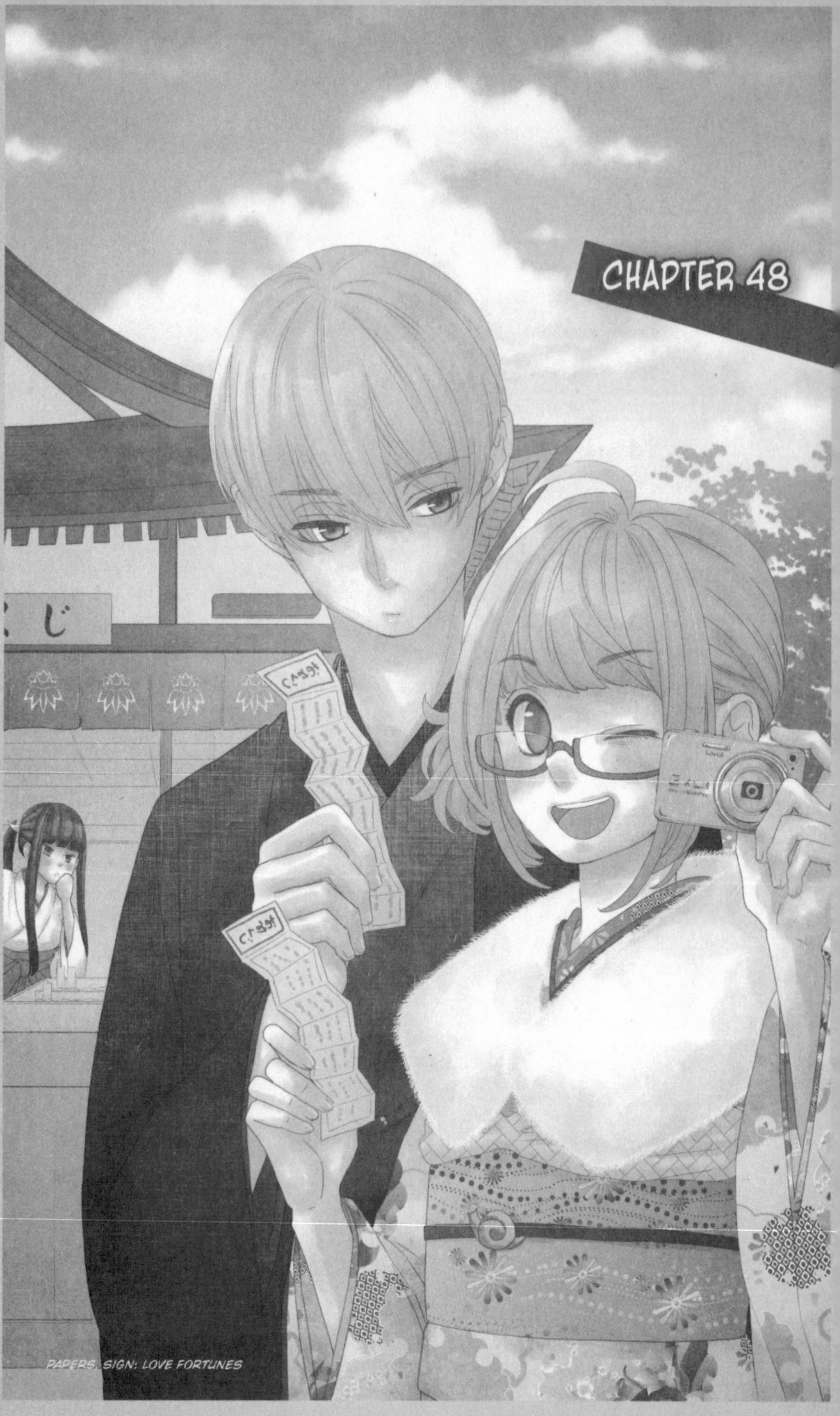
CHAPTER 48
PAPERS, SIGN: LOVE FORTUNES

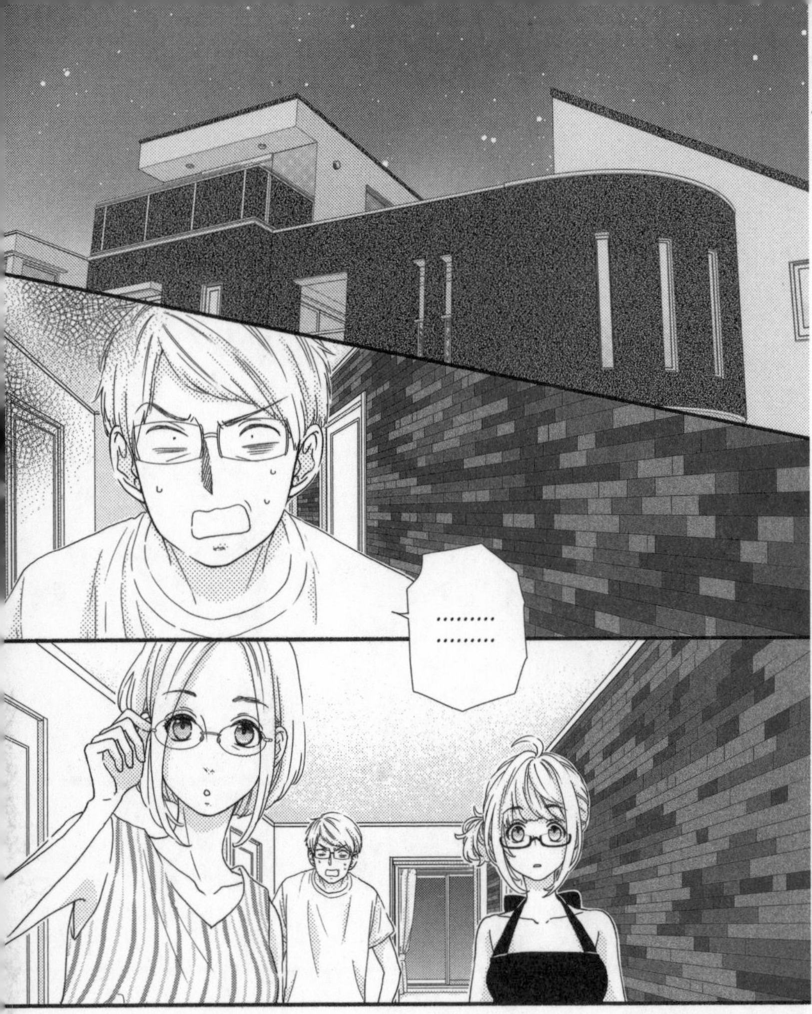
………
………

hatsu haru

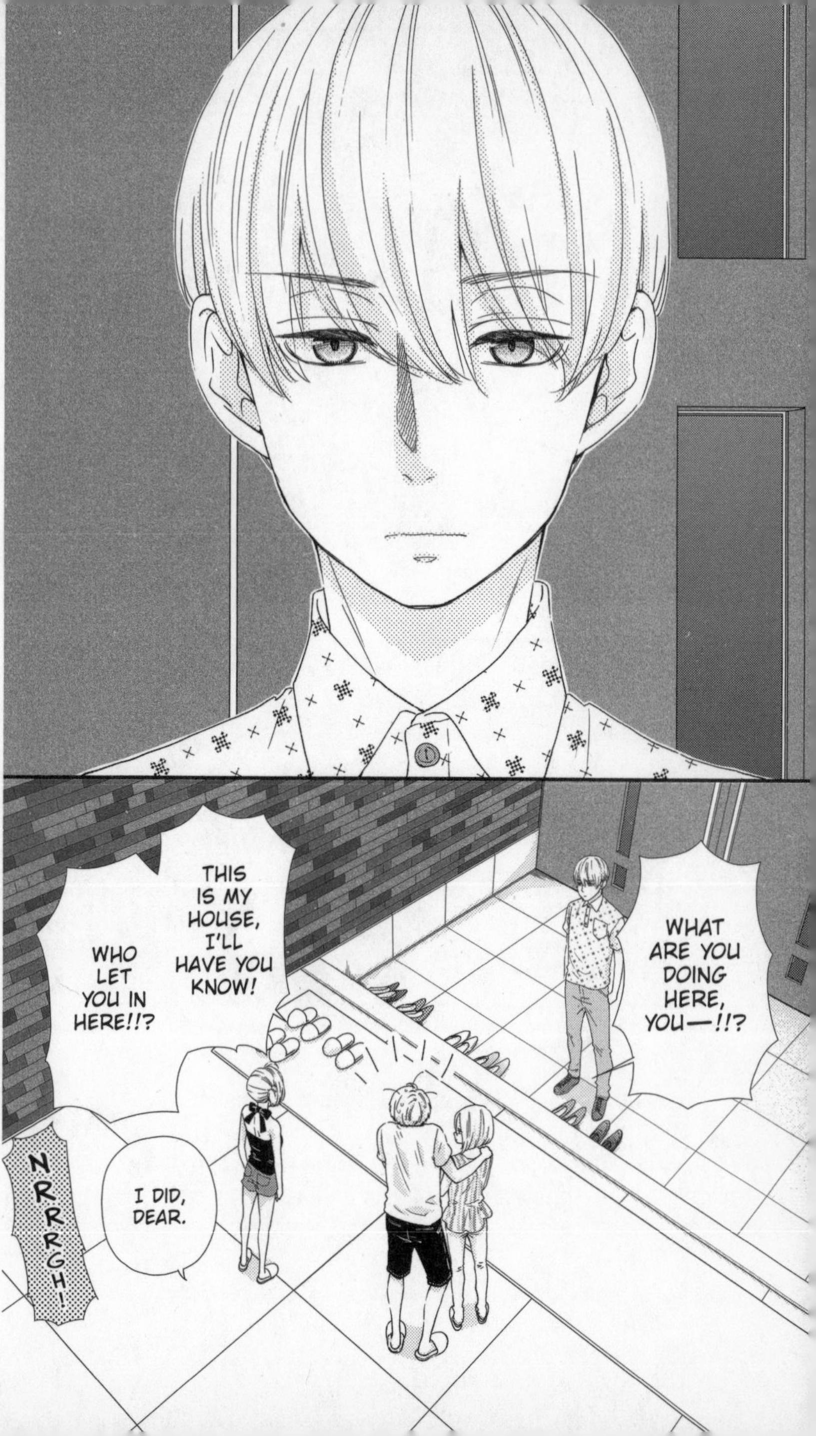
WHAT ARE YOU DOING HERE, YOU—!!?
THIS IS MY HOUSE, I'LL HAVE YOU KNOW!
WHO LET YOU IN HERE!!?
I DID, DEAR.
NRRRGH!

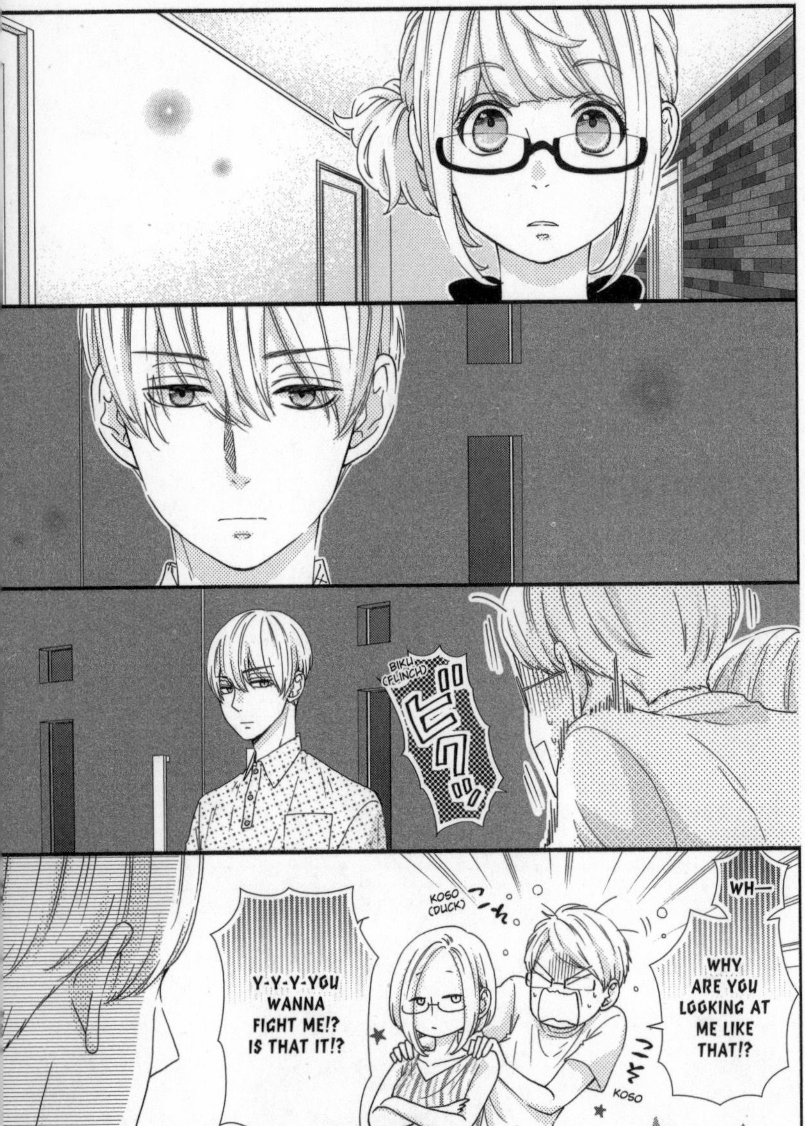
BIKU (FLINCH)
WH—
WHY ARE YOU LOOKING AT ME LIKE THAT!?
KOSO (DUCK)
KOSO
Y-Y-Y-YOU WANNA FIGHT ME!? IS THAT IT!?
...

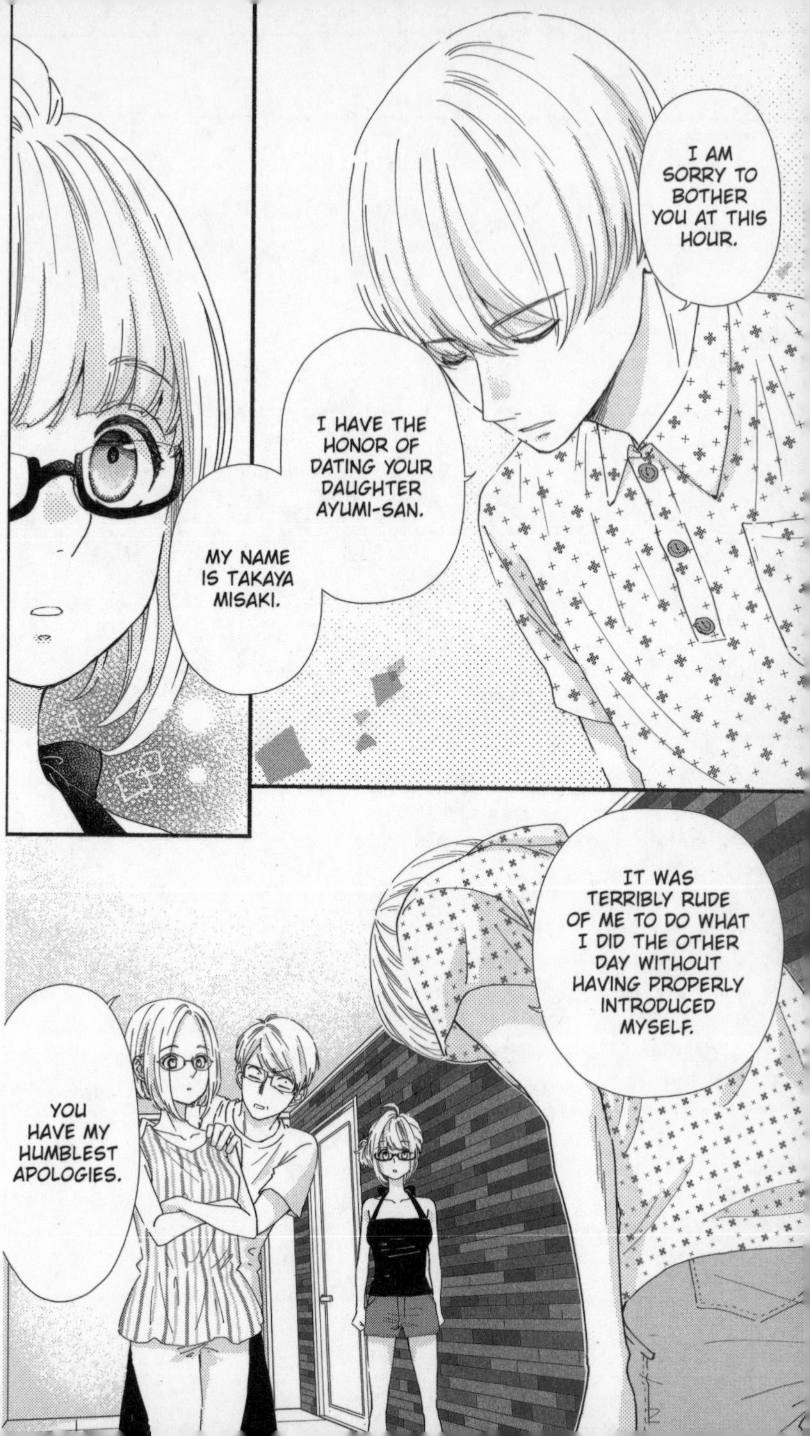
I AM SORRY TO BOTHER YOU AT THIS HOUR.
I HAVE THE HONOR OF DATING YOUR DAUGHTER AYUMI-SAN.
MY NAME IS TAKAYA MISAKI.
IT WAS TERRIBLY RUDE OF ME TO DO WHAT I DID THE OTHER DAY WITHOUT HAVING PROPERLY INTRODUCED MYSELF.
YOU HAVE MY HUMBLEST APOLOGIES.

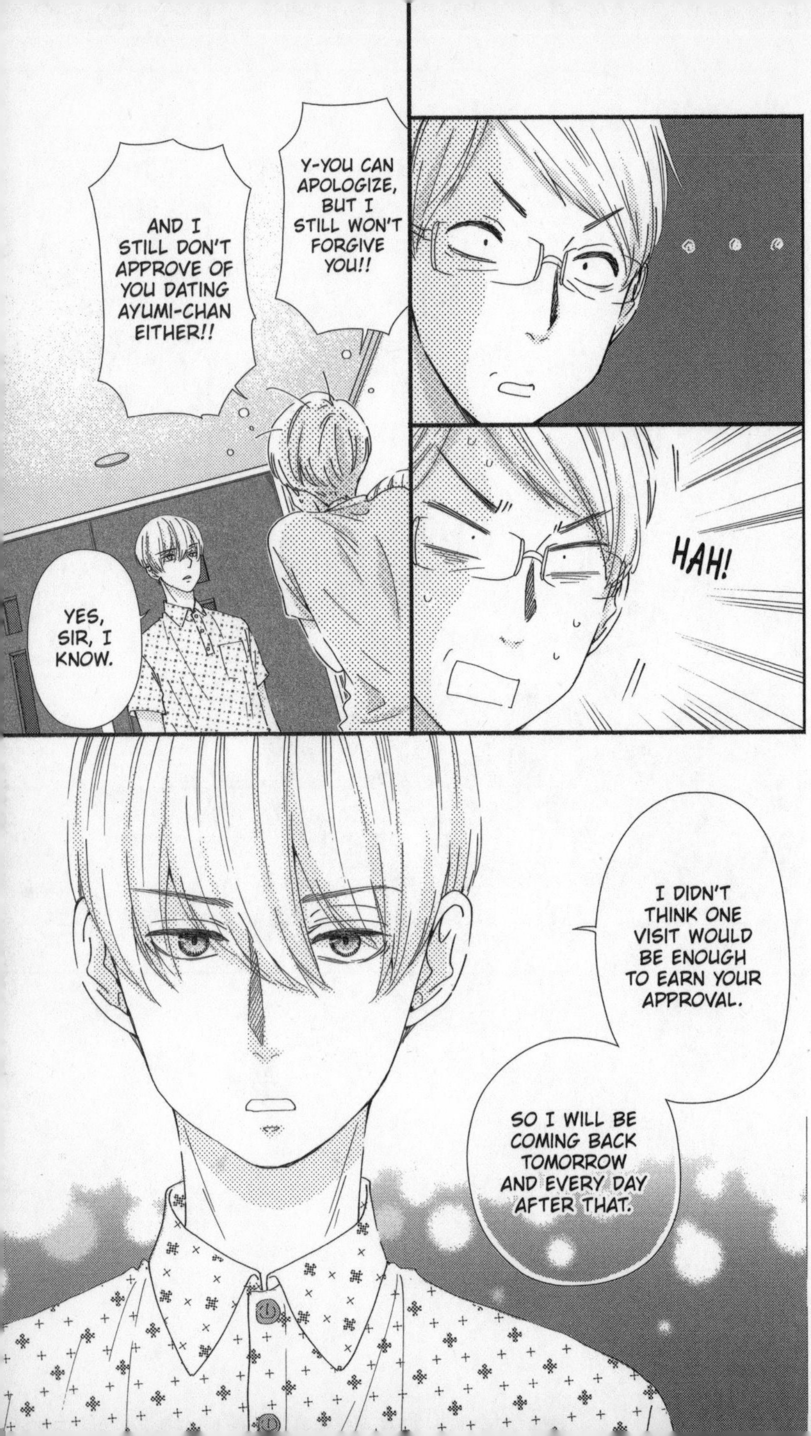
HAH!
Y-YOU CAN APOLOGIZE, BUT I STILL WON'T FORGIVE YOU!!
AND I STILL DON'T APPROVE OF YOU DATING AYUMI-CHAN EITHER!!
YES, SIR, I KNOW.
I DIDN'T THINK ONE VISIT WOULD BE ENOUGH TO EARN YOUR APPROVAL.
SO I WILL BE COMING BACK TOMORROW AND EVERY DAY AFTER THAT.

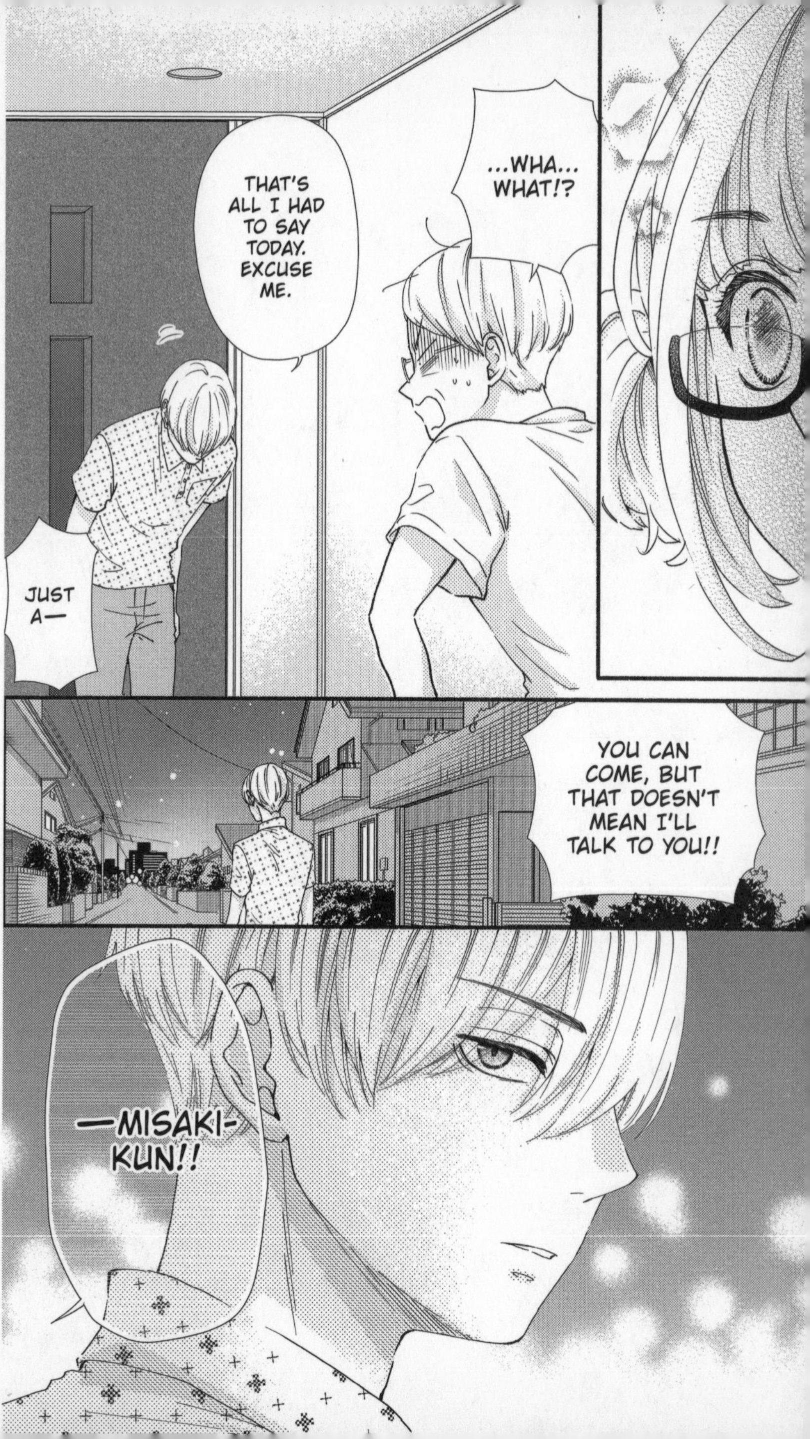
...WHA... WHAT!?
THAT'S ALL I HAD TO SAY TODAY. EXCUSE ME.
JUST A—
YOU CAN COME, BUT THAT DOESN'T MEAN I'LL TALK TO YOU!!
—MISAKI-KUN!!

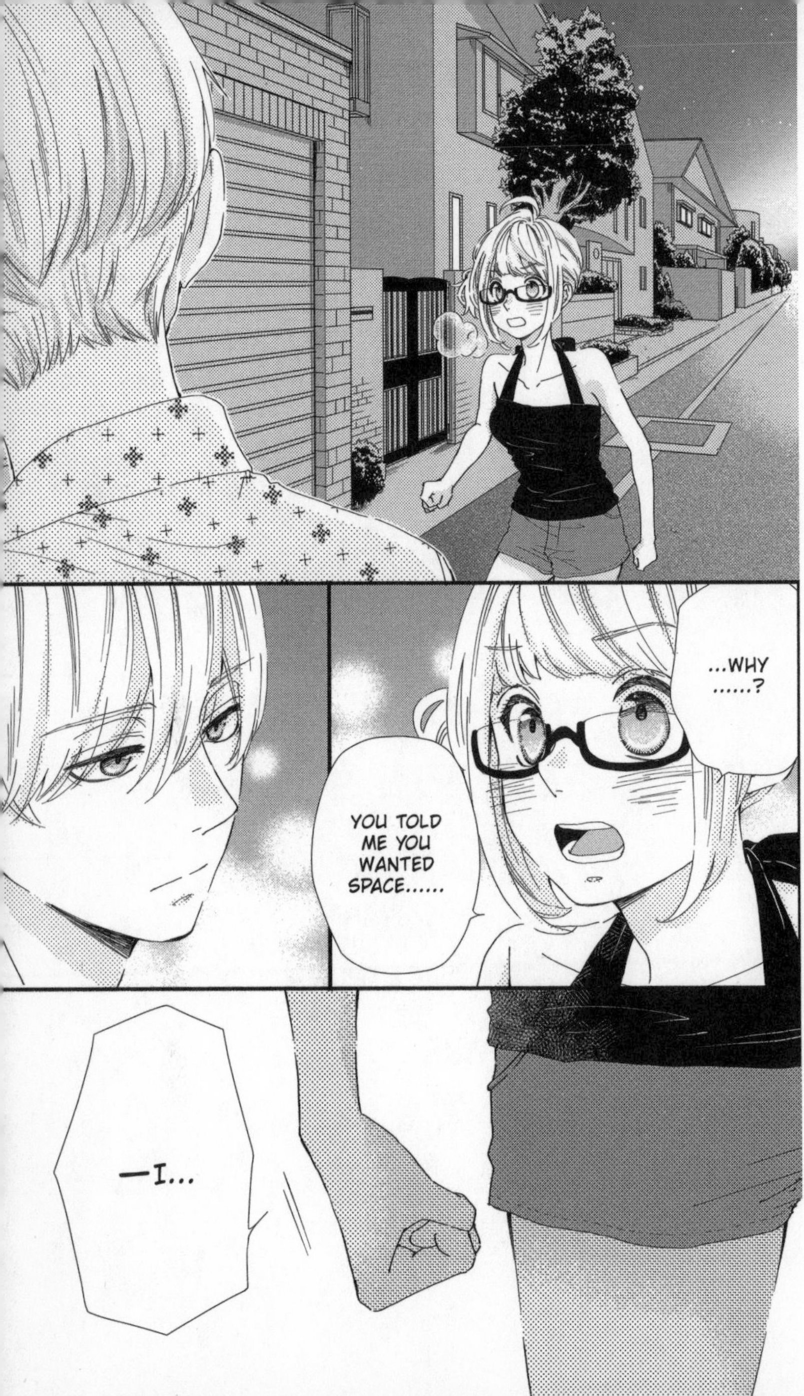
...WHY ......?
YOU TOLD ME YOU WANTED SPACE......
—I...

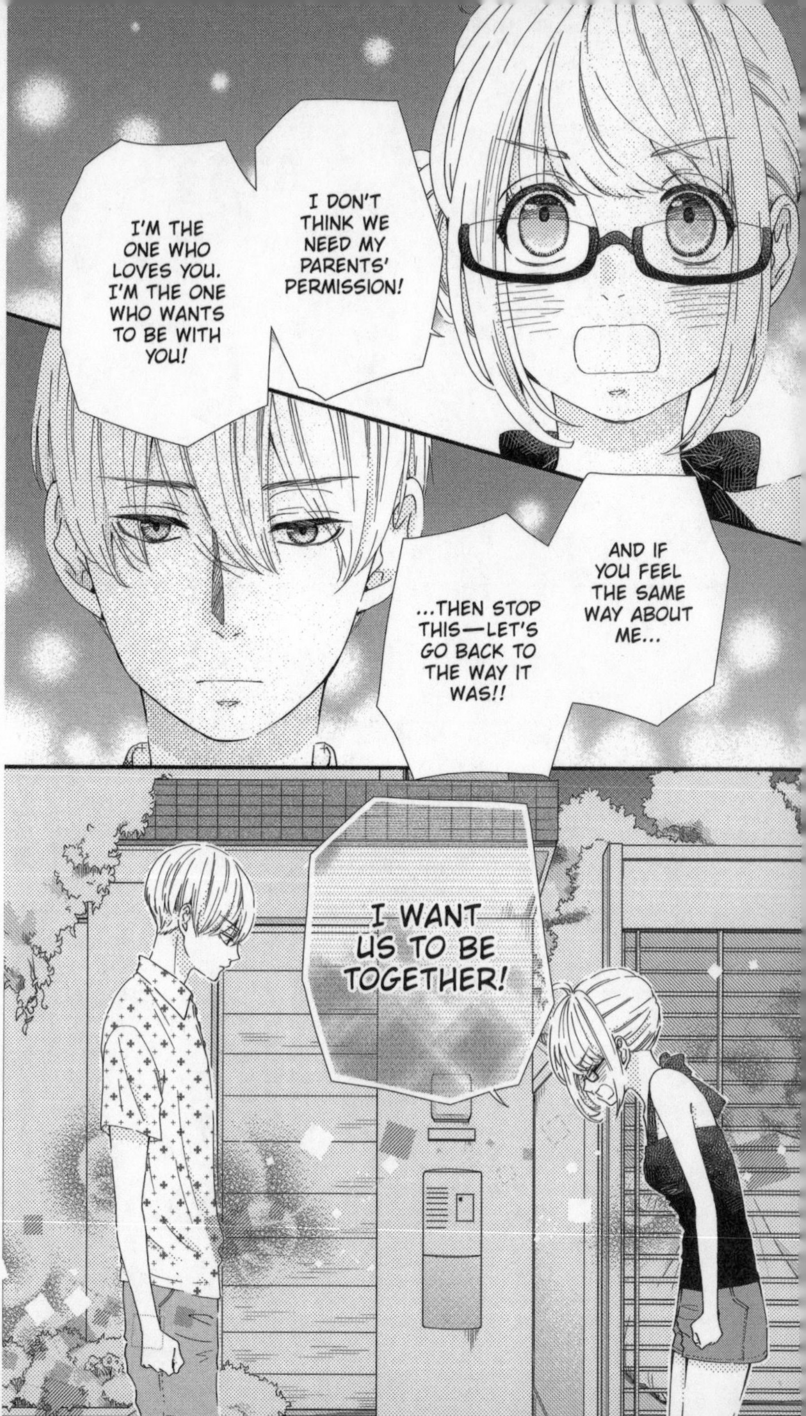
I DON'T THINK WE NEED MY PARENTS' PERMISSION!
I'M THE ONE WHO LOVES YOU. I'M THE ONE WHO WANTS TO BE WITH YOU!
AND IF YOU FEEL THE SAME WAY ABOUT ME...
...THEN STOP THIS—LET'S GO BACK TO THE WAY IT WAS!!
I WANT US TO BE TOGETHER!

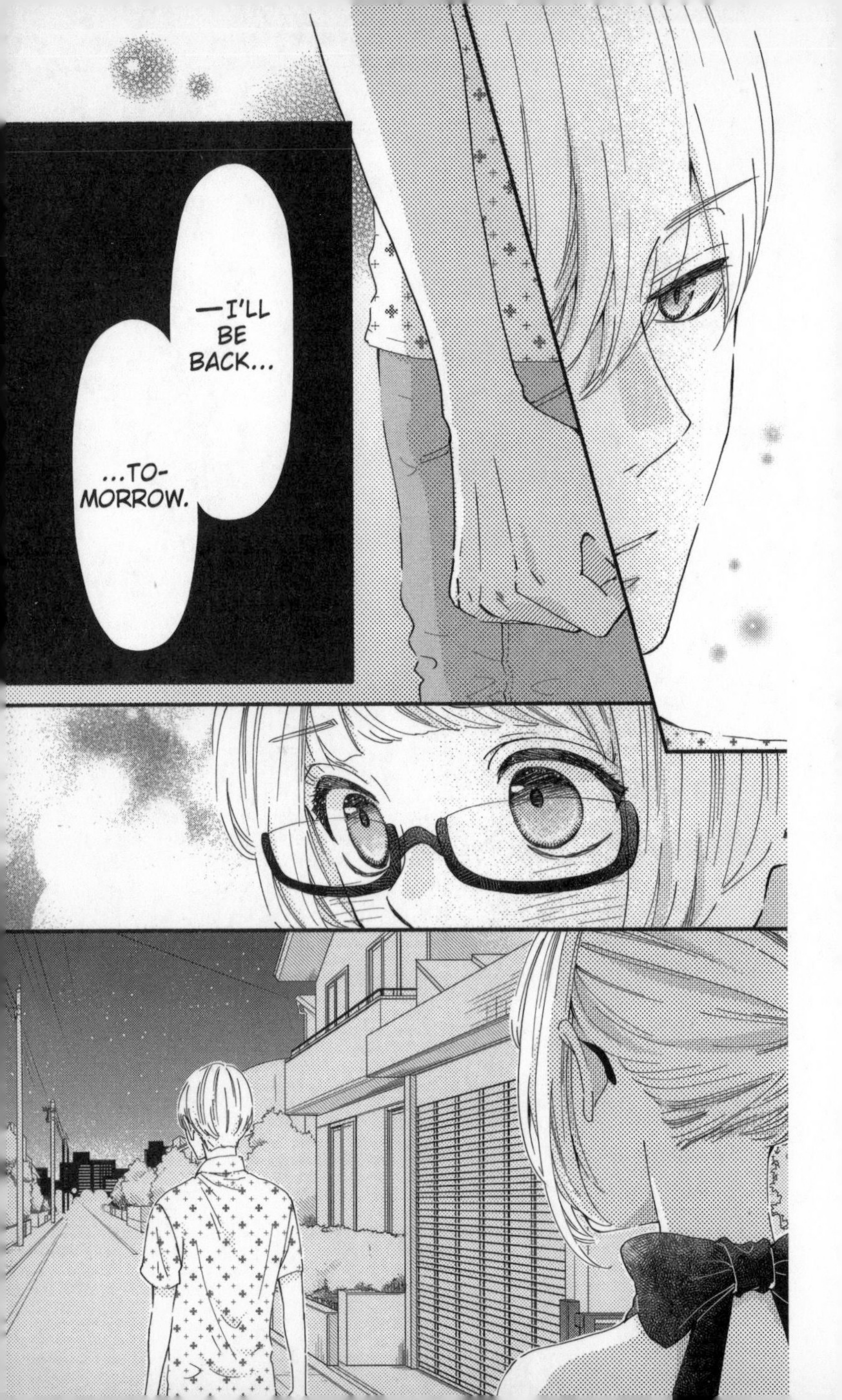
—I'LL BE BACK...
...TO-MORROW.

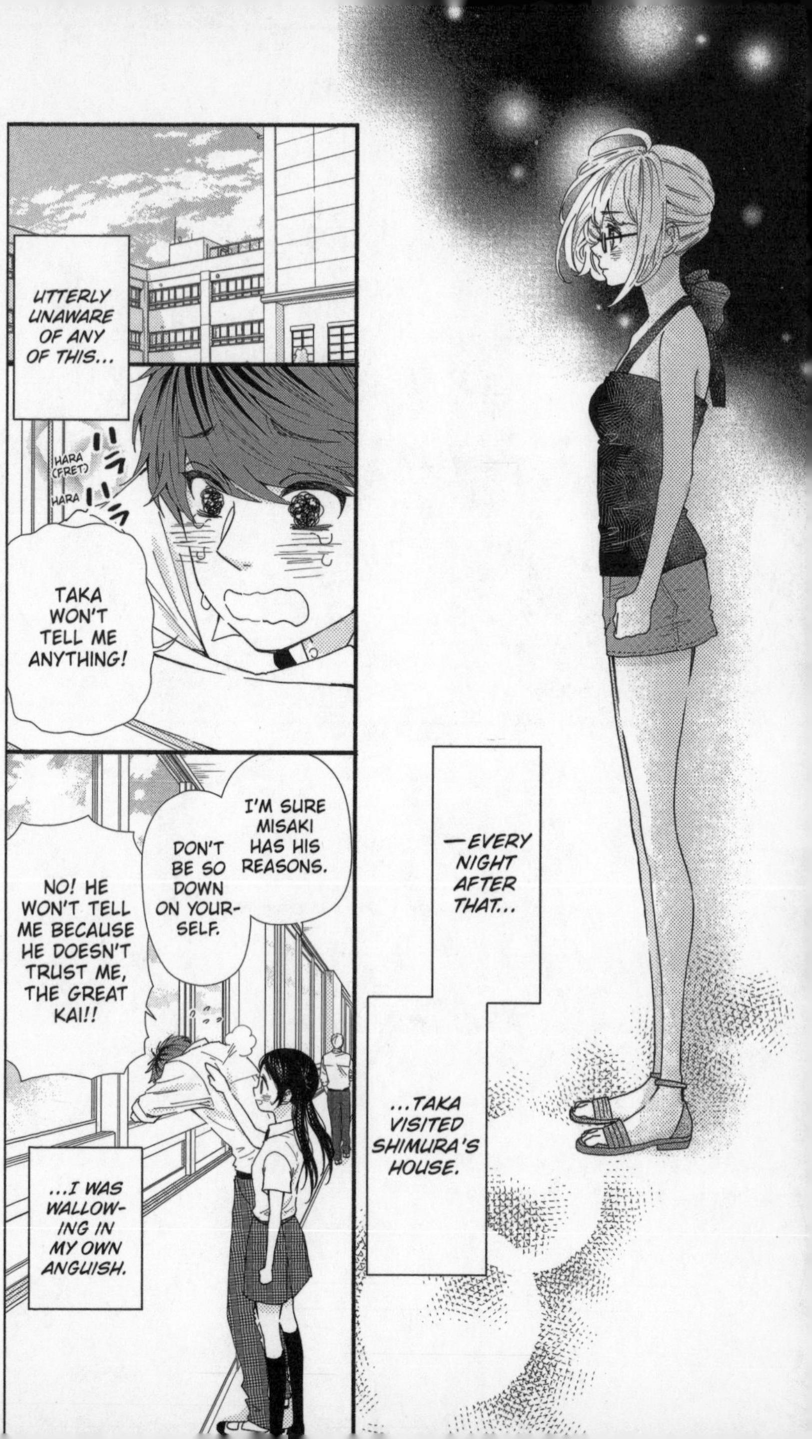
—EVERY NIGHT AFTER THAT...
...TAKA VISITED SHIMURA'S HOUSE.
UTTERLY UNAWARE OF ANY OF THIS...
HARA (FRET)
HARA
TAKA WON'T TELL ME ANYTHING!
I'M SURE MISAKI HAS HIS REASONS.
DON'T BE SO DOWN ON YOUR-SELF.
NO! HE WON'T TELL ME BECAUSE HE DOESN'T TRUST ME, THE GREAT KAI!!
...I WAS WALLOW-ING IN MY OWN ANGUISH.

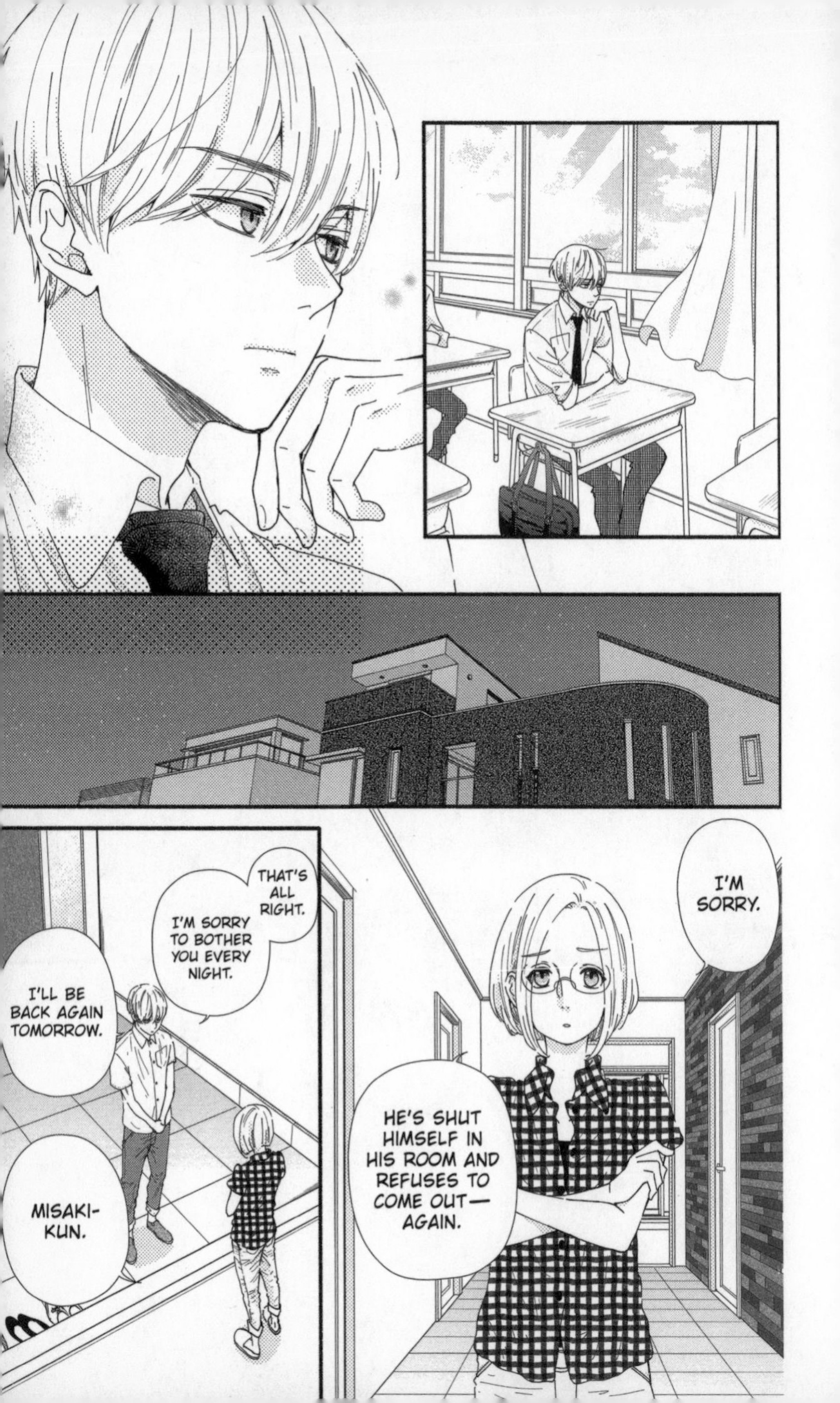
I'M SORRY.
HE'S SHUT HIMSELF IN HIS ROOM AND REFUSES TO COME OUT—AGAIN.
THAT'S ALL RIGHT.
I'M SORRY TO BOTHER YOU EVERY NIGHT.
I'LL BE BACK AGAIN TOMORROW.
MISAKI-KUN.

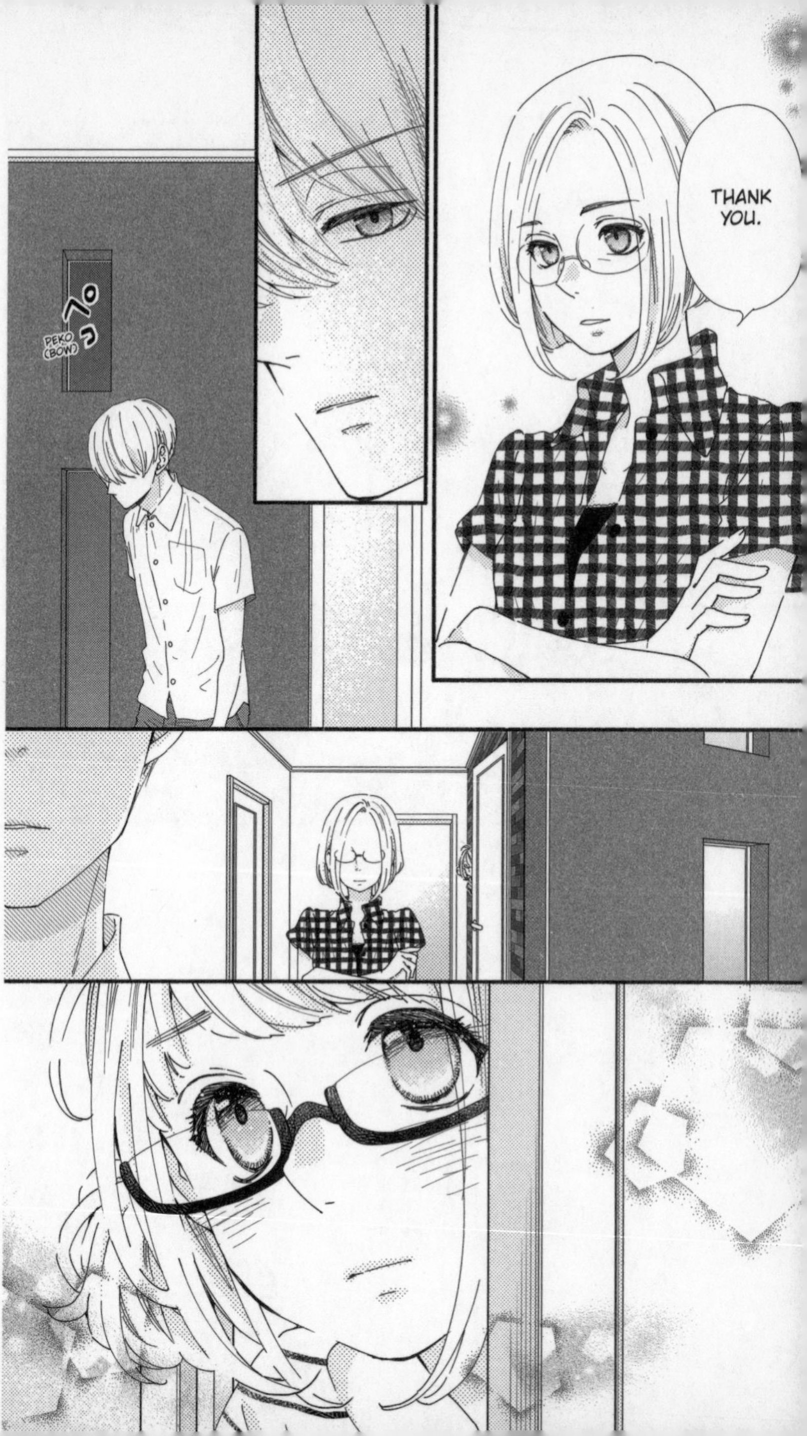
THANK YOU.
ペコ
PEKO (BOW)

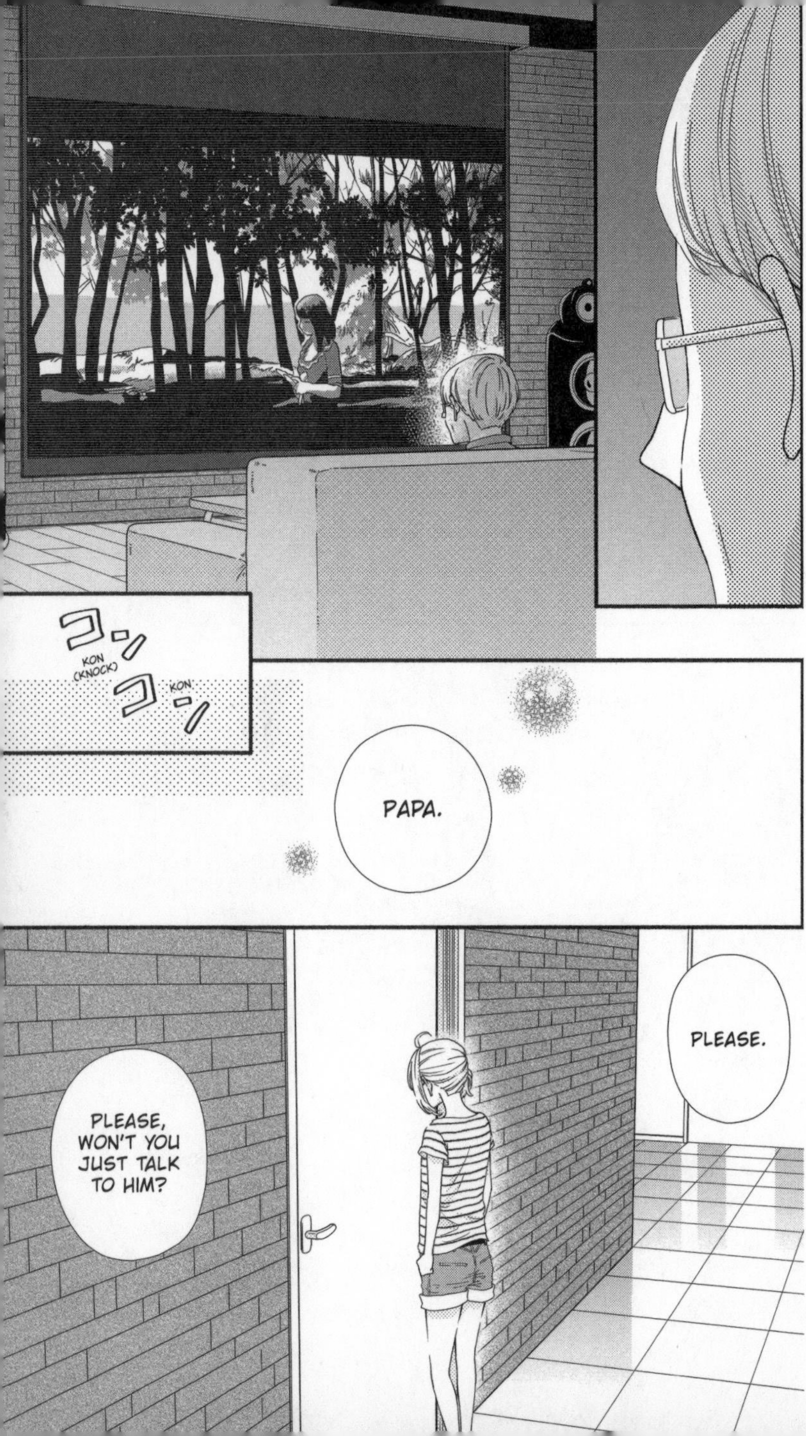
コンコン
KON (KNOCK)
KON
PAPA.
PLEASE.
PLEASE, WON'T YOU JUST TALK TO HIM?

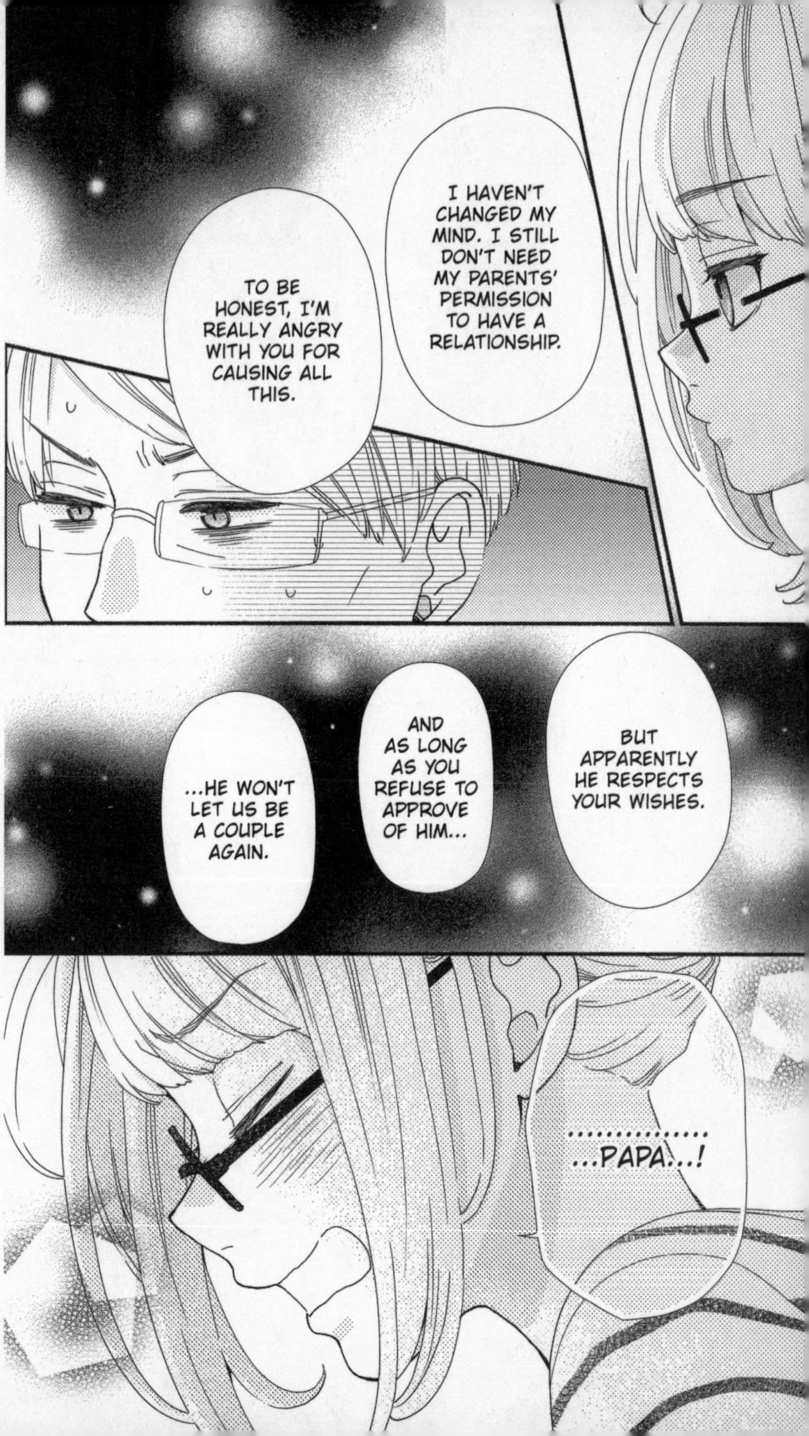
I HAVEN'T CHANGED MY MIND. I STILL DON'T NEED MY PARENTS' PERMISSION TO HAVE A RELATIONSHIP.
TO BE HONEST, I'M REALLY ANGRY WITH YOU FOR CAUSING ALL THIS.
BUT APPARENTLY HE RESPECTS YOUR WISHES.
AND AS LONG AS YOU REFUSE TO APPROVE OF HIM...
...HE WON'T LET US BE A COUPLE AGAIN.
....
...PAPA...!

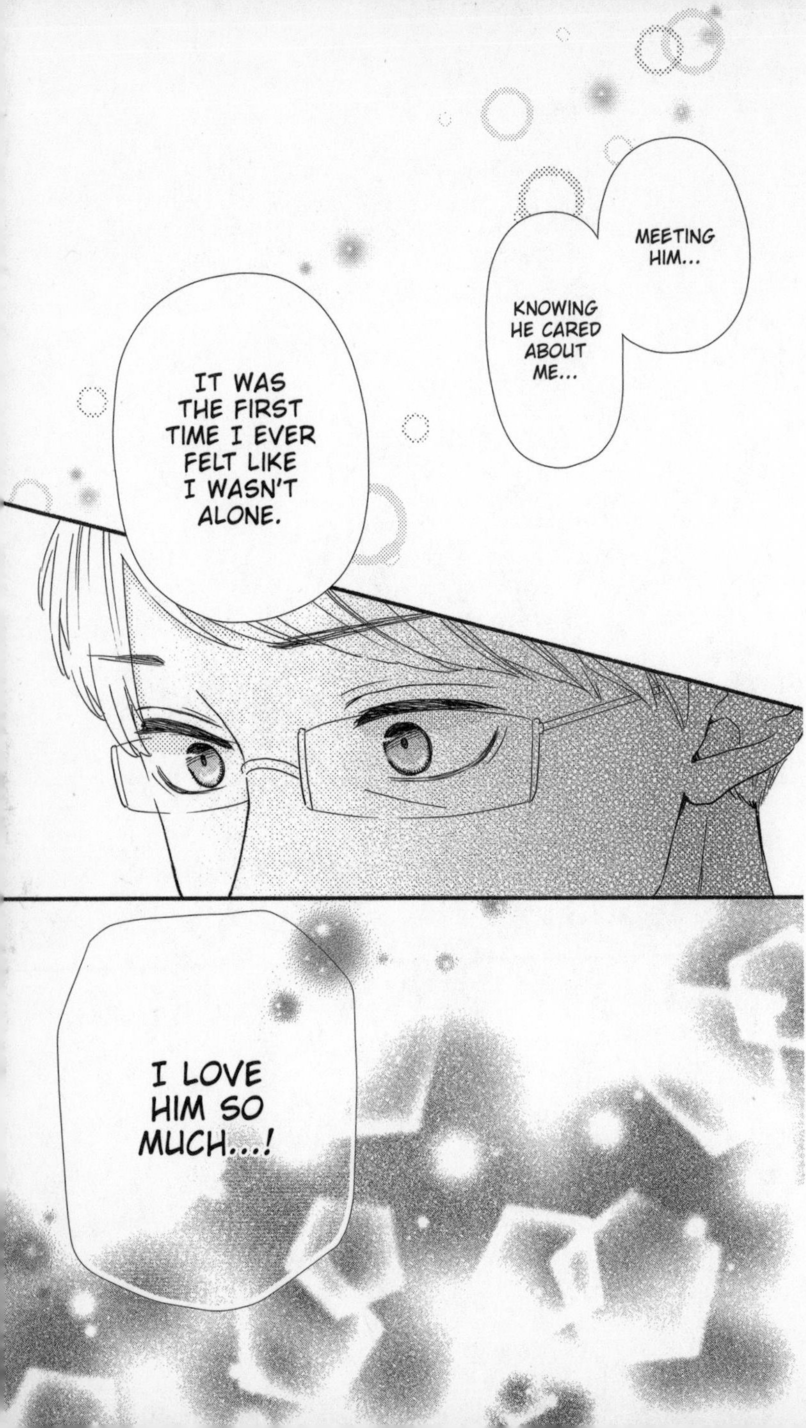
MEETING HIM...
KNOWING HE CARED ABOUT ME...
IT WAS THE FIRST TIME I EVER FELT LIKE I WASN'T ALONE.
I LOVE HIM SO MUCH...!

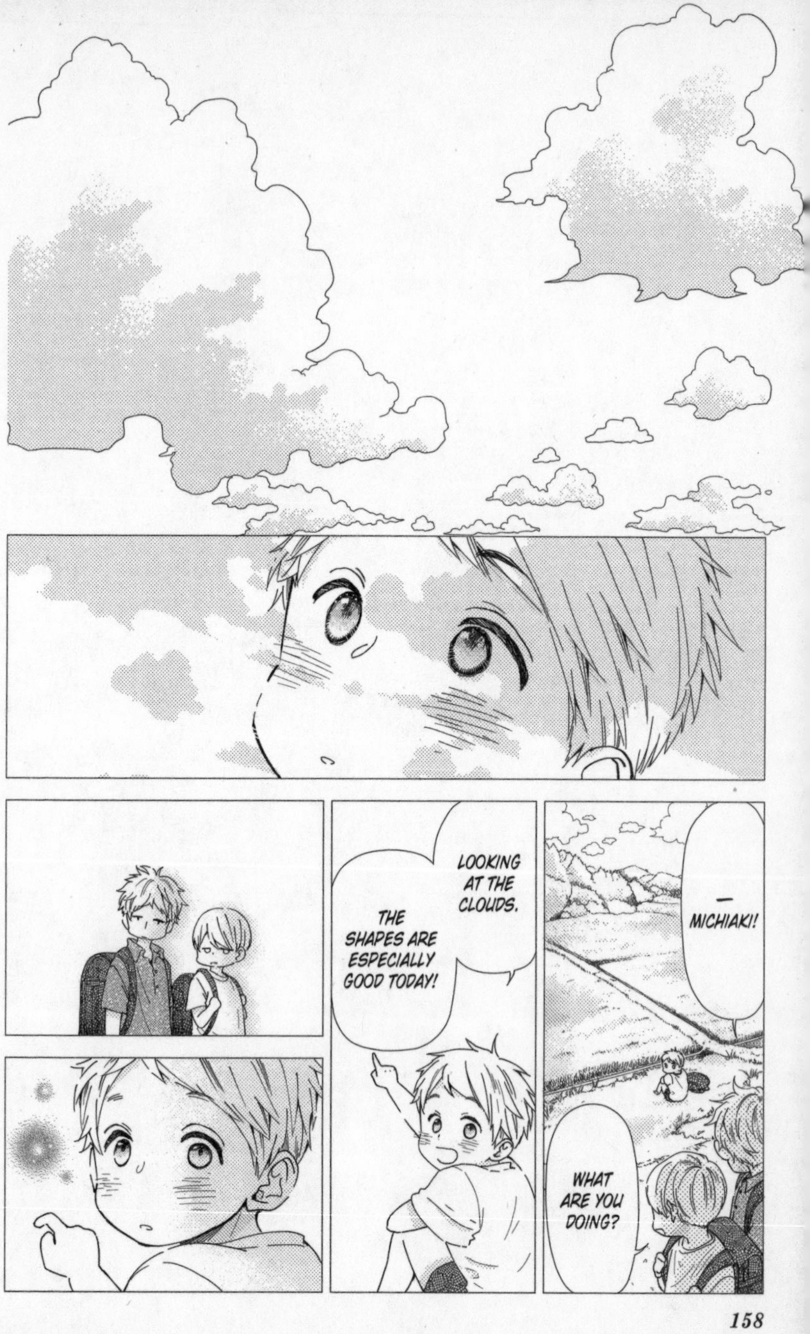
—MICHIAKI!
WHAT ARE YOU DOING?
LOOKING AT THE CLOUDS.
THE SHAPES ARE ESPECIALLY GOOD TODAY!

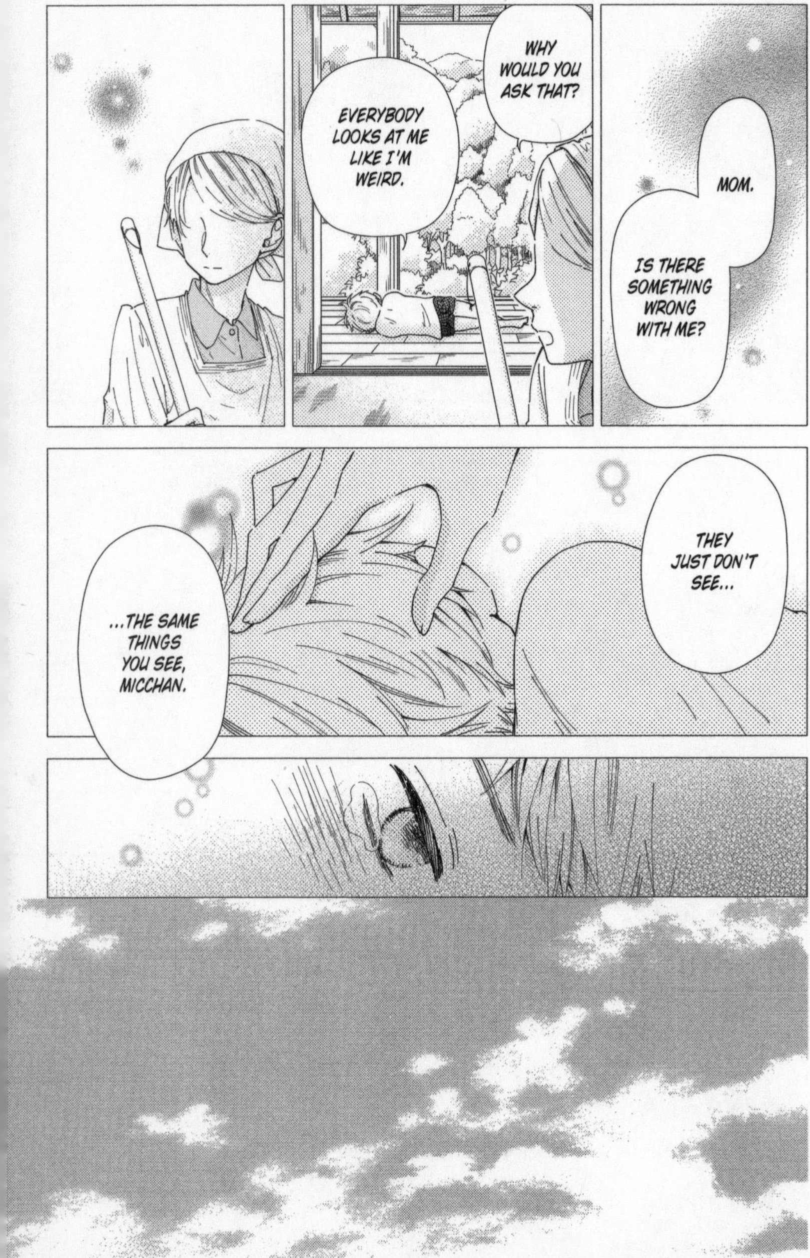
MOM.
IS THERE SOMETHING WRONG WITH ME?
WHY WOULD YOU ASK THAT?
EVERYBODY LOOKS AT ME LIKE I'M WEIRD.
THEY JUST DON'T SEE...
...THE SAME THINGS YOU SEE, MICCHAN.

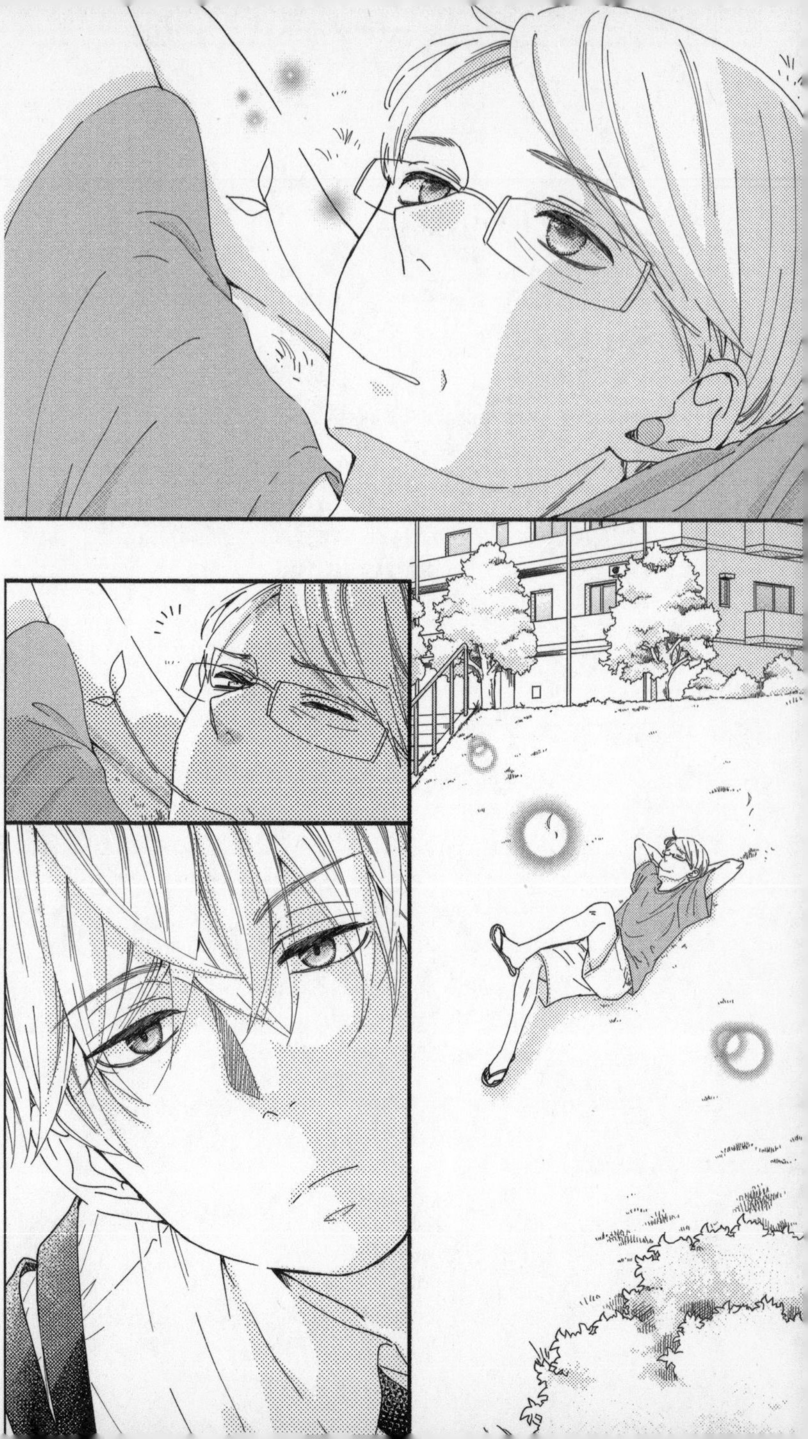

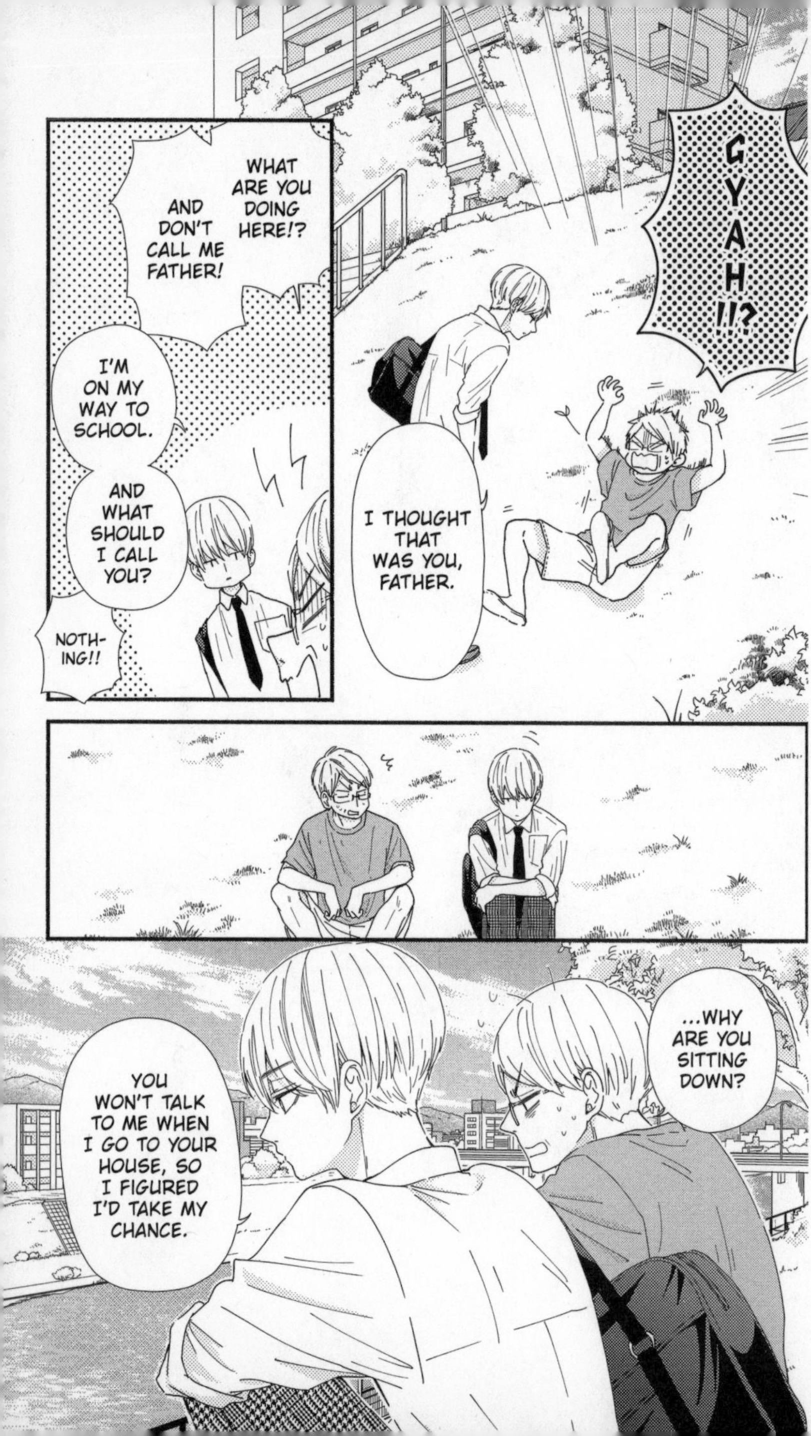
GYAH!!?
I THOUGHT THAT WAS YOU, FATHER.
WHAT ARE YOU DOING HERE!?
AND DON'T CALL ME FATHER!
I'M ON MY WAY TO SCHOOL.
AND WHAT SHOULD I CALL YOU?
NOTH-ING!!
...WHY ARE YOU SITTING DOWN?
YOU WON'T TALK TO ME WHEN I GO TO YOUR HOUSE, SO I FIGURED I'D TAKE MY CHANCE.

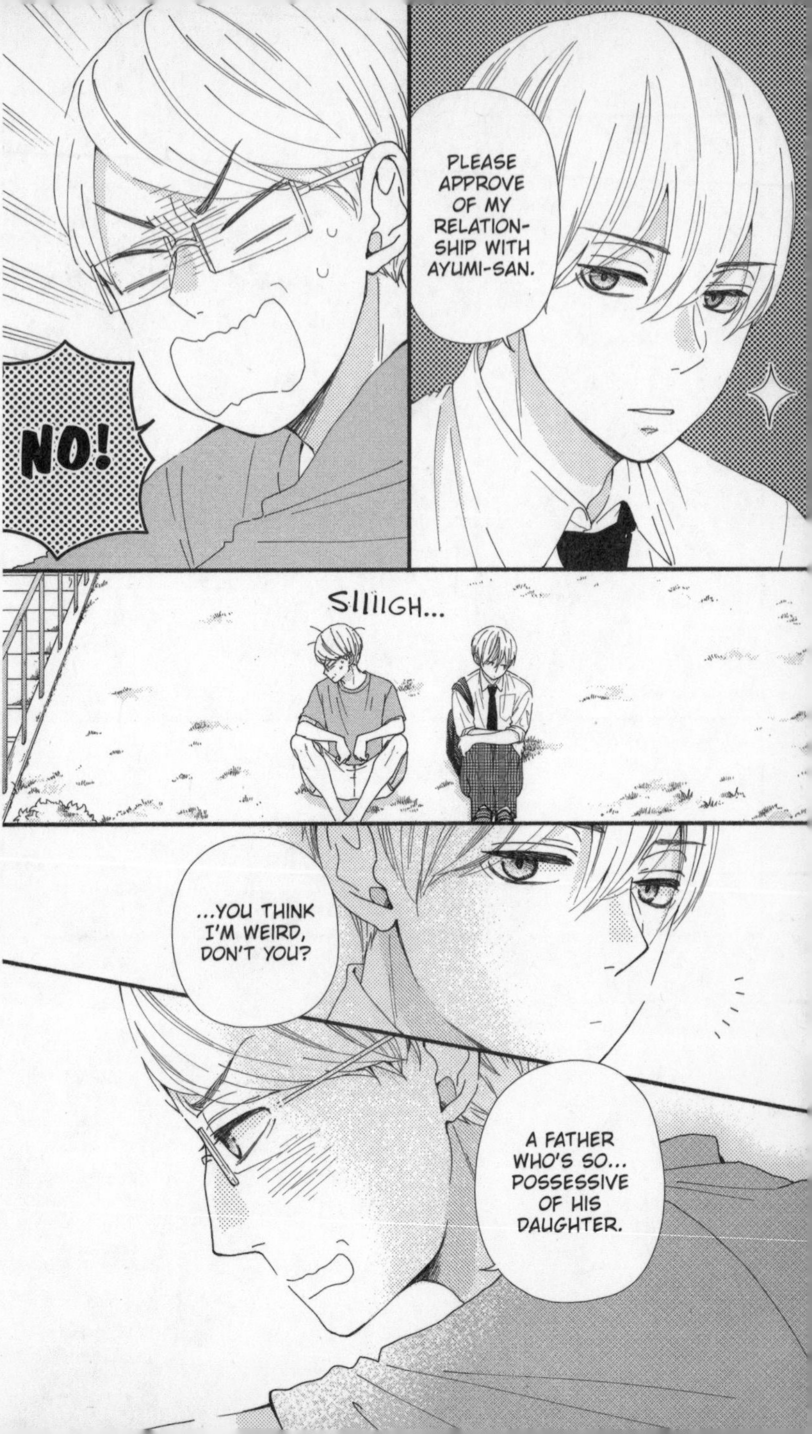
PLEASE APPROVE OF MY RELATION-SHIP WITH AYUMI-SAN.
NO!
SIIIGH...
...YOU THINK I'M WEIRD, DON'T YOU?
A FATHER WHO'S SO... POSSESSIVE OF HIS DAUGHTER.

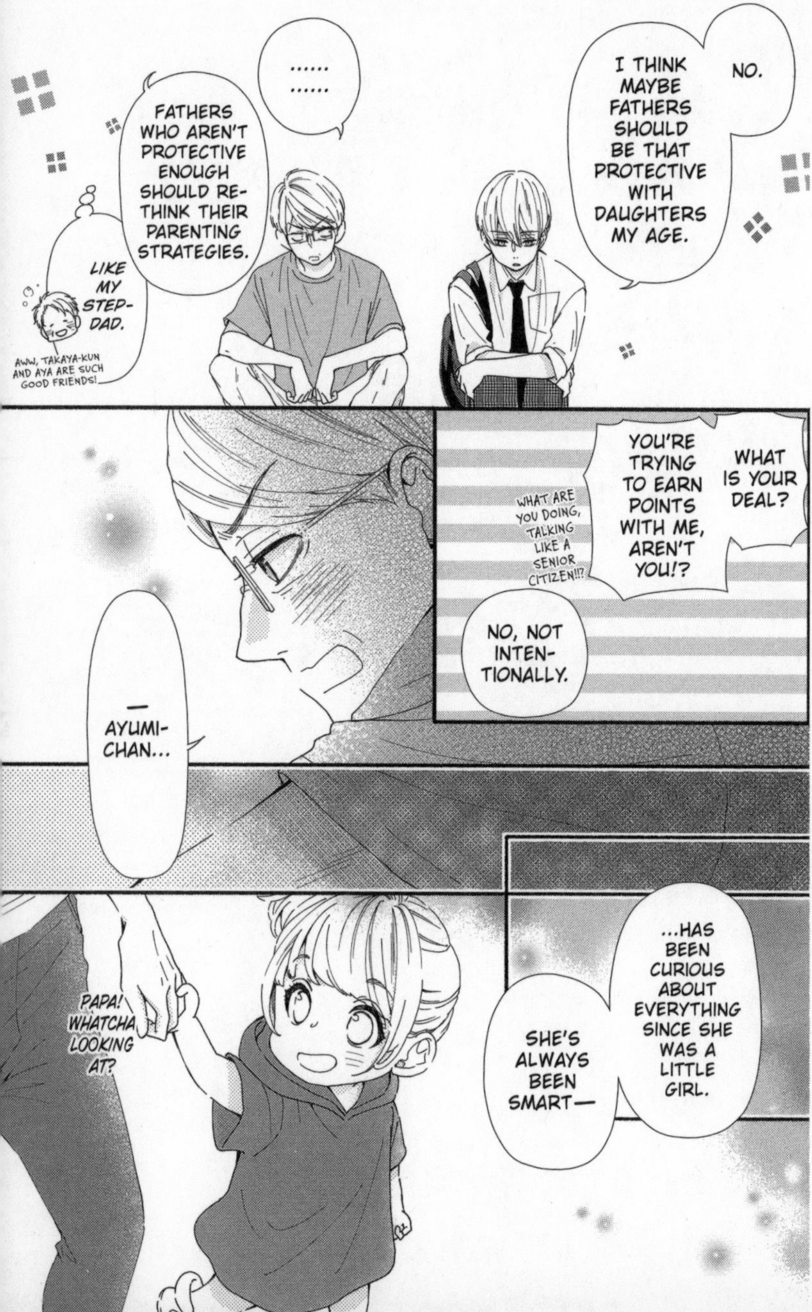
NO.
I THINK MAYBE FATHERS SHOULD BE THAT PROTECTIVE WITH DAUGHTERS MY AGE.
......
......
FATHERS WHO AREN'T PROTECTIVE ENOUGH SHOULD RE-THINK THEIR PARENTING STRATEGIES.
LIKE MY STEP-DAD.
AWW, TAKAYA-KUN AND AYA ARE SUCH GOOD FRIENDS!
WHAT IS YOUR DEAL?
YOU'RE TRYING TO EARN POINTS WITH ME, AREN'T YOU!?
WHAT ARE YOU DOING, TALKING LIKE A SENIOR CITIZEN!!?
NO, NOT INTENTIONALLY.
—AYUMI-CHAN...
...HAS BEEN CURIOUS ABOUT EVERYTHING SINCE SHE WAS A LITTLE GIRL.
SHE'S ALWAYS BEEN SMART—
PAPA! WHATCHA LOOKING AT?

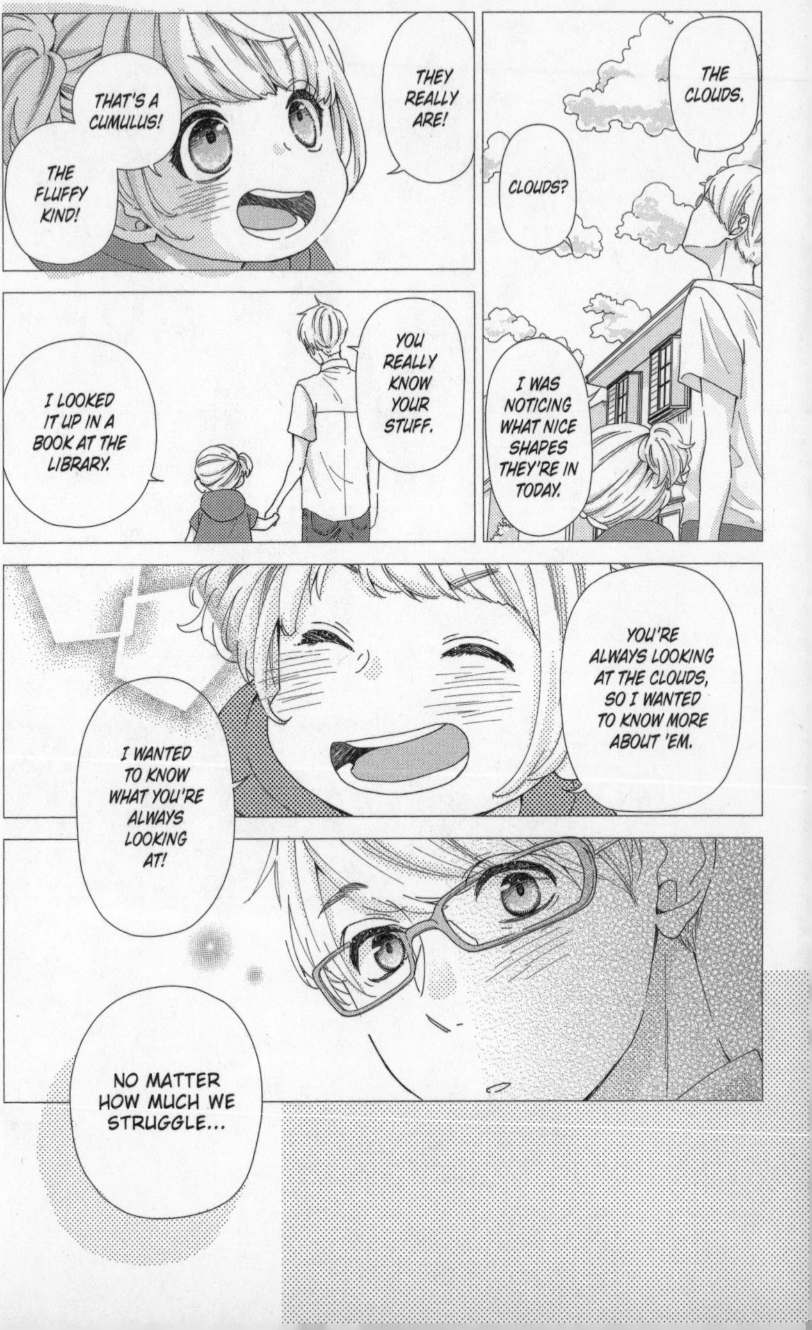
THE CLOUDS.
CLOUDS?
I WAS NOTICING WHAT NICE SHAPES THEY'RE IN TODAY.
THEY REALLY ARE!
THAT'S A CUMULUS!
THE FLUFFY KIND!
YOU REALLY KNOW YOUR STUFF.
I LOOKED IT UP IN A BOOK AT THE LIBRARY.
YOU'RE ALWAYS LOOKING AT THE CLOUDS, SO I WANTED TO KNOW MORE ABOUT 'EM.
I WANTED TO KNOW WHAT YOU'RE ALWAYS LOOKING AT!
NO MATTER HOW MUCH WE STRUGGLE...

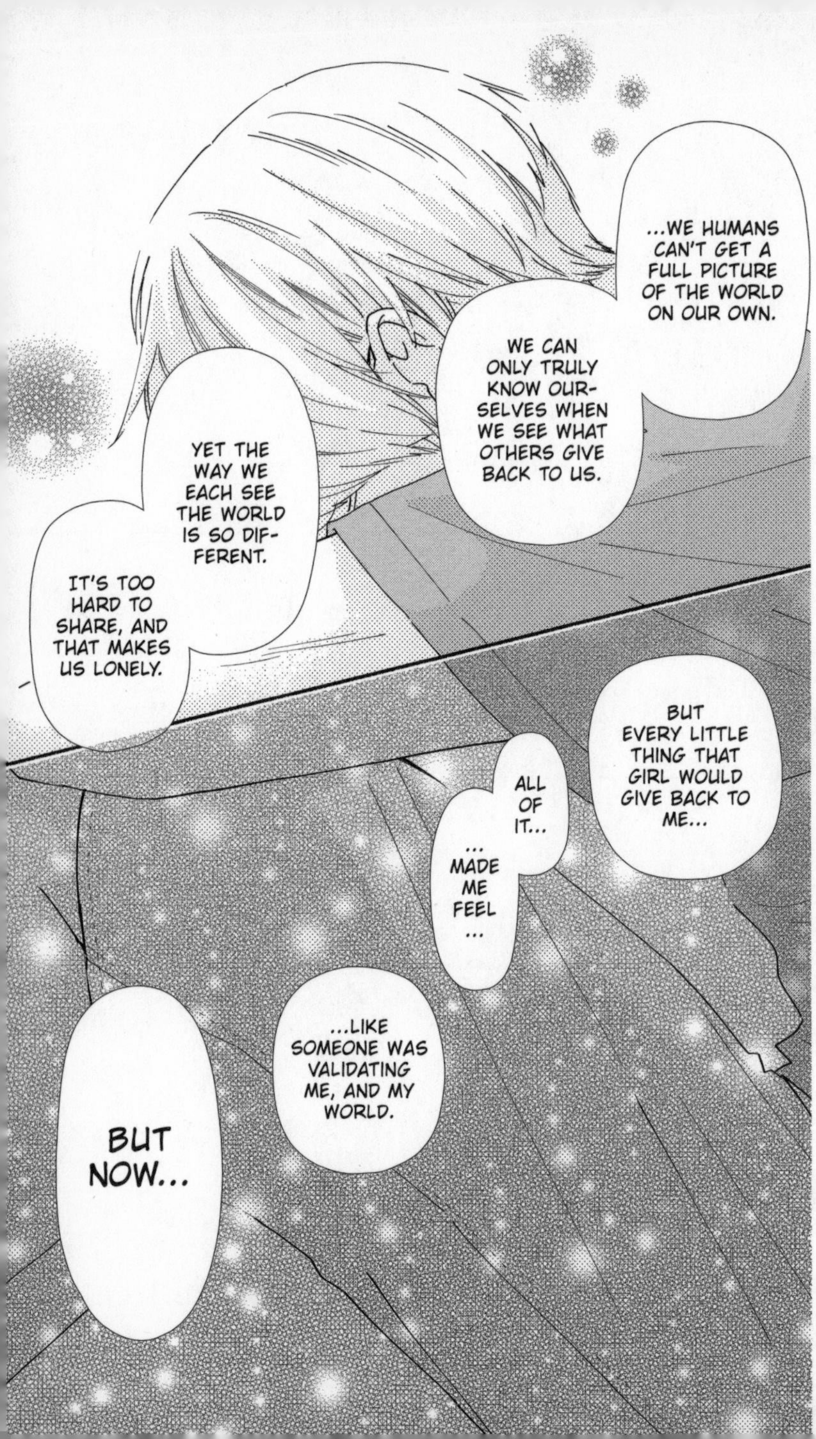
...WE HUMANS CAN'T GET A FULL PICTURE OF THE WORLD ON OUR OWN.
WE CAN ONLY TRULY KNOW OUR-SELVES WHEN WE SEE WHAT OTHERS GIVE BACK TO US.
YET THE WAY WE EACH SEE THE WORLD IS SO DIF-FERENT.
IT'S TOO HARD TO SHARE, AND THAT MAKES US LONELY.
BUT EVERY LITTLE THING THAT GIRL WOULD GIVE BACK TO ME...
ALL OF IT...
...MADE ME FEEL...
...LIKE SOMEONE WAS VALIDATING ME, AND MY WORLD.
BUT NOW...

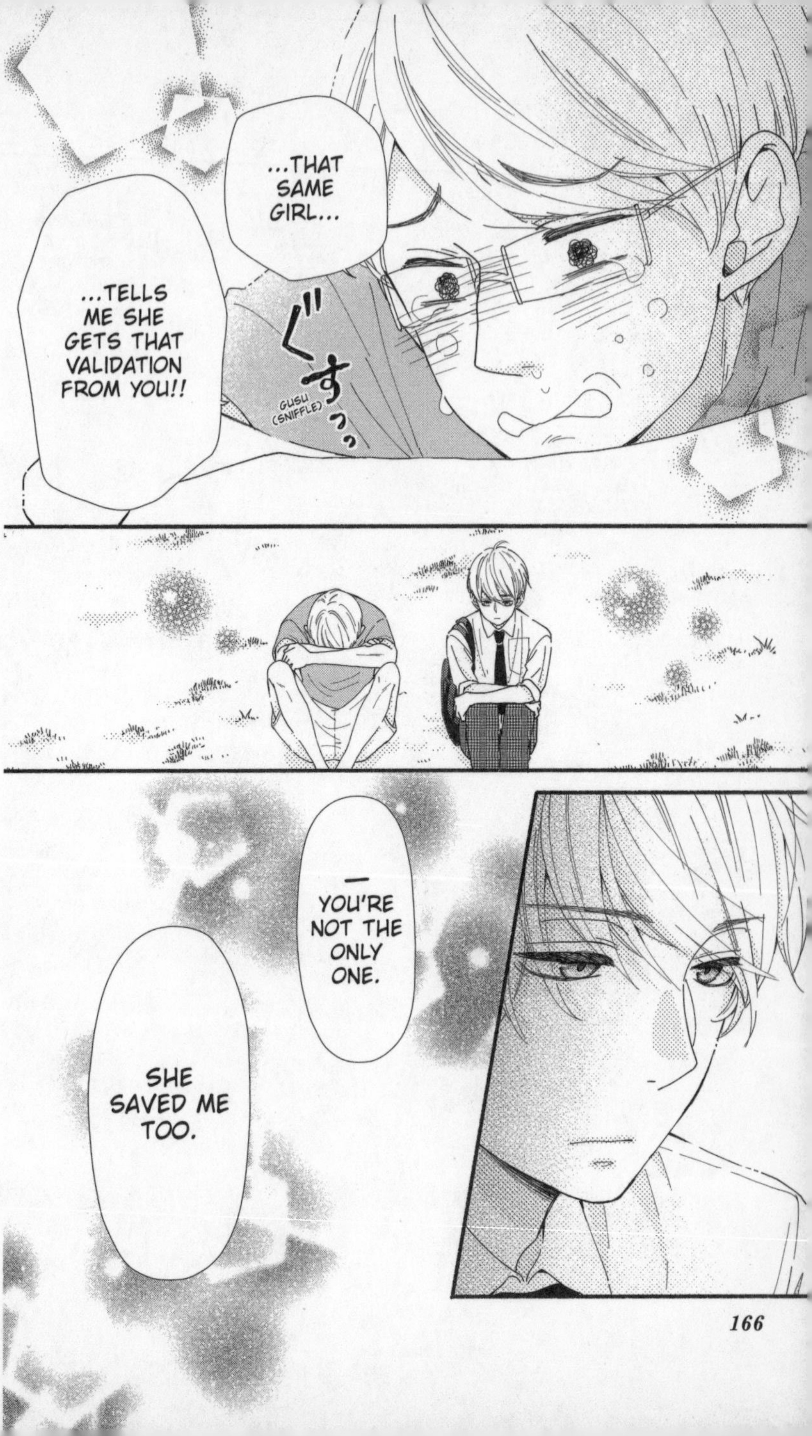
...THAT SAME GIRL...
...TELLS ME SHE GETS THAT VALIDATION FROM YOU!!
ぐすっ
GUSU (SNIFFLE)
— YOU'RE NOT THE ONLY ONE.
SHE SAVED ME TOO.

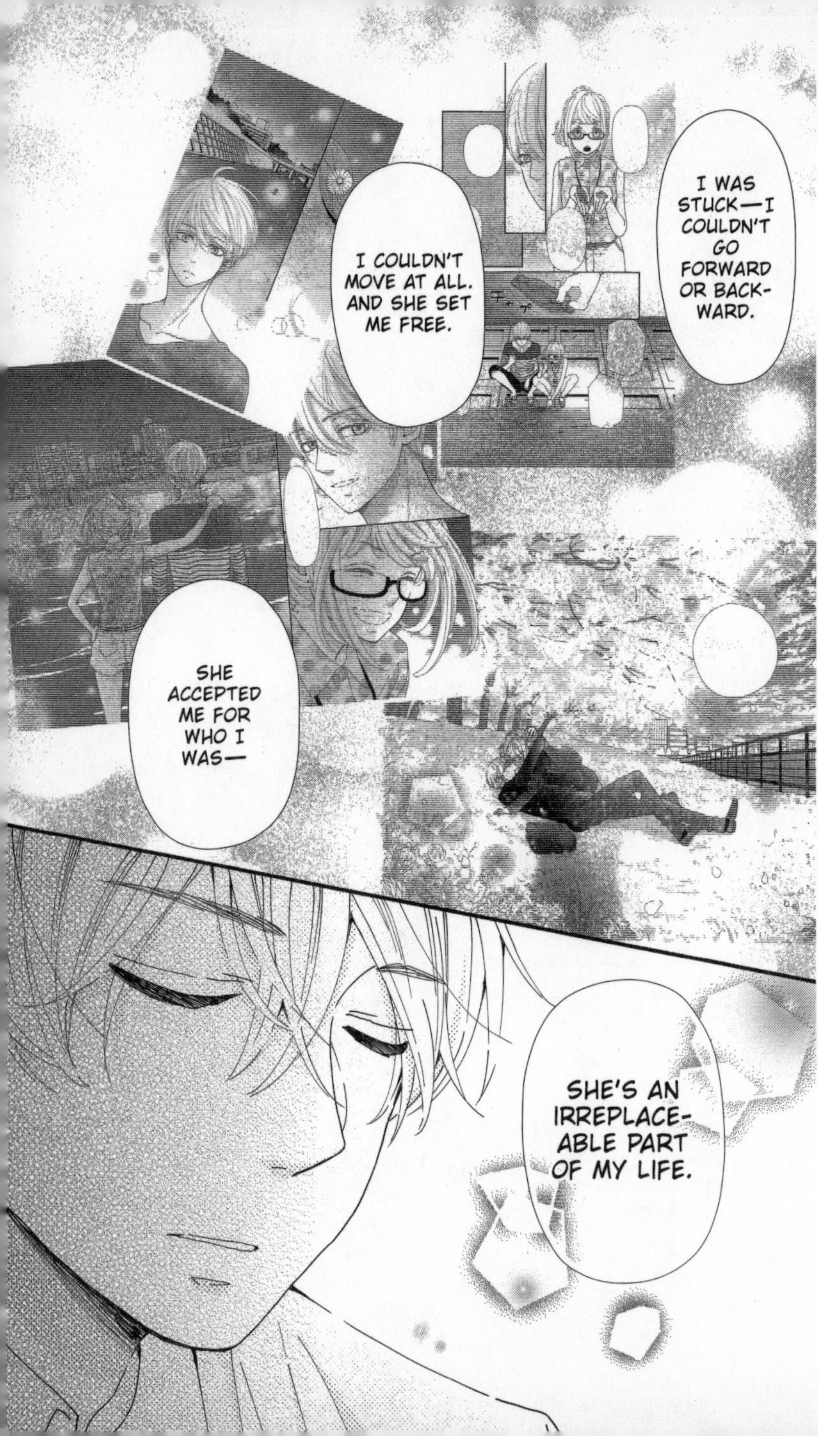
I WAS STUCK—I COULDN'T GO FORWARD OR BACK-WARD.
I COULDN'T MOVE AT ALL. AND SHE SET ME FREE.
SHE ACCEPTED ME FOR WHO I WAS—
SHE'S AN IRREPLACE-ABLE PART OF MY LIFE.

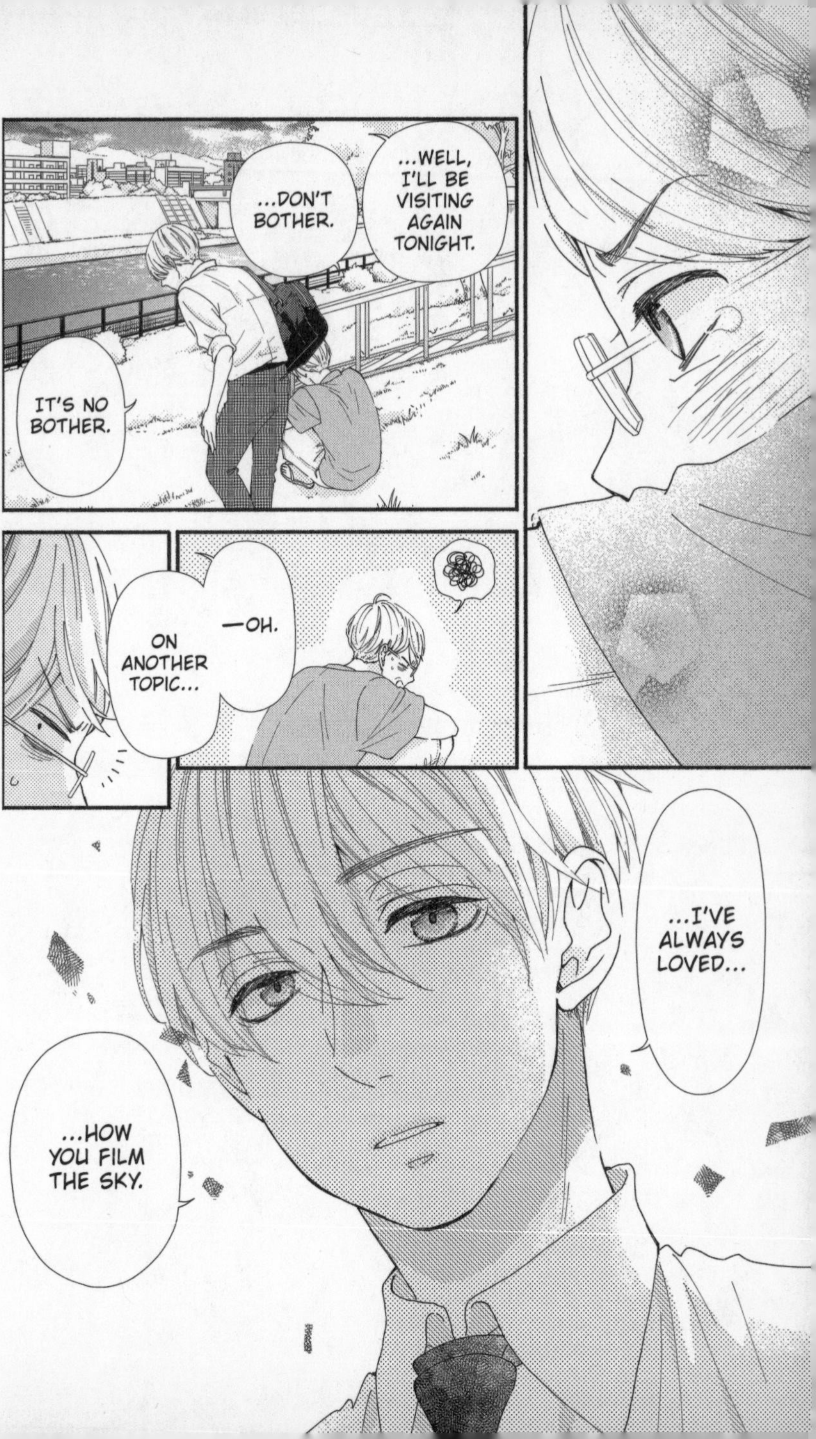
...WELL, I'LL BE VISITING AGAIN TONIGHT.
...DON'T BOTHER.
IT'S NO BOTHER.
—OH.
ON ANOTHER TOPIC...
...I'VE ALWAYS LOVED...
...HOW YOU FILM THE SKY.

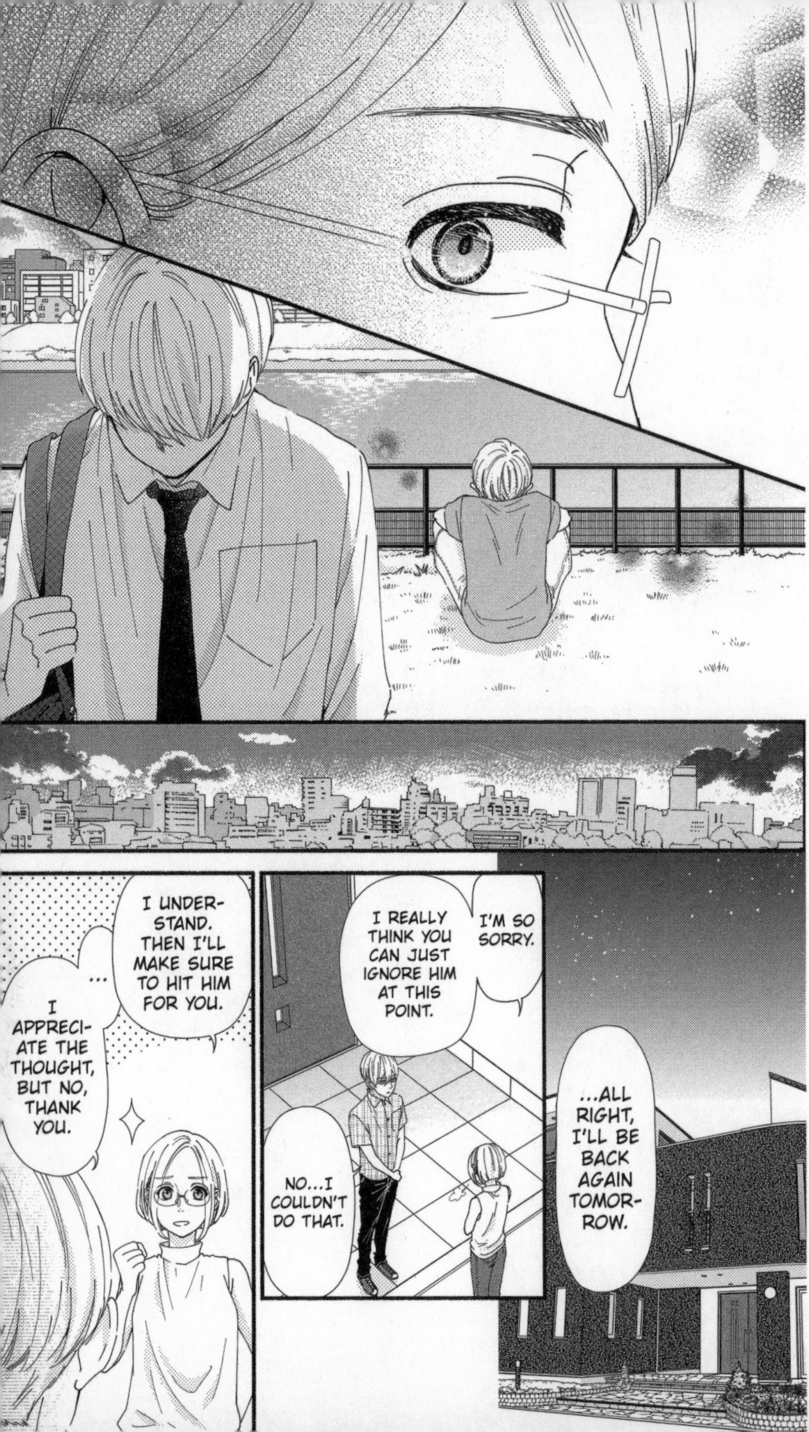
...ALL RIGHT, I'LL BE BACK AGAIN TOMORROW.
I'M SO SORRY.
I REALLY THINK YOU CAN JUST IGNORE HIM AT THIS POINT.
NO...I COULDN'T DO THAT.
I UNDERSTAND. THEN I'LL MAKE SURE TO HIT HIM FOR YOU.
...
I APPRECIATE THE THOUGHT, BUT NO, THANK YOU.

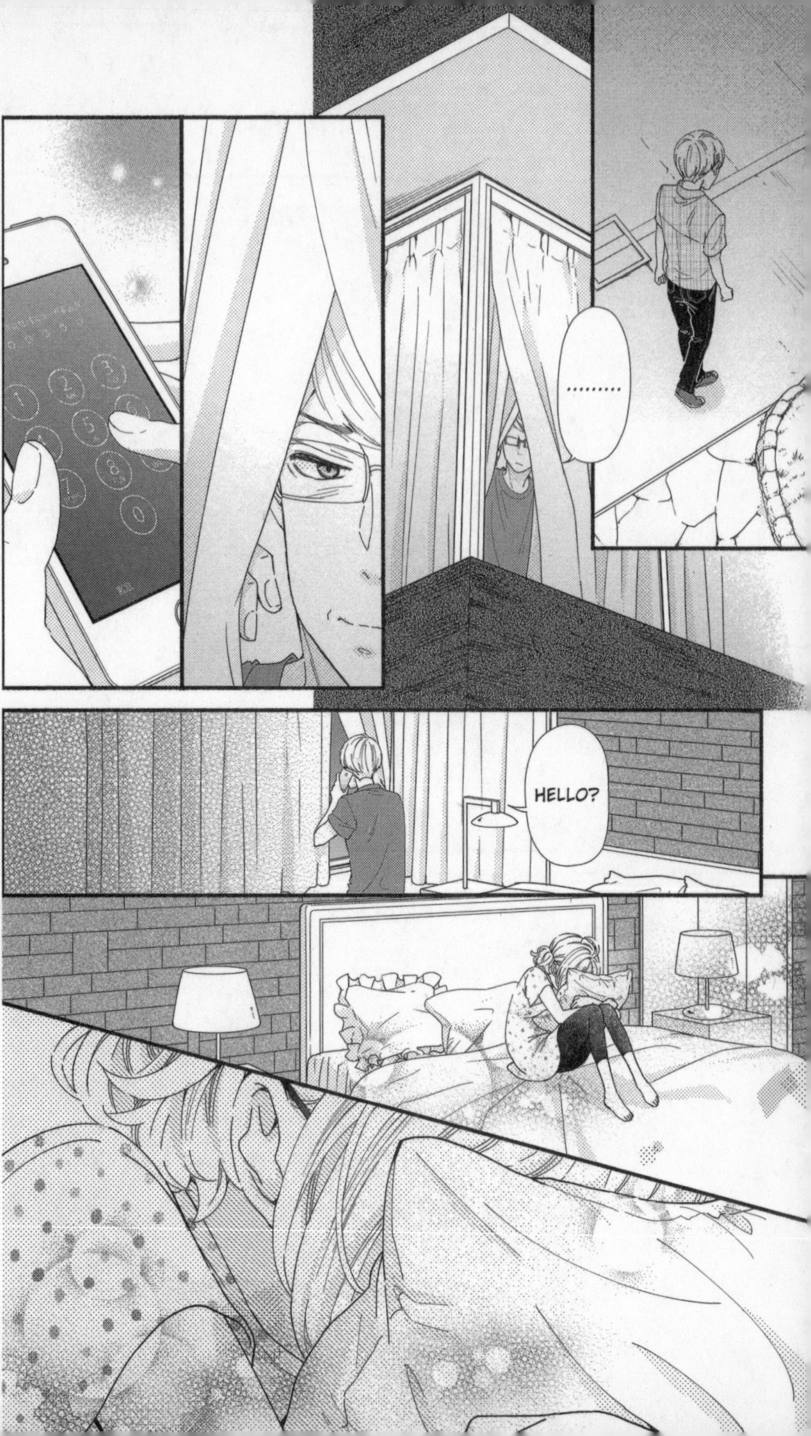
....
HELLO?

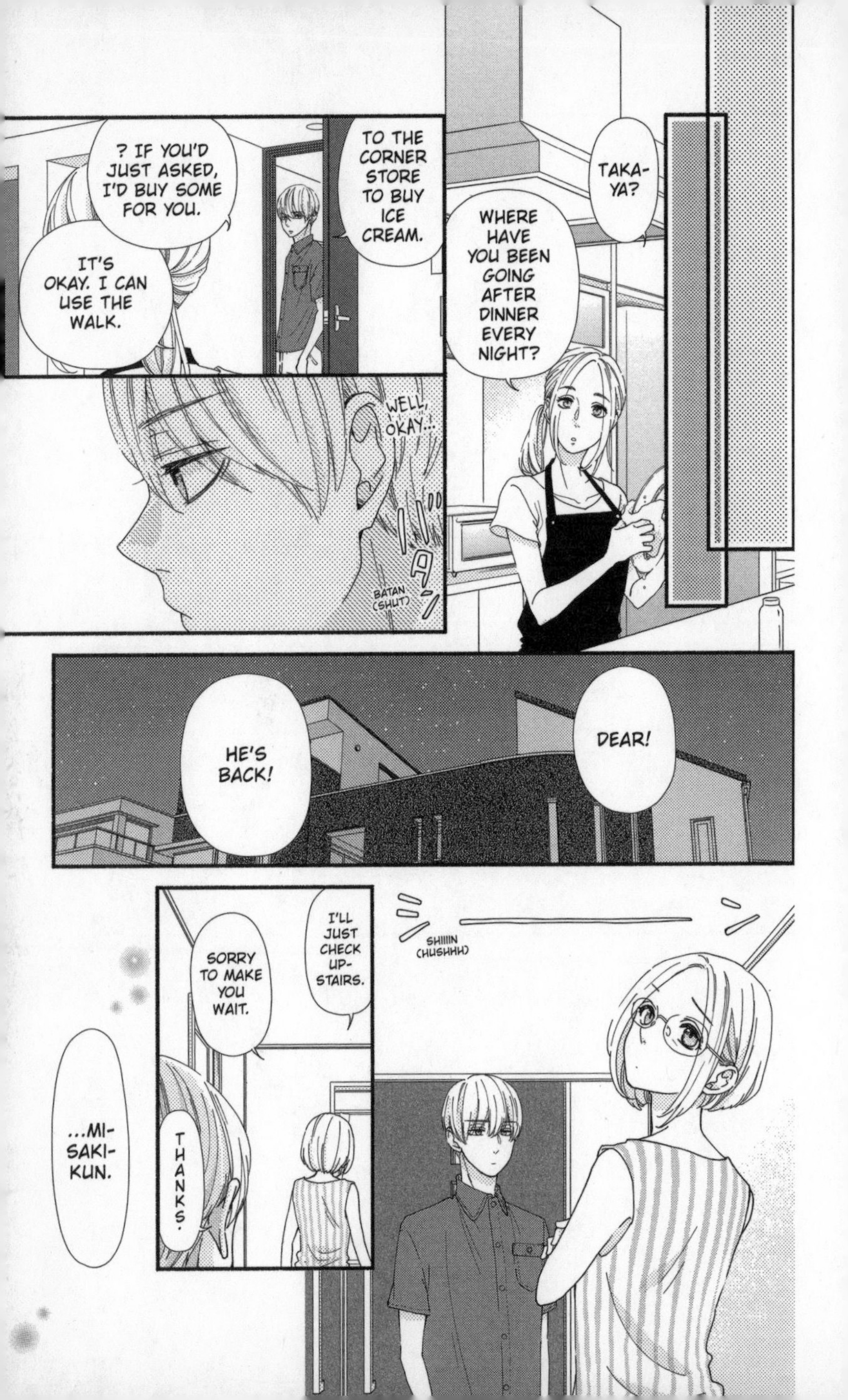
TAKA-YA?
WHERE HAVE YOU BEEN GOING AFTER DINNER EVERY NIGHT?
TO THE CORNER STORE TO BUY ICE CREAM.
? IF YOU'D JUST ASKED, I'D BUY SOME FOR YOU.
IT'S OKAY. I CAN USE THE WALK.
WELL, OKAY...
BATAN (SHUT)
DEAR!
HE'S BACK!
SHIIIN (HUSHHH)
I'LL JUST CHECK UP-STAIRS.
SORRY TO MAKE YOU WAIT.
THANKS.
...MI-SAKI-KUN.

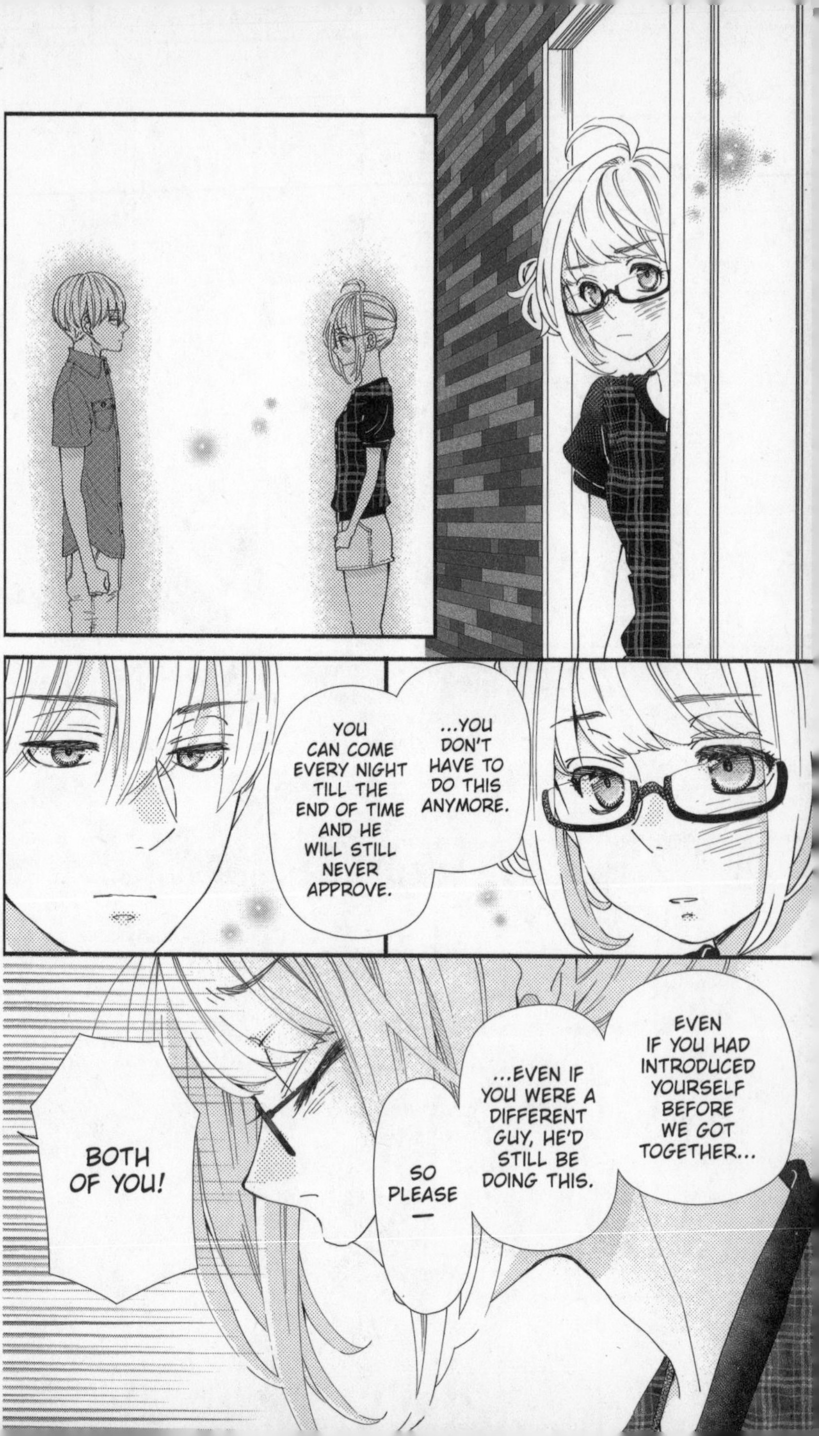
...YOU DON'T HAVE TO DO THIS ANYMORE.
YOU CAN COME EVERY NIGHT TILL THE END OF TIME AND HE WILL STILL NEVER APPROVE.
EVEN IF YOU HAD INTRODUCED YOURSELF BEFORE WE GOT TOGETHER...
...EVEN IF YOU WERE A DIFFERENT GUY, HE'D STILL BE DOING THIS.
SO PLEASE —
BOTH OF YOU!

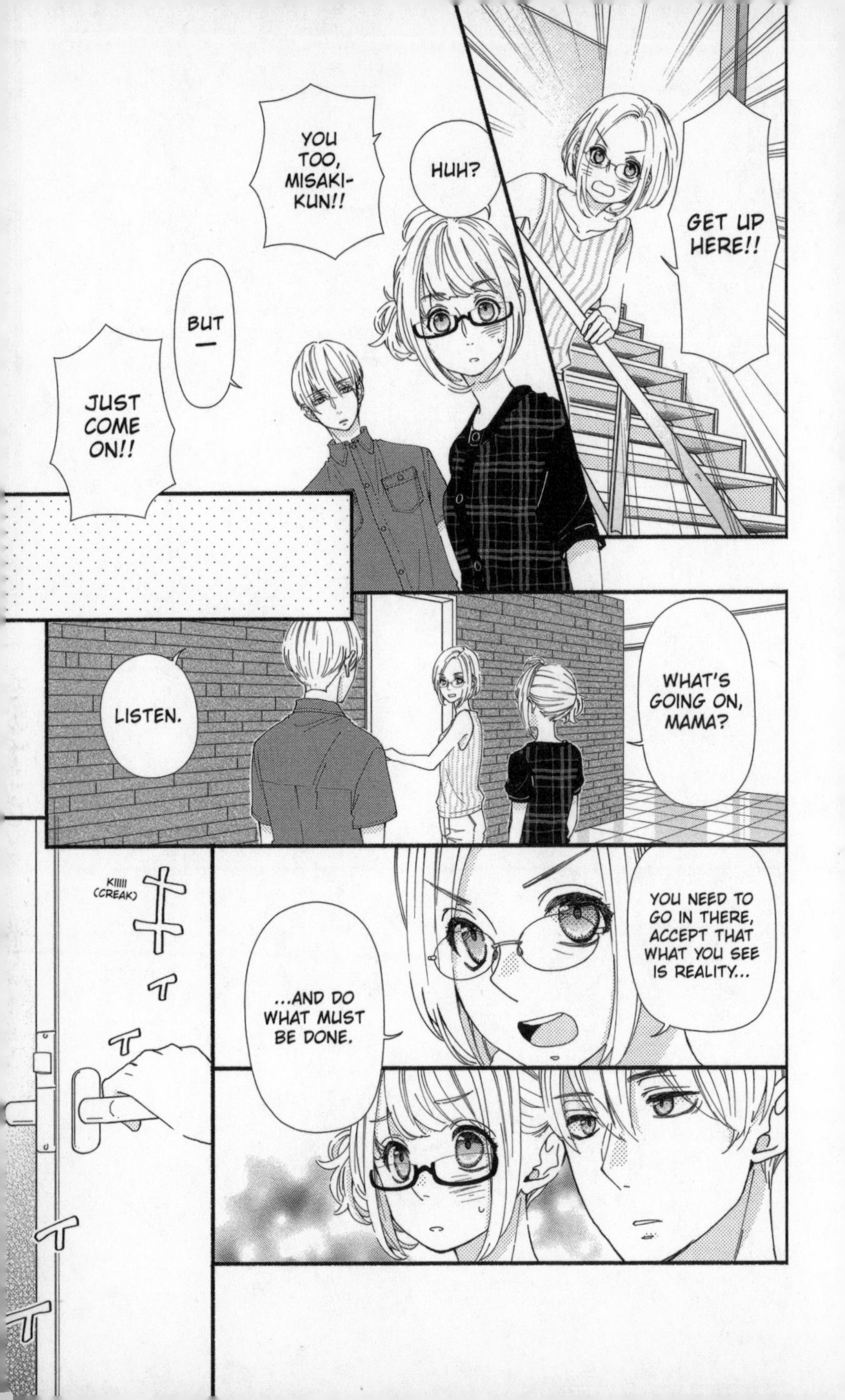
GET UP HERE!!
HUH?
YOU TOO, MISAKI-KUN!!
BUT—
JUST COME ON!!
WHAT'S GOING ON, MAMA?
LISTEN.
YOU NEED TO GO IN THERE, ACCEPT THAT WHAT YOU SEE IS REALITY...
...AND DO WHAT MUST BE DONE.
KIIIII (CREAK)

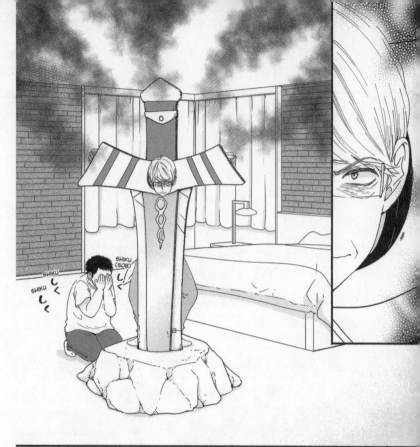

SHIKU
(SOB)
SHIKU
SHIKU

—YOU HAVE DONE WELL TO COME HERE, YOUNG MAN ......

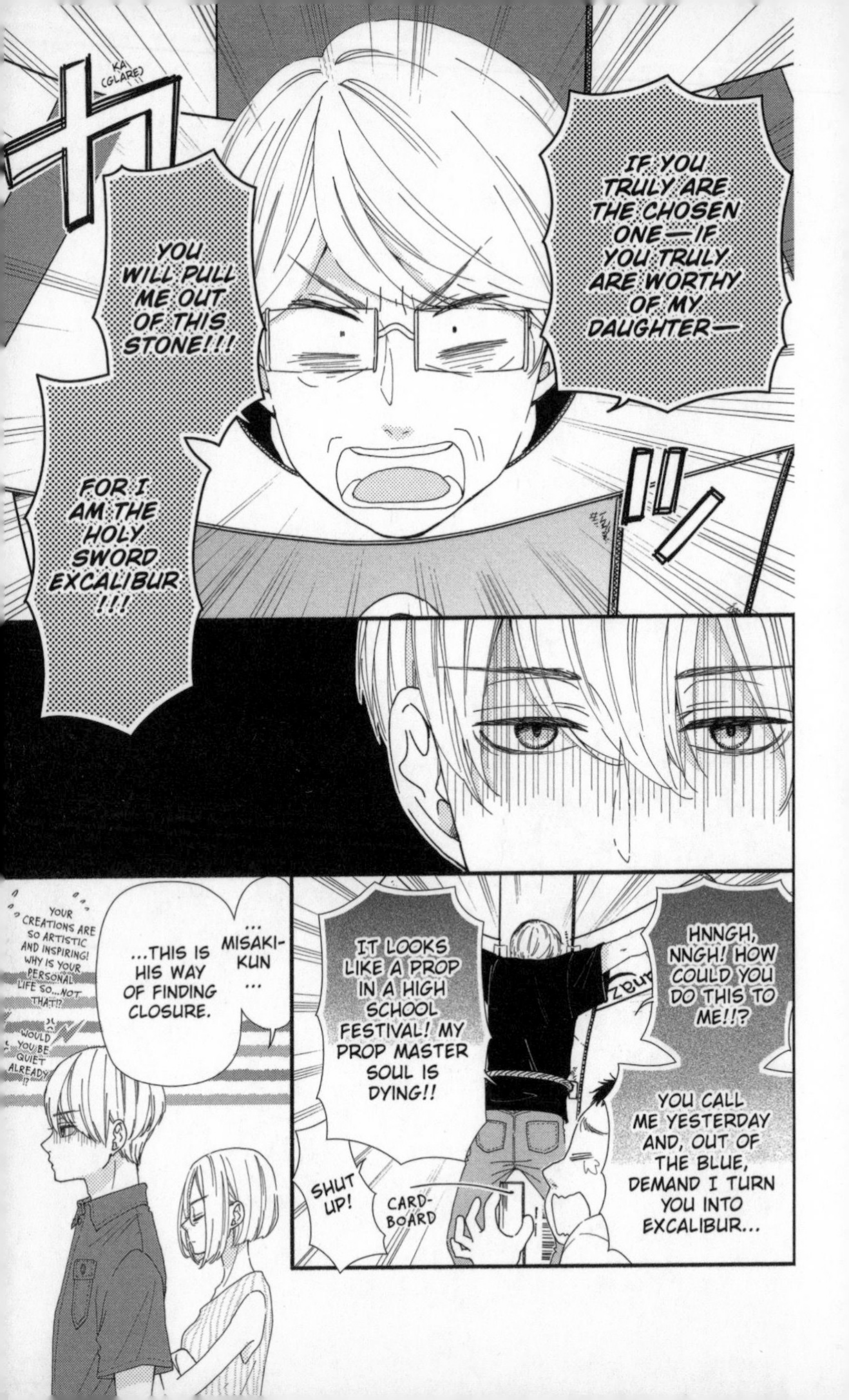
IF YOU TRULY ARE THE CHOSEN ONE—IF YOU TRULY ARE WORTHY OF MY DAUGHTER—
KA (GLARE)
YOU WILL PULL ME OUT OF THIS STONE!!!
FOR I AM THE HOLY SWORD EXCALIBUR!!!
HNNGH, NNGH! HOW COULD YOU DO THIS TO ME!!?
YOU CALL ME YESTERDAY AND, OUT OF THE BLUE, DEMAND I TURN YOU INTO EXCALIBUR...
IT LOOKS LIKE A PROP IN A HIGH SCHOOL FESTIVAL! MY PROP MASTER SOUL IS DYING!!
CARD-BOARD
SHUT UP!
...MISAKI-KUN...
...THIS IS HIS WAY OF FINDING CLOSURE.
YOUR CREATIONS ARE SO ARTISTIC AND INSPIRING! WHY IS YOUR PERSONAL LIFE SO...NOT THAT!?
WOULD YOU BE QUIET ALREADY!?

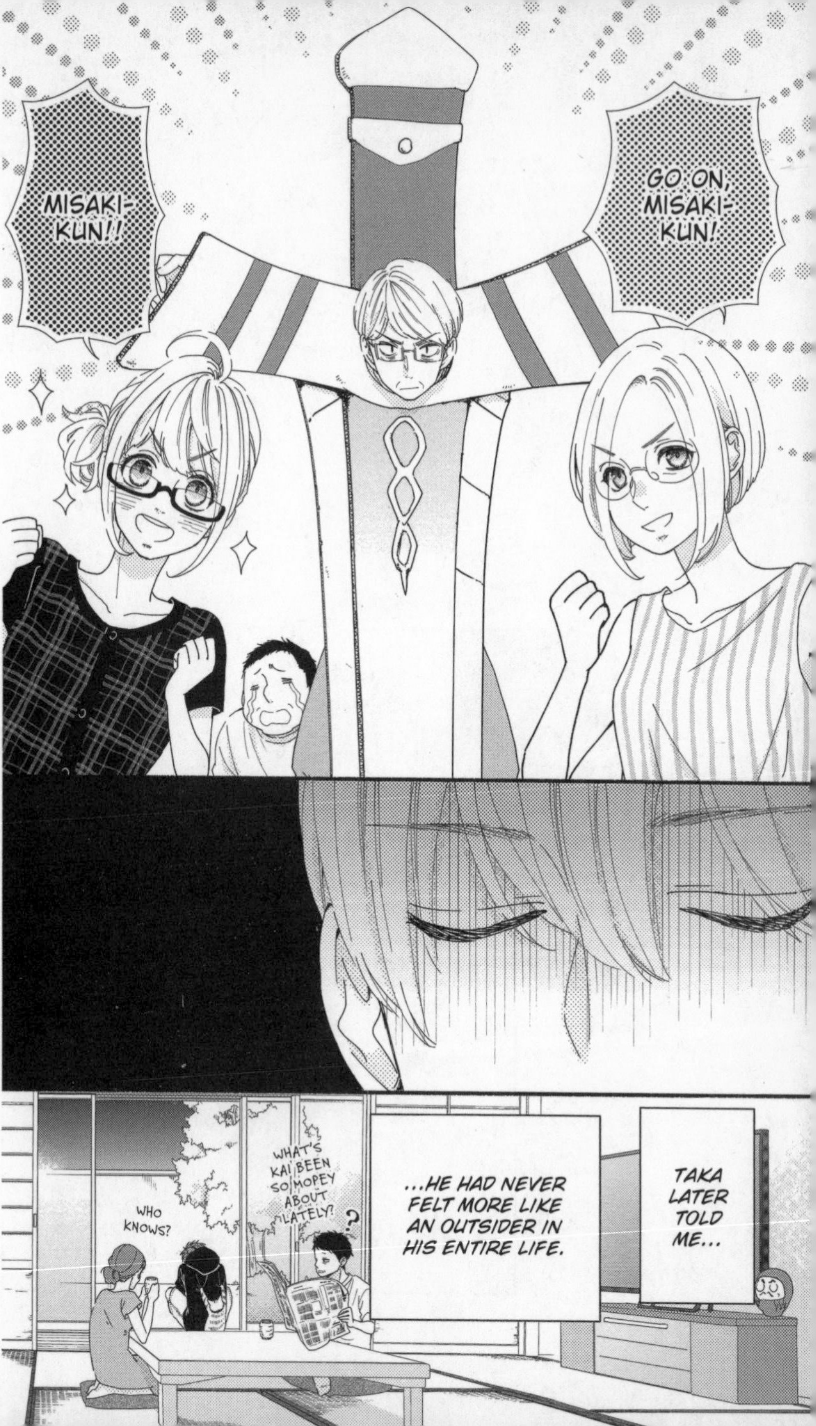
GO ON, MISAKI-KUN!
MISAKI-KUN!!
TAKA LATER TOLD ME...
...HE HAD NEVER FELT MORE LIKE AN OUTSIDER IN HIS ENTIRE LIFE.
WHAT'S KAI BEEN SO MOPEY ABOUT LATELY?
WHO KNOWS?

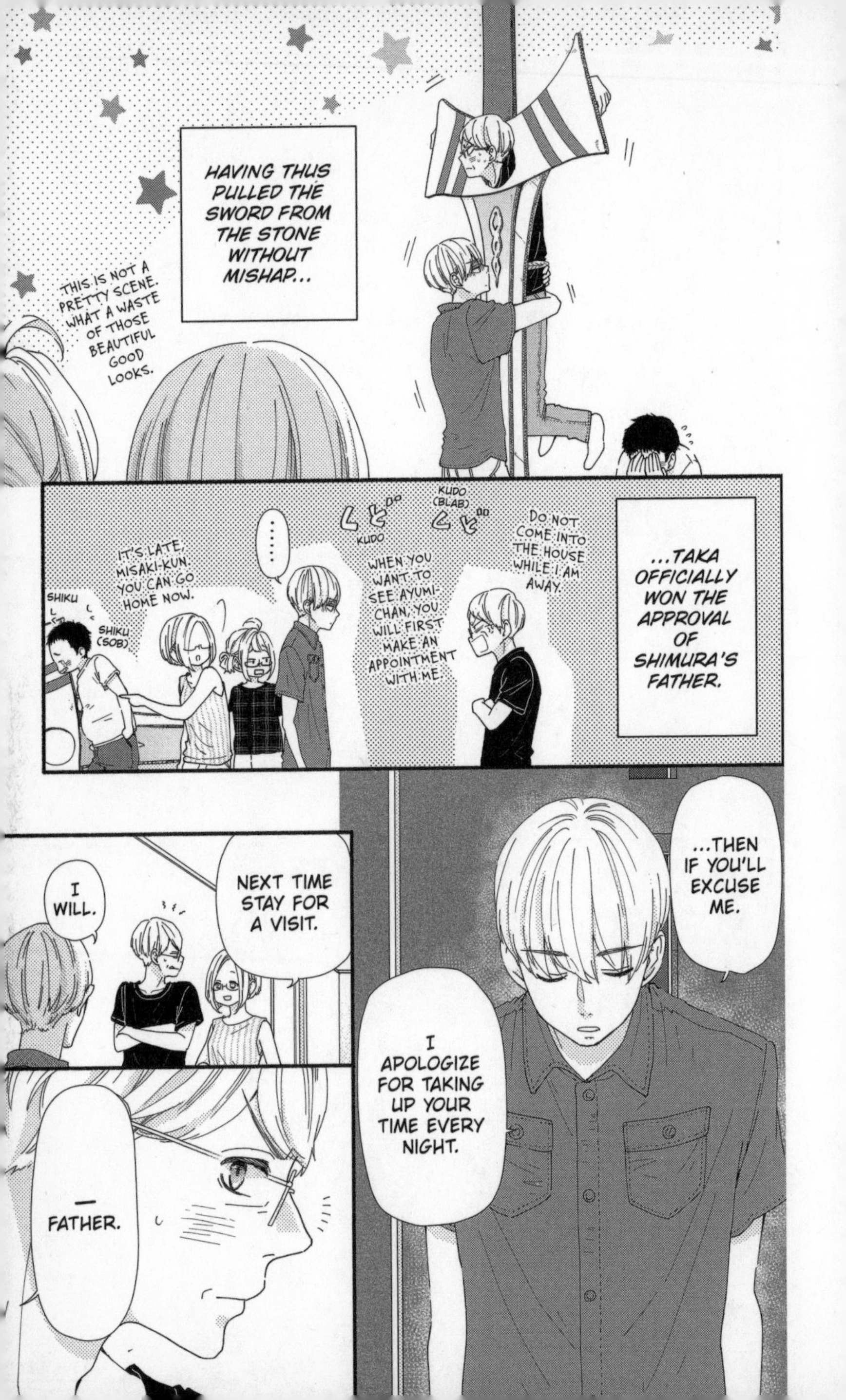
HAVING THUS PULLED THE SWORD FROM THE STONE WITHOUT MISHAP...
THIS IS NOT A PRETTY SCENE. WHAT A WASTE OF THOSE BEAUTIFUL GOOD LOOKS.
...TAKA OFFICIALLY WON THE APPROVAL OF SHIMURA'S FATHER.
DO NOT COME INTO THE HOUSE WHILE I AM AWAY.
KUDO (BLAB)
WHEN YOU WANT TO SEE AYUMI-CHAN, YOU WILL FIRST MAKE AN APPOINTMENT WITH ME.
KUDO
......
IT'S LATE, MISAKI-KUN. YOU CAN GO HOME NOW.
SHIKU
SHIKU (SOB)
...THEN IF YOU'LL EXCUSE ME.
I APOLOGIZE FOR TAKING UP YOUR TIME EVERY NIGHT.
NEXT TIME STAY FOR A VISIT.
I WILL.
— FATHER.

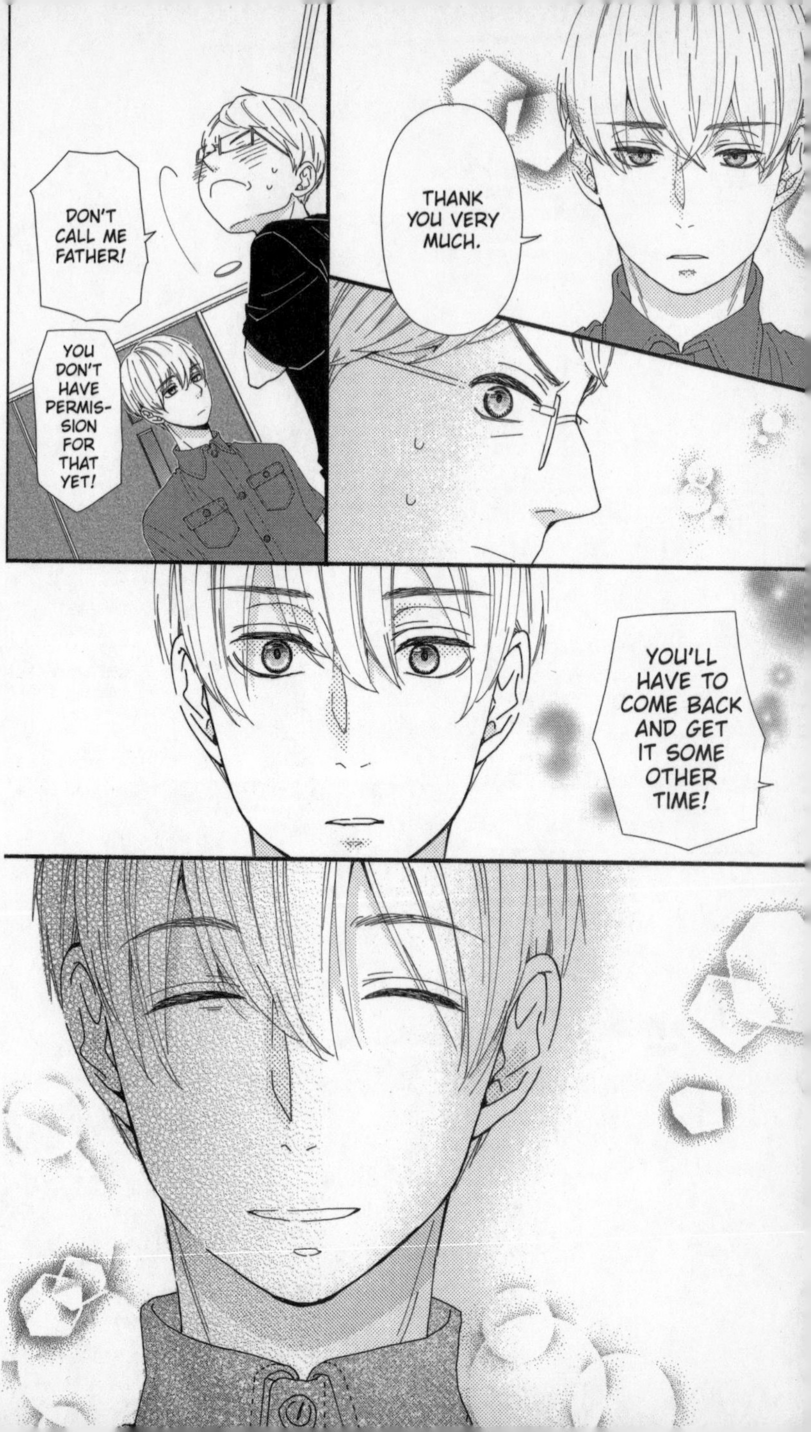
THANK YOU VERY MUCH.
DON'T CALL ME FATHER!
YOU DON'T HAVE PERMIS-SION FOR THAT YET!
YOU'LL HAVE TO COME BACK AND GET IT SOME OTHER TIME!

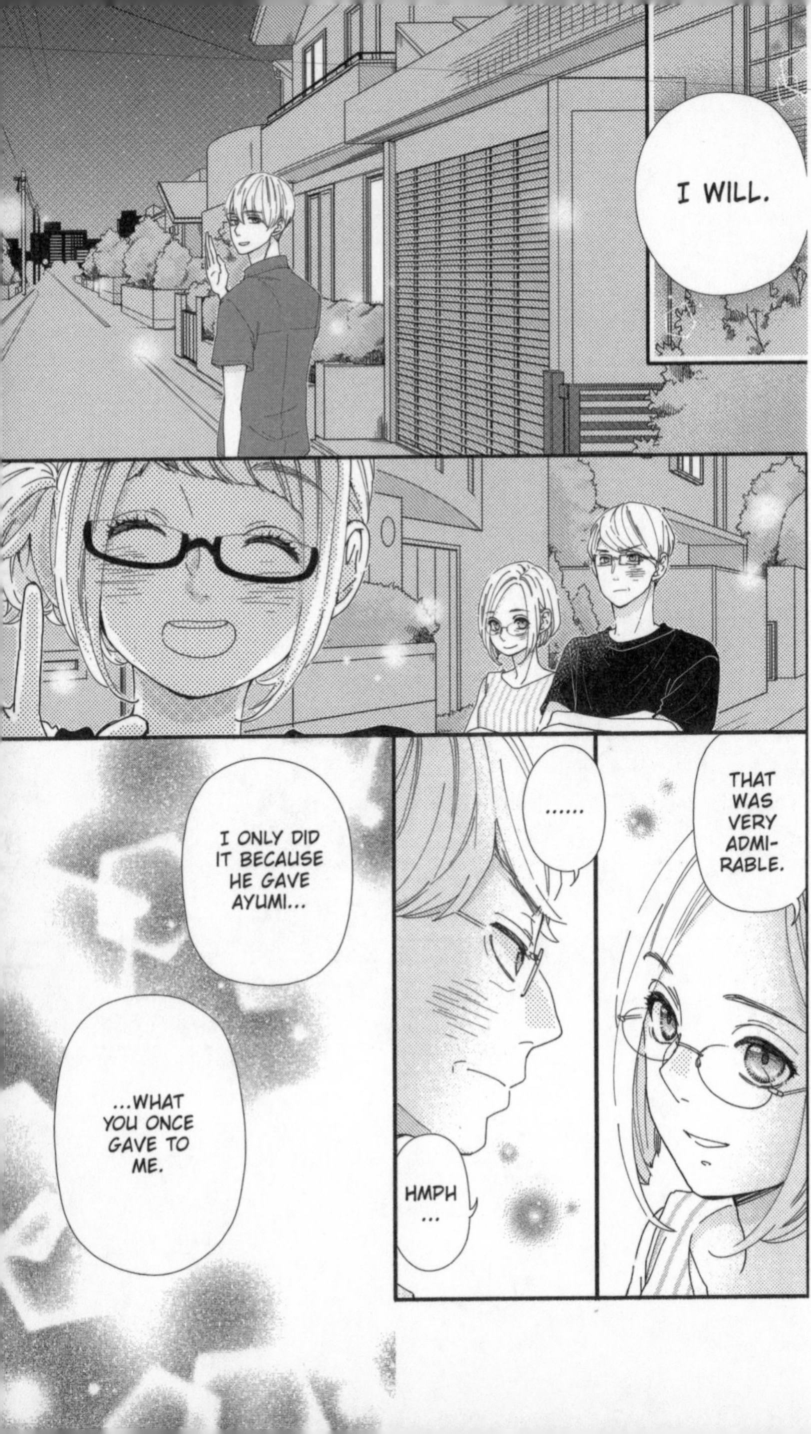
I WILL.
THAT WAS VERY ADMI-RABLE.
......
HMPH ...
I ONLY DID IT BECAUSE HE GAVE AYUMI...
...WHAT YOU ONCE GAVE TO ME.

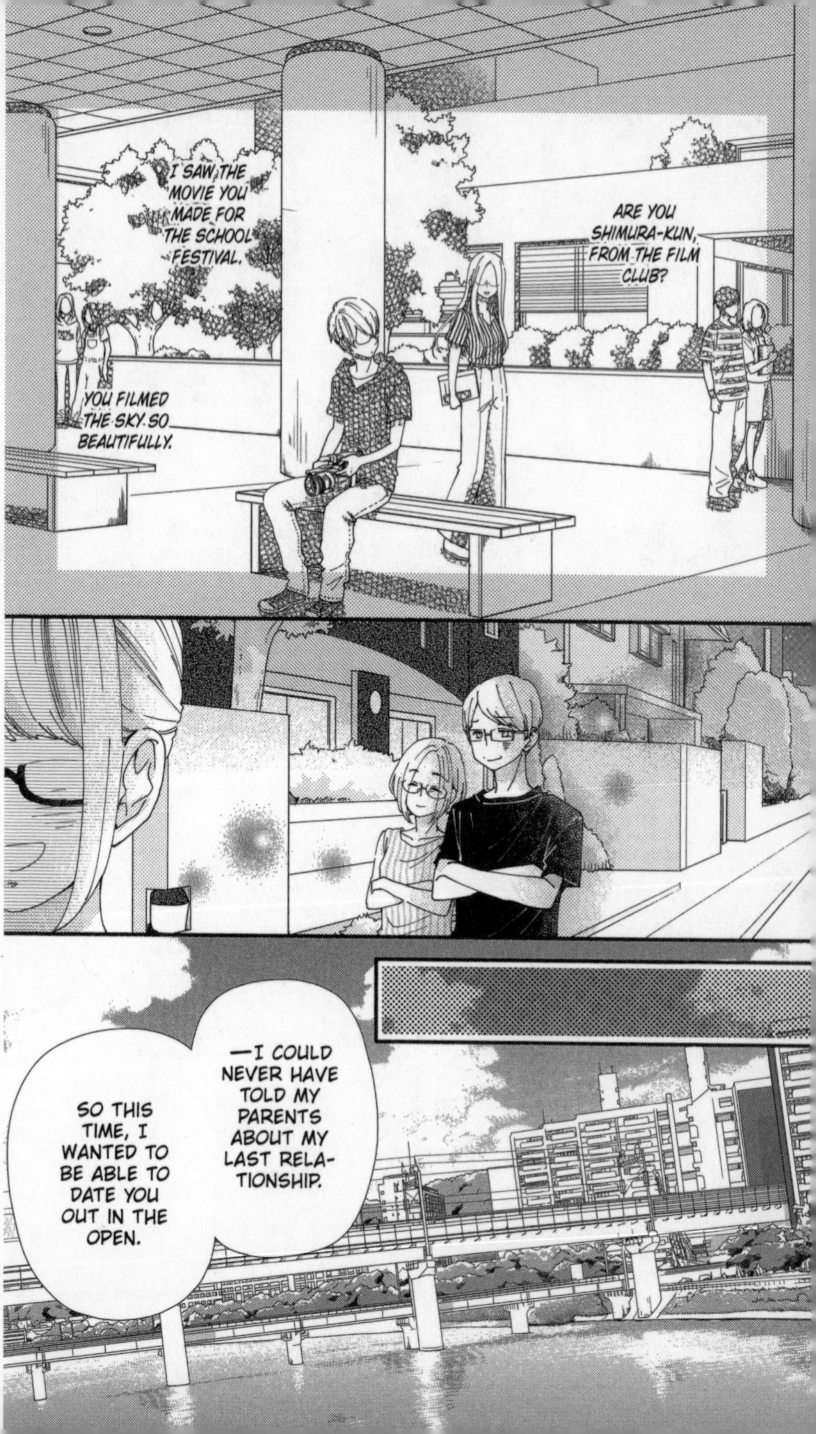
ARE YOU SHIMURA-KUN, FROM THE FILM CLUB?
I SAW THE MOVIE YOU MADE FOR THE SCHOOL FESTIVAL.
YOU FILMED THE SKY SO BEAUTIFULLY.
—I COULD NEVER HAVE TOLD MY PARENTS ABOUT MY LAST RELA-TIONSHIP.
SO THIS TIME, I WANTED TO BE ABLE TO DATE YOU OUT IN THE OPEN.

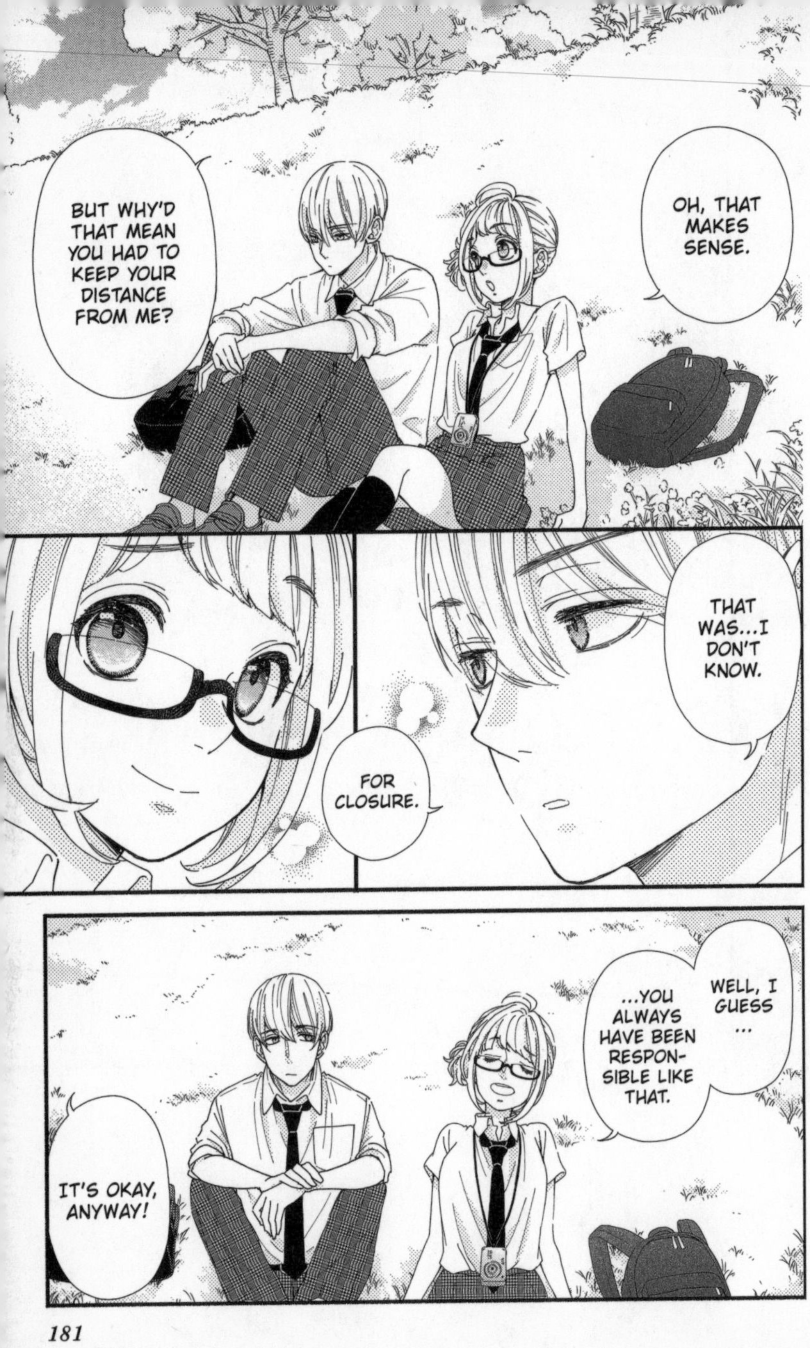
OH, THAT MAKES SENSE.
BUT WHY'D THAT MEAN YOU HAD TO KEEP YOUR DISTANCE FROM ME?
THAT WAS...I DON'T KNOW.
FOR CLOSURE.
WELL, I GUESS ...
...YOU ALWAYS HAVE BEEN RESPONSIBLE LIKE THAT.
IT'S OKAY, ANYWAY!

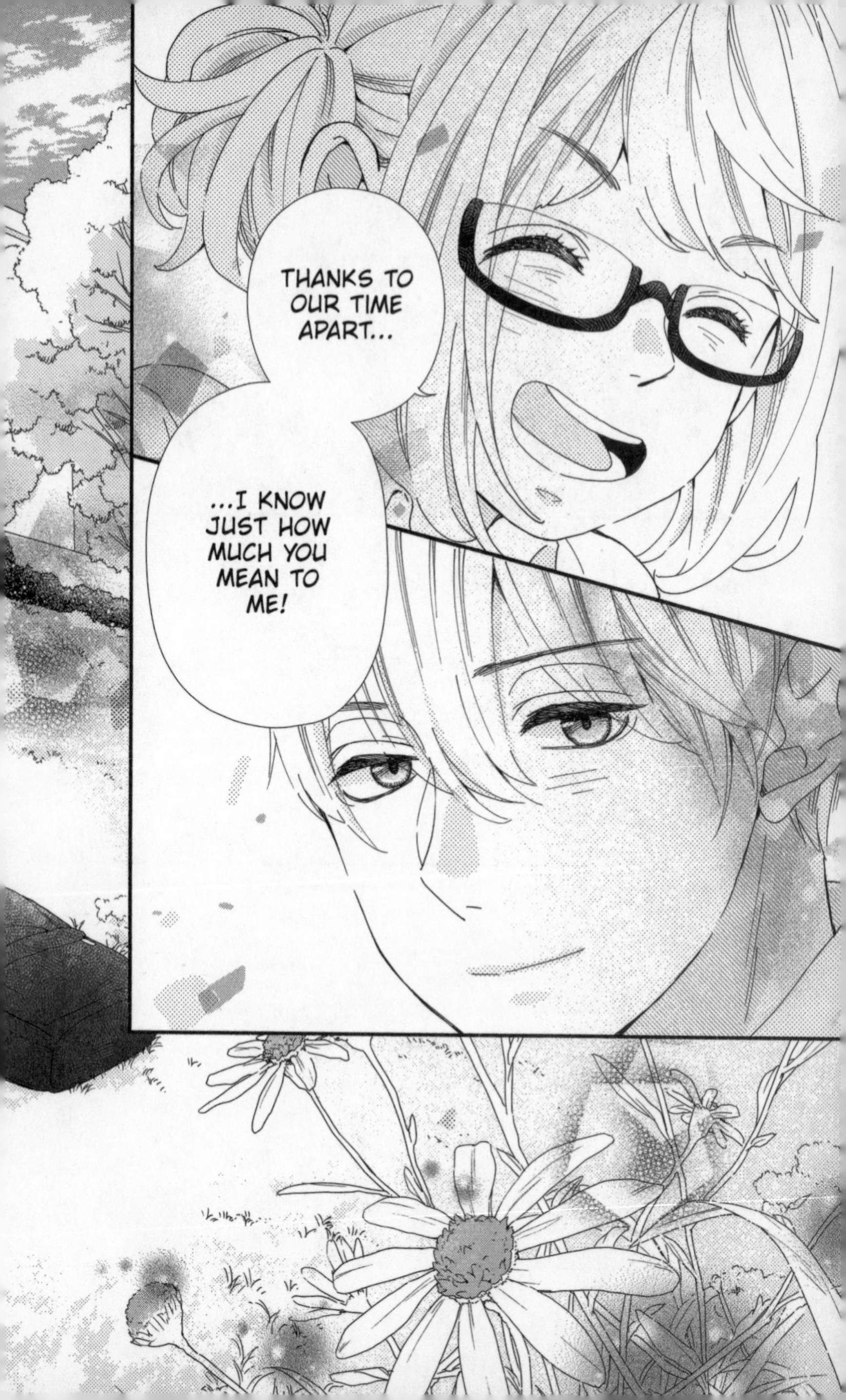
THANKS TO OUR TIME APART...
...I KNOW JUST HOW MUCH YOU MEAN TO ME!

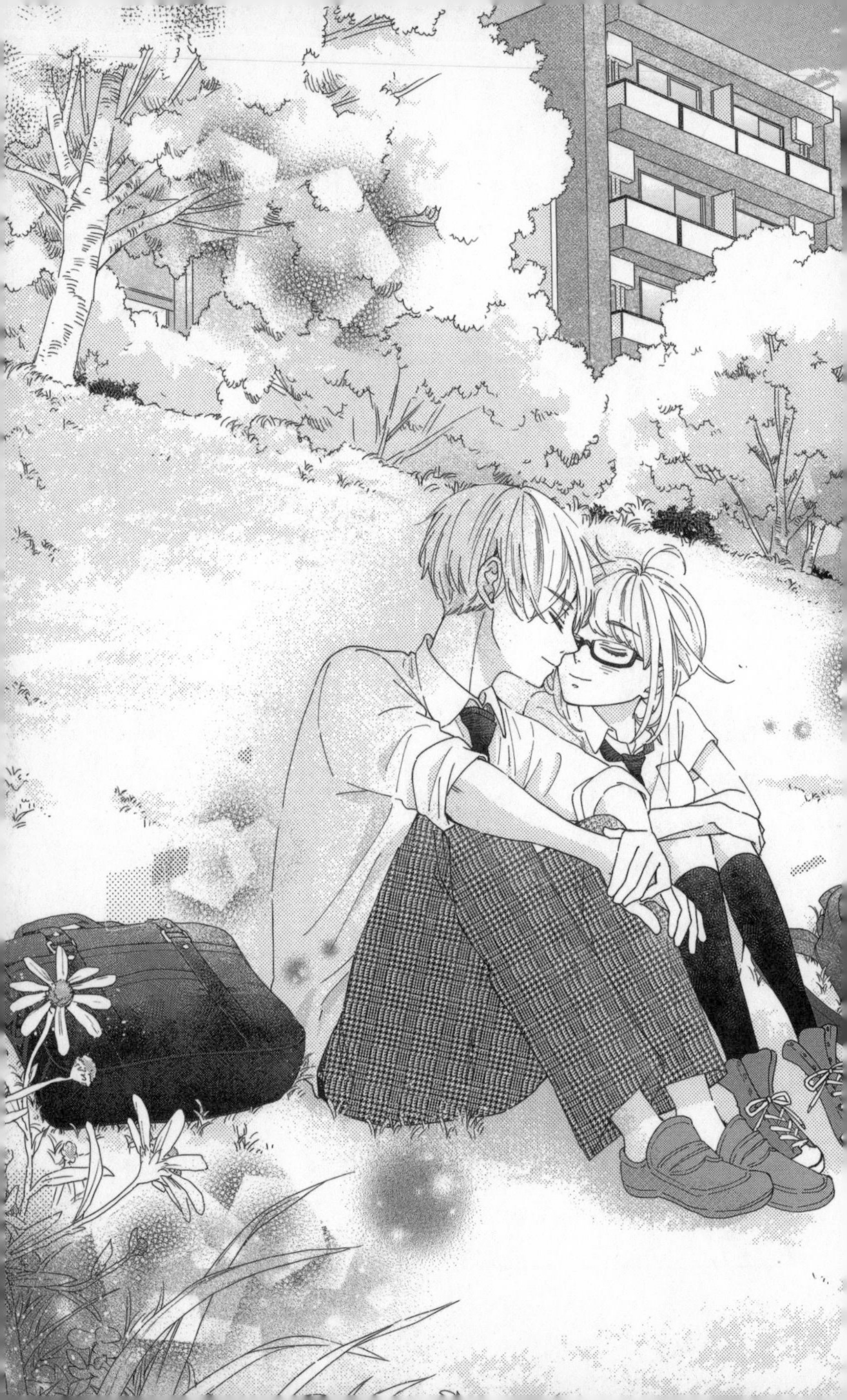

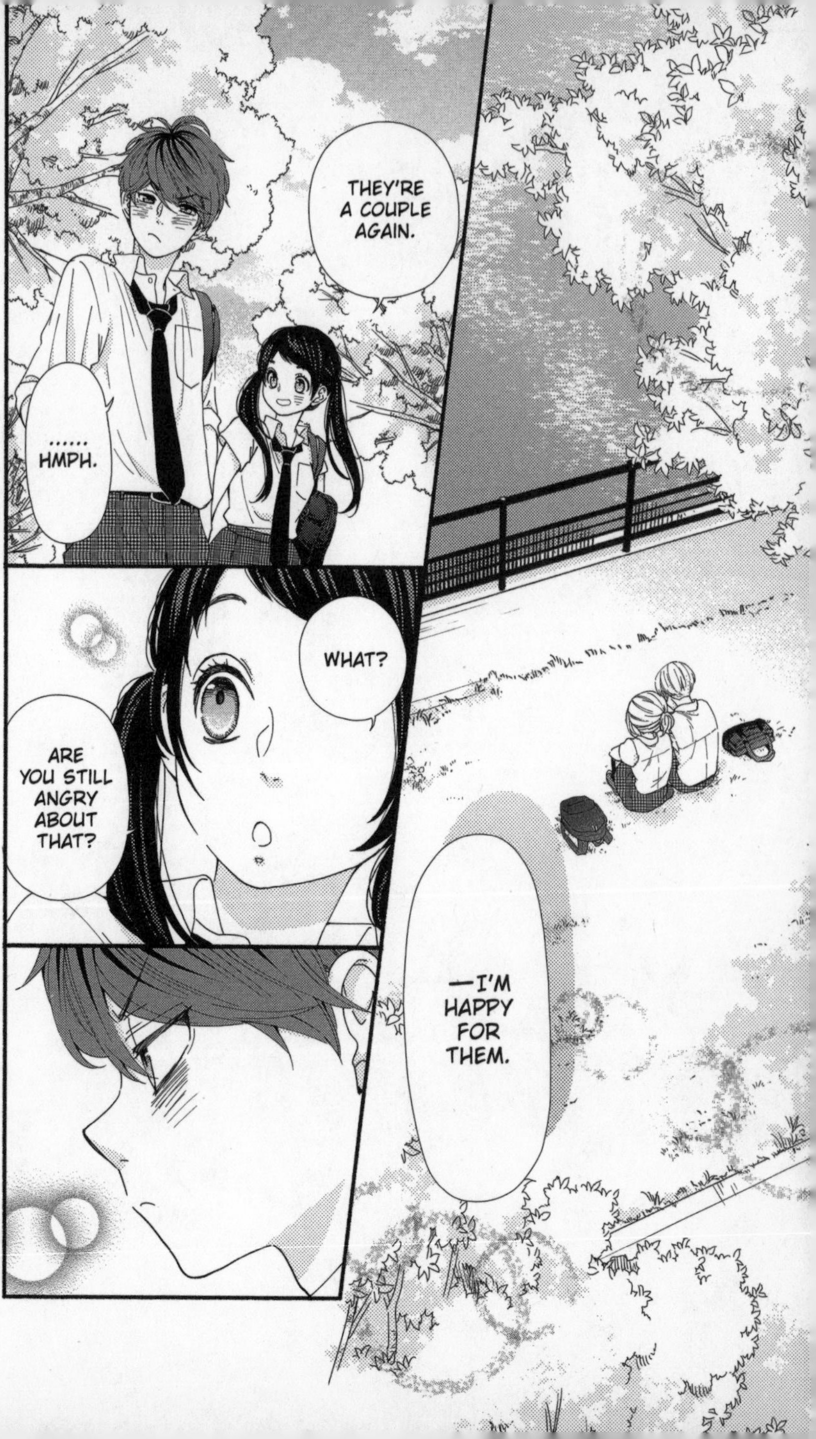
—I'M HAPPY FOR THEM.
THEY'RE A COUPLE AGAIN.
...... HMPH.
WHAT?
ARE YOU STILL ANGRY ABOUT THAT?

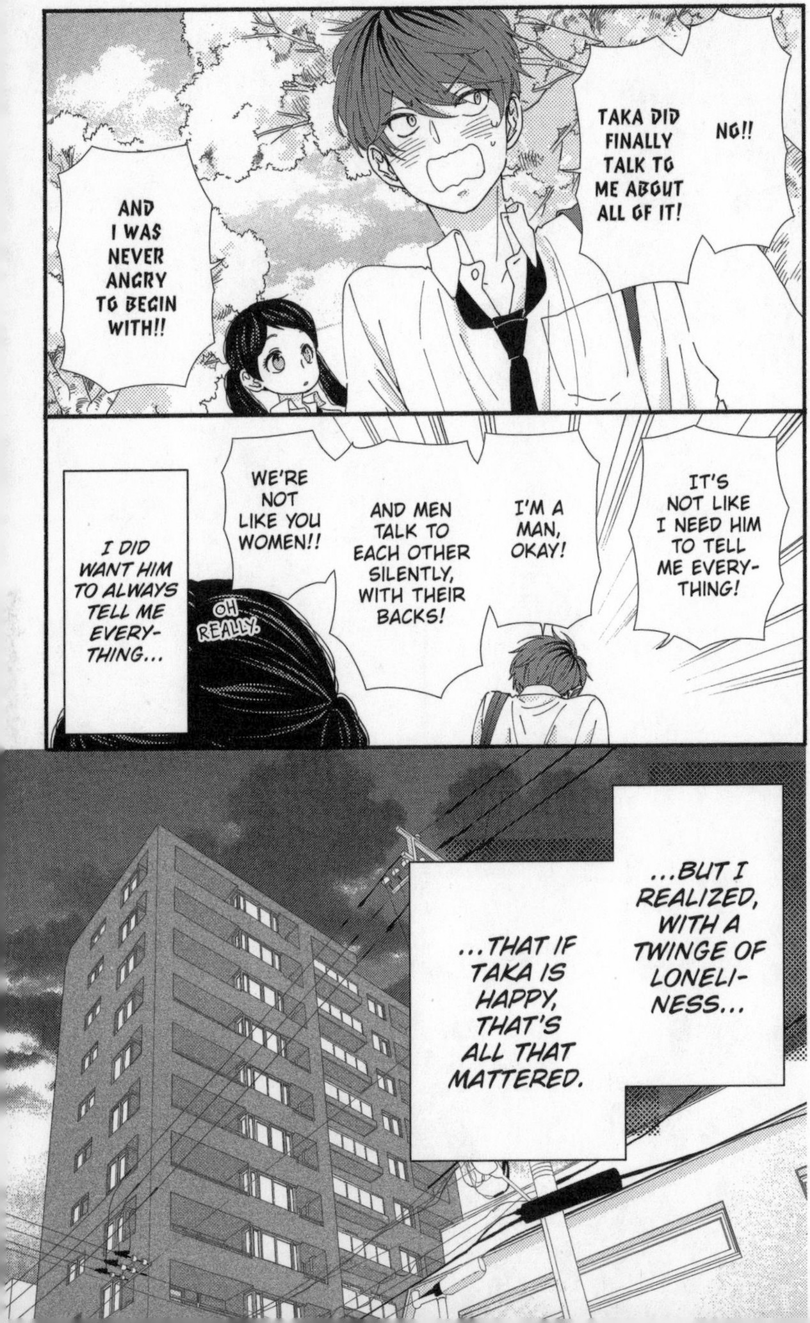
NG!!
TAKA DID FINALLY TALK TO ME ABOUT ALL OF IT!
AND I WAS NEVER ANGRY TO BEGIN WITH!!
IT'S NOT LIKE I NEED HIM TO TELL ME EVERYTHING!
I'M A MAN, OKAY!
AND MEN TALK TO EACH OTHER SILENTLY, WITH THEIR BACKS!
WE'RE NOT LIKE YOU WOMEN!!
OH REALLY.
I DID WANT HIM TO ALWAYS TELL ME EVERYTHING...
...BUT I REALIZED, WITH A TWINGE OF LONELINESS...
...THAT IF TAKA IS HAPPY, THAT'S ALL THAT MATTERED.

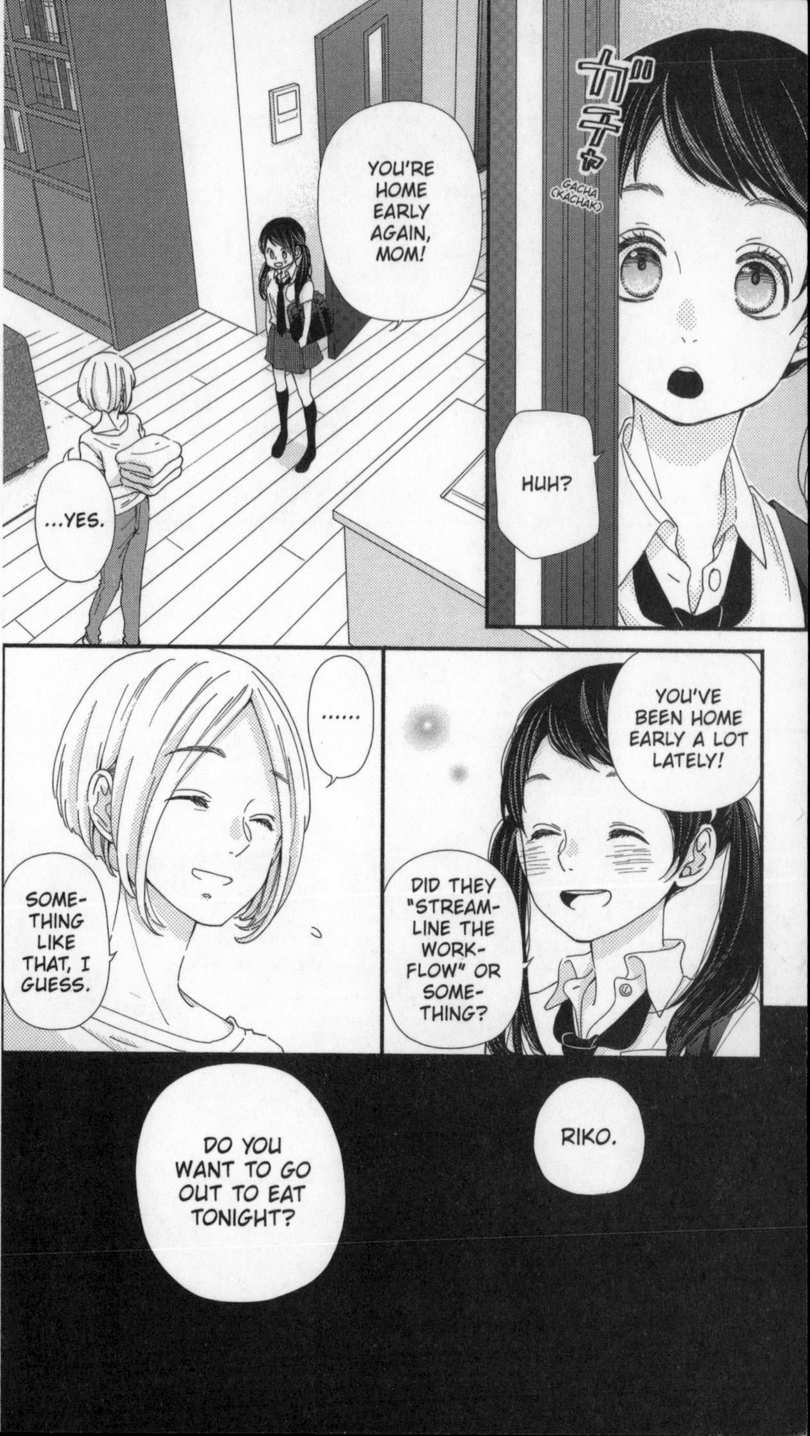
ガチャ
GACHA (KACHAK)
HUH?
YOU'RE HOME EARLY AGAIN, MOM!
...YES.
YOU'VE BEEN HOME EARLY A LOT LATELY!
DID THEY "STREAMLINE THE WORKFLOW" OR SOMETHING?
......
SOMETHING LIKE THAT, I GUESS.
RIKO.
DO YOU WANT TO GO OUT TO EAT TONIGHT?

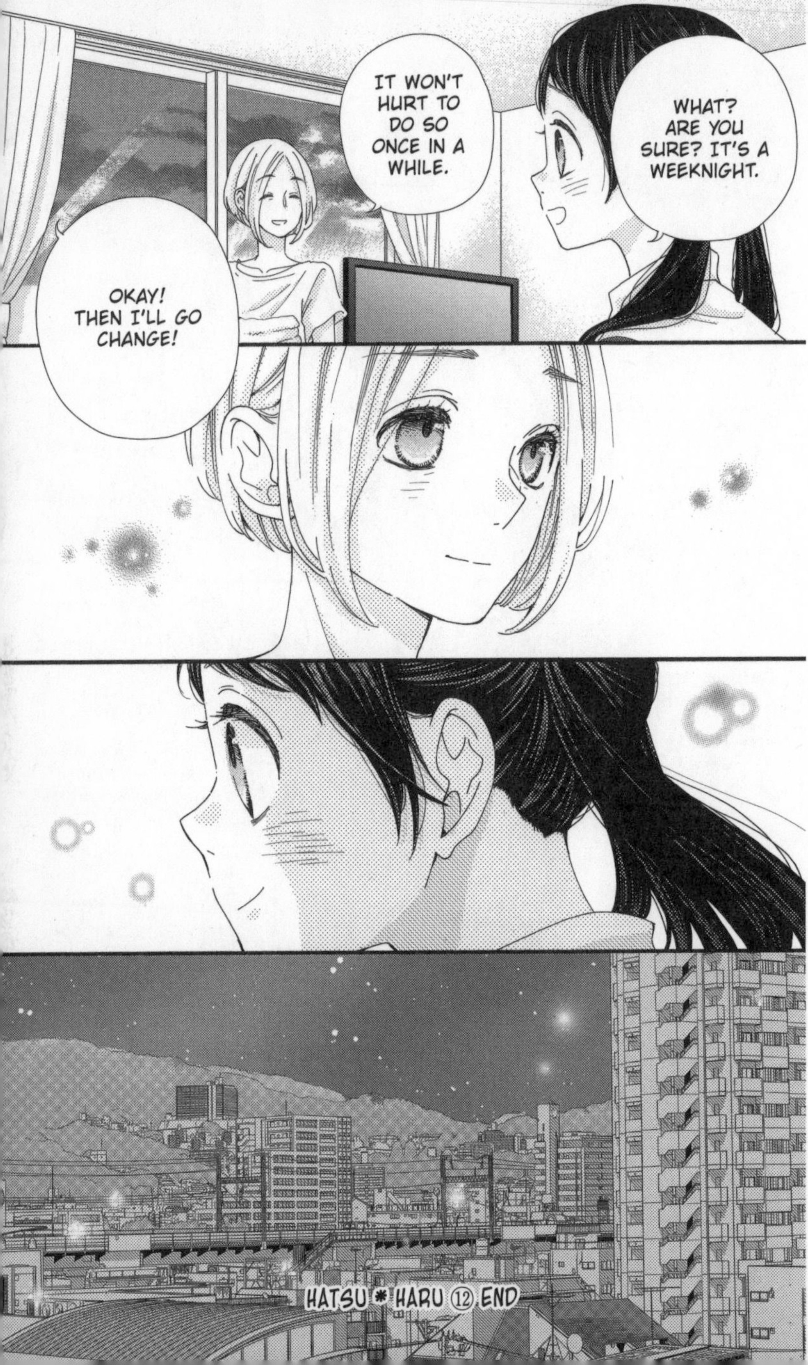
WHAT? ARE YOU SURE? IT'S A WEEKNIGHT.
IT WON'T HURT TO DO SO ONCE IN A WHILE.
OKAY! THEN I'LL GO CHANGE!
HATSU * HARU ⑫ END

Kiyo
Ooshima

Birthday: May 20
Blood Type: A
Height: 5'8"

Favorite Food:
Rice
Favorite Drink:
Milk
Favorite Book:
Shoujo manga

Favorite Type:
A cheerful,
kind person

Kagura
Tatsunami

Birthday: November 18
Blood Type: B
Height: 5'2"

Favorite Sweet:
Dango dumplings
Favorite Book:
Japanese mythology
Daily Routine:
Sweeping her
family's shrine

Favorite Type:
A reliable person
who will protect her

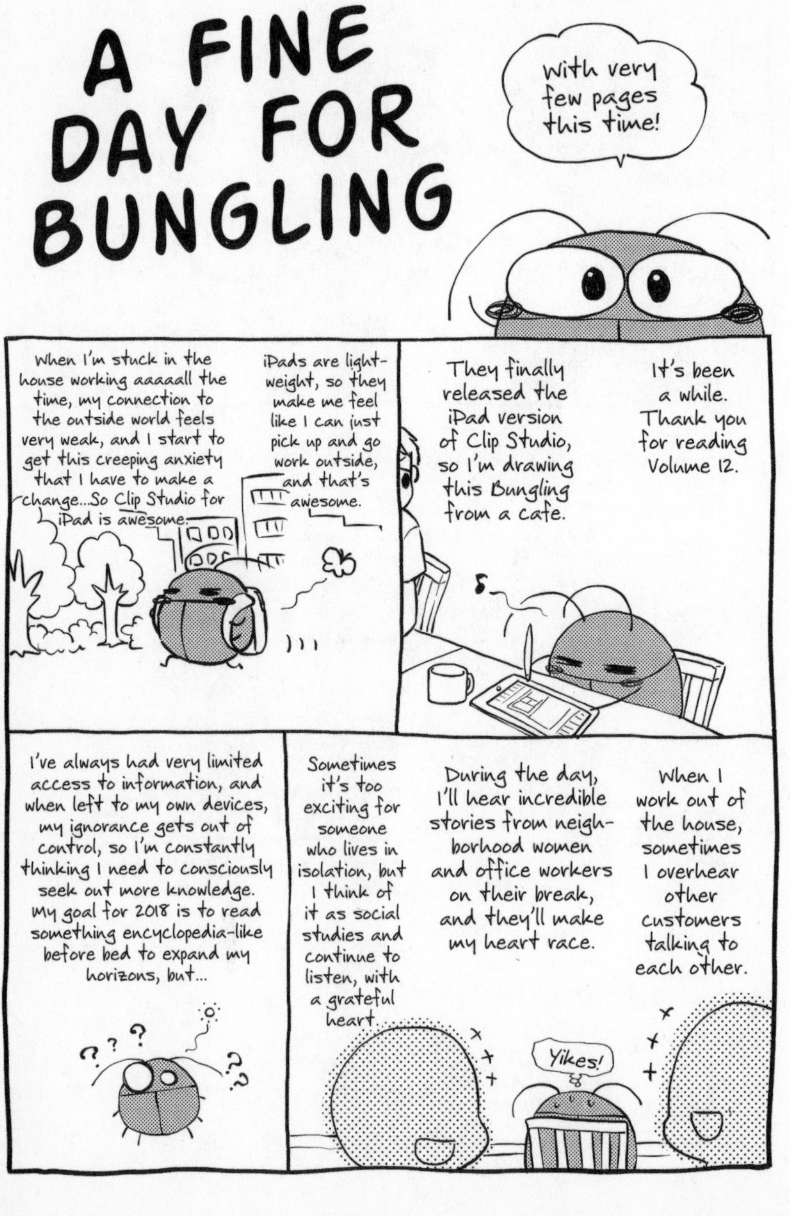
A FINE DAY FOR BUNGLING
With very few pages this time!
It's been a while. Thank you for reading Volume 12.
They finally released the iPad version of Clip Studio, so I'm drawing this Bungling from a cafe.
iPads are lightweight, so they make me feel like I can just pick up and go work outside, and that's awesome.
When I'm stuck in the house working aaaaall the time, my connection to the outside world feels very weak, and I start to get this creeping anxiety that I have to make a change...So Clip Studio for iPad is awesome.
When I work out of the house, sometimes I overhear other customers talking to each other.
During the day, I'll hear incredible stories from neighborhood women and office workers on their break, and they'll make my heart race.
Sometimes it's too exciting for someone who lives in isolation, but I think of it as social studies and continue to listen, with a grateful heart.
Yikes!
I've always had very limited access to information, and when left to my own devices, my ignorance gets out of control, so I'm constantly thinking I need to consciously seek out more knowledge. My goal for 2018 is to read something encyclopedia-like before bed to expand my horizons, but...

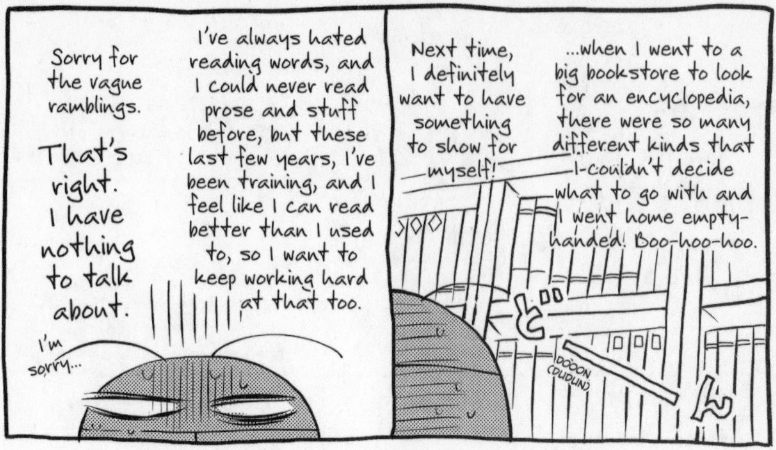
...when I went to a big bookstore to look for an encyclopedia, there were so many different kinds that I couldn't decide what to go with and I went home empty-handed! Boo-hoo-hoo.
Next time, I definitely want to have something to show for myself!
DOOON (DUDUN)
I've always hated reading words, and I could never read prose and stuff before, but these last few years, I've been training, and I feel like I can read better than I used to, so I want to keep working hard at that too.
Sorry for the vague ramblings.
That's right. I have nothing to talk about.
I'm sorry...

This turned into a kind of nonsensical bonus page, but thank you for reading Volume 12. *HATSU * HARU* will be ending in the next volume! To be honest, I didn't think it would go on this long, but thanks to all of you readers, I was able to draw lots of characters. The series is still going on in the magazine too, so I'll do my best to bring it to a proper conclusion............Huh? I still have space...Let's see, let's see, what should I say? I knew I didn't have a lot of bonus pages, so I was determined not to write anything pointless, and my life is made up of boring pointless things, so the reality that I never write anything but stupid things is really being shoved in front of my face right now. And I still have space...!! Let's see, let's see, let's see! This year, I am determined to actually go to bed and wake up at a reasonable hour! (I'm still playing that game with Eda-chan. And I'm always going right back to sleep. I'm sure Eda is too...) I did it!! I filled the space!! I hope you'll read the next volume too.

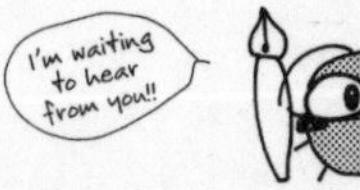
I'm waiting to hear from you!!

Where to send letters:

Yen Press
150 West 30th Street,
19th Floor
New York, NY 10001

web → http://shizukifujisawa.amebaownd.com/

twitter → shizukifujisawa

Special Thanks

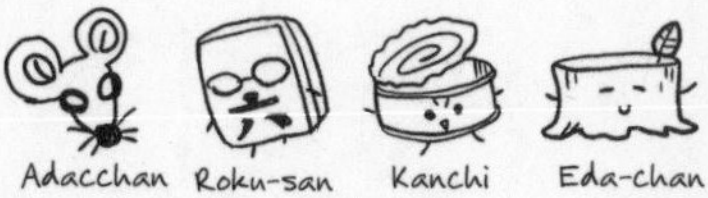

Adacchan Roku-san Kanchi Eda-chan

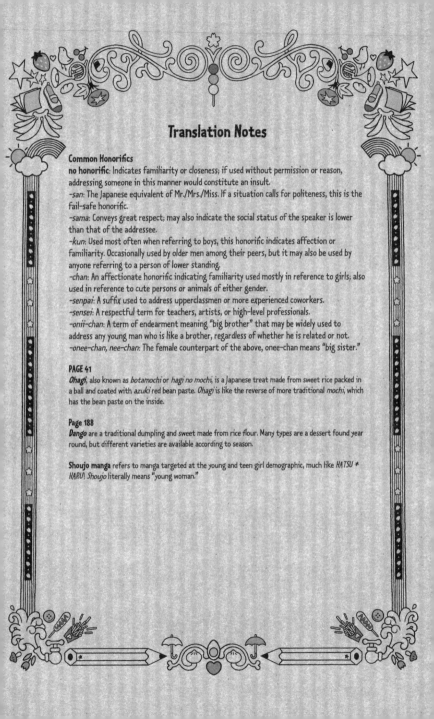

Translation Notes

Common Honorifics

no honorific: Indicates familiarity or closeness; if used without permission or reason, addressing someone in this manner would constitute an insult.

-san: The Japanese equivalent of Mr./Mrs./Miss. If a situation calls for politeness, this is the fail-safe honorific.

-sama: Conveys great respect; may also indicate the social status of the speaker is lower than that of the addressee.

-kun: Used most often when referring to boys, this honorific indicates affection or familiarity. Occasionally used by older men among their peers, but it may also be used by anyone referring to a person of lower standing.

-chan: An affectionate honorific indicating familiarity used mostly in reference to girls; also used in reference to cute persons or animals of either gender.

-senpai: A suffix used to address upperclassmen or more experienced coworkers.

-sensei: A respectful term for teachers, artists, or high-level professionals.

-onii-chan: A term of endearment meaning "big brother" that may be widely used to address any young man who is like a brother, regardless of whether he is related or not.

-onee-chan, nee-chan: The female counterpart of the above, onee-chan means "big sister."

PAGE 41

Ohagi, also known as *botamochi* or *hagi no mochi*, is a Japanese treat made from sweet rice packed in a ball and coated with *azuki* red bean paste. *Ohagi* is like the reverse of more traditional *mochi*, which has the bean paste on the inside.

Page 188

Dango are a traditional dumpling and sweet made from rice flour. Many types are a dessert found year round, but different varieties are available according to season.

Shoujo manga refers to manga targeted at the young and teen girl demographic, much like *HATSU ✻ HARU!* *Shoujo* literally means "young woman."

hatsu*haru 12

Shizuki Fujisawa

Translation/Adaptation: Alethea and Athena Nibley

Lettering: Lys Blakeslee

HATSU * HARU Vol. 12
© 2014 Shizuki FUJISAWA
All rights reserved.
Original Japanese edition published by SHOGAKUKAN.
English translation rights in the United States of America, Canada, the United Kingdom, Ireland, Australia and New Zealand arranged with SHOGAKUKAN
through Tuttle-Mori Agency, Inc.

English translation © 2020 by Yen Press, LLC

Yen Press
150 West 30th Street, 19th Floor
New York, NY 10001

Visit us at yenpress.com ❀ facebook.com/yenpress ❀ twitter.com/yenpress
yenpress.tumblr.com ❀ instagram.com/yenpress

First Yen Press Edition: September 2020

Yen Press is an imprint of Yen Press, LLC.
The Yen Press name and logo are trademarks of Yen Press, LLC.

The publisher is not responsible for websites (or their content) that are not owned by the publisher.

Library of Congress Control Number:
2018935618

ISBN: 978-1-9753-1618-1 (paperback)
       978-1-9753-1619-8 (ebook)

10 9 8 7 6 5 4 3 2 1

WOR

Printed in the United States of America